Jacques Lacan and | **the Other Side of Psychoanalysis**

SIC

A series edited by Slavoj Žižek

SIC stands for psychoanalytic interpretation at its most elementary: no discovery of deep, hidden meaning, just the act of drawing attention to the litter-ality [*sic!*] of what precedes it. A *sic* reminds us that what was said, inclusive of its blunders, was effectively said and cannot be undone. The series SIC thus explores different connections to the Freudian field. Each volume provides a bundle of Lacanian interventions into a specific domain of ongoing theoretical, cultural, and ideological-political battles. It is neither "pluralist" nor "socially sensitive"; unabashedly avowing its exclusive Lacanian orientation, it disregards any form of correctness but the inherent correctness of theory itself.

Reflections on *Seminar XVII*

Jacques Lacan and the Other Side of Psychoanalysis

Justin Clemens
and Russell Grigg,
editors

sic **6**

DUKE UNIVERSITY PRESS   Durham and London 2006

© 2006 Duke University Press

All rights reserved

Printed in the United States

of America on acid-free paper ∞

Typeset in Sabon by Tseng

Information Systems, Inc.

Library of Congress Cataloging-in-

Publication Data appear on the

last printed page of this book.

Contents

Introduction 1

I CLINIC OF THE DISCOURSES

1 Jacques-Alain Miller, *On Shame* 11
2 Paul Verhaeghe, *Enjoyment and Impossibility: Lacan's Revision of the Oedipus Complex* 29
3 Russell Grigg, *Beyond the Oedipus Complex* 50
4 Ellie Ragland, *The Hysteric's Truth* 69
5 Dominiek Hoens, *Toward a New Perversion: Psychoanalysis* 88

II THE OTHER SIDE OF PSYCHOANALYSIS

6 Slavoj Žižek, *Objet a in Social Links* 107
7 Mladen Dolar, *Hegel as the Other Side of Psychoanalysis* 129
8 Alenka Zupančič, *When Surplus Enjoyment Meets Surplus Value* 155
9 Oliver Feltham, *Enjoy Your Stay: Structural Change in* Seminar XVII 179
10 Juliet Flower MacCannell, *More Thoughts for the Times on War and Death: The Discourse of Capitalism in* Seminar XVII 195
11 Dominique Hecq, *The Impossible Power of Psychoanalysis* 216

III DISCOURSES OF CONTEMPORARY LIFE

12 Éric Laurent, *Symptom and Discourse* 229
13 Marie-Hélène Brousse, *Common Markets and Segregation* 254
14 Pierre-Gilles Guéguen, *The Intimate, the Extimate, and Psychoanalytic Discourse* 263
15 Geoff Boucher, *Bureaucratic Speech Acts and the University Discourse: Lacan's Theory of Modernity* 274
16 Matthew Sharpe, *The "Revolution" in Advertising and University Discourse* 292

Contributors 315
Index 319

Justin Clemens
and Russell Grigg | **Introduction**

Much was new in Paris universities in 1969. An old conservative system had been overhauled and restructured following the student uprising of the year before. This included a new, "experimental" university, the Université de Paris VIII (Vincennes), tucked away in the spacious grounds of the Bois de Vincennes east of Paris. Not least of the innovations of this radical and, in its early days, often fractious university was the new Department of Psychoanalysis, the first of its kind in France. The department, overtly Lacanian in orientation—its first chairman was Serge Leclaire—was created under the patronage of the Department of Philosophy, headed by Michel Foucault. The department itself boasted an impressive list of a new breed of philosophers, including Gilles Deleuze, Jacques Rancière, Alain Badiou, and Jean-François Lyotard.

At the same time as this new academic institution was founded, Lacan was obliged to move his seminar from the Ecole Normale Supérieure in the rue d'Ulm (which had hosted his seminar since 1964), to the Faculté de Droit, located a few hundred meters up the hill, in the Place du Panthéon. There he continued to attract what was by then a large and extremely diverse audience. Though the social order was no longer on the brink of collapse as it had been in May 1968, contestation was still in the air—on several occasions, Lacan's seminar was interrupted or even cancelled—and his appearances at the campus at Vincennes proved occasions for agitation and protest.

It is in this context that Lacan delivered what we know as his *Semi-*

nar XVII, *The Other Side of Psychoanalysis*, a yearlong, fortnightly deliberation on psychoanalysis (as always). But he was also deliberating on the contemporary social order. In *Seminar XVII*, Lacan speaks of Freud and Marx by way of Hegel; of changing patterns of social and sexual behavior, and of what will become of them; of the nature and function of science and knowledge. It is pertinent to note that these reflections take place in the context of the foundation of the Department of Psychoanalysis, since for Lacan this raised the question—which had confronted Freud himself—of the place that psychoanalytic knowledge might occupy in the university. But it equally raised the inverse question: what is the impact of *university* knowledge upon psychoanalysis? The new circumstances raised this question in an acute form, particularly as Lacan recognized that unlike, say, psychology or psychiatry, psychoanalysis had always tended to operate outside the university system. Similarly, the Freudian School of Paris, Lacan's school, had the function—to which Lacan's seminar contributed—of training psychoanalysts and transmitting psychoanalysis. Is, then, the extramural nature of psychoanalytic training purely contingent, a consequence of Freud's marginal relationship to the academic institutions of Vienna and the subsequent foundation of an independent International Psychoanalytic Association? Or are there reasons intrinsic to the practice of analysis that have to do with the place of knowledge and the way it functions in the university? Both the new Department of Psychoanalysis and the aspirations of a radical student movement are the immediate causes of this reflection.

Lacan's response to this issue is to set it in a broader context. The introduction and discussion of the four discourses forms a kind of reference point by which Lacan orients himself throughout the year, even as he discusses issues as varied as thermodynamics, Marx, Hegel, Freud's cases, the Oedipus complex, and the university.

At the beginning of the year, Lacan writes out what he takes to be the four structures of discourse, one of his first attempts to use letters to define a fundamental structure of psychoanalysis. The four discourses are given in the form of "mathemes," which, as Jean-Claude Milner puts it, are "atoms of knowledge [*savoir*]"; that is, they are entirely transmissible without loss. The four discourses are as follows:

Figure 1: The Four Discourses

$$\frac{S_1 \rightarrow S_2}{\$ \quad\quad a}$$

$$\frac{\$ \rightarrow S_1}{a \quad\quad S_2}$$

Master's discourse   Hysteric's discourse

$$\frac{a \rightarrow \$}{S_2 \quad\quad S_1}$$

$$\frac{S_2 \rightarrow a}{S_1 \quad\quad \$}$$

Analyst's discourse   University discourse

The terms are as follows:

S_1 Master signifier
S_2 Knowledge, as in *le savoir* or "knowing that—"
$\$$ The divided subject
a both *objet a* and surplus-pleasure.

The places are:

$$\frac{\text{agent} \rightarrow \text{other}}{\text{truth} \quad\quad \text{product}}$$

The four discourses are based on the original matrix that characterizes the signifier as what represents a subject for another signifier:

$$\frac{S_1 \rightarrow S_2}{\$}$$

This matrix captures a number of features: the fact that the subject is a being of language, differing in this respect from an individual; the fact that the subject is divided by language; and, on the other hand, the fact that the signifier is diacritical, that is, each signifier is defined by its difference from and opposition to other signifiers. Lacan calls the place of agent the "dominant," just as he thinks of the master's discourse as the dominant discourse of the four.

The fourth term in the discourses, the *a*, is Lacan's *objet a* viewed in the light of the new theory of *plus-de-jouir*, surplus jouissance or surplus pleasure, which he had introduced at his seminar the previous year.

A rough way of defining surplus jouissance would be to think of it, on analogy with Marx's surplus value, as jouissance that is lost to the subject and recuperated by the Other.

The matrix organizes these four terms in a strict circular order: S_1, S_2, a, $\$$, that allows rotation but no commutation; that is, changing their order relative to one another is not permitted. Through this operation of "circular permutation," four discourses are produced in which each term will occupy one of four different places; one discourse will be transformed into another when the four terms undergo a quarter turn.

The four discourses are not only the most striking aspect of *Seminar XVII* but are fundamental to it. Just as for Aristotle, man thinks with his soul, so, in this seminar, Lacan thinks with his four discourses. The first and perhaps primary question is what purpose Lacan intended that they should serve. This question has been answered in several ways, and many of the papers in this volume address this question in one way or another. At the same time, several of the papers themselves "think with" Lacan's four discourses, thereby demonstrating the productive potential of Lacan's insistent reduction of theory to a kernel of mathemes and formulas. Other of the following papers are more expository or discuss other significant features of the seminar.

In this seminar Lacan also revisits Freud's Oedipus complex, questioning, in particular, the place that the father occupies there. Of interest here is that Lacan's critique of Freud—he speaks of Freud's "prejudices," saying that Freud "falls into error" and that the Oedipus complex is "Freud's dream"—opens up issues that will progressively unfold in later seminars such as *Seminar XX* and the seminar on Joyce, concerning sexuation and sexual difference, the clinical treatment of hysteria, the ends of analysis, and the rethinking of psychosis, in particular.

The contributions to this volume have, somewhat arbitrarily, been grouped into three sections: we have named them "Clinic of the Discourses," "The Other Side of Psychoanalysis," and "Discourses of Contemporary Life."

The first of these sections, on clinical issues, opens with "On Shame" by Jacques-Alain Miller, which explores the consequences for psychoanalysis of a central trait of late capitalism that manifests as a "prohibiting of prohibition." The essays by Paul Verhaeghe, "Enjoyment and Impossibility: Lacan's Revision of the Oedipus Complex," and Russell

Grigg, "Beyond the Oedipus Complex," both address Lacan's critique and revision of earlier views on the Oedipus complex and the implications for our understanding of hysteria. These implications are picked up in Ellie Ragland's "The Hysteric's Truth," which looks at Lacan's reexamination of the subjective division of the hysteric in relation to sexuality and his very interesting reconsideration of Freud's two cases of Dora and the homosexual woman. Dominiek Hoens, in "Toward a New Perversion: Psychoanalysis," provocatively argues that there is a similarity between the analyst's desire and "perversion" in that not only do both analyst and pervert position themselves as *objet a*, but also aim at "the production of the subject qua subject of the signifier." Hoens's argument raises the question of a reevaluation of this old and frequently discarded category of psychoanalysis.

By "the other side of psychoanalysis" Lacan was referring to the master's discourse, and all the articles in the second part explore this discourse in relation to one or more of the three other discourses. In "*Objet a* in Social Links," Slavoj Žižek's approach ranges across the differences between the hysteric's discourse and the university discourse, on the one hand, and that of the analyst on the other. Drawing attention to the historicity of the four discourses, Žižek introduces a number of crucial distinctions in a discussion of work by Miller, Giorgio Agamben, and Antonio Negri and Michael Hardt. Mladen Dolar, in "Hegel as the Other Side of Psychoanalysis," explores the complex or, rather, the *multiple* place that Hegel occupies in the four discourses. For Dolar, Hegel at once functions as a representative of the master's, the hysteric's, and the university discourse, and, ultimately, can be seen to occupy the analyst's place as *objet a* as well. Alenka Zupančič reflects on Lacan's deployment of the four discourses to rework the earlier antithesis between signifier and jouissance in such a way that signifier and jouissance are intertwined. Zupančič gives a convincing demonstration of how, on the one hand, the hysteric's discourse is a reaction to the master's discourse and, on the other, the university discourse has come to be the new form of the master's discourse. In "Enjoy Your Stay," Oliver Feltham discusses a question and a problem that arise out of Lacan's seminar. The first is the question why there are only four discourses and not more, given that the possible number of permutations is twenty-four. The second is the deeper problem of how, in this seminar, Lacan conceives of change. The problem arises because the discourses emerge historically and mutate, which creates the problem for Lacan of how to think structural change without having recourse to a notion of history as sequence. Feltham explores different responses to this problem, both by looking at what Lacan has to offer and by appealing to some of Alain Badiou's work. Juliet Flower MacCannell, in "More Thoughts for the Times on War and Death: The Discourse of Capitalism in *Seminar XVII*," analyzes the master's discourse and, in particular, the new concept of surplus jouissance, introduced by Lacan the previous year but given more extended treatment in *Seminar XVII*. Particularly important is the discussion of the connection between Lacan and Marx around this very point. The discussion of this connection is even more valuable for being the one paper in the collection that explores Lacan's relationship to Marx in detail. In a different way, Dominique Hecq examines the problems of power, impotence, and impossibility as they develop and are treated throughout *Seminar XVII*. Hecq shows how Lacan struggles with certain complexities that arise when jouissance becomes the foundation of any possible link between politics and truth; moreover, how jouissance itself must be reconceived in the breach of such a development.

Part 3 opens with Éric Laurent's "Symptom and Discourse," in which Laurent explores the contemporary place of shame in considerable detail. The essay relates to Miller's, itself in part a response to Laurent's exploration of contemporary mores, foreseen in many ways by Lacan in 1967. Laurent looks at the near-absence of shame as a social phenomena and its relations with other subjective experiences such as guilt, self-hatred, and pride. Discussing the connection with modes of jouissance, Laurent argues that modern science plays a key role in contemporary expressions of subjectivity, and that this has consequences that psychoanalysts cannot ignore. Marie-Hélène Brousse and Pierre-Gilles Guéguen are also interested in the implications of contemporary society for the analyst's discourse. Brousse, in "Common Markets and Segregation," is concerned with the imaginary, symbolic, and real shifts in our contemporary world. She spells out several ways in which a "new universalism" expresses itself, from which she derives a contemporary form of the master's discourse. Guéguen discusses the relationship between intimacy and truth, as it is revealed and treated by literary autobiography and psychoanalysis. Comparing and contrasting truth and intimacy in literature and psychoanalysis, Guéguen makes astute observations on autobiography, the *journal intime*, and the psychoanalytic process itself. In "Bureaucratic Speech Acts and the University Discourse: Lacan's Theory of Modernity," Geoff Boucher, noting that the master's discourse remains the foundation of the social contract, fleshes out the argument for regarding bureaucratic capitalism as the contemporary form of the master's discourse. Through an analysis of speech acts, including a discussion of the shortcomings of Derrida and Foucault on this issue, Boucher pins down what is specific to the bureaucratic expression of the master's discourse. Similarly, Matthew Sharpe, in "The 'Revolution' in Advertising and the Discourse of the University," invokes Lacan's impromptu remark that university discourse provides the contemporary hegemonic matrix of social relations. If Lacan himself considered Stalinist bureaucracy to be exemplary of this development, Sharpe notes that such bureaucracy finds an unexpected analog in the liberal capitalist West: the discourse of marketing. An analysis of this most characteristic form of late-capitalist discourse is used to locate a subtle shift in the place of authority under the master's discourse.

Most but not all of the articles gathered in this volume originated in a conference run jointly by Deakin University and the Lacan Circle of Melbourne with assistance from the Australian Research Council, whose generous support we would like to acknowledge here.

PART I | **Clinic of the Discourses**

Jacques-Alain Miller

1
On Shame

Shame and Guilt

"Dying of shame" is the signifier with which Lacan opens his final lesson of *The Other Side of Psychoanalysis*: "It has to be said, dying of shame is an effect that is rarely obtained." This term *shame* does not open the lesson by chance; Lacan will close this lesson by returning to the concept: "If . . . there are some slightly less than ignoble reasons for your presence here in such numbers, . . . it is because I happen to make you ashamed."

Éric Laurent has given a particularly stimulating presentation in which he wonders whether it really belongs to psychoanalysis to increase this shame, and whether thereby it is not taking the path of the moralist. This led him onto the theme of guilt: "Shame is an affect that is eminently psychoanalytic and belongs to the same series as guilt." This presentation thus offered a perspective not on the actualities of 1970, noticeably different from our own, marked by the blossoming, the excitement of an agitation of which we were contemporaries, but on an anticipation of the moral phase in which we have entered since the collapse of the Berlin Wall, and giving place to an "unfolding of excuses, regrets, pardons, repentances," to the point where being ashamed would have thus become a global symptom. He places a minor key on this construction and opens another way by emphasizing that Lacan has chosen to punctuate shame rather than guilt, adding also that this "being ashamed" does not allow for any pardon. I want to address this disjunction between shame and guilt. Why do shame and guilt evoke one another while being distinct? When he wanted to locate the analytic discourse in the context of a current moment of contemporary civilization, Lacan chose to conclude his seminar with the term *shame* and not *guilt*. In *The Other Side of Psychoanalysis* Lacan implicitly gave us a new edition of *Civilization and Its Discontents*, after having done so more explicitly in his seminar *The Ethics of Psychoanalysis*, which thus makes it possible for us to measure the displacement from one seminar to the other.

No doubt in the intervening period a new relationship has been teased out between the subject and jouissance. The novelty of this relationship stands out in *The Ethics of Psychoanalysis*, where Lacan could say, without any objections being raised, "The movement the world we are living in is caught up in . . . implies an amputation, sacrifices, indeed a kind of puritanism in the relationship to desire that has occurred historically."[1] In 1960, it was still possible to say that capitalism—a term fallen into disuse because it has no antonym—was coordinated with Puritanism. There is no doubt that behind this word coming from the mouth of Lacan was his knowledge of Max Weber's analyses, taken up and reworked, but not really disconfirmed, by the English historian R. H. Tawney, and which conditioned the emergence of the capitalist subject on the repression of enjoyment—accumulating instead of enjoying.[2]

Lacan returns to the theme of the discontents of civilization in his seminar *The Other Side*, indicating that this diagnosis according to which the movement the world is caught up in is now outdated, whereas the new mode—if it bears the mark of a style at all—is rather that of permissiveness, where what can sometimes be the cause of difficulty is the prohibition on prohibiting.

The least that one can say is that capitalism has disconnected itself from Puritanism. In this respect, Lacan's discourse is, in the terms of Éric Laurent, the most anticipatory. In Lacan's terms, this is expressed, in the final chapter of *The Other Side of Psychoanalysis*, in the statement "There is no longer any shame." I will follow Laurent in emphasizing this term *shame*, to the point of declaring that one thereby uncovers the question at work in *The Other Side of Psychoanalysis*, the cards being put on the table only in the final session.

What does it mean for psychoanalysis when there is no longer any shame, when civilization tends to dissolve shame, to make it disappear? This is not lacking in paradox, since it is traditional to suppose that civilization is bound up with instituting shame.

Perhaps we can formulate that shame is a primary affect in relation to the Other. By saying that this affect is primary, one is no doubt seeking to differentiate it from guilt. If one wanted to pursue that path, one would say that guilt is the effect on the subject of an Other that judges, thus of an Other that contains the values that the subject has supposedly transgressed. One would also claim that shame is related to an Other prior to the Other that judges, that it is a primordial Other, not one that judges but instead one that only sees or lets be seen. Nudity can thus be taken to be shameful and covered up, partially if the shame bears upon this or that organ, independently of anything of the order of misdeed, harm, or transgression that might give rise to it. It is moreover in this immediate manner that shame is introduced into one of the great religious mythologies that condition, or used to condition, the movement of our civilization.

Thus one could try saying that guilt is related to desire, whereas shame is related to the jouissance that touches on what Lacan, in his "Kant with Sade," calls "that which is most intimate in the subject."[3] He refers to this in relation to Sadian jouissance, insofar as it traverses the subject's wish and establishes itself in what is for him most intimate, that which is more intimate than his will, and provokes him to go beyond his will and beyond good and evil, attacking him on the point of his modesty— a term that is the antonym of *shame*.

Lacan describes this modesty in a striking and at the same time enigmatic fashion, as being "amboceptive of the conjunctures of being." *Amboceptive* means that modesty is attached, that it takes hold, on the side of both the subject and the Other. It is attached to both subject and Other. As for the "conjunctures of being," the relationship to the Other constitutes the essential conjuncture of the subject's being and demonstrates itself as such in shame. Lacan makes this explicit when he says, "The shamelessness of one forms the veil for the shame of the other."[4]

In this inaugural relationship not only is there shame over what I am or what I do, but if the other goes beyond the limits of modesty, my own modesty is affected by this very fact. This is not exactly the way of making ashamed that Lacan prescribes at the end of his seminar. The experience of shame uncovers, as it were, an amboception or pseudo-coincidence of subject and Other.

The Gaze and Shame

In *Seminar XI*, Lacan refers to a celebrated episode for the appearance of shame, the one sketched out by Sartre in *Being and Nothingness* with respect to the look or the gaze, and which takes place in two moments. The first moment: "I am looking through a keyhole." The second moment: "I hear the sound of footsteps in the hallway, I am being looked at. And so I become ashamed." It is an account of the emergence of the affect of shame as a collapse of the subject. While he is there, "looking through the keyhole," he is "a pure spectator subject, absorbed by the spectacle, unaware of himself." He is not "conscious of himself in a positional mode," as he puts it, and strictly speaking, "in this 'looking through the keyhole,' I am nothing." He attempts to describe for us a moment of the subject's fading, which we could write with its Lacanian symbol, $.

The second moment, bound up with the sound, makes the gaze emerge as such. We can clearly see why the footsteps are necessary. Sartre wants to capture the subject before he recognizes the one who is about to see him. He formulates his "I'm being looked at" before seeing the person's face. The gaze is anonymous. Behind this anonymity there is hidden, no doubt, in Lacanian algebra, the Other's gaze. And Sartre describes the decadence of the subject, who is previously eclipsed in his action and becomes an object, who then finds himself seeing himself, via this mediation, as an object in the world, and Sartre is trying to grasp the subject's fall in the status of this shameful reject. This is where shame is introduced: "I recognize that I am this object that the Other regards and judges. I am that being-in-itself."

The Sartrian conjunction of gaze and judgment perhaps needs to be called into question, or at least unsettled, since it produces what looks like a slide from shame to guilt. Saying "I am this being-in-itself" means that I am thereby cut off from time, from a project. I am seized in the present, a present deprived of my transcendence, of my projection toward my future, toward the meaning that this action could have and which would permit me to justify it. A judgment is something different.

In order to judge, one has to begin to talk. I may have very good reasons for looking through the keyhole. Perhaps what is happening on the other side should be judged and reproached: a present deprived of all transcendence.

I mention this episode only to give some background, a resonance, to Lacan's diagnosis "There is no longer any shame." It can be translated as this: we are at the time of an eclipse of the Other's gaze as the bearer of shame.

Gaze and Jouissance

Éric Laurent, with a striking intuition and construction, has connected this final chapter of *Seminar XVII* with the proposal Lacan addressed to students at Vincennes representing the sublime, the fever of the agitation of the period: "Look at them enjoying!" He remarked that this invitation, this imperative, is in some way echoed today in that fever the media has had, which has abated a little, but which retains its significance as a fact of civilization, for reality shows—*Big Brother*.

This "Look at them enjoying!" recalls the gaze, which previously was the preeminent agency for making one ashamed. For the period in which Lacan is speaking, if it is necessary to recall the gaze, it is because the Other who could be looking has disappeared. The look that one solicits today by turning reality into a spectacle—and all television is a reality show—is a gaze castrated of its power to shame, which it is constantly demonstrating. As if the mission, or at least the unconscious consequence, of this capture of the television spectacle was to demonstrate that shame is dead.

If one can imagine that Lacan evokes this "Look at them enjoying!" in 1970 as an attempt to reactivate the gaze that shames, one can no longer think this is the case for reality shows. The gaze that is distributed there—a mouse click away—is a gaze that carries no shame. It is certainly no longer the gaze of the Other that might judge. What is transmitted in this shameful universal practice is the demonstration that your gaze, far from conveying shame, is nothing other than a gaze that enjoys as well. It is the "Look at them enjoying so as to enjoy!"

This connection that Laurent brings us reveals the secret of the spectacle, which one has even wanted to make into the insignia of contemporary society by calling it, like Guy Debord, the society of the spectacle.[5] The secret of the spectacle is that you look at it because you enjoy it. It is you as subject, and not as Other, that is looking. This television signifies that the Other does not exist. This is why one can hear, in the harmonics of Lacan's proposition, the enactment of the consequences of the death of God, a theme to which Lacan devoted what is effectively a chapter in his *Ethics of Psychoanalysis*. What Lacan describes—and what we have to deal with since it anticipates the path to our current situation—is the death of the gaze of God. I see testimony, perhaps slight, to this in the truly Lacanian phrase that appears in this final seminar: "Appreciate why it was that Pascal and Kant fidgeted about like two valets in the process of acting like Vatel with respect to you."

The Death of the Other

Vatel is better known these days due to a film in which this character is played by Gérard Depardieu.[6] François Vatel, who is known to those who, like the grandmother of Marcel Proust, frequent the correspondence of Mme. de Sévigné, was an organizer of festivities who went into service with Prince de Condé in April 1671. Prince de Condé invites the entire court to spend three days with him at his chateau, and Vatel is in charge of all preparations and service. According to Mme. de Sévigné, he goes without sleep for twelve whole nights and, added to this, apparently, suffers a disappointment in love (embodied in the film by a star who shows how much he happens to be losing). He has provided for a dozen deliveries of fish and seafood, but only two arrive. He comes to the point of desperation—he is visibly depressed—and persuades himself that the feast has been spoiled through his own doing. He goes up to his room, fixes a sword to the door handle, and runs himself through with it two or three times, thereby killing himself and inscribing his name in the history books. Lacan didn't see the film—it is too recent—yet it is the name of Vatel that comes to him as the paradigm of a person who dies from shame, and who was sufficiently in tune with this "dying of shame," despite being not of the nobility in any way, but, as Lacan stresses, a steward instated in a world which is the world of the nobility.

Lacan compares Pascal and Kant with Vatel, and he sees them on the verge of suicide through shame, fidgeting about, constructing their labyrinth in order to escape. In what way were Kant and Pascal tormented by the shame of living and twisting around to the point where they bring the gaze of the big Other into existence, the big Other under which one can be lead to the point of dying of shame? Lacan gives an indication in passing: "There has been a lack of truth up above for the last three centuries." He says this in the twentieth century, but he is referring back to the seventeenth.

Is this not the meaning of Pascal's famous wager we discover here? Pascal's wager is an attempt to sustain the Other's existence. It is a piece of chicanery, agitation, in order to get to the point of stating that there is in effect a God with whom, as Lacan says elsewhere in this seminar, it is worth going to the trouble of playing double-or-nothing surplus jouissance. You cannot rest on the fact that there is a God; you have to make an effort of your own by means of the wager. Pascal's wager is his way of making an effort of his own in order to sustain the Other's ex-sistence.

What does the wager mean? It means that one has to wager one's life in the game—as an object small *a* that one places in the game as a wager, which one accepts might be lost, in the aim of gaining eternal life. This God needs the wager in order to exist. If one makes the effort, if this crutch of a wager is necessary, then it is ultimately the case that this God is on shaky ground, as it were, and that he does not fill his place entirely. This supposes that the Other in question is an Other that is not barred. One is hoping that he will be up to the task.

As for Kant, briefly put, it is a matter not of a wager but of hypotheses. In *Critique of Pure Reason*, both the immortality of the soul and the existence of God are recuperated, not as certitudes, but as necessary hypotheses for morality to have a meaning.

In this vein, it can be said that Pascal and Kant have struck a blow. They have worn themselves out, if I may say so. They have been at work —this is why they are on the side of the valet—so that the gaze of the Other retains a meaning, that is, so that shame exists and that there is something beyond life pure and simple.

Shame and Honor

With respect to the pathetic effort of these great minds, Lacan inscribes Vincennes, which at the time he called "obscene," and which in 1970 he grasps as a place where shame has no currency. He advanced toward this Vincennes. Lacan apparently said it too indirectly for anyone to call out in protest. How did he view it? As the renunciation of what was still the pathetic trembling of Pascal and Kant, and the assumption of the nonexistence of shame. It is an irony of history that Lacan has been classified as a partisan of the 1968 frame of mind. One cannot read anything as severe with respect to '68, but within this severity there was a friendly tone. Lacan has no doubt never been forgiven this.

Why, Laurent asks, and he gave a reply, should the disappearance of shame, in civilization, be of interest to a psychoanalyst? If we take it up from the angle of Vatel, there is a reply: because the disappearance of shame alters the meaning of life. It changes the meaning of life because it changes the meaning of death. Vatel, who died of shame, died for honor, in the name of honor. The term forms a pair with the word *shame*, shame hidden by modesty, but heightened, enlarged, by honor.

When honor retains its value, life does not prevail over honor. Where there is honor, life is purely and simply devalued. This pure and simple life is what is traditionally expressed as *primum vivere*.[7] Live first, we will see why later; saving life is the supreme value. The example of Vatel is there to tell us that even a valet can sacrifice his life for the sake of honor. The disappearance of honor instates the primum vivere as supreme value, the ignominious life, the ignoble life, life without honor. This is why Lacan evokes, at the end of this final seminar, the reasons that could be "less than ignoble."

This can be expressed in mathemes. The matheme in play is the representation of the subject by what Lacan constructs in this seminar as the master signifier S_1.

The disappearance of shame means that the subject ceases to be represented by a signifier that matters. This is why Lacan presents, at the outset of this lesson, the Heideggerian term of being-toward-death as the "visiting card by which a signifier represents a subject for another signifier."[8] He gives this S_1 the value of a visiting card, "the being-towards-death." It is death that is not pure and simple, death conditioned by a value that outclasses it, and once this card is torn up, he says, it is a shame. Its destination is from now on a mockery, since by way of its inscription as $\$$ the subject can be meshed with a knowledge and an order of the world in which he has his place, as a master of ceremonies in this case, but he must maintain his place. As soon as he no longer fulfills his function he disappears, that is to say, he sacrifices himself to the signifier that he was destined to incarnate.

When one has come to the point at which everybody tears up his visiting card, where there is no shame any more, the ethics of psychoanalysis is called into question. The entire seminar, *The Ethics of Psychoanalysis*, and the example taken of Antigone, are there to show us on the contrary that the analytic operation supposes something beyond the primum vivere. It supposes that man, as he put it at that time, has a relationship to the second death. Not to a single death, not to death pure and simple, but to a second death, a relationship to what he is insofar as he is represented by a signifier. This should be sacrificed for nothing in the world. He who sacrifices his life sacrifices all but that which is the most intimate, the most precious in his existence.

Lacan searches for an example of this in the tragedy of Oedipus, precisely when he enters the zone between-two-deaths where he has renounced everything. He is no longer anything other than a cast-off accompanying Antigone. He puts his own eyes out and thus all the goods of this world disappear for him, but, as Lacan notes, "That doesn't prevent him from demanding . . . all the honors due to his rank."[9] In the tragedy, one does not give Oedipus what he has the right to after the sacrifice of a beast—some parts are valued, others not—he is not given what is his, and, although he has already passed beyond the first limit, he highlights what is a slight on his honor as a terrible insult, says Lacan. Even as he abandons all his goods, he affirms the dignity of the signifier that represents him.

The other example that Lacan takes in this respect, that of King Lear, goes in the same direction. Here too is a character who leaves everything, but who, having renounced all his power, continues to hang onto the faithfulness of his own family and onto what Lacan calls a pact of honor.

The Ethics of Psychoanalysis supposes, if not from start to finish, then at least over the first third, the difference between a death that amounts to kicking the bucket and the death of being-toward-death. The death of a being that wishes death is related to the master signifier. It is a death that is risked or a death that is wished for or a death that is assumed, and which is related to the transcendence of the signifier. On the basis of this so unusual accent that Lacan places on this "dying of shame" and this "making ashamed"—which horrified a psychoanalyst colleague, or seemed to him to be displaced, according to Laurent—the signifier *honor*, the word *honor*, continues to have its full value for Lacan when he is trying to found the analytic discourse today.

I said to myself, "Honor, honor, where does he say that?" It is to be found, for example, initially when he gives a summary of one of his late seminars, ". . . Ou pire": "D'autres s' . . . oupirent," "Others sigh or worsen. I undertake not to make it my honor."[10] This word *honor* resonates with the entire configuration that I have been teasing out. It is not only the honor of Lacan, since he adds, "It is a matter of the meaning of the practice of psychoanalysis." The meaning of this practice is not thinkable without honor, is not thinkable if the other side of psychoanalysis is not functioning, this other side that is the master's discourse and the master signifier established in its place. For the subject to spit it out, he has to have been marked by it in the first place. The honor of psychoanalysis derives from the subject's link maintained with the master signifier.

This "honor" is not an anomaly. For example, Lacan feels the need to justify the fact that he is interested in André Gide. Gide deserves our interest because Gide was interested in Gide, not in the sense of a vain narcissism, but because Gide was a subject interested in his own singularity, however fragile it might have been. There is perhaps no better definition of a person who offers to be the analysand. The minimum that can be required is that he is interested in his own singularity, a singularity that draws on nothing else than this S_1, this signifier that is his alone. Lacan, not yet having formalized this master signifier, calls it, in his text on Gide, the subject's "emblem," a term intended to resonate with *honor*: "The emblem that the iron of an encounter has imprinted upon the subject." He also says, "The seal is not only an imprint but a hieroglyph as well."[11]

Each of these terms could be studied for its true value. The imprint is simply a natural mark whereas one deciphers hieroglyphs; but he stresses that in either case it is a signifier, and its meaning is not to have one. One can anticipate that this unusual mark is what he will later call the master signifier that marks the subject with an ineffaceable singularity.

Singularity

At the time Lacan did not recoil from saying that this respect for one's own singularity, this attention to one's signifier singularity, is what makes the subject a master. He opposes it to all words of wisdom, which on the contrary have an air of slavery about them. These wise words that are valid for everyone, these so-called arts of living, all install themselves through neglecting the individual mark in each person that does not allow itself to be reabsorbed into the universal that they proposed. The words of wisdom hiding this mark of the branding iron are hoisted up by the use of this weight, by this travesty, and this is why Lacan imputes an air of slavery to them.

It is no doubt a question, in *The Other Side of Psychoanalysis*, of separating the subject from its master signifier in the analytic operation. But this assumes that he knows he has one, and that he respects it.

Following this line of thought, I would place great weight on what Lacan says, in passing, about his text on Gide, namely that to be interested in one's singularity is the luck of the aristocracy.[12] We are not in the habit of using the term *aristocracy*, but it is nevertheless unavoidable when one returns to Lacan's position in the face of this fact of civilization that was Vincennes. Everything indicates that what he encountered there he classified as belonging to the register of the ignoble, and that, in the face of the emergence of a place from which shame had disappeared, he had an aristocratic reaction. For him this aristocracy is justified because desire is in part bound up with the master signifier—that is to say, with nobility. This is why he can say, in his text on Gide, that the secret of desire is the secret of all nobility.[13] Your S_1 is contingent and, however fragile you may be, places you apart. The condition for being an analysand is to have the sense of what places you apart.

Going even further back, it is something like an aristocratic reaction that motivates the objections Lacan always trotted out in the face of the objectifications to which contemporary civilization constrains the therapist or the intellectual, the researcher. See, for instance, what he offers as an analysis of modern man's ego once he has emerged from the impasse of playing the beautiful soul who censures the course of the world even as he plays his part in it.[14] How does he describe it? On the one hand, this modern man takes his place in universal discourse, collaborates in the advance of science, takes his place as he should, and at the same time forgets his subjectivity, forgets his existence and his death. Lacan did not get to the point of saying, "He watches television," but he mentions crime novels and other diversions.

We have here the outline of a critique of what Heidegger calls inauthentic existence, the realm of the "they." Moreover, in existentialism, even Sartrian existentialism, which included this criticism of the inauthentic, there was also an aristocratic pretension. Do not forget what his existence and his death possessed that was absolutely singular. Here we can see—one does not have to go searching for it or interpret it—Lacan evoking, in contrast with the ego of modern man, what he calls the creative subjectivity, the one that campaigns, he says, for the renewal of the power of symbols.[15] He also says, in passing, "This creation," subjective creation, where the routine masses recite symbols, go around in circles, and extinguish their own subjectivity in futility, "is supported by a small number of subjects." He has hardly formulated this thought when he invites us not to subscribe to it; it is a "romantic point of view." However, there is no mistaking that Lacan places himself among this small number of subjects.

On this basis, at the point in *Television* where he advocates the emergence of capitalist discourse, Lacan writes, "This does not constitute progress if it is only for some." The precise formulation says that the first thought presented there is that it is only for some and not for everyone. The limit of this small number is what Lacan was indicating as this ridiculous thought that one has to distance oneself from and which was "at least me."

When Lacan brings this out at the end of *The Other Side of Psychoanalysis*, I see the traces, the expression of his debate with the aristocracy, his debate with the nobility that is a nobility of desire. The question he asks himself concerning psychoanalysis is this: What is the situation of psychoanalysis in these times when nobility has been eclipsed? Do not forget that when he modified the master's discourse to make it the capitalist's discourse, he inverted the two terms and wrote the barred S above the line, denoting a subject who no longer has a master signifier as referent.

This is confirmed, in this final chapter of *The Other Side*, by a very precise reference to Hegel's *The Phenomenology of Mind*, to the dialectic of noble and vile consciousness, which is the truth of noble consciousness. He relies on this in order to formulate that nobility is destined to become villainy, worthless. The time of the nobility flows into the time where there is no longer any shame. This is why he can say to the students, to the agitators in his public, "The more ignoble you are the better it will be."

One can see why he could speak to the students who crowded into his seminar about their ignominy. He explains it, indirectly, "Henceforth, as subjects, you will be pinned down by signifiers that are only countable signifiers and which will efface the singularity of the S_1." They have begun to transform the singularity of the S_1 into units of value. The master signifier is the singular unit of value, which cannot be quantified, which will not fit into a calculus in which everything is weighed. This is the context in which he proposes to "make ashamed," which has nothing to do with guilt. Making ashamed is an effort to reinstate the agency of the master signifier.

Honesty

There is no doubt a moment in history where the value of honor was found to be exhausted and then eliminated. It has been deplored over the centuries. There was a continual modification of and decline in this honor. Whereas the civilization that bore this honor was the feudal civilization, one can see, bit by bit, this honor becoming twisted, enfeebled, being captured by the court, which Hegel analyzes concerning vile consciousness and noble consciousness. Kojève read it this way, and Lacan did also no doubt, as a reference to the history of France. Captured by the court following the stupidity of the Fronde, which was the final resistance of an ancient form of honor, before honor turned into courtierism. This culminates over the course of the eighteenth century in the renunciation of aristocratic virtue in favor of bourgeois values.

What was aristocratic virtue in its day? A master signifier that was strong enough for the subject to draw upon for his self-esteem and, at the same time, the authorization and the duty to affirm, not his equality with, but his superiority over, others. This is how magnanimity, which is an Aristotelian virtue, was recycled in aristocratic morality, and it can be found in Descartes under the name of generosity in his *Treatise on the Passions*.[16]

On this point even Nietzsche's *Übermensch* finds its historical anchoring point. This aristocratic virtue is in part tied up with heroism. Even if Lacan nuances it—"Everyone is both a hero and a common man, and the goals that he can give himself as a hero he accomplishes as the common man"—a central character that he moves around throughout *The Ethics of Psychoanalysis* is the character of the hero, vehicle of aristocratic virtue, and in particular the virtue—and this is elementary—that enables one to go beyond the primum vivere.

The virtues of what has emerged as the modern man imply the renunciation of aristocratic virtue and of what it obliged in terms of braving death. One of the places this is brought about is in the work of Hobbes, which reveres aristocratic virtue while at the same time deducing that the social bond is above all established in the face of the fear of death, that is, the contrary of aristocratic virtue. Cultivated minds these days refer to this discourse in which one finds the foundation for the claim that security is essential for modern man. This is to affirm that heroism no longer means anything.

This is where new virtues have been proposed—for instance, what the Americans call "greed," and the famous slogan of the 1980s, "Greed is good." Capitalism functions by means of greed. It is also the reign, which does not stop growing, of the profit-loss calculus. When we are constantly offered evaluations of the analytic operation, this is nothing other than the reign of the profit-loss calculus that is making ground within psychoanalysis.

Let us not get on our high horse. There is a place for what Lacan calls, on the first page of his final seminar, honesty. This is a very precise reference to Hegel. When setting out his dialectic of the vile consciousness and the noble consciousness, Hegel evokes honest consciousness, consciousness in repose, which takes "each moment as an essence that endures." For this consciousness, everything is in its place; it "sings the melody of the good and the true." Hegel opposes to it the dissonances made apparent by the fractured consciousness whose paradigm is *Rameau's Nephew*.[17] This fractured consciousness appears in the perpetual reversal of all concepts, all realities, which indicates universal deception—self-deception and deception of others—and testifies to what Hegel calls the impudence of speaking this deception.

Rameau's nephew is the great figure that emerges—and perhaps Diderot kept the manuscript in his drawer out of shame—of the shameless intellectual, in relation to which he who says "I" in *Rameau's Nephew* finds himself in the position of honest consciousness, who sees the propositions that he advances being reversed and denatured by the unleashed nephew of Rameau, and who has the wool pulled over his eyes. At Vincennes—which is reproduced under the title "Analyticon" in the published seminar—Lacan found himself in the position of the ego in relation to *Rameau's Nephew*. He found himself in the position of honest consciousness. He differentiated himself from it in vomiting up the ignoble in his seminar.

Lacan defines the honest person as one who makes it a point of honor not to mention shame. In his seminar he oversteps this limit. It is frankly dishonest to speak like that to people who have received him kindly. The honest person is evidently one who has already renounced honor, renounced its emblem, and who would like it to be the case that shame did not exist—one who enrobes and veils the real of which this shame is the affect.

Even if it is an exaggeration to do so, one cannot help but think that the really honest person that Lacan happens to refer to, and who no doubt held shame at arm's length, is Freud. He could say that "Freud's ideal was an ideal tempered with honesty, patriarchal honesty."[18] Freud was still benefiting from the waning of the Father and, as Lacan demonstrates in his seminar *The Other Side*, psychoanalysis, far from downgrading the Father, has done all it can to try to preserve his status. It has made a renewed effort to found the notion of an all-loving Father.

When Lacan evokes the patriarchal honesty of the Freudian ideal, the reference he takes is Diderot, the Father of the family.[19] Diderot serves as a guide, insofar as he is just on the point of rupture between the patriarchal ideal and the figure of *Rameau's Nephew*, which treats this patriarchal honesty with derision.

Impudence

Lacan never ceases telling the students of the day that they represent a world in which there is no shame anymore. On the contrary, he tried to indicate to them that, with their frivolous [*éventé*] air—one has to hear *éhonté*, "shameless"—they run up against a highly developed "shame at being alive" at every turn. Having censured this absence of shame, he shows them that there is nevertheless shame at being alive behind the absence of shame. This is what psychoanalysis is able to point out, that the shameless are shameful. To be sure, they challenge the master's discourse, the solidarity between the master and the worker, both being a part of the same system. He refers to the Senatus Populusque Romanus, the Senate and the Roman people, who each benefited from the master signifier. He indicates to these students that they are placed with the others in excess, that is to say, the rejects of the system, not with the proletariat but with the *lumpenproletariat*. It is a very precise remark and it runs right across all the years we have lived through since. This enables him to deduce that this system that adheres to the master signifier produces shame. The students, by placing themselves outside the system, put themselves in the place of impudence.

This is where we can see what has changed since then. We are in a system that does not obey the same regulation because we are in a system that produces impudence and not shame, that is, in a system that annuls the function of shame. We no longer apprehend it except in the form of insecurity—a form of insecurity that is imputed to the subject, who is no longer under the domination of a master signifier. The present moment of this civilization is permeated by an authoritarian and artificial return of the master signifier. Everyone must work in their place or be locked up.

While in the system Lacan was in, it was still possible to say "make ashamed." Impudence has progressed greatly since, and today it has become the norm. What does one obtain from saying to the subject, "You owe something to yourself"? There is no doubt that psychoanalysis must define its position in relation to the aristocratic reaction that I have referred to. This is indeed the question that haunts our practice: Is it for everyone?

This is Lacan's fundamental debate. It was never really a debate with ego psychology, nor was it with his colleagues. Lacan's fundamental debate—it is clear in *The Other Side of Psychoanalysis*, as it was already in *The Ethics of Psychoanalysis*—has always been a debate with civilization insofar as it abolishes shame, with the globalization that is in process, with Americanization or with utilitarianism, that is, with the reign of what Kojève calls the Christian bourgeois.

The path that Lacan proposes is the signifier as vehicle of a value of transcendence. This is condensed into S_1. Again, things have changed since *The Other Side of Psychoanalysis*, because the signifier has been affected. Speech itself has been reduced to the pair *listening* and *chattering*. What one attempts to preserve in the analytic session is a space in which the signifier retains its dignity.

The begging pardon that Laurent mentions belongs more to the register of guilt; it helps one to forget the register of shame and honor. Why does one find oneself begging pardon? In this practice, which has become a little outdated since things have tightened up over national and international insecurity, one wanted to make it the case that begging pardon for the S_1s, for the values, which have activated one, and which are deadly or harmful. Throughout this "begging pardon" there is the affirmation of the primum vivere. No value one believes one's self to carry is worth the sacrifice of anyone's life. Hence the careful compilations of the crimes of all the great idealizing forces over the course of history.

We can estimate the difference between today and the period of *The Other Side of Psychoanalysis*. We are at a point where the dominant discourse enjoins one not to be ashamed of one's jouissance anymore. Ashamed of all the rest, yes, of one's desire, but not of one's jouissance.

I had an extraordinary example of this when I met Daniel Widlocher.[20] I conveyed to him one of the results of the careful reading of the papers in this orientation, according to which the practice of the countertransference, the passionate attention the analyst brought to his own mental processes, seemed nevertheless to be a kind of jouissance. You hesitate to say these things to one of its eminent practitioners. And there it was I who was surprised. "Yes, of course," he said. "And it's even an infantile jouissance."

Notes

First published in *La cause freudienne*, no. 54 (2003), 9–19. Lecture from Jacques-Alain Miller's course The Lacanian Orientation III, June 5, 2002. Text and notes edited by Catherine Bonningue. Translated by Russell Grigg.

1 Jacques Lacan, *The Seminar of Jacques Lacan, Book VII: The Ethics of Psychoanalysis*, ed. J.-A. Miller, trans. D. Porter (New York: Norton, 1992), 303.
2 See Max Weber, *General Economic History*, trans. F. Knight (London: George Allen & Unwin, 1923); and R. H. Tawney, *Religion and the Rise of Capitalism* (London: Penguin, 1948).

3 Jacques Lacan, *Ecrits* (Paris: Seuil, 1966), 771.
4 Ibid., 772.
5 Guy Debord, *The Society of the Spectacle* (New York: Zone Books, 1994).
6 *Vatel*, a French, British, and Belgian film released in May 2000, was produced by Roland Joffé.
7 *Primum vivere, deinde philosophari*, live first, then philosophize.
8 Lacan, *Ethics*, 209.
9 Ibid., 304.
10 Jacques Lacan, ". . . ou pire. Compte rendu du séminaire 1971–72," in *Autres écrits* (Paris: Seuil, 2001), 547.
11 Lacan, "Jeunesse de Gide ou la lettre et le désir," in *Ecrits*, 756.
12 Ibid., 757.
13 Ibid.
14 Jacques Lacan, "Function and Field of Speech and Language in Psychoanalysis," *Ecrits: A Selection*, trans. B. Fink (New York: Norton, 2002), 69.
15 Ibid., 283–84.
16 René Descartes, *The Philosophical Writings of René Descartes*, ed. J. Cottingham, R. Stoothoff, and D. Murdoch, vol. 2 (Cambridge: Cambridge University Press, 1985).
17 Denis Diderot, *Rameau's Nephew and D'Alembert's Dream*, trans. and intro. L. Tancock (Harmondsworth: Penguin, 1966).
18 Lacan, *Ethics*, 177. Translation modified.
19 Ibid.
20 Miller's interview with Daniel Widlocher was published in March 2003 in the first issue of the review *Psychiatrie et sciences humaines*.

2

Enjoyment and Impossibility: Lacan's Revision of the Oedipus Complex

Paul Verhaeghe

The strength of the master is determined by the degree of weakness he can bear.
—Jacques Lacan

Seminar XVII, The Other Side of Psychoanalysis, will undoubtedly enter history as the seminar on the four discourses. In this essay I will focus on what grounds the discourse is structured: the prohibition on enjoyment.[1] In classical Freudian thought, this has everything to do with the father, meaning that the function of the father will become our second focus. In *Seminar XVII*, we learn that enjoyment is not so much forbidden as impossible, and that the real father only plays the role of the structural operator. In brief: he is the one "left holding the baby," the one who not only has to pass through and transmit castration but is also subjected to it himself.

In the wider span of Lacan's seminars, *Seminar XVII* sits in opposition to *Seminar VII*, *The Ethics of Psychoanalysis*, and occupies a transitional place between *Seminar XI*, *The Four Fundamental Concepts*, and *Seminar XX*, *Encore*. In his seminar on ethics, jouissance was conceived as real and therefore diametrically opposed to the symbolic. Enjoyment could be reached only through transgression of the law. In *The Other Side of Psychoanalysis*, in contrast, jouissance is of the order of an invasion. Moreover, Lacan will put forward a primordial relationship between jouissance and the signifier. In so doing, certain themes of *Seminar XI* will be taken up again and enhanced, only to reach their full development in *Seminar XX*. These principally concern the *objet a*, the impossibility of the sexual relationship, and the function of the father. The changes in the latter are particularly far reaching: the famous Name-of-the-Father will be replaced by S_1. Furthermore, S_1 can now be any signifier.

Enjoyment and Knowledge: $(a) \mathbin{/\mkern-5mu/} S_2$

Enjoyment is a very ambiguous term, particularly as it always evokes the idea of pleasure. Lacan will never define this concept very clearly, providing us with only vague indications. We learn that "it begins with a tickle and ends in a blaze of petrol" (83). In fact, jouissance is the opposite of pleasure: *Unlust*, *déplaisir* (89). This imprecision is deliberate: for Lacan, enjoyment is by definition undefinable; it is that which escapes symbolization (205). There is no concept of jouissance in Freud, despite the fact that Lacan takes his inspiration for it from Freud.[2] More specifically, he finds it in Freud's conclusion that there must be something "beyond" (*jenseits*) the pleasure principle that works against it and which serves, furthermore, as the cause of a strange repetition—strange, because what is repeated is not exactly what could be called pleasure. This will ground Freud's final conception of the drive in the opposition between Eros and Thanatos.

The heart of this theory is that the human being is driven by two opposing drives, one striving for death (Thanatos), that is, a return to a state of total rest and zero tension, the other (Eros) striving to maintain life through the production of differential tensions. In the end, Thanatos always wins, hence Freud's conclusion that life is nothing but a self-fashioned detour on the way to death. One of the implications of this theory is that the idea of "pleasure" must be reexamined very closely. Indeed, the inescapable conclusion of Freud's new drive theory is that death is the final form of pleasure.

Lacan continues along this same line of reasoning. The surprising new theme in *Seminar XVII* is the idea of an original relationship between jouissance and the signifier, in the sense that the origin of the apparatus of the signifier in the subject is closely bound up with jouissance. This is in diametrical opposition to his *Seminar VII* on ethics, where jouissance is regarded as the opposite of the symbolic. For that matter, the relation between the signifier and jouissance also remains a bit paradoxical in *Seminar XVII*. As we will shortly see, for Lacan the signifier is both the cause of the impossibility of reaching jouissance and, simultaneously, the path to its attainment.

At the beginning of the seminar, Lacan revisits Freud's idea of *Jenseits*. Life is a self-fashioned detour on the way to death and, in most cases, life is in no hurry to reach the end (17–18). One is reminded of the joke about the two alcoholics: "Alcohol is supposed to slowly kill you." "Well, we're not in any hurry, are we?" Lacan connects this detour to the instinct, making a connection between jouissance and a certain form of knowledge. The instinct contains an ancestral knowledge that causes life to dawdle on the road to death (17). As death is the final form of jouissance, this detour is at the same time the road to jouissance. Understanding the instinct as knowledge implies that there is an original connection between a certain form of knowledge and jouissance (54). This gives rise to an even more surprising new thesis in view of his previous theory: the connection between knowledge and jouissance is the foundation for the introduction of the apparatus of the signifier in the subject.

Lacan finds the explanation for this in Freud's theory of repetition (50, 89). Repetition is grounded in an attempt to reach jouissance, which is why one starts out again on the (side) road to jouissance. But, unlike Freud, Lacan presents us with a specific elaboration of the way this detour is paved. The line of reasoning runs as follows: jouissance takes place in the body, through invasions (19). These invasions acquire markings; they are inscribed on the body through the intervention of the Other (55). Walking along the road to jouissance, one will inevitably follow the signs that have previously been erected along this road (89). The instinctual knowledge is then grafted onto this mapping.

One finds the germ of this reasoning in Freud, who posits that every mother "seduces" her child while caring for it. In *Seminar XX*, Lacan describes the real body as an "enjoying substance," during which the initial experiences of jouissance (the invasions) simultaneously imply their inscription on the body.[3] This is their "use value," but in itself this does not suffice for talking about jouissance in terms of the subject. The necessary supplement is the mother's interventions—her "motherly llanguage"— that mark the invasions of jouissance in the course of her interactions with the child. Through these interventions, the original use value enters into a dialectical exchange between the subject and the Other, and the experiences of jouissance acquire an "exchange value." In this way, a map of jouissance is built up through the sign markings.

The conceptual double of "invasion" and "inscription" is important because it sets up an original ambiguity that will only increase from that point onward. Invasion refers to the enjoying body itself, the body as a "being of jouissance." At first sight, this tallies perfectly with Lacan's earlier theory, in which jouissance was regarded as something of the order of the real. Inscription, on the other hand, refers to something or someone who inscribes—that is, to the Other (55). "Jouissance of the Other" then takes on an ambiguous expression in *Seminar XX*, where "the Other" becomes both the body and the Other who marks jouissance on that body.

The simplest form of inscription is the "unary trait." In his *Seminar IX* on identification, Lacan used the unary trait as the starting point for subject formation. The subject identifies with a unary trait that comes from the Other in order to build a singular identity over its lack of being. In *Seminar XVII* he develops this connection between the unary trait and the Other through the concept of jouissance. The Other marks the invasions of the enjoying body through the unary trait. The mandatory repetitions—mandatory because they mark the road to jouissance—lie at the origin of the signifier, says Lacan, and therefore also at the origin of the knowledge that interests us as analysts (52). The surprising conclusion, then, is that the human being learns about the signifier through jouissance. In other words: jouissance is the gateway to the apparatus of the signifier (14, 18, 206).

The repetition of the inscriptions forms the basis of the signifier and gives content to the ancestral, instinctive knowledge. This is an acephalous knowledge, a "knowledge without a head," that is, without self-consciousness, that forms the kernel of what Freud calls primary repression—that which has always been repressed (102). In terms of content, we learn that it concerns life and death, with the detours paved by life toward death. As knowledge, it is inscribed on the body every time the invasions of jouissance on this body are marked by the Other (54–56). Consequently, this knowledge is originally a means to jouissance. In addition, it has little to do with speech in itself; it is a question of structure (57). The theory of discourse is the best illustration of this, as it permits us to chart certain fundamental relations that precede actual speech (11). Later in this essay, I will discuss what effects this has on the positions in the Oedipal structure.

Heads You Win, Tails I Lose: Loss and Gain

Jouissance is the gateway to the apparatus of the signifier because the unary trait is inscribed and repeated as a marking of jouissance. The aim of the repetition is both jouissance in itself (repetition of the inscription as an invasion of jouissance) and that which opposes this jouissance (the unary trait and the signifier always imply a loss). Each repetition will therefore be less than what it tries to repeat (51). This idea appears under different names throughout the seminar: "objet a," "déperdition," "entropy," "plus-de-jouir." However, the signifier is also the cause of the loss, the cause of the division between the subject and the body as organism. Hence the fact that the signifier, as a means for attaining jouissance, necessarily must fail and, in failing, can only further confirm the original loss. Here, we encounter a second ambiguous relation: knowledge, once it has been introduced into the signifier, is both the means to jouissance and the cause of the loss of jouissance.

This idea of loss and lack is central to Lacan. When compared to his previous seminars (particularly *Seminar XI*), his conception of lack in *Seminar XVII* appears strikingly novel and different. Here, lack is described as an effect of the signifier that, as a means for recovering jouissance, precisely confirms its loss. Beginning with his paper on the mirror stage, Lacan always described the loss, whose clearest formulation can be found in *Seminar XI*, in terms of nature. The birth of the individual as a sexed being implies the loss of eternal life (see the myth on the lamella in *Seminar XI*), because sexed life makes death a necessary consequence.[4] But in *Seminar XVII* it is the introduction of the signifier that causes the loss of jouissance, which would seem to be a reversal of his previous position. In my reading, this is not the case. The loss caused by the signifier comes *on top of* the loss caused by the introduction of sexed life. It is not only another iteration of this original loss but an attempt to formulate an answer to this loss. This attempt at an answer must fail, for structural reasons, hence the inevitable "encore"—Freud's repetition compulsion. Elsewhere I have described this as a never-ending but always failing circularity, a flywheel movement whose original cause is the original loss (the loss of the eternal life) that continues to repeat an impossible relation on a different level each time (organism-body; bodily image–ego; ego-subject; man-woman).[5]

In addition, this loss is not solely a loss: the introduction of the signifier results in a form of gain alongside the loss, expressed perfectly by yet another ambiguous expression: *plus-de-jouir*. Lacan connects this idea to Marx's concept of "surplus value" (56). This gain is closely bound up with the repetition that has become necessary because of the loss. This already indicates how this is an ambiguous gain, one that lies elsewhere, in a different place than the original jouissance. The comparison with Marx is not coincidental, because this "elsewhere" has to do with the products of culture and industry that provide us with (an always) temporary and partial satisfaction. As products, they are both the effect of the loss of jouissance and a response to this loss—in this sense, they provide us with a plus-de-jouir. The name Lacan gives this is "slivers of jouissance," *les lichettes de la jouissance*. In this way, Lacan comes quite close to Marx's idea of "surplus value" that has to be not only spent but even squandered (19).

But Lacan's idea of plus-de-jouir goes further still. He will completely redefine the Oedipus complex as a cunning social institution that replaces jouissance with something that has a different origin, that is, this plus-de-jouir. What is of principal interest to us during analysis, Lacan says, is learning how the function of plus-de-jouir is established as a replacement for the prohibition of phallic jouissance (85). I will return to this reading of the Oedipus complex in my discussion of the function of the father.

Master Signifier and Divided Subject: S_1 and $\$$

As we saw, the original knowledge, the means to jouissance, is knowledge "without a head" that functions automatically through the repetition of the signs that mark the invasions of jouissance. These invasions have to do with the body as an enjoying substance in itself, while the inscriptions are from the Other. The result is the automaton, knowledge that functions without knowing itself. The question then is: When and how is the "head" introduced, and what are its effects? As we will see, it is a question of identity development and subject formation, that is, the ego versus the divided subject.

Right from the start of the seminar, we learn that S_2 is already present before there is anything like a subject. S_1 enters the game only later, as an interference in S_2 and as an indication of the subject's position (11–12, 178).[6] The introduction of S_1 is the function of the father as a structural operator (143–46). From the moment that repetition is put in motion in the dialectical exchange between S_1 and S_2, the subject becomes a divided subject (18) that tries to reach S_2 in an attempt to attain jouissance, even while this is precisely the cause of the loss of jouissance.

In contrast, the master—that is, the ego—may try to maintain a certain appearance, to coincide with himself, with the S_1, the jubilatory "That's me!" Recall the master's discourse: the divided subject is located under the bar, covered by the S_1, with all the accompanying illusions (106). This idea can already be seen in Lacan's paper on the mirror stage. The body as an organism, that is, as an enjoying substance, is the reunification of all the partial drives that are bundled together in and by the imaginary body-image into a totality and presented by the other: "That's you!" ("tu es cela!").[7] In this way, an imaginary totality is placed on top of the divided subject, as a "me" (32), a little master who pretends to know. Moreover, he pretends to be identical to "himself" (102), an I that is in control of himself: "m'être/maître à moi-même," to be myself, to belong to myself, to be master of myself (70, 178). This is the illusion of the autonomous ego (83). Nevertheless, the knowledge of the master has nothing to do with that other knowledge, whence the clinical fact that this masterly knowledge goes off the rails from time to time. Hence Freud's famous expression: "The I is not master in its own house." And hence, too, every symptom, with the slip of the tongue as the most elementary example. Furthermore, the essence of the master—the ego—is that he does not know what he wants (34).

Such a use of the signifier—the subject supposedly identical to its "own" signifier, "m'être/maître à moi-même"—implies a split between the master signifier and the body, whereby the other signifiers remain inscribed on the body. This is Freud's primary repressed, that which has always been repressed. The master's knowledge is produced as completely autonomous knowledge, independent of that other, mythical, ancestral knowledge (102–3).

Here, we encounter a double division in which the second comes on top of the first. In a first logical moment, a division occurs between the nonspeaking "being," the body as an enjoying organism, and the master signifier. This latter may maintain the illusion of coinciding with itself. Nevertheless, from the introduction of the S_1 onward, man is perpetually marked by a lack of being. This master signifier intervenes on an already existing S_2 and will represent the subject for any other signifier there. The result is the second division, that of the subject in and among the signifiers. Elsewhere I have interpreted this first process as Freud's primary repression, as what, from a Lacanian point of view, could be regarded as a primary alienation. The second process, then, combines Freud's secondary repression and identification. From a Lacanian point of view, this could be coined as secondary alienation.[8]

It's clear that all this is closely bound up with identity acquisition. Here, the introduction of the master signifier is as necessary as it is paradoxical. S_1 forms the basis both for the ego—that is, an illusory, imaginary unity—and for the divided subject. What is less clear is what identity acquisition has to do with jouissance and the place of the Other in this process. In brief, where does the Oedipus complex fit in?

Lacan's earlier theory in this respect was a retake and extension of Freud's theory in structural terms. With his metaphor of the Name-of-the-Father, he mapped out a structure that explains how a child is freed from the desire of the mother by the intervention of the Name-of-the-Father. The most important new aspect, in comparison with Freud's Oedipal theory, is that the father's intervention is directed not toward the child but toward the mother. This remains, by the way, a fairly classic (that is, patriarchal) view: the mother/woman is the dangerous element whose desire must be constrained. The father takes the role of the savior who must free the child from the mother's threatening desire by the grace of his almighty position.[9]

This idea—which might very rapidly result in maternal blame and a call for stronger fathers—is not so rare in Lacan's earlier theory. In *Seminar XVII* it will appear only once, when he compares the mother to a crocodile from whose jaws the only possible escape is through the phallus (129). It is precisely this aspect of his previous theory that will undergo important changes in this very *Seminar XVII*. Here, both the mother and the father are reduced to little more than pawns in a social shadow play of chess, resulting in the impossibility of jouissance being hidden behind a prohibition (85, 91).

The Oedipus Complex: Social Complicity

In Freud, the Oedipus complex deals with identity acquisition and the regulation of the drive, as summed up in the idea of the superego. Lacan dubs Freud's Oedipal theory a dream, a myth, that calls for extensive correction (135, 159). On the basis of *Seminar XVII*, we can propose the following statement: we are the way in which we (don't) enjoy. At first sight, the negation between the brackets seems paradoxical, but this negation is significant because it indicates our dividedness toward "our" enjoying "being." If we "were" our enjoyment, we could not ex-sist as a subject.[10] One's ex-sistence as a subject simultaneously implies a divided stance toward jouissance. Note that this was also one of Freud's earliest discoveries, which became one of the starting points of psychoanalysis: there is a division and a defense within ourselves in relation to what we desire and enjoy. Hence the need for an *Abwehr*, a defense system.

The divided stance toward jouissance—why do we not go full speed at it?—has to do with the threat that enjoyment poses to life itself. This is what Freud understood in his study of *Jenseits* in the opposition between the life and death drives. Lacan offers another take on this: enjoyment and death lie very close to one another; the road to enjoyment is the road to death. Hence the need for an internal, instinctive brake prior even to the onset of a divided subject and an identity. Once subject formation proper begins, this internal brake takes the form of what constitutes the subject: signifiers and, hence, the Other. The distribution of roles in this are as follows: the mother acquires the part of jouissance, the father plays both the role of the brake and that of the brake's guarantee through his prohibition. The price to pay is castration, not just for the mother and the child, but for the father, too. The fact that, in Lacan, "castration" acquires a completely different meaning than in Freud is quite clear—as we will shortly see.

Where does jouissance stem from? It stems from the body as an enjoying substance. This, in itself, is not enough in the sense that jouissance can only ever be experienced as jouissance by being inscribed through the repetitions centered around these inscriptions. The oyster "knows" no enjoyment because it lacks a signifier. At most, it can only "be" enjoyment, a "being of enjoyment" (206). The signifier that inscribes enjoyment in man comes strictly from the Other who, through his or her gestures, marks the body, even the skin, as an object of enjoyment. This means that the subject receives its "own" enjoyment—in actual fact, the enjoyment of the body—in the form of the Other's enjoyment. It is not by accident that in this context Lacan refers to Freud's idea of the lost object, the mythical primordial enjoyment that can be never refound (55). Following on from this, the inscriptions will be repeated in an attempt (not) to attain jouissance: the signifier is both the means for arriving at enjoyment and the cause of its loss. The subsequent articulation of this process leads to subject formation, where the dialectical exchange of alienation and separation—the original division between organism and enjoyment—now becomes both a division within the subject and a division between subject and Other.

Hence, the living being's original divided stance toward its enjoyment—founded on an instinctive knowledge that the road to enjoyment leads to death and therefore must be slowed down—becomes, from the point of the introduction of the Other's signs onward, redistributed. In this way, the original internal division and internal impossibility can be externalized onto the Other. It is she who carries the enjoyment in her, with the result that it is to her that the demand will be addressed and upon whom the prohibition will be put. But the structural impossibility ensures that this demand will never fully be met. This will have far-reaching consequences for the sexual relationship—I refer you here to normal, that is, hysterical desire and the distribution of roles between the genders.

Lacan describes this as a "cunning" transition that replaces the impossibility of jouissance with the prohibition of enjoyment. What makes this possible is the social apparatus that results in the Oedipus complex (85). The question now is how the impossibility is replaced by prohibition and how this emerges as what he calls "*plus-de-jouir*." Here, woman takes on an unavoidably central role. As a mother, she dominates the inscriptions of jouissance; any attempt to repeat jouissance must be addressed to her. The child becomes the demanding party and inhabits a position of dependence toward her. Whereas the original (im)possibility of jouissance was previously located in the living body as a "being of enjoyment," now the possibility for jouissance and the simultaneous need for its failure are displaced onto the mother. She leads her little one toward the plus-de-jouir, as the roads toward jouissance are opened for the child on condition that it renounce the enjoyment that from now on (i.e., from the first moments of inscription) is situated in the mother (89). Lacan locates the cause for this shift in what he calls "social complicity": as the child fixates on the mother, she becomes the chosen seat of the prohibitions through which absolute enjoyment can be avoided (91). This immediately becomes the cause of desire.

The next question is what the role of the father is. At this level, Freud's theory is contradictory, to say the least. The few descriptions he gives of the Oedipus complex are fairly crude. Briefly summarized, his theory goes like this: the child—that is, the male child—wants to kill the father so as to have sexual access to the mother. Out of fear of the father and his threat of castration, the child renounces his incestuous desires and directs his desire toward a future, an elsewhere. The drives become regulated by a special identification that results in the formation of the superego. Once one takes a closer look at Freud's theory, however, it becomes obvious that his reasoning does not make sense, clinically, conceptually, or historically.

The Oedipus Complex: Freud's Dream

What we find in Freud's case studies is diametrically opposed to what he asserts in his theory. From *Studies on Hysteria* onward, we find only weak, ill fathers who need taking care of, frequently by the person who later becomes Freud's patient. Lacan talks of the "father-out-of-service" and refers to the function of the idealized father (108). In Freud's wider case studies, this is even more striking. We encounter an impotent father who barters his daughter with his mistress's husband (Dora); a father who, in several meanings of the word, is very much a "noncommissioned officer" living off his wife's fortune, for which he left his poorer lover (the Rat man); a melancholic father who wanders from one sanatorium to another (the Wolf man); and a father who learns from Freud that he must assume his Oedipal place, despite it being quite clear that he is a weakling (little Hans).

The last case study is the most instructive for noting the gap between Freud's theory and his clinical practice. Hans's mother wears the pants, so the threat of castration comes from her. When Freud produces his famous interpretation, this can be read only—in light of the clinical material—as a suggestive construction: "Long before he [Hans] was in the world, I went on, I had known that a Little Hans would come who would be so fond of his mother that he would be bound to feel afraid of his father because of it; and I had told his father this."[11] This last part was essential, and it operated in a therapeutic-suggestive way. Freud's theoretical model—the child longing for the mother; the severe, castration-threatening and forbidding father; the child thereby renouncing his desire—does not in the slightest correspond with the clinical picture. A Lacanian reading is much closer to the clinical material. Confronted with an invasion of enjoyment—recall his initial phallic "wiwi" experiences—Hans does not know how to handle it and looks for protection. He associates the threat arising from his own enjoyment with his mother and looks to his father for protection. This is why Freud's backup was necessary, although it took on a strange form: desire for the mother, anxiety about the father. Lacan will introduce his first important correction to Freud's Oedipal theory on this point. In Lacan's previous conception, the dominant desire is the mother's desire; the fatherly intervention must be directed toward the mother, thereby freeing the child from his mother and opening up the possibility for a desire of his own. This is the standard reading of the metaphor of the Name-of-the-Father, and it is precisely this reading that undergoes serious changes in *Seminar XVII*.

Freud's theory (of the strong, prohibiting father) thus clearly contradicts his own clinical practice (weak fathers). In *Totem and Taboo*, he will try to solve this inconsistency through a self-invented myth that is designed to save the Oedipal father, that is, his image of this figure. Later he will write that when the individual's reality does not follow the expected and needed model, the child can call on a supraindividual, historical reality that, in one way or another, has been preserved in the collective memory of mankind.[12] Hence, it is no big deal if one is unlucky enough to have a weak father. One can always fall back on this archaic figure. What comes through from this part of the "theory," albeit differently than Freud intended, is the need for a specific father figure. In fact, what he is doing here is giving form to neurotic desire and elevating it, moreover, to a supposedly historical reality.[13]

Now, if we take a closer look at his myth, we are in for another surprise. As Lacan observes, the result of the primal murder is precisely the opposite of its aim in Freud's model (137–38). Once the primal father has been murdered by the sons, they realize that they are brothers and together they collectively install the incest prohibition—that is, they make enjoyment definitively unreachable. In Freud's story, the threat of castration, let alone the actual castration by the primal father, is barely mentioned. As a result, the conclusion is the exact opposite of Freud's: the murder of the primal father is what installs the enjoyment prohibition (139). Freud's reading of Sophocles's tragedy, for that matter, is just as odd. In contradiction to Freud's reading, Oedipus does not gain access to his mother because he has murdered his father. His mother is given to him as a wife because he has solved an existential question. The sequence of the story—during which he confronts truth for a second time—ends in a symbolic equivalent of self-inflicted castration as he puts out his own eyes (139–40).

The conclusion is that, needing a defense against jouissance, the child calls for help from a supposedly almighty father figure. We find this not only in Freud's clinical studies, but also appearing more fully in his revised version of the myth of the primal herd. The murder of the primal father is thus an expression of a death wish whose aim is to make the father immortal and, therefore, almighty (141). In the revised version of the myth (*Moses and Monotheism*), it is the youngest son who, in the face of a matriarchy, elevates the (meanwhile murdered) primal father to divine proportions.[14] Moreover, it appears as though this enjoyment is somehow associated with a dangerous femininity, with the woman/mother. This is as famous as it is misunderstood (witness the three religions of the Book).

As I said above, in the first instance Lacan corrects Freud's theory on this point. It is not so much the child's desire that has to be restrained. Rather, it is the dangerous jouissance that comes from the mother; it is her desire that needs to be signified through the symbolic Name-of-the-Father so as to enable the child to develop its own desire. That such a theory would rapidly form the basis for patriarchal interpretations along the lines of the religions of the Book, is easy enough to predict in hindsight. There are calls everywhere today for the reintroduction of strong father figures, along with the mother-at-the-hearth. The renewed fascism in Europe is, alas, no exception—with the United States coming in right behind—and what Klaus Theweleit described with regard to the male-female relationship and the onset of fascism during the interwar years, is now repeating itself in a contemporary version.[15]

In the end, with his Oedipal theory Freud did nothing but "scientifically" confirm the neurotic's fundamental fantasy. It is no coincidence that the very same Oedipal figure is constructed in the neurotic's all too familiar "family romance."[16] We are invariably tempted to elevate our father to unknown proportions in order to combat a danger we locate in the woman/mother, a danger that, in one way or another, always has to do with jouissance and our fear of becoming its victim.

Beyond the Oedipus Complex:
The Real Father as a Structural Operator

Lacan's reworking in *Seminar XVII* distances itself from any psychologizing, moralizing interpretation. The idea of an almighty father, enjoying all women, is an illusion; the father is scarcely capable of satisfying one woman (114, 144). Lacan's thesis is that man and woman, father and mother, are inevitably invested in certain positions on the basis of an already existing fact: the impossibility of jouissance. The social complicity ensures that this impossibility is translated into a prohibition, leaving man the illusion that it can be transgressed. This is nothing but the Oedipus complex, whatever the form it might take in different cultures.

As far as the Oedipal theory is concerned, Lacan notes an important difference between Freud and the post-Freudians. Freud will systematically put the emphasis on the father, regarding the first identification with the father as primordial. Both the post-Freudians and contemporary attachment theorists stress the earliest relation between mother and child (100, 113). In general, one could say that the post-Freudians have very little interest in Freud's Oedipal theory: the castration complex has almost entirely disappeared. Lacan returns to Freud's focus on the father but will give it a structural interpretation that enables him to put forward a different theory of castration. In place of Freud's castrating primal father, he will offer the castrated father who must hand on a certain function to the child—the S_1.

It is clear that Lacan defines the notion of castration in a completely different way than Freud. For Freud, the emphasis is on castration-anxiety in which the Oedipal boy fears being castrated by the father in punishment for his incestuous desire for the mother. For Lacan, *symbolic* castration is the inevitable consequence of the fact that man becomes a subject and must therefore pass through the signifier in order to gain jouissance, with the simultaneous implication that jouissance is impossible. Becoming a subject, being "taken in" by language, takes place through the S_1, more specifically, through a primary identification with the S_1. This also means that symbolic castration is determined by that S_1, and it is here that Lacan locates the function of the father.

As opposed to the supposedly almighty Freudian patriarch, here the father becomes nothing more than a structural operator (143) that performs the job of the "agency of the master" (146). It is not by chance that Lacan has previously already discussed the humiliated father and that he will end this seminar with a lesson on shame. What the father has to pass on to his son is the S_1 that gives the subject the illusion of coinciding with itself. This is Freud's primary identification with the father figure. The introduction of the S_1, however, inevitably implies the division of the subject and, hence, castration — that is, the impossibility of attaining jouissance (141). In fact, the S_1 intervenes in the already existing S_2 that divides the subject through the chain of signifiers, making enjoyment impossible to reach. In sum, the intervention of the master signifier S_1 on S_2, that is, on knowledge as a means for attaining jouissance, induces and determines symbolic castration (101). And this applies for the father as well; from the moment he enters the master discourse, the father is also symbolically castrated (115).

The role of the social apparatus is to convert this into a prohibition on jouissance, closely linked with woman, and to combine it with the fantasy of the imaginary father-castrator. Jouissance is ascribed to woman because it is the mother who inscribes the invasions of jouissance on the body. The child's "own" jouissance comes from the Other. Next, the need to keep jouissance at bay, to create a halt on the road to jouissance, takes the form of defining both the mother and her jouissance as prohibited, presumably by the father, punishable by castration. This imaginary castration covers up and conceals a fundamental truth which is that enjoyment is impossible from the moment that one speaks: this is symbolic castration, as a given of structure. Its agent is the real father (149). Both "real" and "agent" must be understood in Lacanian terms. "Real" means impossible, which is why Freud needed a primal father who was dead (143–45). The living father can never coincide with this function. Accordingly, "agent" must be regarded as very far removed from the idea of the almighty primal father. Agent here is nothing but an executive, "my agent," who is or ought to be paid to do a certain job, that of the master agency (146, 197). This job is to pass the lack on from father to son (141).

For Lacan, symbolic castration is structurally bound up with the introduction of the master signifier in the relationship between the sexes (149). This can be understood in the following way: the signifier is the means for attaining jouissance, which it can accomplish only through a repetition that is linked to a demand. "Repetition" because the inscriptions on the body must be repeated; "demand" because the inscriptions stem from the Other. The result of this repetitive demand is precisely the opposite of its aim; a plus-de-jouir is installed: the loss of jouissance and the possibility of gaining it elsewhere in another form. Here the master signifier, indeed every signifier, runs up against an impotence. For Lacan, this is the same impotence of the child in its demand to the mother.[17] No matter what she answers, it will never be enough.

As a consequence, the father and child join forces; the child is the father of man. As the agent of the master agency, the father confronts impotence from the moment he speaks and, hence, makes a demand. The child itself begins with an original impotence and helplessness. The mediation between them is what Lacan calls the "instance of the master" insofar as this instance produces the master signifier. At this point, Lacan adds an important nuance, thereby considerably changing his previous theory regarding the Name-of-the-Father: the master signifier can be produced by *any* signifier (144). This nuance can be understood in terms of the evolution of his theory of the Name-of-the-Father to the Names-of-the-Father to, finally, any signifier whatsoever so long as it is produced as an S_1 by the instance of the master (101). It is clear that we are a long way from the exclusive signifier of the Name-of-the-Father.

This is doubtless the most difficult theme that will be taken up again in *Seminar XX*: in order to make subject formation possible, the intervention of the S_1 is necessary. The question then is: Where does this S_1 come from? Lacan provides a tautological answer: the S_1 comes from the signifier "One," as in the axiom: "There is a One" ("Y a de l'Un"). The S_1 based on this can be any signifier, hence his homonymic word-play, an S_1, *un essaim* (swarm). It is a question not of the signifier's specific nature but rather of its function: to offer an envelope in which the entire chain of signifiers can subsist.[18] With this, Lacan takes up a line of thought already put forward in his seminar on identification, albeit with the same deadlock. In *Seminar IX*, he places the subject's origin on the identification with a unary trait that comes from another subject, thereby inscribing the subject as a singular "one." In this seminar, too, the unary trait is said to need repeating, because the "one" comes on top of an absence—there is no underlying substantial subject, only a *hupokeimenon*, a supposed presence. This is the very same relationship as between the signifier and the thing; the signifier can only refer to another signifier, while the thing-in-itself insists outside the chain of signifiers.

The deadlock in this line of reasoning concerns the question of the origin, which, as Lacan says repeatedly throughout his oeuvre, is impossible to answer. Subject formation derives from an S_1 that stems from a unary trait that needs to be repeated over an underlying absence. In my reading, this is the very same deadlock that Freud ended with, and on the very same topic. In order to found the father, he needed a primal father. No wonder that Freud ended this circular reasoning with the "Credo quia absurdum"—I believe it because it is absurd.[19]

The Strength of the Master Is Determined
by the Degree of Weakness He Can Bear

From the moment the subject is introduced into discourse, jouissance becomes impossible. This impossibility is translated by the social apparatus into a prohibition that assigns specific positions to the two sexes. We find the fullest expression of this in the statement "There is no sexual relationship," through which psychoanalysis demonstrates how the sexual relationship must be understood in terms of the plus-de-jouir (179).

The effect of discourse on the man, his being introduced into the symbolic order, is that he is unable to attain jouissance except by way of the plus-de-jouir, *objet a*, which is at the same time the cause of his desire. The implication is that man must reduce woman to this *objet a*, if he wishes to walk the jouissance road (186). These roads contain knowledge, founded on the Other's inscriptions of the invasions of jouissance.

These inscription points are well known. The privileged, yet not exclusive, places where the *objet a* is inscribed are the breast, ass, voice, and gaze, with their accompanying phallicization. Man can walk the road to jouissance only by reducing woman to these points. This is why Lacan could note that man, insofar as he aims for the Woman as such, inevitably must end in perversion.[20] The least form of it, which is also the most widespread, is fetishism, which Freud described as an avoidance of castration.[21]

The effect of discourse on woman is that she is reduced to *objet a*, that is, to what is for her as a subject an empty place of jouissance, empty because it involves nonsubstance and is unformed and unnameable (186). Consequently, she demands that the man assume an almighty position from which to be able to name her and provide her with an identity of her own. Should she ever find such a man, The Man, she will find psychosis.[22] This is, at the same time, the age-old illusion of the master, imagining that he can form a woman (186; see also *Pygmalion*, *My Fair Lady*, and *Pretty Woman*). If a man presents himself as a master, he will inevitably be subjected to symbolic castration and be unable to give woman what she demands. Hence Lacan's statement that man's castration has woman's privation as an effect (179). Hence, too, the clinical experience that attempting to answer the hysterical demand only heightens a woman's—in Freudian terms—"penis envy," that is, her reproach to the mother for not having given her what she needed (112).

Incidentally, this reproach is itself an effect of the cunning social apparatus: the supposedly absolute jouissance is impossible anyway, and this has nothing to do with a mother who answers or refuses to answer, or with a father who may or may not be almighty. Both are branded by the structure that exists before them. The fact that either may add their own pathologies to the positions they are assigned is testified to in clinical praxis. In the best of cases, the sexual relationship is a creative sublimation on top of the impossibility of jouissance and the resulting social forms that it takes through prohibition. Today's tragedy is that both prohibition and lack are refused by ascribing it to what has become an invisible master signifier, its invisibility being one of the effects of the latest form of capitalism (207). What is visible everywhere, on the other hand, are the traces of jouissance that have thereby become possible.

Everyone is saying these days that there are no more fathers. This is doubtless true, except that we don't know what we are saying. The call for the father is a neurotic demand for a primal father who will reinstall the prohibition—something that he was never capable of in the first place. In contrast, in a Lacanian reading, the position of the father is one of shame, and it is precisely this position that has become so rare. Shame, because he must represent a master signifier in the full consciousness that this is impossible: "But it was perhaps simply someone who was ashamed, who pushed himself forward, like that. . . . That is perhaps what it really is, the hole from which the master signifier springs" (218). Shame, too, because he will never be able to fill in the lack, because he can only pass it on to the next generation—which is, incidentally, also an expression of love: giving what you don't have ("L'amour, c'est donner ce qu'on n'a pas").

Notes

Many of the ideas in this essay were developed from a roundtable on *Seminar XVII* with G. Deneckere, L. Jonckheere, S. Matthé, and H. Van Hoorde. Comments by V. Palmans, who read a first version, were very helpful as well. My thanks to each of them.

1 Jacques Lacan, *Le séminaire, livre XVII: L'envers de la psychanalyse*, ed. J.-A. Miller (Paris: Seuil, 1999), 205. Parenthetical citations in text list page numbers from the French edition of the *Seminar*.

2 Sigmund Freud, *Beyond the Pleasure Principle* (1920), in *The Standard Edition of the Complete Psychological Works of Sigmund Freud*, ed. J. Strachey et al. (London: Hogarth, 1978), 13:7–64.

3 Jacques Lacan, *The Seminar of Jacques Lacan, Book XX: Encore or On Feminine Sexuality, The Limits of Love and Knowledge*, ed. J.-A. Miller, trans. B. Fink (New York: Norton, 1993), 23, 97.

4 Jacques Lacan, *The Four Fundamental Concepts of Psycho-analysis*, ed. J.-A. Miller, trans. A. Sheridan (London: Penguin, 1994), 197–99.

5 See Paul Verhaeghe, *Beyond Gender, from Drive to Desire* (New York: Other, 2001), 99–132.

6 At the end of the seminar, Lacan once again stresses the necessary presence of a master signifier within knowledge. Indeed, he says it is the master signifier that determines the readability of a story. Without it, the story doesn't work (218). The same reasoning can be applied to the subject. As the subject is an effect of the chain of signifiers and is represented by a signifier for another signifier, the subject needs a master signifier in order to be able to read "itself." In *Seminar XX*, Lacan states that the

master signifier presents an envelope through which the whole chain of signifiers—knowledge—can subsist (*Seminar XX*, 141–43).

7   See Jacques Lacan, "The Mirror Stage as Formative of the Function of the I," in *Ecrits: A Selection*, trans. B. Fink (New York: Norton, 2002), 3–9.

8   Verhaeghe, *Beyond Gender*, 65–97.

9   Of course, this reading is post-Lacanian. Lacan's theory itself is purely formal and structural. The psychological interpretations were made by the post-Lacanians. Note that in Lacan's theory, even the idea of prohibition is absent. The Oedipal transition is due to a signifying process: the desire of the mother (her incomprehensible comings and goings) is signified through the signifier of the Name-of-the-Father. This process reassures the child because it puts a name, a signifier, to a previously all-too-real process.

10 To ex-sist is to stand outside the real, in the symbolic; this is the ex-sistence of the subject as a subject of the signifier.

11 Sigmund Freud, "Analysis of a Phobia in a Five-Year Old Boy," in *The Standard Edition*, 10:42.

12 See Sigmund Freud, "Introductory Lectures on Pycho-Analysis," in *The Standard Edition*, 15–16:374; Freud, "From the History of an Infantile Neurosis," in *The Standard Edition*, 17:119.

13 Here, as a subject, Freud wants to elevate his own father to what he felt he needed as the almighty father. This is Lacan's interpretation of certain of Freud's dreams (141–51). In this connection, recall Freud's dream about Rome. The accompanying associations are without doubt the most instructive. In these, the following memory emerges: "I may have been ten or twelve years old, when my father began to take me with him on his walks and reveal to me in his talk his views upon things in the world we live in. . . . 'When I was a young man,' he said, 'I went for a walk one Saturday in the streets of your birthplace; I was well dressed, and had a new fur cap on my head. A Christian came up to me and with a single blow knocked off my cap in the mud and shouted: "Jew! Get off the pavement!"' 'And what did you do?' I asked. 'I went into the roadway and picked up my cap,' was his quiet reply. This struck me as unheroic conduct on the part of the big, strong man who was holding the little boy by the hand. I contrasted this situation with another which fitted my feelings better: the scene in which Hannibal's father, Hamilcar Barca, made his boy swear before the household altar to take vengeance on the Romans. Ever since that time Hannibal had had a place in my phantasies." Freud, *The Interpretation of Dreams*, in *The Standard Edition*, 6:197. To which let me add, not only in Freud's fantasies, but clearly in his theory as well.

14 Freud, "Moses and Monotheism," in *The Standard Edition*, 23:80–84, 130–32.

15 See Klaus Theweleit, *Male Fantasies*, Vol. 1: *Women, Floods, Bodies, History*, trans. S. Conway (Minneapolis: University of Minnesota Press, 1987) and *Male Fantasies*, Vol. 2: *Male Bodies: Psychoanalyzing the White Terror*, trans. C. Turner and E. Carter (Minneapolis: University of Minnesota Press, 1989).

16 Freud, "Family Romances," in *The Standard Edition*, 9:235–44.

17 The presumed omnipotence of the child in psychoanalysis is an illusion and comes down to an identification with a presumed omnipotence of the mother.
18 Lacan, *Seminar XX*, 141–43.
19 Freud, *Moses and Monotheism*, 118.
20 Jacques Lacan, *Television: A Challenge to the Psychoanalytic Establishment* (1974), trans. and ed. D. Hollier, R. Krauss, and A. Michelson (New York: Norton, 1990), 37–38.
21 See Freud, "Fetishism," in *The Standard Edition*, 21:149–58.
22 Lacan, *Television*, 40.

3

Beyond the
Oedipus Complex

Russell Grigg

Oedipus, the Limit of Psychoanalysis

It is well known that the Oedipus complex plays a central role for Lacan. In his early seminars, including *The Psychoses*, *The Object Relation*, and *Formations of the Unconscious*, he refers to the Oedipus complex constantly, recurrently, and persistently. Indeed, his conceptual edifice revolves around it. The mother's desire, the phallus as object of the mother's desire, the child that initially wants *to be* the phallus and then comes to accept *to have* the phallus; the Name-of-the-Father—none of this would make any sense outside its reference to the function of the Oedipus complex. This is all so much magnificent and complex machinery that depends on, indeed is a part of, the Oedipus complex, which, for Lacan, we must invoke if we are to explain pretty well anything that is at all relevant to psychoanalysis, whether it be a phobia in a child, the nature of hysteria and obsessional neurosis, why psychosis and not neurosis, the conditions for fetishism and transsexualism to be set in place, or, of course, the engendering of masculinity and femininity. In all of this, the particular dynamics of the Oedipus complex in each particular case are invoked, in the constant belief that this is where we have to look to understand the origin and nature of the different clinical structures that are the psychoanalyst's daily fare. Without the Oedipus complex, there is no possibility of understanding neurosis, psychosis, or perversion, no way of thinking about sexuation. The constant return to the Oedipus complex indicates Lacan's belief that nothing can be understood in the absence of a reference to it as the cornerstone of psychoanalysis. Whereas Freud called it the "nucleus of the neuroses," Lacan went further, declaring that the Oedipus complex covers the entire field of analytic experience, marking the limit that our discipline assigns to subjectivity.[1]

Lacan discusses, elaborates, and develops Freud's theory of the Oedipus complex at great length in his early seminars. See, for instance, his discussion of the "three moments" of the Oedipus complex in *Seminar V*; or, in *Seminar IV*, the detailed breakdown of the Oedipus complex in terms of the real father, the imaginary father, and the symbolic mother; symbolic castration, imaginary frustration, and real privation; the imaginary phallus, the symbolic phallus, and the real breast. All this is discussed and elaborated in the 1950s—and in a way, it must be said, that is very compelling, clarifies a great number of issues in psychoanalysis, and is clinically useful.

Critique of the Oedipus Complex

Then something unexpected happens. At about the time of *Seminar XVI*, *Seminar XVII*, *Seminar XVIII* (1968–71) Lacan gradually came to dismiss the Oedipus complex as being at best useless and irrelevant and, at worst, liable to lead us into significant errors of judgment in the clinical setting. Most analysts ignore it altogether, he says, even those trained in his school. Those who make it a point of reference for their work get into all sorts of bother—one need look no further than Freud's own cases. This turnaround is particularly apparent in *Seminar XVII*, *The Other Side of Psychoanalysis*, and *Seminar XVIII*, *D'un discours qui ne serait pas du semblant*, where Lacan adopts a surprisingly new approach to the Oedipus complex and to what up till then had been the key signifier the Name-of-the-Father. Quite suddenly Lacan starts referring to the Oedipus complex as "Freud's dream." If it is a dream, he says, it can no longer be a theoretical construction to be unpacked, dissected, and rebuilt; it can no longer be the bedrock of psychoanalysis. If it is Freud's dream, it is a formation of the unconscious and that implies that it calls for interpretation.[2]

Why this turnaround from seeing the Oedipus complex as the bedrock of psychoanalysis to the judgment that it is a dream of Freud's? While there are probably a number of reasons, one factor is absolutely crucial: the introduction, in the late 1960s, of the theory of the four discourses and, in particular, the role played within the four discourses of the concepts of master, master signifier, S_1, and master's discourse.

$$\frac{S_1}{\$} \rightarrow \frac{S_2}{a}$$

The master's discourse

Many things follow from this, in particular, the hysteric's discourse, the analyst's discourse, and the university discourse, which are derivatives of the principal discourse, the master's discourse.

When Lacan calls the Oedipus complex Freud's dream, we have to understand that he is distinguishing it from myth. It is *also* a myth, one that takes two forms in Freud's work: the Oedipus complex that derives from Sophocles's play and a myth of Freud's own invention, which is the myth of the primal father that is advanced for the first time in *Totem and Taboo*. But by calling it a dream he is implying that there is a place for it to be treated psychoanalytically and not anthropologically.

The difference between anthropology and psychoanalysis is important, and even though Lacan always appreciated it, it took some time for him to realize its full significance. Lacan initially thought that psychoanalysis could draw upon Lévi-Strauss's anthropology of myths, and he engaged in some serious efforts to make use of Lévi-Strauss's work in his own work on individual analytic cases. His approach in *Seminar IV* in 1957 to the analysis of Little Hans draws heavily upon Lévi-Strauss's study of myths and analysis of the Oedipus myth, or myths, in particular. He takes a similar approach in "The Neurotic's Individual Myth," conceived analogously to Freud's thesis on religion, when he takes obsessional neurosis to be an individual religion of the neurotic. Here, it seems, the analyst has much to learn from the anthropologist's method for the analysis of myths, which comprises a comparative study of all the different versions of the myth that are known to exist. If one applies this method to Little Hans, as Lacan does, then the evolution of his phobia can be regarded as exhibiting a number of versions of the key Oedipal myth, as the young boy grapples with the questions of his existence and his sexual identity.

In "The Structural Study of Myth," Lévi-Strauss develops a method for uncovering the underlying structure of myths and takes the myth of

Oedipus as a case study.³ Noting that the myth can be found all around the world, though disguised in various ways, he gathers together all its known variants for analysis. For Lévi-Strauss, the meaning of the myth resides not in the story narrated but in the way in which the elements of the myth, the "mythemes," are combined with one another. A mytheme is a phrase or proposition, not unlike a fantasy, at least as Lacan understands it, such as, for example, "A child is being beaten."

Lévi-Strauss's method consists of writing the themes of a myth out from left to right, with different myths located one above the other, as if they were each the parts of the one orchestral score. When the elements from different myths express the same theme or idea, one locates them one above the other, without taking any account of the order in which the elements occur in the original myth. Take, by way of illustration, Sophocles's *Oedipus Rex* and Sophocles's *Antigone*, which Lévi-Strauss considers to be variants of the same myth. This gives:

Myth of Oedipus

1	2	3	4
Oedipus marries his mother, Jocasta.	Oedipus kills his father, Laius.	Oedipus immolates the sphinx.	"Labdacos" means lame. "Laius" means left.
Antigone buries her brother, Polynices, in defiance of the law.	Eteocles kills his brother, Polynices.		"Oedipus" means swollen foot.
Blood ties are overrated.	Blood ties are underrated.	The destruction of monsters	Difficulties in walking properly
Contraries		Contraries	
Human origins		Autochthonous origins	
	Contraries		

Note the following about the four columns: Columns 1 and 2 are contraries; and so, too, are Columns 3 and 4, although it is less apparent because the opposition appears in symbolic form. In column 4 the difficulty with walking represents the terrestrial, or autochthonous, origins of humans, while in column 3 the destruction of monsters signifies the negation of these autochthonous origins. Thus, columns 1 and 2, on the one hand, and columns 3 and 4, on the other, form two contrary pairs.[4] Now, if we also consider the fact that columns 1 and 2 concern the question of human origins, and columns 3 and 4 concern the question of autochthonous origins, then, again, we can see that the key term in the opposition around which the contrary relations in the left-hand pair revolve is contrary to the key term in the opposition around which the right-hand side contraries revolve. These myths thus use this "bridging" technique to move from an initial problem—"Is one born from one or from two?"—that is the inevitable question and enigma of human reproduction, to another, derivative issue, "Is the same born out of the same or out of something that is different?"

This, then, according to Lévi-Strauss, gives us the structural law of the Oedipus myth. It confronts the impossibility of passing from belief in the autochthonous origins of humans to the recognition of birth from two parents. A myth is a kind of logical instrument for resolving contradictions such as these. It typically fails to resolve the contradictions, since the contradictions it confronts are nevertheless real ones. However, for Lévi-Strauss, the mere fact that the motivation for myth is to resolve a contradiction means that mythical and scientific reasoning are no different in kind; mythical reasoning is not a "primitive" form of thought that scientific reasoning has superseded.

Concerning Freud's Oedipus complex, note that Lévi-Strauss's analysis is somewhat double-edged as far as psychoanalysis is concerned. On the one hand it claims that the Oedipus complex is universal and that it can be found in widely different cultures that have had no contact with one another. Yet this discovery, which in appearance psychoanalysis can claim to have made, is a sign that psychoanalysis's epistemological pretensions are unjustified, for Freud's Oedipus complex turns out to be just another version of this myth, alongside all the others. In Lévi-Strauss's analysis of the Oedipus myth, with all its variants, the Freudian version becomes so much grist to the anthropologist's mill: psychoanalysis cannot claim to have revealed "the truth," the true meaning, of the myth; rather, the psychoanalytic version becomes merely a modern version of the myth, indistinguishable from all the others in being just one more variant. In Freud's version, the question of autochthony disappears, it is true, but the other theme, *How is one born from two?*, remains. For Lévi-Strauss this merely shows the continuing importance and relevance of the Oedipus myth across very different cultural and social contexts.

Lacan takes a different view from Lévi-Strauss about the relationship between science and myth, and also about the place of the Freudian Oedipus complex. He agrees that at the heart of myth there is a point of impossibility, a "contradiction." Lacan's name for this impossibility is the real, and in the Oedipus complex this "bit of real" is the impossibility of any sexual relationship between man and woman. However, he differs from Lévi-Strauss in thinking that myth covers over this bit of impossibility by giving it a sense, a "bit of meaning," in the form of a fiction. The myth is, thus, a fictional story woven around this point of impossibility, or the real, which is why Lacan says that there is indeed truth in myth, but that it is truth that has the structure of fiction.

Lacan thinks that science does the opposite to this activity of myth of covering over points of impossibility. Whereas myth is something that generates sense and meaning, which is its function, the tendency of science is to reduce meaning and sense to the point of eliminating them. Science pares them away to the point where it can demonstrate an impossibility. Lacan also claims that writing is essential to this process and that there is no science, and he includes mathematics in this, without writing. It is therefore significant that myth, on the other hand, proceeds by way of speech, which is crucial to the way in which myth expresses the truth. Myth, for Lacan, accomplishes this "bridging" mentioned by Lévi-Strauss by producing something that is a mixture of the imaginary and the symbolic, and it is in actual fact a way of papering over the impossible, real kernel around which the myth is constructed and for which it was originally formulated. Science cannot write the impossible, any more than myth can *say* it; here they are on common ground. However, science differs from myth in that it can, and does, use symbolic means to demonstrate and expose this impossibility, whereas myth constantly revolves around the impossibility in recurrent attempts at resolving questions that have no answers.

For Lacan, Lévi-Strauss's analysis of myth actually makes myth much closer to fantasy than to science. At least, it does if we think of fantasy in the way Lacan does, as a phrase or proposition—"A child is being beaten," for instance—that takes the place of a point of impossibility, a "contradiction," such as the sexual relationship between man and woman, which both indicates the place of the impossibility and, at the same time, occludes it by means of a fantasmatic profusion of meaning.

We need, then, to distinguish four domains: myth, fantasy, science, and psychoanalysis. The difference between science on the one hand and fantasy and myth on the other comes down to the response each makes to the real. Lacan's insight was to see that this was the point at which psychoanalysis was on common ground with science, and his ambition was to make psychoanalysis more scientific at this point.

A dream is not a myth, however, and if Lacan is right in thinking that the Oedipus complex was "Freud's dream," then the Oedipus complex is not a myth either. If it is a dream then it will have been formed according to different laws. As we know from Freud, the dream is a product, a "formation," of the unconscious. The dream work distorts and disguises the latent content of the dream in the service of unconscious desire according to the two processes by which the latent material is encoded: condensation and displacement, which are equivalent to the linguistic operations of metaphor and metonymy. These unconscious processes are both unknown to myth. This is why Lacan was able to point out the limitation of Lévi-Strauss's analysis with great precision. In "Radiophonie," a radio broadcast of 1970 prepared over the course of *Seminar XVII*, Lacan says, "Myths, in their elaboration by Lévi-Strauss, refuse everything that I have promoted in the instance of the letter in the unconscious. They perform no metaphor, nor even any metonymy. They do not condense; they explain. They do not dislodge; they lodge, even to the point of changing the order of the texts."[5]

The mechanisms of dream formation make dreams specific to the language (or, as sometimes happens, languages) in which they are dreamed. Dreams rely on the features of a language, its polysemies, ambiguities, and so on, that constitute the language as llanguage, *lalangue*, in one

Beyond the Oedipus Complex 57

word. This language-specific character of dreams contrasts with the universality of the Oedipus myth. Lacan continues the radio address by adding that the myth is "untranslatable." This seems an odd thing to say, given that one and the same myth can be found in different linguistic communities with very little variation, that myth has something universal about it, and therefore that myths do indeed "translate" from one linguistic community to another. However, what Lacan has in mind is that a myth is not rooted in any given language. A myth is neither embedded in nor an expression of a particular language. Rather, it is part of language in the same way that proper names are, passing untranslated from one language to another.

While it was only in 1970 that Lacan became fully aware of the distance separating psychoanalysis from anthropology, with hindsight it is possible to see that the crucial development in Lacan's move away from Lévi-Strauss's views occurs in 1958 with the development of the theory of the paternal metaphor, where the metaphoric process of substitution of the Name-of-the-Father for the mother's desire places us squarely within the field of formation of the unconscious. By 1970, Lacan is aware of the significance of metaphor and metonymy and how they differ from the operations at play in the construction of myths; we can get an idea of the time it took for Lacan to understand by the degree of lag between, on the one hand, the elaboration of a theory of metaphor and metonymy and the Lévi-Straussian analysis of Little Hans in *Seminar IV*, and on the other the critique of Lévi-Strauss in 1970.

Castration and the Oedipus Complex

A dream disguises; the dream work is a work of distortion. According to Lacan, then, the place given to the father in Freud's work covers up and papers over its underlying structure, presenting it in disguised form. Nevertheless, the father does not occupy just one place in Freud's work but varies from one version of the Oedipus complex to the next, from *The Interpretation of Dreams*, through *Totem and Taboo* and *Civilization and Its Discontents*, and down to Freud's final work, *Moses and Monotheism*. Nevertheless, all versions of the myth consistently paper over the same form of the real as impossible: the sexual relationship between man and woman. There is a further element that for Freud is part of the father's role and is essential to and recurrent in Freud's account of the Oedipus complex, present in all versions, but which is absent from the original myth of Oedipus: the castration complex.

Psychoanalysts since Freud have had difficulty knowing what to do with or how to understand the castration complex and have proposed a number of candidates as the source of the threat or fear of castration. The most popular of these is that the trauma of castration originates in the registration of the anatomical difference between the sexes, the ensuing recognition of a "lack," and the child's aggression toward the father, which comes to be turned back around upon him or (less persuasively) her in the form of the threat of castration.[6] By the same token, however, there is no real reason to specifically invoke castration in the case of the primal horde father. Why should the threat from the primal father be the threat of castration? And in the Oedipal myth, in either Freud's version or Sophocles's version, there is, strictly speaking, no particularly prominent place given to castration.

Indeed, there is no inherent link between castration and its mythical, Oedipal, settings. Given this fact, it might be fruitful to acknowledge the point and begin to treat them as separate and distinct. This is what Lacan undertakes in *Seminar XVII*. Thus, on the one hand Lacan explores the question of the castration complex independently of the Oedipal context in which it is embedded. This line of approach eventually leads him to the formulas of sexuation that we are familiar with from *Seminar XX, Encore*. On the other hand, we can enquire into the reasons why Freud holds so strongly to the Oedipus complex itself. If we follow Lacan well enough, we may be able to see why he thinks that the Oedipus complex in Freud is designed to "save the father."

For Lacan castration is not a fantasy, and, a fortiori, is not a fantasy about a castrating father or any supposed encounter with the opposite sex. These are at best precipitating causes for what is a real operation, which is brought about by language itself. For Freud, in the case of the little girl the castration complex acts as a trigger for her to pass into the Oedipus complex, whereas the little boy exits the Oedipus complex as a result of his encounter with castration. For Lacan castration is an operation that is brought about by language and determined by the master signifier, S_1, and arises from a confrontation between the signifier and enjoyment.

Lacan's four discourses in *The Other Side of Psychoanalysis* are an attempt to formalize the structure of this relationship between signifier, in the form of semblant, and enjoyment. All four discourses, but particularly the master's discourse, share a common aim with the myth of the primal horde in Freud's *Totem and Taboo*, in that Freud's work is as much an attempt to give an account of the social bond that binds people together, along with an account of what segregates them, as it is an account of the origin of religion.

All of this in Freud is constructed on the basis of the father's murder. There is of course no question of the father's murder describing an actual historical event, even though Freud believed it had to be true, and even though this was the work he took perhaps greatest pride in. The primal-horde tale takes precisely the place of a myth, describing as it does an ahistorical event that, as Lévi-Strauss puts it, "evokes an abolished past" that is projected into all eternity, and a fortiori into the present. If we reject the thesis that the father's murder has any role to play as a historical event, if we consider that its status is that of a myth, and, further, if we also consider castration to be a real operation of language, stemming from the symbolic, then the question arises of what role the father's murder plays in Freud's work.

Lacan, who raises this question in *Seminar XVII*, gives as his response the thesis that the father's murder is set in place as a myth in order to cover up the castration that institutes *both* the law *and* fantasy, which is a consequence of the law. There is a fundamental fantasy at issue here, that of the father who enjoys—and, in particular, who enjoys all the women. This fantasy of the father who enjoys is of course an impossibility—as Lacan comments, a man generally finds it hard enough to satisfy just one woman, and even then, he must not boast about it. The fantasy is also a retrospective effect of the institution of the prohibition of jouissance, which I am inclined to think is the sense of a difficult remark Lacan makes when he gives the myth of the father's murder the status of a "statement [*énoncé*] of the impossible."[7] The father who is retroactively created as the father who enjoys is what Lacan calls the real father; this is the real father of *Totem and Taboo*.

Lacan does not, however, completely abandon all reference to the Oedipus complex, at least not to the father of the primal horde. This might seem a little bit surprising, given that the entire thrust of his thought in *Seminar XVII* has been first to remove the link between the castration complex and the Oedipus complex and then to dismiss the family romance of the Oedipus complex itself. Yet while Lacan does separate the castration complex off from the dead father, he nevertheless retains the function that the dead father has in myth, specifically the *Totem and Taboo* myth, which is the function of both enjoyer (that is, the one who enjoys) and also prohibitor of jouissance. If castration is a function of language, in the form of the master, then why does he retain this vestige of a father, this residual father, whom he refers to, somewhat obscurely, as a statement of the impossible?

The following reasoning has been suggested by Geneviève Morel.[8] If we assume that castration is a universal function of language that comes into play for any subject who both speaks and enjoys, then we have no way of explaining the fact that this function sometimes works and sometimes does not, and that sometimes it works better than other times. I have in mind the clinic of psychoanalysis, which includes the discovery of the foreclosure of phallic signification in psychosis and the implications this has for the way the psychotic enjoys, on the one hand, and all the possible vicissitudes of neurotic sexuation and psychopathology on the other. Yet if castration is automatic and is a mere fact of language, why isn't its effect the same in all cases? There must be individual factors, contingent elements, alongside the automatic operation of language. In other contexts, such as his discussion of *tyche* and *automaton* in *Seminar XI, The Four Fundamental Concepts of Psychoanalysis*, Lacan is very aware both of how important it is that there be a place for the contingent and of the inclination in psychoanalysis to a type of immanentism. What Lacan calls the real father is invoked as the agent necessary to explain the contingency of the encounter with castration; the real father is a contingent agent of a universal operation, which explains why there is no identity across cases, why there is contingency in the universality of language.

Lacan makes the further claim that it is impossible for any subject to know this real father; even though the real father is specific to each subject, the subject does not have access to him. There is something that does not enter into the universal operation of castration but will remain an operator unknown to the subject.

Lacan refers to this real father as master-agent and guardian of enjoyment.[9] Although impossible to analyze, he says in *Television*, it is quite possible to imagine the real father.[10] What the subject has access to in analysis is figures of the imaginary father in his multiple representations: castrating father, tyrannical, weak, absent, lacking, too powerful, and so on.

Saving the Father

I mentioned earlier that there was a second issue to explore in this seminar, which was why Freud holds so tenaciously to the Oedipus complex itself. We now need to explore why Lacan claims it has to do with Freud wanting to "save the father."

The first thing to note is that there are some important and indeed puzzling differences between the two forms of the myth of the father in Freud—that is, the Oedipus complex and the myth of the primal horde—of which the most striking is the inversion in the relationship between desire and the law. The Oedipus complex is meant to explain how desire and jouissance are regulated by the law. Both the Oedipus myth "borrowed from Sophocles" and the primal-horde myth involve the murder of the father, but the consequences of this murder are exactly opposite in the two cases, and the reason for this is the different place occupied by the law in each. Both deal with what Lacan had been calling the Name-of-the-Father, which as signifier is closely bound up with jouissance and its regulation by the law, but, oddly enough, the relationship between the law and jouissance that unfolds in each ends up inverted. In Freud's Oedipal myth the law is there from the outset; it is an inexorable law, demanding punishment even when the transgression has been committed unwittingly or unconsciously, and exists for the subject as an unconscious sense of guilt. The law precedes enjoyment, and enjoyment henceforth takes the form of a transgression. The relationship is the inverse of this in *Totem and Taboo*, where enjoyment is present at the outset, and the law comes afterward.

The contrast between the two forms of Oedipus leads Lacan to say that there is "*une schize*, a split, separating the myth of Oedipus from *Totem and Taboo*,"[11] raising the question of the reason for the two versions. Why does Freud initially introduce the Oedipus complex and then subsequently insist upon the primal-horde father whose relationship to jouissance is so different? One suggestion is that we should see them as responses, respectively, to the clinical experience of hysteria and obsessional neurosis. On this view the Oedipus complex would be the myth that Freud creates in response to the clinic of hysteria; the myth of the primal-horde father of *Totem and Taboo* his response to the clinic of obsessional neurosis. I think this is, in rough terms, Lacan's view in *Seminar XVII*.

Lacan's thesis in *Seminar XVII* is that the Oedipus complex is something Freud produces in response to his encounter with hysteria. It is not that the Oedipus complex is invented or introduced by the hysteric; the Oedipus complex is Freud's response to hysteria, a response, moreover, designed to protect the place of the father. Let me explain, with reference to the case of Dora.

Right from the outset, whenever Lacan discussed Dora he was always critical of Freud's treatment. He criticized Freud for missing the fact that the object of Dora's desire was a woman, Frau K., whereas Freud had relentlessly pursued the case as if her real object was a man, Herr K. From Freud's point of view, Dora's problem was that, as a hysteric, she was unable to acknowledge her desire for this man, whereas everything would have had a good chance of being brought to a successful resolution if only she could be brought to this realization. Throughout the entire analysis Freud persists in hammering away at this fact: you refuse to acknowledge that it's Herr K. that you desire. However, as Freud came to realize many years later, in assuming that Dora's object was a heterosexual one he had missed the crucial fact that the object of Dora's desire was a woman, Frau K.

As it happens, Freud's confusion in the face of hysteria did not stop there. For what he had also failed to grasp was the place and significance of the structure of desire in hysteria and in particular the role played in it by a desire for an unsatisfied desire. His failure to realize this meant that in his treatment of hysteria Freud would invariably look for some particular object or other as the object of the hysteric's desire. It is true that this object is, for Freud, typically a man, and that Freud thus misses the significance of the woman for the hysteric. But the point I am making is the slightly different one that, by failing to recognize that what the hysteric desires is a desire that is unsatisfied, his search for an object of the hysteric's desire always ends up coming up with something that is forced and in one way or another rejected or resisted by his patient. This is apparent at every turn in the case of Dora.

We owe to Freud the first real insight into the crucial, even essential, role that lack plays in female sexuality. But his conclusion from this was that a woman can never be fully satisfied until she has filled this lack by receiving the phallus and, moreover, by receiving it from the father. Freud's solution to the woman's lack was motherhood, and this solution keeps insisting in his treatment of hysteria. He thinks that the hysteric will not be properly "cured" until she has this desire to receive the phallus from the father, or rather, since Freud is in no doubt that she does indeed have this desire, until she acknowledges it. This is why we see Freud relentlessly pursuing his efforts at getting Dora to acknowledge her desire for the father's substitute, Herr K., even to the point where this eventually brings about the early and abrupt termination of the treatment. This much is clear and can be demonstrated in Freud's case history.[12]

What is Dora's attitude toward this father of hers? Lacan emphasizes the importance of the role that the impotence of Dora's father plays. His impotence has for her the signification of his castration. Lacan takes this to indicate that seeing her father as deficient in this way is to measure him against some symbolic, ideal function of the father. The father is not merely who he is or what he is, but he is also someone who carries a title or fills an office. He is, as he puts it, an *ancien géniteur*, a former begetter, which, Lacan says, is a bit like the title of what in French is called the *ancien combatant*, former or ex-soldier, that is, a veteran, or a returned soldier, as we say in Australia. He carries this title of *ancien géniteur* with him. Even when he is "out of action," he maintains this position in relation to the woman. Using resources of English not available to the French, we could sum up this emphasis upon the father as he who begets or engenders by appeal to the pleonasm "The father fathers." As a matter of fact, one might suggest a new French verb, *perrier*, which would mean "to father." Not only would this recycle a word already in existence, but it would have other advantages as well. "The father fathers" would then come out as "Le père perrie."[13] In any case, Lacan calls this fathering father, the father who begets or engenders, "the idealized father," and he is at the core of the hysteric's relation to the father.

On the one hand, then, there is the figure of the idealized father, and on the other, the hysteric's desire for an unsatisfied desire. The introduction of the Oedipal myth of psychoanalysis short-circuits the question of the hysteric's desire by guiding the hysteric's desire in the direction of the father. In this sense Lacan says that the Oedipus complex gives consistency to the figure of the idealized father in the clinical setting.

Lacan's conclusion is that the introduction of the Oedipal myth was "dictated to Freud by the hysteric's insatisfaction" and also by what he calls "her theater."[14] The Oedipus complex, which derives from the myth whose dynamics revolve around the father and his death, merely gives consistency to the figure of the idealized father. The complex undoubtedly has explanatory value, but this merely redoubles the hysteric's wish to produce knowledge that can lay claim to being the truth. For the hysteric the Name-of-the-Father comes to fill the place of the master signifier S_1, where it acts as a point of blockage for this discourse that determines it.

I have suggested a link between obsessional neurosis and the myth of the primal horde. We can begin with Lacan's comment that *Totem and Taboo* is a "neurotic product." I take this to mean that the work is a product of Freud's neurosis, and that the "something unanalyzed" in Freud crops up again in his encounter with obsessional neurosis. If this is so, then *Totem and Taboo* comes out of this encounter; it is Freud's response to the clinic of obsessional neurosis, just as the Oedipus complex is the product of his encounter with hysteria. As with the Oedipus complex, it needs to be interpreted.

I would like to return to the significant differences between the myth of the primal horde and the Oedipus complex. The first difference, which I outlined above, is that in *Totem and Taboo* the relationship between the law and enjoyment is inverted in comparison with the Oedipus complex, since here the primal father's enjoyment of all the women precedes his murder at the hands of his sons and the establishment of the law. His enjoyment is in a sense the condition for the establishment of the law; in the Oedipus complex, on the other hand, the law precedes transgression.

Note a second difference, related to but different from the first, between the father of the Oedipus complex and the primal father. Of course, whereas the father of the Oedipus complex is himself subject to the law he transmits to his children, with the figure of the primal father we have an exception to this very law. The father of the primal horde is the *père sévère* ($\exists x \overline{\Phi} x$), who is egotistical and jealous, a sexual glutton, a father who enjoys, who is not limited by any submission to the law of an order transcendent to him. His death, moreover, is no liberation for the sons, for his power to prohibit is only increased by his disappearance. Through his death the sons are even more strongly bound to the law of prohibition that returns in the form of his son's identification with him.

Third, note the striking development from the Oedipus complex to the myth of the father of *Totem and Taboo* and later of *Moses and Monotheism*. At the outset, the father's function is clearly to pacify, regulate, and sublimate the omnipotence of the figure of the mother, called by Freud "the obscure power of the feminine sex." But by the end the father himself has assumed the power, obscurity, and cruelty of the omnipotence his function was supposed to dissipate in the first place.

In the context of this critique of the Oedipus complex, Lacan introduces the four discourses. Central to the four discourses is the master's discourse; or, more specifically, the concept of the master itself. The interest of the four discourses is that Lacan would like to dispense with the Oedipus complex—"Freud's dream," he calls it—and the primal-horde myth and replace them with a reference to the discourses. "A father," says Lacan, "has with the master only the most distant of relationships. . . . What Freud retains, in fact if not in intention, is very precisely what he designates as the most essential in religion—namely, the idea of an all-loving father."[15]

There is one further consideration about Freud's *Totem and Taboo* that should be mentioned. The reference in this passage to the son's identification with the father, in relation to the ideal of acquiring his father's position, suggests that an answer to the question of how in this myth the incest taboo arises should be sought in terms of an identification with the father and not merely in terms of a vaguely sociological theory of a social contract between equals. In the primal-horde myth Freud attributes a crucial role in the establishment of prohibitions to the son's love for the primal father: "[The primal father] forced [the sons] into abstinence and *consequently* into the emotional ties with him and with one another which could arise out of those of their impulses that were inhibited in their sexual aim."[16] Now, there should be identification with the renounced object, whereas the actual vehicle of the frustration draws the subject's hatred and aggression upon himself. However, here, "forced abstinence" produces an emotional tie with the agent, in a way that runs counter to what we should expect on the theory.

There is a hiatus in Freud's views on identification, which I have discussed elsewhere; it is a hiatus concerning the identification with the father at the very moment at which he is also the agent who deprives the subject of his erotic satisfactions. The importance of this for the Oedipus complex should be obvious; as Lacan says, "Love . . . relates to the father by virtue of the father's being the vehicle of castration. This is what Freud proposes in *Totem and Taboo*. It is in so far as the sons are deprived of women that they love the father—a bewildering remark that is sanctioned by the insight of a Freud."[17] This brings us back to the relationship between the myth of the primal horde and obsessional neurosis. For if the myth is a product of an encounter with obsessional neurosis, then so too is the idea of an all-loving father. Yet this father-love combines with the father-who-enjoys, to form the obsessional's master, the object of his *hainamoration*.

The consequences for the sons of murdering the father of the primal horde are not the ones expected by the sons—principally access to a jouissance without limit—since no one accedes to the omnipotence of the vacated position. The prohibitions before the murder continue just as strongly afterward because the sons agree upon them among themselves so that total and mutual destruction does not ensue. As Freud writes in *Moses and Monotheism*, "Each individual renounced his ideal of acquiring his father's position for himself and of possessing his mother and sisters. Thus the *taboo on incest* and the injunction to *exogamy* came about."[18]

Lacan's conclusion is that the Oedipus complex is "strictly unusable" in the clinical setting, so by implication it is unusable with respect to all hysteria. He adds, "It is odd that this didn't become clearer more quickly."[19] Given Lacan's long and detailed treatment of the Oedipus complex over many years, he is most likely directing this remark at himself. What takes the place of the Oedipus complex are the new reference points unfolding in this seminar: the introduction of a new concept of knowledge, S_2, the split between it and truth, and, importantly, the concept of master, which has "only the most distant of relationships" to the concept of father. These developments enable the Oedipus complex to play the role of knowledge claiming to be truth, which is to say that in the figure of the analyst's discourse knowledge is located in the site of truth.

$$\frac{a}{S_2} \rightarrow \frac{\$}{S_1}$$

Analyst's discourse

The Oedipus complex does not regulate the hysteric's desire; it is rather the result, the product—in the form of knowledge claiming to be truth—of the discourse by which it is determined, and which Lacan writes in the following way:

$$\frac{\$}{a} \rightarrow \frac{S_1}{S_2}$$

Hysteric's discourse

The hysteric presents as a subject divided by his or her symptoms ($\$$); he or she produces knowledge (S_2) and solicits the master signifier in the other (S_1): "She doesn't hand her knowledge over. She unmasks . . . the function of the master with whom she remains united, . . . [and] which she evades in the capacity of object of his desire. This is the . . . function . . . of the idealized father."[20] She wants the other to be a master, that he know many things, but all the same not that he know enough not to believe that she is the supreme price of all his knowledge. In other words, as Lacan puts it, she wants a master over whom she can reign; that she should reign, and that he not govern.

Notes

1 Jacques Lacan, "Function and Field of Speech and Language," *Ecrits: A Selection*, trans. B. Fink (New York: Norton, 2002), 65.
2 Jacques Lacan, *Le séminaire, livre XVII: L'envers de la psychanalyse*, ed. J.-A. Miller (Paris: Seuil, 1991), 159.
3 Claude Lévi-Strauss, "The Structural Study of Myth," *Journal of American Folklore* 78 (1955): 428–44.

4   Two propositions are contraries when both cannot be true, though both can be false; contradictories are propositions that cannot be either true together or false together.
5   I am reading, along with Geneviève Morel, "textes" for "tentes." Morel gives a very interesting account of the comparison between myth and dream in *Oedipe Aujourd'hui* (Lille: Association de la Cause Freudienne, 1997).
6   See Russell Grigg, Dominique Hecq, and Craig Smith, *Female Sexuality: The Early Psychoanalytic Controversies* (New York: Other, 1999).
7   Lacan, *Le séminaire, livre XVII*, 145. I refer you to my earlier comment about the real as impossible.
8   See Geneviève Morel, *Oedipe Aujourd'hui*, 51.
9   See the discussion of "agent" in chap. 8 of *Seminar XVII*.
10 "I hold that it is out of the question to analyze the real father; for better the cloak of Noah when the Father is imaginary" (Jacques Lacan, *Television: A Challenge to the Psychoanalytic Establishment*, trans. and ed. D. Hollier, R. Krauss, and A. Michelson [New York: Norton, 1990], 19).
11 Jacques Lacan, *Séminaire XVIII, D'un discours qui ne serait pas du semblant*, session of June 9, 1971. Unpublished.
12 The fact that we can do this, incidentally, indicates what is absolutely remarkable about Freud's case histories: even when Freud misses something crucial, traces of it can still be found in the text.
13 This is of course homophonic with *le père périt*, the father perishes.
14 Lacan, *Seminar XVIII*, session of June 9, 1971.
15 Lacan, *Le séminaire, livre XVII*, 114.
16 Freud, *Group Psychology and the Analysis of the Ego* (1921), in *The Standard Edition of the Complete Psychological Works of Sigmund Freud*, ed. James Strachey (London: Hogarth, 1955), 18:24. My emphasis.
17 Jacques Lacan, *Le séminaire, Livre XXIII: Le sinthome*, published in *Ornicar?*, no. 11 (1977): 7.
18 Sigmund Freud, *Moses and Monotheism*, in *The Standard Edition*, 23:82.
19 Lacan, *Le séminaire, livre XVII*, 113.
20 Ibid., 107.

4

Ellie Ragland | **The Hysteric's Truth**

Lacan says in *Seminar XVII*, "It is clear that there is no question more burning than what, in discourse, refers to enjoyment. Discourse is constantly touching it, by virtue of the fact that this is where it originates."[1]

What is the relation between jouissance and the primary dissatisfaction of the hysteric's jouissance? What does Lacan mean when he says that Dora wants to give the cherished object of her satisfaction—Frau K.—to another, as does the witty butcher's wife (84–85)?

One possible avenue of investigation regarding how the hysteric treats herself in the position of truth as *objet a* bears on her confusion in the imaginary regarding a viable image of her body as a woman's body. Given that the hysteric's fundamental question in the signifier is "Am I a woman or a man?" she is at risk of being overtaken by the real in both the symbolic and the imaginary. How does she dispose of a body that cannot locate itself in terms of the masculine or the feminine? She is, indeed, troubled by being on both sides of the sexuation graph at once. Doubtlessly, this division renders her anxious.

One might say that this division causes the blockage of the *a* in the place of truth in the hysteric's discourse. It, thus, supports the division of the subject one finds at the surface of her discourse. In the treatment, there will hopefully be some resolution of this split.

Why is anyone, not only the hysteric, a slave in discourse? One reason is that language translates the gaze of the Other. I shall try to get at what enslaves the hysteric in discourse and in jouissance by looking at the Dora case and the case of the young homosexual woman. Bringing together the series, gaze, phallus, jouissance, ideal ego, and anxiety, we might arrive at a conclusion as to what these two young women deprive themselves of in jouissance and why. What we are working with is the proximity of $\$$ and a to the ideal ego as an image in the real. To arrive at an understanding of how these are linked in the two cases I've mentioned, we must keep in mind that Lacan says, "Of course, there is only the phallus in the sexual relations. Only, what this organ has as privileged, let us propose that in some way, one can isolate its *jouissance*. It is thinkable as excluded" (86). The hysteric's preoccupation with the place of the phallus illuminates its exclusion, for her interest in the father's desire concerns the place of the phallus, the issue of the organ, and the proximity of desire and the law.

At one level, hysteria concerns the hysteric's seeing her father's castration and trying to hide it from others, as well as denying her own to herself. As a part of this issue, hysterics question their own gender identifications—their sexuation—around the question of what the father desires. This ties together Dora and the young homosexual woman. But, I would say that it is not Dora's identification with Frau K. per se that is at issue, or the young homosexual woman's identification with the Lady, but the identification each has with the woman in question in relation to her father's desire. He desires as castrated. That is the truth of the master. In other words, castration enters the field here (110). Indeed, Lacan says the father is castrated even before he enters the terrain of the master discourse (115). That means that he can be a father only as a signifier of difference from the mother. As a third term that intervenes in the infant/mother duality, he is the Name-of-the-Father. Dora's father lacks his health and possibly his sexual potency. The young homosexual woman's father shows his castration in not being able to control his daughter's anger at him. Unlike Dora, the young homosexual woman is not angry at her father because he is castrated, and she certainly does not try to hide his castration. Rather, she castrates him in the eyes of others. In this she attests to the importance to him of carrying on his name via the control of his daughter's sexual choice, if one can call this a kind of castration.

The reason I place the young homosexual woman beside Dora as a hysteric concerns, rather than the issue of castration, the hysteric's confusion over whether she is a woman or a man. Because of this she elevates the Other woman to a sexual position in order to reject her own identification with the maternal body, favoring, instead, a question regarding the sexual body. In order to develop the picture of Dora and the young homosexual woman as hysterics who have no solid imaginary identification with a woman's body, and no signifier attaching them chiefly with the mother, I would like to explain why I place the young homosexual woman as a hysteric, rather than in some other structure. In *Seminar IV*, Lacan calls her perverse,[2] yet elsewhere he says that only males can be truly perverse. He also describes hysteria as a negative perversion—one that fails to realize its own jouissance. It has been argued that the young homosexual woman is psychotic because of her passage to the act of violence in jumping over the tram bridge when her father gave her a scalding glance as he promenaded the Lady upon whom her affections were centered.[3]

It is noteworthy that the young homosexual woman's crisis follows from the birth of a baby brother when she is sixteen years old. She feels displaced in her father's affections. But it is not her mother she is angry with, as Freud argued, calling the Lady a substitute for her mother. It is not the maternal body that is at issue but the sexual body. The question of how to identify herself as subject and as an object is fundamental to the hysteric and is decided by her position in reference to the phallus. In consequence of the hysteric's not knowing where to place herself as man or woman, she often deprives herself of jouissance. Lacan says in *Seminar X*, regarding the young homosexual woman, that she is "the girl for whom the attachment to the father and the disappointment because of the birth . . . of a young brother" is paramount.[4] Indeed, this disappointment was the turning point of her life. What will she do? "Make of her castration as a woman," he says, "what the knight does with respect to his lady, to whom precisely he offers the sacrifice of his virile prerogatives to make of her the support of what is linked in the relationship by an inversion to this sacrifice, namely the putting in place of the lack, precisely what is lacking to the field of the other, namely the supreme guarantee, the fact that the law is well and truly the desire of the father, that one is sure of it, there is a law of the father, an absolute phallus, Φ."[5] By making herself a lover, the young homosexual woman imagines that she has the phallus. We remember that Little Hans's symptom appeared upon the birth of a baby sister. He became obsessed with the question of the phallus. Lacan's point about the young homosexual woman's wanting to take the place of the mother in her father's eyes goes hand in hand with Freud's description of this young woman as taking up the masculine position, that of the lover.

Lacan portrays the young homosexual woman as castrated, not psychotic. Whether he means her castration as a subject, or her castration as a woman in sexuation, she would not be psychotic, given that the psychotic—identified with The Woman—does not appear on the sexuation graph. Indeed, the young homosexual woman has not foreclosed the Name-of-the-Father at all. He is central to her dilemma. Lacan portrays her as suddenly unsure about her sexual identifications. Freud details how she had dropped all her attention to her female toiletry and taken up the position of a man in relation to a woman. As Jacques-Alain Miller has argued in "To Interpret the Cause: From Freud to Lacan,"[6] this is not an easy thing for any human subject—to take up a position of a man or woman. Children try to ascertain gender identity and sexual identity from the parental couple M ◊ F. They try to get W ◊ M or B ◊ G from M ◊ F. But the parental couple and the sexual couple are different.[7] There is no holistic image or signifier that will yield up the answer to this question. So we are left sorting this out through identifications with the masculine or the feminine in a given culture. Once those identifications are solidified, then we choose a partner on the basis of masculine and feminine traits, not on the basis of some pregiven heterosexual or homosexual being.

If we look at Dora and the young homosexual woman as confused about sexual identifications, we have examples of acting out and passage to the act in both young women.[8] Lacan says that Dora's position in the K. household is an acting out, while the young homosexual woman's very public courtship of the Lady is an acting out. Indeed, acting out prevents each girl from taking up her place in the discourse chain of the symbolic order. Lacan says that acting out is the sign that one is preventing many things.[9] When one brings together the structure of the hysteric's discourse with Lacan's explanation of acting out, one sees that in the position of subject, the hysteric is lacking, even that she incarnates the lack-in-being, while aiming her desire at some master signifier in the place of the other: $\$ \rightarrow S_1$ (44). In acting out, Lacan says "something in the behavior of the subject shows itself. The demonstrative accent, the orientation toward the Other of every acting out, is something that ought to be highlighted."[10] While Freud believed that the young homosexual woman wanted a baby from her father, I would argue, rather, that she wanted to remain primary in the field of his gaze.

But can one say that the withdrawal of the father's gaze was enough to send the young homosexual woman to an act of attempted suicide, jumping over a railway bridge into the ditch below? I would say not. Rather, there is a coming together of the ideal ego as a real image; the identification with the Lady as "nothing," occasioned by her father's gaze; and the unconscious realization that she is not the phallus. She has tried to incarnate the phallus, but when she fails in that effort, she produces a spontaneous gesture on the side of the *objet a*, the passage to the act. She throws herself off the stage. She drops herself as an object that has been rendered nothing; nothing if not the apple of her father's eye. Freud says she wanted to have her father's child. Lacan says she tries to embody the phallus she is not. Indeed, she tries to give the phallus to the Lady, becoming the servant by sacrificing what she imaginarily assumes herself to have. We saw this in her acting out of a courtship where desire affirmed itself as a truth of the object.

Lacan says that acting out is the demonstration—the veiled showing, veiled as subject insofar as it speaks. It shows its cause, which is a division at the place of the Other that is nonauthenticable. The Other's refusal of her identification throws the young homosexual woman back upon herself as a subject who lacks. She herself literally tumbles as in a falling domino chain into the position of the *objet a*. We can say that the *a* emerges in the hysteric's discourse as the truth of that discourse, as the extra pound of flesh. One acts out to try to get that pound of flesh. The young homosexual woman will pay her father back. She will ruin his reputation and have her pound of flesh. What is the problem, then? The problem is that she wants to realize his desire; in this case, the desire of being the phallus he cherishes in his newborn son.

The young homosexual woman is "othered" in her fictional structure, the subject taking on the structure of fiction in its efforts to get the love that will validate the real image of the ideal ego unconscious formation. In *Seminar X*, Lacan gives another example of getting this pound of flesh—that which any discourse structure seeks in its relation to the object. He reminds us in "The Direction of the Treatment" of Ernst Kris's patient who thinks his book is not original, but plagiarized.[11] Kris reads the book and does everything to convince his patient by true facts that the book is indeed original; others are the plagiarizers, not him. This has no effect on the patient who knows he has not gotten his pound of flesh. He manifests this in his acting out by going to a restaurant to eat "fresh brains," his new object identification. The *objet a* sought by the witty butcher's wife is to be both plump and thin at the same time, thus having all her husband's desire. The pound of flesh Dora is aiming at is something like being her father's mistress via a triangulation of desire with her father and Frau K. We can look at this in relation to Dora's passage to the act. When Herr K. tries to kiss her by the lake, she passes to the act of violence and slaps him. He has touched upon her ideal ego, has pushed her from her subject position to the side of the object. He has called the woman who is her father's desire, and with whom she identifies—for example, via traits of Frau K.'s beautiful white body—"nothing to him." If Frau K. is nothing, then so is Dora. There is no time to reflect, to act out by huffing away. She passes to the act in the slap.

While passing to the act concerns the object and the real, acting out, on the other hand, is a symptom that shows itself as other. The proof is that it has to be interpreted, but only on conditions that are added to the symptom present in the first place. Here Lacan takes a symptom by its very nature to be a backhanded kind of jouissance, a displeasure. What is the displeasure of Dora? Of the young homosexual woman? Of the witty butcher's wife? Dora lives her sexual jouissance vicariously, interestingly enough, staring for hours at a picture of the Dresden Madonna, the quintessential virgin. The young homosexual woman also lives her pleasure vicariously, chasing a Lady who spurns her. Freud comments upon her genital chastity. The Lady has, so far, only allowed her to kiss her hand. And Lacan stresses that she takes the position of the phallus that fulfills her desire vis-à-vis the father, not sexual pleasure per se. The witty butcher's wife keeps herself from the jouissance of a dinner party with a friend, holding on, instead, to a jealousy of her husband's attraction to her thin friend.

Freud argues that there is no transference in the case of the young homosexual woman. In her dreams she says she will marry, and she tells him she will because that will give her more time to spend with women.

Freud thinks she is lying, and Lacan comments that it is a lie that tells the truth. "Freud," Lacan says, "refuses to see the structure of fiction at the origin of truth."[12] In a sense, fiction and acting out are one and the same. You try to convince the Other that your demand is valid by taking the place of the other, by incarnating what is lacking in the game. One can see what kind of cataclysm will ensue for the hysteric when her connection to the master signifier, as positivized phallus, is thrown into doubt. She is left looking lack and loss in the face. It is not surprising that anxiety will push her to a passage to the act in such moments. Her anchor is her father's desire, her attachment to him as phallic signifier.

Indeed, the young homosexual woman sets up the kind of triangle characteristic of the hysteric, who obtains sexual identification via an unconscious desire. This has been commented upon by Jacques-Alain Miller in his article "Le trio de mélo."[13] Dora is in three triangles—one with her father and Frau K., another with Frau K. and Herr K., and another with Herr K. and her father. And both are in a triangle with Freud. The young homosexual woman is in a triangle with her father and the Lady. The witty butcher's wife is in a triangle with her friend and her husband. In all these cases there is a perturbation concerning the phallus. Who is it? Who has it? How does it confer sexuality? What the hysteric knows is that the phallus confers being at the point where she lacks. The clinical question that arises here is whether to allow a hysteric the equilibrium provided by maintaining her symptom, or challenging it such that the ideal ego image in the real will be shattered. What happens when this image is touched upon? Anxiety is produced. When she falls as *objet a* in the place of truth, the hysteric has lost the precious thing that maintained her pseudo-balance. The object has suddenly become the void. One sees in the hysteric's discourse structure—in that the truth of the real resides in the *objet a*—that she can readily become object of the excruciating gaze of the Other, rather than object of her fantasy. In her fantasy, she has the phallus and is the precious object of her father's/husband's/lover's desire. Indeed, the young homosexual woman's bitterness toward men, which follows her suicide attempt, is, Lacan says, the neurotic bitterness of the hysteric confronting her own castration.

Anxiety introduces us to lack, says Lacan.[14] The hysteric, then, is proximate to lack insofar as her subject position is to live consciously with the lack-in-being at the surface of her discourse and desire. But, I would claim, the hysteric does not desire lack of jouissance in and of itself. Rather, given that her sense of identity is split between the masculine and the feminine, she bears the mark of the sexual nonrapport at the surface of her consciousness. The reason her desire is not to be the daughter to her mother is because it is the conferring of sexual identification she questions. She turns, rather, to her father's desire, her desire to be the phallus to him, either the phallus he lacks or the phallus he wants. In this sense, one can say the hysteric denies the father's castration.

$$\frac{S \Diamond o}{-\Phi}$$

As Lacan puts it, the Oedipal myth means that the father's desire and his law are one and the same.[15] Dora supports the desire of a lawless father, while the young homosexual woman passes to the act of suicide when she confronts her father as father of the law. But in each case, when the hysteric confronts a primordial identification with the woman who incarnates desire in her scenario, she responds to a negative identification with the woman she emulates with anxiety that is productive of a passage to the act.

Lacan says that anxiety responds to primordial helplessness and is taken up by the ego in reference to slighter dangers.[16] In neurosis, the *a* appears and acts out to stop the tragedy—the insult to the ideal ego as real—that is in play.[17] Insofar as both Dora and the young homosexual woman are searching for identification as subject—either masculine or feminine—and the search takes its measure in terms of the phallus, when Herr K. insults his wife, with whom Dora identifies, and when the young homosexual woman's father insults her Lady, each young woman suddenly identifies herself in the object at the site of truth as a piece of trash, a *déjet*, a *rejet*.

Covering up the father's castration is not the same as realizing the father's desire. Both Dora and the young homosexual woman are trying to understand where they are in a subject position by acting out and in an object position via their dreams and their passage to the act. While Dora has often been said to hide her father's impotence—partly because she observed Frau K. and her father in the act of fellatio—this is no proof of her father's impotence. What is clear is that his relationship with Frau K. was complex and ongoing. Yet, insofar as the hysteric wants to enable her father to accomplish his desire, Dora facilitates her father's relationship with Frau K. The young homosexual woman tries to be the boy her father wants. The hysteric creates herself in conformity with what she imagines her father's desire to be—creates herself for his gaze. She is, in turn, dependent upon the judgment of that gaze, Lacan says in *Seminar X*:

> If you think you know the function of the maternal breast, or that of the turd, you know well how much obscurity remains in your minds about the phallus, and when it is the object which comes immediately after that is concerned. I will give it to you all the same, as a way of giving your curiosity something to feed on, namely the eye as such, about it you know nothing at all. This is why it should only be approached with prudence, and for the best of reasons. This is the object involved since, when all is said and done, it is the object without which there is no anxiety, it is because it is a dangerous object.[18]

When Marilyn Monroe lost her position as object of desire in John Kennedy's gaze, she passed to the act of suicide. I would call it a hysterical suicide, not a psychotic one.

If what shakes the hysteric to the core is her loss of a strong attachment to the phallus, one can understand Lacan's claims that in the case of the young homosexual woman what is involved in her elevating of the Lady to the position of a desired object is "a certain promotion of the phallus as such to the place of *a* and it is here," he says, "in the object choice [*Objektwahl*] which Freud distinguishes as such, as including the mechanisms which are original, everything turns effectively around this relationship as the young homosexual woman between the subject and *a*."[19] Indeed, Dora does the same with her phallus—Frau K.—promoting her to the place of Dora's *a*.

Lacan reproaches Freud for his treatment of the young homosexual woman. Freud decides she is not in transference with him and is lying in her dreams, so he lets her fall as an object. He drops her, handing her over to a female colleague.[20] If acting out is a subject position, then passing to the act concerns the subject as object, as *objet a*. Indeed, in passing to the act the subject is obliterated, falls off the stage, out of the picture. She falls out of her fiction, away from her acting out on the stage of the Other. Why does this engage the ideal ego as real? Lacan says when there is an ambiguity between identification and love, between having and being, the object is liable to fall.

> This is why one can rediscover along the regressive path, in the form of identification to being, this *a*, what one no longer has. It is exactly what makes Freud put the term regression at the point where he specifies the relationships between identification and love. But in this regression where *a* remains what it is, the instrument, it is with what one is that one can . . . have or not have. It is with this real image constituted here, when it emerges, as i(*a*), that one catches or not what remains in the neck of this image, the multiplicity of the *a*-objects represented in [Lacan's] schema by the real flowers caught up or not in the constitution . . . of the symbol of something . . . which ought to be rediscovered in the structure of the cortex, as the foundation for a certain relationship between man and the image of his body and different objects which can be constituted from this body are, or not caught, grasped at the moment when i(*a*) has the opportunity of constituting itself.[21]

Specularization is strange, Lacan says, space being the dimension of what can be superimposed.[22]

The important thing for the hysteric is that she has no image of her body as being either strictly feminine or strictly masculine. She is not, like the schizophrenic, subject to the bodily fragmentation that shows the "subjectification of the *a* as pure real."[23] She is not the woman in the masquerade who puts on her feminine garb as the armature of a given sociohistorical moment and then calls herself a woman. Dora identifies with her father's cigar smoke, the young homosexual woman with her image of what a body looks like. Both are split because they know they are girls or women. Lacan says that in clinical practice, when an analysand cannot find himself or herself in the mirror, he or she is seized by a depersonalizing vacillation. Indeed, the removal of the father's positive gaze for the young homosexual woman—in Dora's case, Herr K.'s disturbance of her unconscious identification with his wife—throw the hysteric into disarray. Not finding herself in the mirror places her topologically at the edge, at the point of anxiety, an edge phenomenon.[24] Continuing in a topological vein for a moment, Lacan argues in an address published in *Scilicet* that the body is a sphere by its surface and the knot that ties together the imaginary, symbolic, and the real image of the ideal ego.[25] Its subversion in regards to the hysteric's fantasy of the father's desire causes her to subvert the father's discourse in trying to reestablish her imaginary relation to his gaze.

What the hysteric cannot support, Lacan says in *Seminar XVII*, is confronting her own castration. Why? Generally, Lacan says, one talks of the primary identification of a person as being to the mother. However, if we go to Freud's "Group Psychology and the Analysis of the Ego" (1921),[26] the identification to the father is given as primary, and for this reason he merits love (100). In other words, the father introduces difference into the mother-infant dyad and as such is himself the first countable value.[27] If his name and his law do not intervene, there is no castration and psychosis follows. The result is that the master signifier, S_1, determines castration. Jacques-Alain Miller has spoken of this signifier as commensurate with the unary trait. Identification with the father is identification with him as the voice of difference, of being as being castrated.

What is the function of this master signifier? Its function, as Lacan often said, is to represent the subject for another signifier. It is precisely this function that fails in psychosis. If the young homosexual woman were psychotic, she would not be parading a woman around town, asking implicitly for the town's judgment of her behavior. Moreover, she would have picked a woman who was responsive to her gestures of love. Lacan's point about the signifier's representing a subject for another signifier is that the subject is not univocal. It is both represented and not. Something of it remains hidden (101). What remains hidden? Hegel says self-knowledge (101). Lacan says, rather, that it is something concerning the body. It may seem strange to say that a hysteric acts out vis-à-vis the Other to try to ascertain where the phallus is for her. "More simply," says Lacan, "it is a matter of the fact that there is a use of the signifier that we can define by starting out from the master's signifier split from this body . . . the body lost by the slave which becomes nothing other than the body in which all the other signifiers are inscribed" (102).

The slave fetches and carries, allowing the master repose. The question hiding in this rapport is the one concerning who has the phallus. If the slave does not do his job, he deprives the master of jouissance and the slave has the phallus.

All this means that from the start there is a headless knowledge, Lacan says (102). Indeed, the master's knowledge can be constituted by something other than a mythical knowledge—something one calls science (102–3). But how does this knowledge concern truth? How does it separate itself from truth? The "they say" of science concerns the field of language. "Iraq has weapons of mass destruction and is a gathering threat to the United States of America," Bush says. And the Americans go to war. This knowledge justifies itself in a science of supposedly documented reports issued by the CIA and other agencies. Lacan goes somewhere quite different to make the distinction between science and truth.

We find the truth of the unconscious, that of subject division and object confusion, with the hysteric, he says. The master discourse is written as

$$\frac{\text{master signifier}}{\text{subject}} \rightarrow \frac{\text{knowledge}}{\text{jouissance}}$$

$$\frac{S_1}{\$} \rightarrow \frac{S_2}{a} \;\; (\leftarrow)$$

What is repressed is the subject of desire and the knowledge of jouissance. The hysteric is written as

$$\frac{\text{subject}}{\text{jouissance}} \rightarrow \frac{\text{master signifier}}{\text{knowledge}}$$

$$\frac{\$}{a} \rightarrow \frac{S_1}{S_2} \;\; (\leftarrow)$$

Her knowledge is of the jouissance that supports the subject in his illusion of knowing the master signifier. For this reason, the hysteric subverts master-discourse knowledge. The hysteric knows the truths of desire and jouissance, that they govern the language that calls itself the

The Hysteric's Truth 81

master discourse. While desire is on the side of the Other, which is the side of acting out, jouissance is on the side of the object, the side of passing to the act. Lacan rewrites the hysteric's discourse as

$$\frac{\text{desire}}{\text{truth}} \quad \begin{array}{c} \rightarrow \\ \leftarrow \end{array} \quad \frac{\text{Other}}{\text{loss}}$$

In the place of knowledge, S_2, she knows about loss. This brings her to the realization that truth concerns the *objet a*. In Lacan's words,

> This is where the discourse of the hysteric gets its price. It has the merit of maintaining in the discursive institution the question of what the sexual relation is, namely how a subject is able to maintain it or, to express it better, is unable to maintain it.
>
> As a matter of fact, the answer to the question how he is able to maintain it is the following—by leaving speech to the Other, and precisely qua locus of repressed knowledge.
>
> What is interesting is the truth, that what is there in sexual knowledge is yielded up entirely as foreign to the subject. This is what in Freudian discourse was originally called "the repressed." (106)

Dora's father claims that he must have the presence of Frau K. as his nurse, for his health. Dora sees another truth there. The young homosexual woman's father has no protest other than that he has a new son who has produced strange behavior in his daughter. His daughter sees another truth there. She has lost the position of phallus in his gaze. It is, for the hysteric, a sexual question. Where do I place my jouissance? What body will I incarnate?

Lacan persists, pointing out something that history has always repressed: "I mean that the discourse of the hysteric is not the testimony that what is inferior is down below. On the contrary, as a battery of functions it is indistinguishable from those assigned to the discourse of the master.... It's simply that the discourse of the hysteric reveals the discourse of the master's relation to *jouissance*, in the sense that in it knowledge occupies the place of *jouissance*" (106–7). While jouissance is located in the master discourse in the place of repressed knowledge (fantasy as repressed), in the hysteric's discourse it is in the place of truth;

because it dwells in a repressed place in the master discourse, it can be aimed at by the hysteric, subverted. Herr K.'s jouissance is thwarted by Dora. The young homosexual woman's father's jouissance in having a typical family, a daughter who will marry and bear him grandchildren, is thwarted by his daughter.

"The subject himself, the hysteric is alienated from the master signifier as he whom this signifier divides—'he' in the masculine represents the subject—he who refuses to make himself its body. People speak about somatic compliance," and this is Freudian, Lacan says (107). Rather, in hysteria, a refusal of the sexual body is in question. Dora refuses to have a sexual life of her own. The young homosexual woman refuses to give her body to anyone—male or female—insofar as the Lady is cold to her and she remains a virgin. The witty butcher's wife refuses to give her body to a social occasion where she will have to compete sexually—in the gaze of her husband—with her thin friend. One can say that she refuses to give her body as a sexual body. Lacan says that jouissance and sexual union are always in the closest possible relationship.[28] The hysteric refuses to follow the effect of the master signifier. She will not make herself its object, its slave (107). This differs from the woman in the sexual masquerade who plays whatever game is required of her.

The hysteric is on strike, Lacan says. She does not deliver her knowledge. What is her knowledge? She knows that the master is castrated and that jouissance resides in the place of truth. Yet, paradoxically, she unmasks the function of the master with whom she remains in solidarity by putting into value the master's linkage with the One. She puts it into value by subtracting herself from it by the title of object of his desire. Herr K. is left lacking, castrated, as is the young homosexual's father regarding this reputation. Lacan says this concerns the question of the idealized father (107). Dora fails her father in not accommodating Herr K., and the young homosexual woman fails her father in taking up a position of a boy. Freud stresses Dora's symptoms in being disgusted by Herr K., a thing he considers neurotic (107). Lacan says, rather, Dora's father is castrated (108). He wants to fulfill his desire of jouissance the best he can with Frau K. Any help Dora can give him in this scenario will help him keep his castration at bay.

Lacan says the hysteric's father is deficient in the symbolic. Dora's father is certainly deficient. Not only is he sick, he does not take up the position of symbolic father for his daughter. The young homosexual woman's father's protest is that she will not allow him to be a symbolic father. She is subversion incarnate in her loud protest at having lost her place in his gaze. But Dora is always the most typical hysteric. Lacan points out the obvious. She knows that truth is sexual truth and she goes to find it, not only with Frau K., the object of her father's desire, but with Herr K. because he clearly has the organ. When he embraces her when she is fourteen years old, she does not run away, nor does she upset the relations between the two families. Herr K. gives her the phallus while her father deprives her of the phallus, giving that position, rather, to Frau K. In her first dream about the jewel box being saved, Lacan points out that it is the box she wants to save, not the jewel; she wants to save the envelope of the precious organ (109), not the jewel in the dream, who is Frau K.

Dora's question—what am I as a woman?—is answered not only in her identification with Frau K., but also in Herr K.'s offering her his jouissance. My wife is nothing to me, he says. In the moment he offers her this knowledge as jouissance, she passes to the act of pointing out to him that he is castrated. Her answer is found by remaining faithful to her castrated father and his desire for Frau K. Yet she suffers not only in her division of identification—am I my father's daughter, identified with his cough, his cigar smoke, or am I a beautiful sexual woman like Frau K., or am I a virgin mother like the Madonna?—but in having to deal with her father's castration. In her second dream, she realizes that her symbolic father is dead and confronts an empty place (110). When she returns home, confused and lost, she finds, instead of a father, a big dictionary about sex (111).

What lies, Lacan says, what does not tell the truth, is the analysand's desire.[29] The young homosexual woman dreams that she desires to marry. The witty butcher's wife dreams that she cannot give a dinner party.[30] The dream is the demand, Lacan says, the signifier in liberty (149). Both the young homosexual woman and the witty butcher's wife pose obstacles to their desire to be as women, as does Dora. But the fundamental confusion about being vis-à-vis the phallus is not a matter of simple wish fulfillment. It is a problem of structure. One might surmise that by adoring Frau K. and the Madonna, Dora takes her revenge on the penis. Lacan says in *Seminar XVII* that the witty butcher's wife would actually be happy to leave the phallic object to another. This is only one solution, one interpretation of her dream, he says (85). He places the hysteric, then, on the side of the symptom, on the side of displeasure, pointing out that other than phallic jouissance, there is the function of the plus-de-jouir (excess in jouissance). The excess in jouissance concerns a withholding of pleasure from another. Indeed, there is a kind of sadistic joy in the hysteric's jouissance. One sees the irruptions of these unary traits through the acting out. Dora is asked to go out with an attractive young man, eighteen years old, and she faints. She withholds her body from sexual pleasure, as does the young homosexual woman and the witty butcher's wife.

This presents a paradox. Indeed, living the division of the subject at the surface of agency of speech is a paradox. The hysteric's speech itself is an act, an act of the truth of jouissance that hides behind desire (145). But the paradox is this: the hysteric's great concern is the sexual body, yet she has this strange feature, as, Lacan says, does all feminine jouissance, of being foreign to the mother (89). Not only is the necessity of separating herself from the mother a given of psychoanalysis, so is the fact that the male organ is excluded from reality in some sense. This, says Lacan, is the Other side of psychoanalysis (90). This is why he so prizes the hysteric's discourse. It speaks for the inverse side of discourse, for the Other side of psychoanalysis.

We think of the hysteric's problem as concerning the symbolic father, even the imaginary father. But Lacan says the real father does the work of agency-master (146). But what is this real father? In *Seminar IV*, Lacan calls him the agent of symbolic castration.[31] In *Seminar XVII*, he says he is an effect of language (147). The hysteric in analysis reweaves her identifications around the signifiers for daughter and for mother. Lacan says, "Castration is a real operation that is introduced through the incidence of a signifier, no matter which, into the sexual relationship [*rapport du sexe*]. . . . It is now a question of knowing what this castration means, which is not a fantasy and the result of which is that the only cause of desire is produced by this operation and that fantasy dominates the entire reality of desire, that is to say, the law" (149). The hysteric in analysis changes her fantasies, changes her relation to the phallic signifier. She comes to accept her father's castration in accepting her own.

To answer Freud's question regarding what a woman wants, Lacan says one must go to the hysteric (150). One gets many versions of "I want to be my father's daughter," and so on. As one hysteric said to me upon awaking in a hospital after an overdose of sleeping pills, "It would have all been OK if I had just married my father." What does the hysteric want in Lacan's estimation? She wants a master, she wants the other to be a master, to know many things. But she does not want him to know enough not to believe that she is the supreme prize of all his knowledge. She wants to reign and does not want him to govern (150). Yet, the father is the one who knows nothing of the truth, the one who speaks from the agency of the master signifier as ruler of the symbolic order (151).

How, then, does the hysteric reveal a truth worth noting? Subversion for its own sake or acting out is not admirable. Lacan certainly does not elevate the hysteric's suffering, for it too is nothing to admire. It is, rather, this, that the subject, any subject except a psychotic, is divided. In varying ways, all individuals who are divided suffer from this. The master represses it in the place of truth. The academic puts it in the place of repressed knowledge. The analyst interrogates it. But the hysteric lives it; it is her badge of honor that she lives castration at the surface of her life and discourse. "It is on the basis of the cleavage, the separation between *jouissance* and the henceforth mortified body, it is from the moment that there is a play of inscriptions, a mark of the unary trait, that the question arises [be it via a paralyzed limb or in anxiety itself].... The subject's division is without doubt nothing other than the radical ambiguity that attaches itself to the very term 'truth'" (206). Am I a woman or a man? Am I going to be a mother like my mother or a sexual partner? The hysteric does not say, as poststructuralists would claim, I am man and woman, the difference makes no difference, mother and sexual body. For her it is an either/or question.

This is the heart of Lacanianism: either/or. Either one is masculine or one is feminine. One is not both, except in the suffering of hysteria. Both is the position of suffering, not liberation. It is this truth of the hysteric to which Lacan pays heed. The hysteric's discourse points him toward *Seminar XX*, where he gives us the logic of the masculine and the feminine in the sexuation graph.[32] Finally, one might say of Lacan, as one says of Freud, that his knowledge comes in large part from taking seriously the discourse of the hysteric, her truth, opposed as it is to the master signifier, to the discourse of science, following Lacan to his new science of the real.

Notes

1. Jacques Lacan, *Le séminaire, livre XVII: L'envers de la psychanalyse*, ed. J.-A. Miller (Paris: Seuil, 1991). All further references appear parenthetically, citing Grigg's translation.
2. Jacques Lacan, *Le séminaire, livre IV: La relation d'objet*, ed. J.-A. Miller (Paris: Seuil, 1994).
3. Roland Broca, "Act and Psychosis," trans. C. Linse *(Re)-Turn: A Journal of Lacanian Studies* 1 (2003): 63–78.
4. Jacques Lacan, *The Seminar of Jacques Lacan, Book X: Anxiety*, trans. C. Gallagher from unedited French typescripts; Jacques Lacan, *Le séminaire, livre X: L'angoisse*, ed. J.-A. Miller (Paris: Seuil, 2004), 130.
5. Ibid., 130–31.
6. Jacques-Alain Miller, "To Interpret the Cause: From Freud to Lacan," *Newsletter of the Freudian Field* 3.1–2 (1989): 36.
7. Ibid.
8. Sigmund Freud, "Fragment of an Analysis of a Case of Hysteria" (1905), in *The Standard Edition of the Complete Psychological Works of Sigmund Freud*, ed. J. Strachey (London: Hogarth, 1953), 7:1–122; Sigmund Freud, "The Psychoanalysis of a Case of Homosexuality in a Woman" (1920), in ibid., 18:145–72.
9. Lacan, *Seminar X*, 150.
10. Ibid., 145.
11. Jacques Lacan, "The Direction of the Treatment and the Principles of Its Power," (1958), *Ecrits: A Selection*, trans. B. Fink with Fink and Grigg (New York: Norton, 2002), 215–70.
12. Lacan, *Seminar X*, 152.
13. Jacques-Alain Miller, "Le trio de Mélo," *La cause freudienne, Revue de la psychanalyse* 31 (1995), 9–19.
14. Lacan, *Seminar X*, 155.
15. Ibid., 126.
16. Ibid., 162.
17. Ibid., 164.
18. Ibid., 125.
19. Ibid., 132–33.
20. Ibid., 133.
21. Ibid., 139.
22. Ibid., 142.
23. Ibid., 140.
24. Ibid.

25 Jacques Lacan, "Massachusetts Institute of Technology, 2 decembre 1975," *Scilicet, tu peux savoir ce qu'en pense l'École freudienne de Paris*, nos. 6–7 (1976): 53–61.
26 Sigmund Freud, "Group Psychology and the Analysis of the Ego" (1921), in Strachey, *The Standard Edition* 18:65–81.
27 Ellie Ragland, *The Logic of Sexuation: From Aristotle to Lacan* (New York: SUNY Press, 2004).
28 Lacan, *Seminar X*, 176–77.
29 Ibid., 152.
30 See Lacan, "Direction of the Treatment and the Principles of Its Power," 215–70.
31 Lacan, *Le séminaire, livre IV: La relation d'objet*, ed. J.-A. Miller (Paris: Seuil, 1994), 269.
32 Jacques Lacan, "A Love Letter," in *The Seminar of Jacques Lacan, Book XX: Encore, or on Feminine Sexuality, The Limits of Love and Knowledge*, ed. J.-A. Miller, trans. with notes by B. Fink (New York: Norton, 1998), 78–89, esp. the sexuation graph on 78.

Dominiek Hoens

5

Toward a New
Perversion:
Psychoanalysis

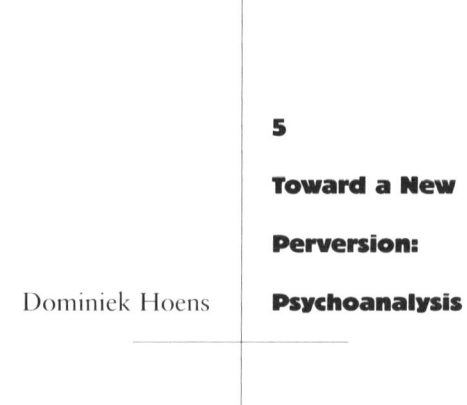

Comment venir à bout de notre amour?
—Aurélia Steiner de Melbourne

Considering psychoanalysis as an "event," with the meaning and significance Alain Badiou has given to this word, can help us to understand what Lacan's "return to Freud" is about.[1] The position of Lacan seems to be that any return to Freud is a return to the *event* of Freud and that this return inscribes itself in the postevental truth procedure called psychoanalysis.[2]

It is Freud—someone coming from the neurosciences and with a very broad interest ranging from philosophy over literature to archaeology—who in a censored passage from *The Question of Lay-Analysis* warns us of "open-mindedness."[3] The word is in English in the German text because it was directed against the American branch of the International Psychoanalytic Association in order to prevent a schism. On the advice of Ernest Jones and Max Eitington, the most vehement passages got censored. Leaving the historical context and details of Freud's self-censoring aside, one should notice Freud's awareness of the threat that psychoanalysis would disappear not by closing itself off from "the outside" (the influence of other disciplines, theories, etc.) but by an openness provoked by an insecurity about and, in the end, infidelity to its own cause. Psychoanalysis is a hybrid theory relying on psychology, linguistics, philosophy, and sociology, among other disciplines, and its emergence can be considered symptomatic of the historical shift named "modernity" and its entailments. Its "being there" can only be problematic, because through its existence it not only constitutes the platform where the aforementioned disciplines meet in an unforeseen way, but it also resists reduction to one of them. This resistance is the point where one could accuse it of being (hysterically) deaf and blind to what conditions it.

In the current context of the two main and conjoined attacks on psychoanalysis, it is more than interesting to see how psychoanalysts react. As a reply to the first attack, the one coming from the sciences and the philosophy of science, which can be summarized as "psychoanalysis does not follow a scientific method," one can discern a tendency to show how some or even most psychoanalytic theses are similar to and in conformity with findings in, for example, evolutionary psychology and the neurosciences.

As a reply to the second attack, the one coming from the psychotherapeutic field, which argues that psychoanalysis is too time-consuming and is not effective, one often hears that psychoanalysis is in the end more effective because it does not heal on the superficial level of the symptoms but on the more important, yes, *effective* level of the causes of those symptoms.

However valuable these replies may be, they remain replies—they are reactive. Sometimes these reactions are accompanied by a critical attitude toward the attacks directed against psychoanalysis: one questions the ideological background from where these attacks stem, that is, the current obsession with scientific explanations joined to the idea of quality control in education, governing, and healing. It could be argued that this was already the case in Freud's time, because the 1927 text I was referring to, *The Question of Lay-Analysis*, originated in Freud's defense of Theodor Reik. Reik was accused of doing psychotherapy without being a doctor and thus trying to heal without being a healer. Freud's reply, in brief, consisted in pointing out how a medical training was quite irrelevant for the psychoanalytic praxis.

Psychoanalysis is a strange phenomenon: how much it may have been produced by and how well it may be imbedded in Europe's history and culture, it remains alien to it. Indeed, isn't it a strange thing that during a long period two people meet three or more times a week and one of them is lying down, being invited by the other to talk nonsense? This other, the analyst, seems to be convinced of one thing: "Away you go, say whatever, it will be marvelous."[4] Lacan's "return to Freud" consists in trying to conceptualize this "psychoanalytic scene" and to understand what one is doing when one engages in this practice.

Here we find a third position toward the attacks on psychoanalysis. Whereas the first position is inclined to minimize the differences between psychoanalysis and other "human sciences" and is looking for a consensus,[5] and while the second one defends psychoanalysis against critique by questioning the value of this critique, the third position seems to be convinced of the uniqueness of psychoanalysis. While not being deaf to external criticisms, it treats them as if they are missing the point. One is tempted to qualify this position as "arrogant naïveté." This position, however, does not prevent one from questioning the theoretical assumptions and their implications, not despite but because one is engaged in psychoanalysis as a praxis.

In order to formulate his theory, Lacan's first and most important reference is to what he calls "l'expérience analytique," psychoanalytic experience, qualified in *Seminar XVII* as a "precise experience" (89). One of Lacan's aims in *Seminar XVII* is to distinguish psychoanalysis qua social bond from other discourses. Besides this differentiation, Lacan is also reflecting on how psychoanalysis depends on other discourses and the historical context in which it originated and exists. This way of questioning psychoanalysis does not end up by promoting it as a solution to cultural problems (e.g., the current dominance and the use made of the university discourse). On the contrary, Lacan's basic view on psychoanalysis consists in emphasizing its eccentricity with respect to this culture and the fact that it can only adopt an important but weak position, that of exploring both the effects and conditions of a cultural dynamic.

In this seminar one also finds the elements for understanding what is specific to and problematic about the psychoanalytic discourse. Paying attention to these elements will show how the analytic discourse can potentially be qualified as "perverse." Instead of refusing this proximity between psychoanalysis and perversion, one could ask whether it is not precisely there that one of the arguments in favor of psychoanalysis can be found. This essay aims, first, to show what the notion of discourse means within the Lacanian framework, and, second, to point out some promising difficulties pertaining to psychoanalytic discourse.

Discourse and signifier

Lacan's basic axiom is the following: when someone is speaking, one can suppose a subject of this speaking. This subject is supposed and functions as the *hypokeimenon*, as that what underlies the speaking.[6] This subject is neither a substance nor a pregiven entity. As he says, "It is not a question of beings in the effect of language. It is only a question of a speaking Being. At the outset we are not at the level of beings, but at the level of Being" (94). The condition of possibility of any subject is the intervention of a signifier, formalized as S_1. Through this S_1 the subject $\$$ gets represented for another signifier S_2.[7] This process leaves a remainder, qualified as *objet a*. These four terms $\$$, S_1, S_2 and a — in this order — form the master's discourse. This sounds like the well-known Lacan, but it is worth paying attention to some implications:

1. What Lacan calls the master's discourse is the condition of possibility of the subject (of the unconscious) and as such of the analytic discourse.[8]
2. Discourse stands in between language (*langage*) and speech *parole*). Language is a necessary condition for discourse,[9] but discourse can exist without speech. (11)
3. "Discourse" is Lacan's most elaborate way of formulating an alternative to the idea of "intersubjectivity" that presupposes a (relative) autonomy and independence of the subjects involved.

Let's start with the last point, because it is against the background of his critique of intersubjectivity that we can appreciate his theory of the discourses. In *Seminar VIII*, Lacan makes the provocative statement that where love is concerned he hopes that his auditors treat the other not as a subject but as an object.[10] Later in the seminar he will explain that love indeed implies two subjects, but only on the basis of a desire that aims at an object.[11] The "subject(ivity)" Lacan is denouncing here is the one propagated by a humanism of the individual and an ethics of the fellow human being (*semblable*). This "fellow," however, is not only the one who from a psychoanalytic point of view is essentially an uncanny Doppelgänger; he also haunts the psychoanalytic, Lacanian theory itself. Whereas in Freud one can ask how and at what point an autoerotic infant comes to relate itself to others, according to Lacan a human being is always already in a relation with others. In the 1930s and 1940s, when Lacan tried to formulate a theory of identification for the first time, he could rely on only one imaginary mechanism. I find myself first in the other and can hold on to a feeling of self only as far as I can at the same time distance myself from this other. From this description, the problem Lacan had to face can be easily deduced: the ego (what I think I am) continuously seesaws between two possible threats: either I merge with and disappear in the other, or there is no identification and therefore no identity. On the clinical level it is, on the one hand, logical that Lacan described a cure as a "guided paranoia" but, on the other hand, it is difficult to see what the outcome of such a process can be.[12] *L'enfer, c'est les autres*, and at that moment of Lacan's thinking there is nothing but a *huis clos*.

In his 1945 text on "logical time" Lacan conceives a way out of this difficulty.[13] Like the prisoners in the sophism, it is through following the intersubjective logic to its end that the possibility of a nonimaginary identification arises.[14] The possibility consists in being able to say "I am x."[15] This x indicates not an ideal image but a signifier. This signifier, S_1, is a signifier isolated from the rest of the symbolic universe (S_2). As such it is the necessary exclusion that guarantees a more or less coherent world. On a social level, however, Lacan was convinced of witnessing a decline of this guarantor. Lacan scholarship has shown in ample detail how much Lacan is indebted to the French sociology of the late nineteenth and early twentieth centuries that dealt with the question and problem of the dissolution of the family and community.[16]

The problem Lacan was facing resided in the precarious status of this symbolic identification, because it is a mechanism that works only in a symbolic universe that itself is organized by a master signifier that divides the world into places.[17] Lacan, following Alexandre Kojève and Alexandre Koyré, argues throughout his seminar that Christianity meant a break with the ancient, Greek world. If we agree with Badiou that (Pauline) Christianity founded universalism, on the level of the subject this means that we are all equal.[18] In contrast, the Greek aristocratic master's discourse was founded on inequality. Already in *Seminar II*, and in a much more developed manner in *Seminar XVII*, the model for the master's discourse is the one that divides the roles into master and slave, formalized as S_1 and S_2 respectively.[19] The master is master only in relation to a slave. In contrast, in a Christian world, no one is anyone else's master. We are *free* and *equal* subjects and without a given "one that divides into two."

In *Seminar XVII*, Lacan seems to draw the consequences of this historical shift. There is an old and waning master's discourse (some of us are masters), a recent, bureaucratic university discourse (all of us are slaves), the hysteric's discourse (I am the master of a master become impotent), and the analyst's discourse. I will return to this fourth discourse, but looking at this discourse as one of the four social bonds, one can remark the following concerning the intricate relation between the master and analytic discourses. In the lower part of the formula of the master's discourse one can discern a double bar between $\$$ and a ($\$ // a$), which indicates that the master's discourse works without a fantasmatic support.[20] Hystericization (a prerequisite of any analytic cure) means not only that a master's "repressed" subjectivity is made present (from S_1 to $\$$), but, more importantly, also that the object produced by the master's discourse comes to stand in a relation to the $\$$ ($\$/a$). The analytic discourse qua social bond works with and somehow *creates* desire, that is, a desire caused by an object that is neither imaginary nor symbolic. This implies that the subjects involved in an analysis relate to each other neither as imaginary equals, nor as individuals occupying the place and position guaranteed by a symbolic order. They relate as radically different, that is, as singulars.[21] The promise of the analytic discourse seems to be that in the current context of the replacement of the particular (master's discourse) by abstract universality (university discourse), there is a scene where, and a social bond in which, the singularity of the subject qua desire can have a place.

My second point, which is that discourse stands in between language and speech, allows Lacan to add a third dimension to his *linguisterie*. As is well known, *language* refers to the synchronic, paradigmatic, and atemporal system of signifiers that is the condition for any speech act.[22] Speech is the diachronic, syntagmatic, and temporal concatenation of signifiers. Discourse stands in between the two, referring to the point where the two intersect. This point of intersection is the point where language gets subjectified (and where a human being becomes subjected to language) and the starting point of any possible speech. Lacan has been dealing with this enigmatic point of departure throughout his oeuvre. For example, his first formulation of fantasy is tantamount to "staging one's own disappearance under the signifier."[23]

The master's discourse, logically speaking the "first" discourse, is the discourse where the subject disappears under an originary signifier, making it possible for a human being to access the symbolic order qua language. The subject has to "die" in order to be able to live.[24] This can explain the famous but obscure sentence from *Seminar XX*: "There is some emergence of analytic discourse with each shift from one discourse to another."[25] The analytic discourse produces the S_1 that is the prerequisite for any discourse. The analytic discourse is not only one of the four discourses, but is also the only discourse in which the origin of any discourse (S_1) is produced. Put differently, the analytic discourse allows one to confront the origin of speech (the point where the subject gets represented in its disappearance) and as such allows one to be engaged in a discourse. If being able to shift discourses is a sign of health, then psychoanalysis might be the necessary condition.[26]

The Lacanian notion of discourse is another way of answering older questions about the advent of the subject, the signifier and intersubjectivity. What is new in *Seminar XVII* is the substitution of four discourses implying the three dimensions of the imaginary, the real, and the symbolic for an understanding of intersubjectivity in terms of either imaginary rivalry or symbolic rigidity. In the next section we will take a closer look at the analytic discourse as the discourse that produces S_1, the point of subjectivation, and the affect "of which there is only one, namely the affect of being caught in a discourse."

Discourse and Affect (Love and Shame)

The first aspect of the "analytic experience" is the signifier, and the second aspect concerns the fact that two people are talking to each other and that this talking is both made possible and modeled by transference. There is something in or next to or, maybe, beyond speaking that one could call "the affective." Again, here as well, Lacan as a psychoanalyst does not feel obliged to give us an account of how *the mind* works. Affect is relevant to the extent that it can explain what happens in the analytic cure. Although Lacan repeats over and over that transference is not an affect, it is most often in a context of dealing with the phenomenon of transference that Lacan has the most to say about affect.[27]

One of the surprises in *Seminar XVII* is to read Lacan quoting Freud affirmatively on the claim that "the analytic relation is founded on love of truth" (192–93). It is surprising because one would expect Lacan to criticize the claim that love, and especially "love of truth," is a foundation of psychoanalysis. Although psychoanalysis works with (transference) love, isn't its aim to show how much it is an imaginary lure veiling the dimension of desire? And doesn't one always talk about the analyst's *desire*? We can understand that there is an analysand's love for the analyst, who is supposed to have a certain knowledge. As Lacan puts it elsewhere, "I insist: it is love that addresses itself to knowledge. Not desire."[28] But then again, the goal of analytic cure is to "frustrate" this love and to unveil the transcendental structure of desire this love (of knowledge) is based upon.

What about the love of truth? If the love of truth is not to be located on the side of the analysand, maybe it can be found on the side of the analyst. One could argue that this is the case. Referring to *Seminar VIII*, one could say that the analyst, in order to become an analyst, has left the place of the *eromenos* (beloved) for the place of the *erastes* (lover). This shift is what Lacan calls "the miracle of love." It means that one is desired as an object and is capable of desiring back from this object position. "To love" means to desire the other as the subject of a desire.[29] It is this kind of desire that one finds on the upper part of the analytic discourse: $a \rightarrow \$$. The analyst loves the analysand not for this or that personal trait (love *de dicto*) and not because of some essential humanity (love *de re*), but for an inhuman desire.[30] This is how Lacan understands Freud's quote: love of truth is love of the essential weakness human beings are marked by. "What is the love of truth?" he asks. "The love of truth is the love of this weakness whose veil we have lifted, it's the love of what truth hides, which is called castration. . . . That there is a love of weakness is no doubt the essence of love" (58).

It is not the first time that a similarity has been remarked upon between the upper part of the analytic discourse, $a \rightarrow \$$, and the form of the pervert's fantasy: $a \lozenge \$$.[31] The pervert positions himself at the place of *a* (the instrument of the Other's *jouissance*) in order to transfer the castration he denies onto a $. The pervert's fantasy secures for him the fact that it is not he but the others who are castrated. What a sadist aims at is not to cause an innocent victim physical or mental pain but to bring the victim to the point where (s)he is revealed as subjected to the signifier.[32] The comparison between the analyst and the pervert concerns not only the similar position they adopt (the place of *objet a*), but also what they aim at, namely, the production of the subject qua subject of the signifier.[33]

From this perspective the final, already strange and murky session of *The Other Side of Psychoanalysis* takes on a specific significance. Lacan starts this lesson with the remark "It does have to be said that it is unusual to die from shame." It is indeed unusual, and what Lacan is suggesting is that its rare occurrence has become close to being absent. This absence has to be situated in a cultural context that does not refer to "honor" (*honneur*), "honesty" (*honnêteté*) or "glory" (*gloire*) (three forms of fidelity to an S_1) as an ethical guideline, but to enjoyment. Lacan continues: "Yet it is the one sign—I have been talking about this for a while, how a signifier becomes a sign—the one sign whose genealogy one can be certain of, namely that it is descended from a signifier. After all, any sign can fall under the suspicion of being a pure sign, that is to say, obscene." The first question one has to ask is where Lacan has been talking about a "signifier becoming a sign." There are at least two passages in his work one can think of. The first one that immediately comes to our mind is the analysis devoted to the first part of the Paul Claudel trilogy, *The Hostage*, in *Seminar VIII*.[34] The heroine of the play, Sygne de Coûfontaine, living in Napoleonic times, has decided to dedicate her life to saving and bringing together what is left of the family property in order to preserve the noble name "Coûfontaine" for the future. As such, she is a master:[35] faithful to a name and committed to a project (she can betray and die of shame for). At a certain moment, however, she is asked by a priest (Badilon) to marry Toussaint Turelure in order to save the Pope's life. After a long and perversely refined talk (in the genre "I, Badilon, cannot ask you this and there is no reason to do so, but still it would be great if you were to"), she decides to marry this Turelure.[36] At the very end of this play she is fatally wounded, and when asked by Turelure for a last forgiveness, she can make only an obscene sign (*un signe que non*). Without going into the details of the play, what we can see here is this reduction of a signifier to a sign, a tic. For Sygne as subject this means that she has been represented by a signifier (Coûfontaine), a signifier she has an ambiguous relation to, that is, has a certain distance from, but ultimately, through the complete betrayal of her name, she is reduced to an ugly sign. One possible reading of the play consists in pointing out how a Christian "love" meets and destroys an old, aristocratic "desire." What the priest asks of Sygne is not an act that runs counter to her basic commitment and desire, but a sacrificial act that annuls this commitment. By betraying her cause she, as a subject, is no longer *re*presented as a signifier but presented as a sign. Isn't this what Lacan is also referring to in *Seminar IV*?

> In the fantasy there is something like a symbolic reduction, which has progressively eliminated the entire subjective structure of the situation, only allowing a residue to subsist that is entirely desubjectivated and ultimately enigmatic, because it preserves the whole charge—but the charge as unrevealed, unconstituted, and not assumed by the subject. . . . At the level of the perverse fantasy all the elements are there, but everything concerning signification, namely the intersubjective relation, is lost. What one can call signifiers in a pure state are maintained without any intersubjective relation, emptied of their subject. We have here a sort of objectivation of the signifiers of the situation. What is indicated here, in the sense of a fundamental structuring relation of the subject's history at the level of perversion, is at the same time maintained, contained, but it is so in the form of a pure sign.[37]

What is said here about the perverse fantasy could perfectly fit the analytic operation: in the end the subject appears as pure and autistic sign.

The analytic discourse reminds us of perversion not only through the $a \rightarrow \$$, but also because of what it aims at, namely, to make the S_1 qua sign appear, that is as a signifier isolated from the others (cf. the lower part of the discourse: $S_2 \mathbin{/\mkern-6mu/} S_1$). Nonetheless, Lacan talks about it not in terms of perversion, but in terms of shame. The shame he is talking about is the shame in relation to the betrayal of an S_1.[38] And Lacan states that he (read, as an analyst) happens to make people ashamed (223). This can be easily understood on the basis of the formula of the analytic discourse: it aims at the production of a master signifier. And as Jacques-Alain Miller remarks, "It is no doubt a question, in *The Other Side of Psychoanalysis*, of separating the subject from its master signifier in the analytic operation. But this assumes that he knows he has one, and that he respects it."[39]

Can we equate this inducing of shame with a perverse strategy? The first problem one encounters trying to answer this question has to do with the word *perversion*. In Lacan's work, the word not only takes on different meanings, but it remains unclear whether it can be clearly differentiated from neurosis and psychosis and, more important, whether Lacan has a clear and unambiguous evaluation of it. This concerns the similarity between the analytic discourse and perversion: the similarity is striking and puzzling, but it is too often and too quickly dismissed as something that certainly cannot/should not be the case. This has to do with the exclusive focus on the position of the analyst ($a \rightarrow \$$). If we add, however, the aim, in this position, of taking the appearance of the subject as an isolated signifier ($\$ / S_1$), that is, as a sign, one could think of a specific intersubjective relation we can call love. "This love without limits and outside the law" is possible only in a very specific context, the analytic scene.[40]

What to think of this kind of intersubjective relation? How to evaluate this kind of practice? At the end of his teaching Lacan makes a suggestion concerning the role psychoanalysis can play in culture:

> If we are following what Freud says then we have to consider that human sexuality is perverse. He never succeeded in conceiving this sexuality in any other way than perverse. And it is at this point that I am questioning the fruitfulness of psychoanalysis. You have heard me more than once saying that psychoanalysis did not even succeed in inventing a new perversion. That is sad. Because, after all, if perversion is the essence of man, what kind of unfruitfulness in this practice![41]

Here we see how the word *perversion* takes on two different but related meanings. The Spinozistic perversion refers to what Lacan calls *jouissance*. The invention of a new perversion seems rather to refer to perversion as what a culture perceives as perverted or to a praxis that could be analyzed as perverse. One could think here of the Greek *pai-*

deia, or courtly love.⁴² This new perversion would be a (sub)culture of desire. The suggestion is not that psychoanalysis should be or become this "new perversion," but that maybe it can help in creating the conditions for the appearance of a scene where this desire is possible.

Notes

I would like to thank David Blomme, Justin Clemens, Russell Grigg, Sigi Jöttkandt, Dany Nobus, and Ed Pluth for their various and helpful comments on an earlier draft of this text.

1   See Alain Badiou, *L'être et l'événement* (Paris: Seuil, 1988).
2   Whether or not psychoanalysis can be considered as a truth procedure is an unanswered question. Badiou seems to reply negatively to it. Nonetheless there are good (but nonconclusive) reasons to consider it as one; see D. Hoens and Ed Pluth, "Working Through as a Truth Procedure," in "Miracles Do Happen: Essays on Alain Badiou," ed. Dominiek Hoens, special issue, *Communication and Cognition* 37 (2004): 279–92.
3   Ilse Grubrich-Simitis, *Zurück zu Freuds Texten: Stumme Dokumente sprechen machen* (Frankfurt am Main: Fischer, 1993), 226–29. Many thanks to David Blomme for pointing out this passage to me.
4   Jacques Lacan, *Le séminaire, livre XVII: L'envers de la psychanalyse*, ed. J.-A. Miller (Paris: Seuil, 1991), 27, 62. All references to *Seminar XVII* refer to the French edition, but the quotes are taken from Russell Grigg's forthcoming translation of this seminar.
5   In that sense this position reminds us of the one labeled by Melanie Klein as "depressive." The self-reproach could sound like: "As psychoanalysts we are dealing with partial objects and feel guilty about the fact that their very existence constitutes a gap in the big Other of Unified Science and Health Care, so we should stop existing and the world will be a better place."
6   Lacan often uses the Aristotelian notion of *hypokeimenon* to explain his theory of the subject, as in *Seminar XVII*, 12, 53. One should not understand this "subject" as a person's "subjectivity," one's feeling of "self." In *Autres écrits* (Paris: Seuil, 2001), referring to Aristotle, Lacan states explicitly that his aim is to scrub off (*décrotter*) the "subjective" from "the subject" (248).
7   Lacan formulates the mutual implication of signifier and subject in these terms no earlier than in 1961; see the unpublished *Seminar IX, Identification*, lesson of December 6, 1961.
8   The notion of discourse is not new in Lacan's work. He used it frequently, at least since *Seminar III*. See Jacques Lacan, *The Seminar of Jacques Lacan, Book III: The Psychoses*, ed. J.-A. Miller, trans. with notes by R. Grigg (New York: Norton, 1993), 54. In the title of *Seminar XVII*, the "other side" of the analyst's discourse is the master's discourse.

9   Lacan argued that "the notion of discourse should be taken as a social link, *founded on language*" (Jacques Lacan, *The Seminar of Jacques Lacan, Book XX: Encore, or On Feminine Sexuality, The Limits of Love and Knowledge*, ed. J.-A. Miller, trans. with notes by B. Fink [New York: Norton, 1998], 17; my emphasis).
10 Jacques Lacan, *Le séminaire, livre VIII: Le transfert*, ed. J.-A. Miller (Paris: Seuil, 2001), 50.
11 "In desire it is a question of an object, not a subject," Lacan says in *Seminar VIII*, 207. The "miracle of love" Lacan talks of does *not* concern what goes on between two amorous subjects, but rather refers to the metaphorical substitution of the subjective act of desiring the other qua subject for the object position one is put in by the desire of this other.
12 Jacques Lacan, "Aggressiveness in Psychoanalysis" (1948), in *Ecrits: A Selection*, trans. B. Fink (New York: Norton, 2000), 17.
13 Jacques Lacan, "Logical Time and the Assertion of Anticipated Certainty: A New Sophism," trans. B. Fink and M. Silver, *Newsletter of the Freudian Field*, 2.2 (1998): 4–22.
14 For an explanation of how this possibility arises for the prisoners in the sophism, see David Blomme and Dominiek Hoens, "Anticipation and Subject: A Commentary on an Early Text by Lacan," in D. Dubois, ed., *Computing Anticipatory Systems: CASYS'99—Third International Conference* (New York: American Institute of Physics, 2000), 117–23.
15 This version of symbolic identification is simplified and begs a detailed account of how at that time Lacan was thinking "signifier," "negation," "castration," and "temporality" together.
16 See Bertrand Ogilvie, *Lacan: La formation du concept de sujet (1932-1949)* (Paris: Presses Universitaires de France, 1987), and Markos Zafiropoulos, *Lacan et les sciences sociales: Le déclin du père (1938-1953)* (Paris: Presses Universitaires de France, 2001).
17 That may be why Lacan invented so many names for this "point," which makes it difficult for any student of Lacan to distinguish them from one another: ego ideal, quilting point, Name-of-the-Father, unary trait, master signifier, and, finally, *sinthome*. In this context it is worth noticing that in *Seminar XVII* Lacan is again dealing with the unary trait (introduced in the final part of *Seminar VIII* and developed in *Seminar IX*), neither distinguishing it from nor identifying it with the master signifier S_1 (see lesson 11). Our hypothesis would be that Lacan is aware both of the decline of the master's discourse (in favor of the university discourse) and of the persistence of the symbolic qua order of subjectivation, that is, containing an element by which a subject gets represented in that order.
18 See Alain Badiou, *Saint Paul: The Foundation of Universalism*, trans. R. Brassier (Stanford, Calif.: Stanford University Press, 2003).
19 S_2 stands for "knowledge." According to the classical Hegelian scheme the slave works and obtains knowledge, while the master is enjoying.
20 Isn't this what makes Aristotle exclude what he names "bestiality" (*thèriotès*) from his reflection on desire? See *Nichomachean Ethics*, 1148b15–1149a24.

21 Lacan writes, "The desire of the analyst is not a pure desire. It is a desire to obtain an absolute difference" (Jacques Lacan, *The Four Fundamental Concepts of Psychoanalysis*, ed. J.-A. Miller, trans. A. Sheridan [London: Penguin, 1994], 276).
22 In *Seminar XVII* as well Lacan says that one should not ask about the origin of language; language is always already there: "It is 'there' " also means that it is absent: in any speech act language is the system from which one selects the signifiers that have a meaning effect on the basis of all the signifiers one does *not* choose (181).
23 Jacques Lacan, *Le séminaire, livre V: Les formations de l'inconscient*, ed. J.-A. Miller (Paris: Seuil, 1998), 236–42, 345.
24 Lacan never left behind the Heideggerian idea that death is the precondition to our understanding of *Dasein* as temporal. This, Lacan states, distinguishes him from de Sade: "It is just that, being a psychoanalyst, I can see that the second death is prior to the first, and not after, as de Sade dreams it" (*Seminar XVII*, 76).
25 Lacan, *Seminar XX*, 16.
26 The quote continues: "I am not saying anything else when I say that love is the sign that one is changing discourses." One could argue that love too is related to that point where a subject shows itself as a subject of the signifier, that is as a sign (see section 2). There is no sign of love, but love itself is revealed as a *sign*.
27 One could easily object that the seminar on affect is the one on anxiety (*Seminar X*) and thus not on transference. Let's not forget, however, that the theoretical precursor of the object of anxiety, *objet a*, is the *agalma*. The genesis and the development of *objet a* can indeed be traced back to his earlier theorizing of transference in *Seminar VIII*. However, to do full justice to Lacan's teaching one should mention that his teaching from 1958 until 1961 pivots around the difference between modern, "Christian," and ancient, "Greek," tragedy. In that respect, agalma (*Seminar VIII*) and *das Ding* (*Seminar VII*) need to be differentiated from *objet a*, which he discovers while analyzing *Hamlet* (*Seminar VI*). The basic point to be made about the development in *Seminar VI* through to *Seminar X* is not only that Lacan invents his *objet a*, but also that he struggles with theorizing "the signifier" qua representation of the subject in the symbolic order, given the fact that this symbolic order is no longer the *orthos logos* Aristotle is referring to, nor the logos supported by the god of medieval theology, but a logos of which human beings have to be the "support." That is why in *Seminar VIII*, after his analysis of Plato's *Symposium*, he analyzes a modern, Christian tragedy (by Paul Claudel) for which he does not use "Greek" notions like das Ding or the agalma but shows how being the support, the "subject," of an impotent order can result in the sacrifice not only of one's life but also of the representation of one's subjectivity (S_1). Ultimately one is reduced not to a signifier but to an obscene sign. That's why Lacan starts to think about the special form of identification designated by Freud as the identification with an *einiger Zug*. One can discern in Lacan, to use Jacques Taminiaux's famous expression, "a nostalgia for Greece" and one could describe the aim of a Lacanian psychoanalytic cure as liberating Greek desire from Christian love.
28 Lacan, *Autres écrits*, 558.
29 There is a minimal but important difference in the case of the hysteric's desire. The

hysteric either identifies with the other's desire or provokes it. In both cases (which correspond to the formula "desire is desire of and desire for the other") the underlying question is "what am I in this desire?" This desire does not desire the other qua (subject of) desire but as the one who should answer the question of what it means that there is something like desire. The hysteric ultimately sticks to the object position, without being able to subjectify this position, that is, to desire back. Besides, any Lacanian theory of love should take into account the perverse moment of desiring from an object position.

30 Desire can be qualified as "inhuman" because it aims at jouissance, an enjoyment that is singular and extrasymbolic. At the same time it is what makes us "human," in the sense that this differentiates us from animals. In lesson one Lacan repeats Freud's basic insight that all animals have instincts (an unconscious knowledge, S_2), but that humans are perverse because these instinctual mechanisms are used for the production of pleasure and become drives (*Triebe*).

31 See Serge André, *L'imposture perverse* (Paris: Seuil, 1993); Dany Nobus, *Jacques Lacan and the Freudian Practice of Psychoanalysis* (London: Routledge, 2000); Slavoj Žižek, "Herrschaftsstruktur heute—eine lacanianische Sicht," in *Über Žižek: Perspektiven und Kritiken*, ed. Erik Vogt and Hugh J. Silverman (Vienna: Turia + Kant, 2004), 210–30. In *Seminar XVII*, Lacan himself seems to be aware of the proximity between the analyst and the sadist, because in the lesson after the one I quoted from he refers to de Sade as someone, like the analyst, who loves truth (76). The formalization of the pervert's fantasy as $a \lozenge \$$ was presented by Lacan in *Le Séminaire, Livre X: L'angoisse* (Paris: Seuil, 2004), 62; see also *Lacan, Seminar XI*, 181–82.

32 In *Seminar VI*, Lacan calls this "la douleur d'exister."

33 Isn't the aim of psychoanalysis the "traversal of fantasy" (*traversée du fantasme*) instead of the emergence of the subject qua signifier? Although I cannot develop this here, I think they amount to the same. That may be why Lacan himself referred once or twice to the "traversal of fantasy" as the aim of analysis but never repeated it.

34 Lacan, *Seminar VIII*, 315–38.

35 "The supreme image of the master is that character from the tragedy by Paul Claudel, namely Sygne de Coûfontaine," Lacan, *Seminar XI*, 200.

36 He had been held captive by Napoléon and is now looking to be rescued. Turelure knows where the Pope is hiding and, in order to keep this secret, he asks, as a reward, that Sygne marry him.

37 Lacan, *Seminar IV*, 119.

38 I leave two other forms of shame out of consideration: the (imaginary) shame of being caught in the gaze of the other and appearing as a blameful object and the (real?) shame (*pudeur*) concerning sexuality as a traumatic thing. The shame Lacan is referring to has a lot in common with the Greek *aidos*, which means, simplifying several connotations, both "shame" and "courage" (for example, as a support to people who are about to undertake an important task, meaning: "Do not betray your cause"). See Bernard Williams, *Shame and Necessity* (Berkeley: University of California Press, 1993); and, for a meticulous analysis of this word and its vicissitudes,

Philipp Steger, "Die Scham in der griechisch-römischen Antike: Eine philosophiehistorische Bestandsaufnahme von Homer bis zum Neuen Testament," in *Scham— ein menschliches Gefühl: Kulturelle, psychologische und philosophische Perspektiven*, ed. R. Kühn, M. Raub, and M. Titze (Opladen: Westdeutscher Verlag, 1997), 57–73.

39 Jacques-Alain Miller, "On Shame," in this volume, 21.
40 Jacques Lacan, *Seminar XI*, 276. Translation modified.
41 Jacques Lacan, *Le séminaire, livre XXIII: Le Sinthome*, ed. J.-A. Miller (Paris: Seuil, 2005), 153.
42 Courtly love is dealt with in *Seminar VII*, in the context of the development of a theory of sublimation, and is intended as a reply to the problem, at the end of *Seminar VI*, of how to differentiate "sublimation" and "perversion." Paideia can be found in *Seminar VIII* in the context of an analysis of transference (love). Lacan emphasizes that, although this paideia was socially accepted, it still needs to be considered as a perversion! To the extent that this paideia serves as the model for the analytic cure, one has to investigate in what way the last takes over, or fails to take over, the perverse characteristics of the former. For more about the difference between sublimation and perversion, see Marc De Kesel's excellent *Eros and Ethics: On Lacan's Seminar VII* (Albany: SUNY Press, forthcoming 2006).

PART II | **The Other Side of Psychoanalysis**

6

Slavoj Žižek

Objet a in Social Links

Although Lacan's notion of "university discourse" circulates widely today, it is seldom used in its precise meaning (designating a specific "discourse," social link). As a rule, it functions as a vague notion of some speech being part of the academic interpretive machinery. In contrast to this use, one should always bear in mind that, for Lacan, university discourse is not directly linked to the university as a social institution—for example, he states that the Soviet Union was the pure reign of university discourse. Consequently, not only does the fact of being turned into an object of the university interpretive machinery prove nothing about one's discursive status—names like Kierkegaard, Nietzsche, or Benjamin, all three great antiuniversitarians whose presence in the academy is today all-pervasive—demonstrate that the "excluded" or "damned" authors are the IDEAL feeding stuff for the academic machine. Can the upper level of Lacan's formula of the university discourse—S_2 directed toward a—not also be read as standing for the university knowledge endeavoring to integrate, domesticate, and appropriate the excess that resists and rejects it?

Lurking behind the reproach of belonging to university discourse is, of course, the question of the relationship between psychoanalysis and cultural studies. The first fact to note here is that what is missing in cultural studies is precisely psychoanalysis as a social link, structured around the desire of the analyst. Today, one often mentions how the reference to psychoanalysis in cultural studies and the psychoanalytic clinic supplement each other: cultural studies lack the real of clinical experience, while the clinic lacks the broader critico-historical perspective (say, of the historic specificity of the categories of psychoanalysis, Oedipal complex, castration, or paternal authority). The answer to this should be that each of the approaches should work on its limitation from within its horizon—not by relying on the other to fill up its lack. If cultural studies cannot account for the real of the clinical experience, this signals the insufficiency of its theoretical framework itself; if the clinic cannot reflect its historical presuppositions, it is a bad clinic. One should add to this standard Hegelian dialectical paradox (in fighting the foreign or external opposite, one fights one's own essence) its inherent supplement: in impeding oneself, one truly impedes one's external opposite. When cultural studies ignore the real of clinical experience, the ultimate victim is not cultural studies itself but the clinic, which remains caught in pretheoretical empiricism. And, vice versa, when the clinic fails (to take into account its historical presuppositions), the ultimate victim is theory itself, which, cut off from clinical experience, remains an empty ideological exercise. The ultimate horizon is here not the reconciliation of theory and clinic: their very gap is the positive condition of psychoanalysis. Freud already wrote that, in the conditions in which it would finally be possible, psychoanalysis would no longer be needed. Psychoanalytic theory is ultimately the theory of why its clinical practice is doomed to fail.

One of the telltale signs of university discourse is that the opponent is accused of being "dogmatic" and "sectarian." University discourse cannot tolerate an engaged subjective stance. Should not our first gesture be, as Lacanians, to heroically assume this designation of being "sectarian" and engage in a "sectarian" polemic?

The Historicity of the Four Discourses

University discourse as the hegemonic discourse of modernity has two forms of existence in which its inner tension ("contradiction") is externalized: capitalism, its logic of the integrated excess, of the system reproducing itself through constant self-revolutionizing, and the bureaucratic "totalitarianism" conceptualized in different guises as the rule of technology, of instrumental reason, of biopolitics, as the "administered world." How, precisely, do these two aspects relate to each other? We should not succumb to the temptation of reducing capitalism to a mere form of appearance of the more fundamental ontological attitude of technological domination; we should rather insist, in the Marxian mode, that the capitalist logic of integrating the surplus into the functioning of the system is the fundamental fact. Stalinist "totalitarianism" was the capitalist logic of self-propelling productivity liberated from its capitalist form, which is why it failed: Stalinism was the symptom of capitalism. Stalinism involved the matrix of general intellect, of the planned transparency of social life, of total productive mobilization — and its violent purges and paranoia were a kind of a "return of the repressed," the "irrationality" inherent to the project of a totally organized "administered society." This means the two levels, precisely insofar as they are two sides of the same coin, are ultimately incompatible: there is no metalanguage enabling us to translate the logic of domination back into the capitalist reproduction-through-excess, or vice versa.

The key question here concerns the relationship between the two excesses: the economic excess/surplus integrated into the capitalist machine as the force that drives it into permanent self-revolutionizing and the political excess of power-exercise inherent to modern power (the constitutive excess of representation over the represented: the legitimate state power responsible to its subjects is supplemented by the obscene message of unconditional exercise of Power—laws do not really bind me, I can do to you whatever I want, I can treat you as guilty if I decide to, I can destroy you if I say so).

Perhaps the key to this problem is provided by the historicity inscribed in Lacan's matrix of the four discourses, the historicity of modern European development. The master's discourse stands not for the premodern master, but for the absolute monarchy, this first figure of modernity that effectively undermined the articulate network of feudal relations and interdependences, transforming fidelity to flattery: it is the "Sun-King" Louis XIV with his *L'état, c'est moi* who is the master par excellence. Hysterical discourse and university discourse then deploy two outcomes of the vacillation of the direct reign of the master: the expert-rule of bureaucracy that culminates in the biopolitics of reducing the population to a collection of *homo sacer* (what Heidegger called "enframing," Adorno "the administered world," Foucault the society of "discipline and punish"); the explosion of the hysterical capitalist subjectivity that reproduces itself through permanent self-revolutionizing, through the integration of the excess into the "normal" functioning of the social link (the true "permanent revolution" is already capitalism itself).

Lacan's formula of the four discourses thus enables us to deploy the two faces of modernity (total administration and capitalist-individualist dynamics) as two ways to undermine the master's discourse: doubt about the efficiency of the master-figure (what Eric Santner called the "crisis of investiture") can be supplemented by the direct rule of the experts legitimized by their knowledge, or the excess of doubt, of permanent questioning, can be directly integrated into social reproduction. Finally, the analyst's discourse stands for the emergence of revolutionary-emancipatory subjectivity that resolves the split of university and hysteria. In it, the revolutionary agent (a) addresses the subject from the position of knowledge that occupies the place of truth (i.e., which intervenes at the "symptomal torsion" of the subject's constellation), and the goal is to isolate, get rid of, the master signifier that structured the subject's (ideologico-political) unconscious.

Or does it? Jacques-Alain Miller has recently proposed that today the master's discourse is no longer the "obverse" of the analyst's discourse.[1] Today, on the contrary, our "civilization" itself—its hegemonic symbolic matrix, as it were—fits the formula of the analyst's discourse. The agent of the social link is today a, surplus enjoyment, the superego injunction to enjoy that permeates our discourse; this injunction addresses $\$$ (the divided subject) who is put to work in order to live up to this injunction. The truth of this social link is S_2, scientific-expert knowledge in its different guises, and the goal is to generate S_1, the self-mastery of the subject, that is, to enable the subject to cope with the stress of the call to enjoyment (through self-help manuals, etc.). Provocative as this notion is, it raises a series of questions. If it is true, in what, then, resides the difference between the discursive functioning of civilization as such and the psychoanalytic social link? Miller resorts here to a suspicious solution: in our civilization, the four terms are kept apart, isolated; each operates on its own, while only in psychoanalysis are they brought together into a coherent link: "in civilization, each of the four terms remains disjoined . . . it is only in psychoanalysis, in pure psychoanalysis, that these elements are arranged into a discourse."

However, is it not that the fundamental operation of the psychoanalytic treatment is not synthesis, bringing elements into a link, but, precisely, analysis, separating what in a social link appears to belong together? This path, opposed to that of Miller, is indicated by Giorgio Agamben, who, in the last pages of *The State of Exception*, imagines two utopian options of how to break out of the vicious cycle of law and violence, of the rule of law sustained by violence.[2] One is the Benjaminian vision of "pure" revolutionary violence with no relationship to the law. The other is the relationship to the law without regard to its (violent) enforcement, such as Jewish scholars do in their endless (re)interpretation of the Law. Agamben starts from the right insight that the task today is not synthesis but separation, distinction: not bringing law and violence together (so that right will have might and the exercise of might will be fully legitimized), but thoroughly separating them, untying their knot. Although Agamben confers on this formulation an anti-Hegelian twist, a more proper reading of Hegel makes it clear that such a gesture of separation is what the Hegelian "synthesis" is effectively about. In it, the opposites are not reconciled in a "higher synthesis"; it is rather that *their difference is posited "as such."*

The example of Paul may help us to clarify this logic of Hegelian reconciliation: the radical gap that he posits between life and death, between life in Christ and life in sin, is in no need of a further synthesis; it is itself the resolution of the "absolute contradiction" of Law and sin, of the vicious cycle of their mutual implication. In other words, once the distinction is drawn, once the subject becomes aware of the very existence of this other dimension beyond the vicious cycle of law and its transgression, the battle is formally already won. So, with regard to the old question of the passage from Kant to Hegel, Hegel's move is not to overcome the Kantian division, but, rather, to assert it as such, to *drop the need for its overcoming*, for the additional reconciliation of the opposites, that is, to gain insight—through a purely formal parallax shift—into how positing the distinction as such already is the looked-for reconciliation. The limitation of Kant is not in his remaining within the confines of finite oppositions, in his inability to reach the Infinite, but, on the contrary, in his very search for a transcendent domain beyond the realm of finite oppositions. Kant is not unable to reach the Infinite—what he is unable to see is how he *already has* what he is looking for.

However, is this vision not again the case of our late capitalist reality going further than our dreams? Are we not already encountering in our social reality what Agamben envisages as a utopian vision? Isn't the Hegelian lesson of the global reflexivization-mediatization of our lives that it generates its own brutal immediacy? This has best been captured by Etienne Balibar's notion of excessive, nonfunctional cruelty as a feature of contemporary life, a cruelty whose figures range from "fundamentalist" racist and/or religious slaughter to the "senseless" outbursts of violence performed by adolescents and the homeless in our megalopolises, a violence one is tempted to call Id-Evil, a violence grounded in no utilitarian or ideological reasons. All the talk about foreigners stealing work from us or about the threat they represent to our Western values should not deceive us: under closer examination, it soon becomes clear that this talk provides a rather superficial secondary rationalization. The answer we ultimately obtain from a skinhead is that it makes him feel good to beat foreigners, that their presence disturbs him. What we encounter here is indeed Id-Evil, that is, the Evil structured and motivated by the most elementary imbalance in the relationship between the ego and jouissance, by the tension between pleasure and the foreign body of jouissance in the very heart of it. Id-Evil thus stages the most elementary short circuit in the relationship of the subject to the primordially missing object cause of his desire. What bothers us in the other (Jew, Japanese, African, Turk) is that he appears to entertain a privileged relationship to the object — the other either possesses the object treasure, having snatched it away from us (which is why we don't have it), or he poses a threat to our possession of the object.

What one should propose here is the Hegelian "infinite judgment," asserting the speculative identity of these "useless" and "excessive" outbursts of violent immediacy, which display nothing but a pure and naked ("non-sublimated") hatred of the Otherness, with the global reflexivization of society. Perhaps the ultimate example of this coincidence is the fate of psychoanalytic interpretation. Today, the formations of the unconscious (from dreams to hysterical symptoms) have definitely lost their innocence and are thoroughly reflexivized: the "free associations" of a typical educated analysand consist for the most part of attempts to provide a psychoanalytic explanation of their disturbances, so that one is quite justified in saying that we have not only Jungian, Kleinian, Lacanian, and so on, interpretations of the symptoms, but symptoms themselves that are Jungian, Kleinian, Lacanian, and so on, that is, whose reality involves implicit reference to some psychoanalytic theory. The unfortunate result of this global reflexivization of interpretation (everything becomes interpretation, the unconscious interprets itself) is that the analyst's interpretation itself loses its performative "symbolic efficiency" and leaves the symptom intact in the immediacy of its idiotic jouissance.

What happens in psychoanalytic treatment is strictly homologous to the response of the neo-Nazi skinhead who, when really pressed for the reasons for his violence, suddenly starts to talk like social workers, sociologists, and social psychologists, quoting diminished social mobility, rising insecurity, the disintegration of paternal authority, the lack of maternal love in his early childhood—the unity of practice and its inherent ideological legitimization disintegrates into raw violence and its impotent, inefficient interpretation. This impotence of interpretation is also one of the necessary obverses of the universalized reflexivity hailed by the risk-society-theorists: it is as if our reflexive power can flourish only insofar as it draws its strength and relies on some minimal "prereflexive" substantial support that eludes its grasp, so that its universalization comes at the price of its inefficiency, that is, by the paradoxical reemergence of the brute real of "irrational" violence, impermeable and insensitive to reflexive interpretation. So the more today's social theory proclaims the end of nature or tradition and the rise of the "risk society," the more the implicit reference to "nature" pervades our daily discourse: even when we do not speak of the "end of history," do we not put forward the same message when we claim that we are entering a "postideological" pragmatic era, which is another way of claiming that we are entering a postpolitical order in which the only legitimate conflicts are ethnic/cultural conflicts? Typically, in today's critical and political discourse, the term *worker* has disappeared from the vocabulary, substituted or obliterated by *immigrants* or *immigrant workers*: Algerians in France, Turks in Germany, Mexicans in the United States. In this way, the class problematic of workers' exploitation is transformed into the multiculturalist problematic of "intolerance of otherness," and the excessive investment of the multiculturalist liberals in protecting immigrants' ethnic rights clearly draws its energy from the "repressed" class dimension. Although Francis Fukuyama's thesis on the "end of history" quickly fell into disrepute, we still silently presume that the liberal-democratic capitalist global order is somehow the finally found "natural" social regime, we still implicitly conceive conflicts in the Third World countries as a subspecies of natural catastrophes, as outbursts of quasi-natural violent passions, or as conflicts based on the fanatic identification to one's ethnic roots (and what is "the ethnic" here if not again a code word for "nature"?). And, again, the key point is that this all-pervasive renaturalization is strictly correlative to the global reflexivization of our daily lives.

What this means, with regard to Agamben's utopian vision of untying the knot of the Law and violence is that, in our postpolitical societies, this knot is already untied: we encounter, on the one hand, the globalized interpretation whose globalization is paid for by its impotence, its failure to enforce itself, to generate effects in the real, and, on the other hand, explosions of the raw real of a violence that cannot be affected by its symbolic interpretation. Where, then, is the solution here, between the claim that, in today's hegemonic constellation, the elements of the social link are separated and as such to be brought together by psychoanalysis (Miller), and the knot between Law and violence to be untied, their separation to be enacted (Agamben)? What if these two separations are not symmetrical? What if the gap between the symbolic and the raw real epitomized by the figure of the skinhead is a false one, since this real of the outbursts of the "irrational" violence is generated by the globalization of the symbolic?

When, exactly, does the *objet a* function as the superego injunction to enjoy? When it occupies the place of the master signifier, that is, as Lacan formulated it in the last pages of his *Seminar XI*, when the short circuit between S_1 and a occurs. The key move to be accomplished in order to break the vicious cycle of the superego injunction is thus to enact the separation between S_1 and a. Consequently, would it not be more productive to follow a different path, that is, to start with the different modus operandi of *l'objet a*, which in psychoanalysis no longer functions as the agent of the superego injunction—as it does in the discourse of perversion? This is how Miller's claim of the identity of the analyst's discourse and the discourse of today's civilization should be read: as an indication that this latter discourse (social link) is that of perversion. That is to say, the fact that the upper level of Lacan's formula of the analyst's discourse is the same as his formula of perversion ($a\_\$$) opens up a possibility of reading the entire formula of the analyst's discourse also as a formula of the perverse social link: its agent, the masochist pervert (the pervert par excellence), occupies the position of the object instrument of the other's desire, and, in this way, through serving his (feminine) victim, he posits her as the hystericized/divided subject who "doesn't know what she wants." Rather, the pervert knows it for her, that is, he pretends to speak from the position of knowledge (about the other's desire) that enables him to serve the other; and, finally, the product of this social link is the master signifier, that is, the hysterical subject elevated into the role of the master (dominatrix) whom the pervert masochist serves.

In contrast to hysteria, the pervert knows perfectly what he is for the Other: a knowledge supports his position as the object of his Other's (divided subject's) jouissance. The difference between the social link of perversion and that of analysis is grounded in the radical ambiguity of *objet a* in Lacan, which stands simultaneously for the imaginary fantasmatic lure/screen and for that which this lure is obfuscating, for the void behind the lure. Consequently, when we pass from perversion to the analytic social link, the agent (analyst) reduces himself to the void, which provokes the subject into confronting the truth of his desire. Knowledge in the position of "truth" below the bar under the "agent," of course, refers to the supposed knowledge of the analyst, and, simultaneously, signals that the knowledge gained here will not be the neutral objective knowledge of scientific adequacy, but the knowledge that concerns the subject (analysand) in the truth of his subjective position.

Recall, again, Lacan's outrageous statements that, even if what a jealous husband claims about his wife (that she sleeps around with other men) is all true, his jealousy is still pathological. Along the same lines, one could say that, even if most of the Nazi claims about the Jews were true (they exploit Germans, they seduce German girls), their anti-Semitism would still be (and was) pathological—because it represses the true reason the Nazis *needed* anti-Semitism in order to sustain their ideological position. So, in the case of anti-Semitism, knowledge about what the Jews "really are" is a fake, irrelevant, while the only knowledge at the place of truth is the knowledge about why a Nazi *needs* a figure of the Jew to sustain his ideological edifice. In this precise sense, the analyst's discourse produces the master signifier, the swerve of the patient's knowledge, the surplus element that situates the patient's knowledge at the level of truth: after the master signifier is produced, even if nothing changes at the level of knowledge, the same knowledge as before starts to function in a different mode. The master signifier is the unconscious *sinthome*, the cipher of enjoyment, to which the subject was unknowingly subjected.

The crucial point not to be missed here is how the late Lacan's identification of the subjective position of the analyst as that of *objet petit a* presents an act of radical self-criticism. Earlier, in the 1950s, Lacan conceived the analyst not as the small other (*a*), but, on the contrary, as a kind of stand-in for the big Other (A, the anonymous symbolic order). At this level, the function of the analyst was to frustrate the subject's imaginary misrecognitions and to make them accept their proper symbolic place within the circuit of symbolic exchange, the place that effectively (and unbeknownst to them) determines their symbolic identity. Later, however, the analyst stands precisely for the ultimate inconsistency and failure of the big Other, that is, for the symbolic order's inability to guarantee the subject's symbolic identity.

One should thus always bear in mind the thoroughly ambiguous status of *objet a* in Lacan. Miller recently proposed a Benjaminian distinction between "constituted anxiety" and "constituent anxiety": while the first designates the standard notion of the terrifying and fascinating abyss of anxiety that haunts us, its infernal circle that threatens to draws us in, the second stands for the "pure" confrontation with *objet a* as constituted in its very loss.[3] Miller is right to emphasize here two features: the difference that separates constituted from constituent anxiety concerns the status of the object with regard to fantasy. In a case of constituted anxiety, the object dwells within the confines of a fantasy, while we get the constituent fantasy only when the subject "traverses the fantasy" and confronts the void, the gap, filled up by the fantasmatic object. Clear and convincing as it is, Miller's formula misses the true paradox or, rather, ambiguity of *objet a*: when he defines *objet a* as the object that overlaps with its loss, that emerges at the very moment of its loss (so that all its fantasmatic incarnations, from breasts to voice and gaze, are metonymic figurations of the void of nothing), he remains within the horizon of *de-*

sire—the true object cause of desire is the void filled in by its fantasmatic incarnations. While, as Lacan emphasizes, *objet a* is also the object of the drive, the relationship is here thoroughly different. Although in both cases, the link between object and loss is crucial, in the case of *objet a* as the object cause of *desire*, we have an object which is originally lost, which coincides with its own loss, which emerges as lost, while, in the case of *objet a* as the object of the drive, the "object" *is directly the loss itself*. In the shift from desire to drive, we pass from the *lost object* to *loss itself as an object*. That is to say, the weird movement called "drive" is not driven by the "impossible" quest for the lost object, but by a push to directly enact the "loss"—the gap, cut, distance—itself. There is thus a double distinction to be drawn here: not only between *objet a* in its fantasmatic and postfantasmatic status, but also, within this postfantasmatic domain itself, between the lost object cause of desire and the object loss of the drive. Far from concerning an abstract scholastic debate, this distinction has crucial ideologico-political consequences: it enables us to articulate the libidinal dynamics of capitalism.

Following Miller himself, a distinction has to be introduced here between lack and hole. Lack is spatial, designating a void within a space, while the hole is more radical—it designates the point at which this spatial order itself breaks down (as in the "black hole" in physics). Therein resides the difference between desire and drive: desire is grounded in its constitutive lack, while drive circulates around a hole, a gap in the order of being. In other words, the circular movement of drive obeys the weird logic of the curved space in which the shortest distance between two points is not a straight line, but a curve: the drive "knows" that the shortest way to attain its aim is to circulate around its goal-object. At the immediate level of addressing individuals, capitalism of course interpellates them as consumers, as subjects of desires, soliciting in them ever new perverse and excessive desires (for which it offers products to satisfy them); furthermore, it obviously also manipulates the "desire to desire," celebrating the very desire to desire ever new objects and modes of pleasure. However, even if it already manipulates desire in a way that takes into account the fact that the most elementary desire is the desire to reproduce itself as desire (and not to find satisfaction), at this level, we do not yet reach the drive. The drive inheres to capitalism at a more fundamental, systemic level: drive propels the entire capitalist machinery;

it is the impersonal compulsion to engage in the endless circular movement of expanded self-reproduction. The capitalist drive thus belongs to no definite individual—it is rather that those individuals who act as direct "agents" of capital (capitalists themselves, top managers) have to practice it. We enter the mode of the drive when (as Marx put it) the circulation of money as capital becomes "an end in itself, for the expansion of value takes place only within this constantly renewed movement. The circulation of capital has therefore no limits." One should bear in mind here Lacan's well-known distinction between the aim and the goal of drive: while the goal is the object around which drive circulates, its (true) aim is the endless continuation of this circulation as such.

Objet a as the Inherent Limit of Capitalism

This capitalist dynamics is the central reference of Michael Hardt's and Toni Negri's *Empire* and *Multitude*, arguably the ultimate exercises in Deleuzian politics. These two books are such refreshing reading because they refer to and function as the moment of theoretical reflection of —one is almost tempted to say "are embedded in"—an actual global movement of anticapitalist resistance. One can sense, behind the written lines, the smells and sounds of Seattle, Genoa, and Zapatistas. So their limitation is simultaneously the limitation of the actual movement.

Hardt's and Negri's basic move, an act by no means ideologically neutral—and, incidentally, one totally foreign to their philosophical paradigm, Deleuze!—is to identify (name) "democracy" as the common denominator of all today's emancipatory movements: "The common currency that runs throughout so many struggles and movements for liberation across the world today—at local, regional, and global levels— is the desire for democracy."[4] Far from standing for a utopian dream, democracy is "the only answer to the vexing questions of our day. . . . the only way out of our state of perpetual conflict and war" (xviii). Not only is democracy inscribed into the present antagonisms as an immanent telos of their resolution; even more, today, the rise of the multitude in the heart of capitalism "makes democracy possible for the first time" (340). Until now, democracy was constrained by the form of the One, of the sovereign state power; "absolute democracy" ("the rule of everyone by everyone, a democracy without qualifiers, without ifs or buts" [237]) becomes possible only when "the multitude is finally able to rule itself" (340).

For Marx, highly organized corporate capitalism already was "socialism within capitalism" (a kind of socialization of capitalism, with the absent owners becoming more and more superfluous), so that one needs only to cut off the nominal head to get socialism. For Hardt and Negri, however, the limitation of Marx was that he was historically constrained to centralized and hierarchically organized, machinical, automatized industrial labor, which is why his vision of "general intellect" was that of a central planning agency; only today, with the rise of "immaterial labor" to the hegemonic role, does the revolutionary reversal become "objectively possible." This immaterial labor extends between the two poles of intellectual (symbolic) labor (production of ideas, codes, texts, programs, the figures of writers and programmers) and affective labor (those who deal with our bodily affects, from doctors to baby-sitters and flight attendants). Today, immaterial labor is "hegemonic" in the precise sense in which Marx proclaimed that, in nineteenth-century capitalism, large industrial production is hegemonic as the specific color giving its tone to the totality—not quantitatively, but playing the key, emblematic structural role: "What the multitude produces is not just goods or services; the multitude also and most importantly produces cooperation, communication, forms of life, and social relationships" (339). What thereby emerges is a new vast domain of the "common": shared knowledge, forms of cooperation and communication, and so on, which can no longer be contained by the form of private property. Far from posing a mortal threat to democracy (as conservative cultural critics want us to believe), this opens up a unique chance of "absolute democracy." In immaterial production, the products are no longer material objects, but new social (interpersonal) relations themselves—in short, immaterial production is directly biopolitical, the production of social life. Marx emphasized how material production is always also the (re)production of the social relations within which it occurs; with today's capitalism, however, the production of social relations is the immediate goal of production: "Such new forms of labor . . . present new possibilities for economic self-management, since the mechanisms of cooperation necessary for production are contained in the labor itself" (336). The wager of Hardt and Negri is that this directly socialized, immaterial production not only renders owners progressively superfluous (who needs them when production is directly social, formally and as to its content?); the producers also master the regulation of social space, since social relations (politics) is the stuff of their work: economic production directly becomes political production, the production of society itself. The way is thus open for "absolute democracy," for the producers directly regulating their social relations without even the detour of democratic representation.

This vision gives rise to a whole series of concrete questions. Can one really interpret this move toward the hegemonic role of immaterial labor as the move from production to communication, to social interaction— in Aristotelian terms, from *techne* as *poiesis* to *praxis*, as the overcoming of the Arendtian distinction between production and *vis activa*, or of the Habermasian distinction between instrumental and communicational reason? How does this "politicization" of production, where production directly produces (new) social relations, affect the very notion of politics? Is such an "administration of people" (subordinated to the logic of profit) still politics, or is it the most radical sort of depoliticization, the entry into postpolitics? Last but not least, is democracy by necessity, with regard to its very notion, nonabsolute? There is no democracy without a hidden, presupposed elitism. Democracy is, by definition, not "global"; it has to be based on values and/or truths that one cannot select "democratically." In democracy, one can fight for truth, but not decide what IS truth. As Claude Lefort and others have amply demonstrated, democracy is never simply representative in the sense of adequately re-presenting (expressing) a preexisting set of interests and opinions, since these interests and opinions are constituted only through such representation. In other words, the democratic articulation of an interest is always minimally performative: through their democratic representatives, people establish what their interests and opinions are. As Hegel already knew, "absolute democracy" could actualize itself only in the guise of its "oppositional determination," as *terror*. There is, thus, a choice to be made here: do we accept democracy's structural, not just accidental, imperfection, or do we also endorse its terrorist dimension? However, much more pertinent is another critical point that concerns Hardt and Negri's neglect of the *form* in the strict dialectical sense of the term.

Hardt and Negri continuously oscillate between their fascination for global capitalism's "deterritorializing" power and the rhetoric of the struggle of the multitude against the One of capitalist power. Financial capital, with its wild speculations detached from the reality of material labor, this standard bête noire of the traditional Left, is celebrated as the germ of the future, capitalism's most dynamic and nomadic aspect. The organizational forms of today's capitalism—decentralization of decision making, radical mobility and flexibility, interaction of multiple agents—are perceived as pointing toward the oncoming reign of the multitude. It is as if everything is already here, in "postmodern" capitalism, or, in Hegelese, the passage from In-itself to For-itself—all that is needed is just an act of purely formal conversion, like the one developed by Hegel apropos the struggle between Enlightenment and Faith, where he describes how the "silent, ceaseless weaving of the Spirit . . . infiltrates the noble parts through and through and soon has taken complete possession of all the vitals and members of the unconscious idol; then 'one fine morning it gives its comrade a shove with the elbow, and bang! crash! the idol lies on the floor.' On 'one fine morning' whose noon is bloodless if the infection has penetrated to every organ of spiritual life."[5]

Even the fashionable parallel with the new cognitivist notion of the human psyche is not missing here: in the same way brain sciences teach us there is no central Self in the brain, how our decisions emerge out of the interaction of a pandemonium of local agents, how our psychic life is an "autopoietic" process without any imposed centralizing agency (a model, incidentally, explicitly based on the parallel with today's "decentralized" capitalism). So the new society of the multitude that rules itself will be like today's cognitivist notion of the ego as a pandemonium of interacting agents with no central deciding Self running the show. However, although Hardt and Negri see today's capitalism as the main site of the proliferating multitudes, they continue to rely on the rhetorics of the One, the sovereign Power, against the multitude. How they bring these two aspects together is clear: while capitalism generates multitudes, it contains them in the capitalist form, thereby unleashing a demon it is unable to control. The question to be asked here is if Hardt and Negri do not commit a mistake homologous to that of Marx: is their notion of the pure multitude ruling itself not the ultimate capitalist fantasy, the fantasy of capitalism's self-revolutionizing perpetual motion freely exploding when freed of its inherent obstacle? In other words, is the capitalist form (the form of the appropriation of surplus value) not the necessary form, formal frame and condition, of the self-propelling productive movement?

Consequently, when Hardt and Negri repeatedly emphasize how *Multitude* "is a philosophical book" and warn the reader "do not expect our book to answer the question, What is to be done? or propose a concrete program of action" (xvi), this constraint is not as neutral as it may appear: it points toward a fundamental theoretical flaw. After describing multiple forms of resistance to the Empire, *Multitude* ends on a messianic note, pointing toward the great Rupture, the moment of Decision when the movement of multitudes will be transubstantiated into the sudden birth of a new world: "After this long season of violence and contradictions, global civil war, corruption of imperial biopower, and infinite toil of the biopolitical multitudes, the extraordinary accumulations of grievances and reform proposals must at some point be transformed by a strong event, a radical insurrectional demand" (358). However, at this point, when one expects a minimum theoretical determination of this rupture, what we get is again withdrawal into philosophy: "A philosophical book like this, however, is not the place for us to evaluate whether the time for revolutionary political decision is imminent" (357). Hardt and Negri perform here an all-too-quick jump: of course one cannot ask them to provide a detailed empirical description of the Decision, of the passage to the globalized "absolute democracy," to the multitude that rules itself; however, what if this justified refusal to engage in pseudo-concrete futuristic predictions masks an inherent notional deadlock/impossibility? That is to say, what one does and should expect is a description of the notional structure of this qualitative jump, of the passage from the multitudes *resisting* the One of sovereign Power to the multitudes directly *ruling* themselves. Leaving the notional structure of this passage in a darkness elucidated only by vague homologies and examples from the movements of resistance cannot but raise the anxious suspicion that this self-transparent direct rule of everyone over everyone, this democracy tout court, will coincide with its opposite.[6]

Hardt and Negri are right in rendering problematic the standard Leftist revolutionary notion of "taking power": such a strategy accepts the formal frame of the power structure and aims merely at replacing one bearer of power ("them") with another ("us"). As it was fully clear to Lenin in his *State and Revolution*, the true revolutionary aim is not to "take power," but to undermine, disintegrate, the very apparatuses of state power. Therein resides the ambiguity of the "postmodern" Leftist calls to abandon the program of "taking power": do they imply that one should ignore the existing power structure, or, rather, limit oneself to resisting it by way of constructing alternative spaces outside the state power network (the Zapatista strategy in Mexico); or do they imply that one should disintegrate, pull the ground from, the state power, so that the state power will simply collapse, implode? In the second case, the poetic formulas about the multitude immediately ruling itself do not suffice.

Hardt and Negri form here a kind of triad whose other two terms are Ernesto Laclau and Giorgio Agamben. The ultimate difference between Laclau and Agamben concerns the structural inconsistency of power: while they both insist on this inconsistency, their position toward it is exactly opposite. Agamben's focusing on the vicious circle of the link between legal power (the rule of Law) and violence is sustained by the messianic utopian hope that it is possible to radically break this circle and step out of it (in an act of the Benjaminian "divine violence"). In his *Coming Community*, he refers to Saint Thomas's answer to the difficult theological question: What happens to the souls of unbaptized babies who have died in ignorance of both sin and God? They committed no sin, so their punishment

> cannot be an afflictive punishment, like that of hell, but only a punishment of privation that consists in the perpetual lack of the vision of God. The inhabitants of limbo, in contrast to the damned, do not feel pain from this lack. . . . they do not know that they are deprived of the supreme good. . . . The greatest punishment—the lack of the vision of God—thus turns into a natural joy: irremediably lost, they persist without pain in divine abandon.[7]

Their fate is for Agamben the model of redemption: they "have left the world of guilt and justice behind them: the light that rains down on them is that irreparable light of the dawn following the *novissima dies* of judgment. But the life that begins on earth after the last day is simply human life."[8] (One cannot but recall here the crowd of humans who remain on stage at the end of Wagner's *Twilight of Gods*, silently witnessing the self-destruction of gods—what if they are the happy ones?) And, mutatis mutandis, the same goes for Hardt and Negri, who perceive resistance to power as preparing the ground for a miraculous Leap into "absolute democracy" in which multitude will directly rule itself— at this point, the tension will be resolved, freedom will explode into eternal self-proliferation. The difference between Agamben and Hardt and Negri could be best apprehended by means of the good old Hegelian distinction between abstract and determinate negation: although Hardt and Negri are even more anti-Hegelian than Agamben, their revolutionary Leap remains an act of "determinate negation," the gesture of formal reversal, of merely setting free the potentials developed in global capitalism, which already is a kind of "Communism-in-itself"; in contrast to them, Agamben—and, again, paradoxically, in spite of his animosity to Adorno—outlines the contours of something much closer to the utopian longing for the *ganz Andere* (wholly Other) in late Adorno, Horkheimer, and Marcuse, to a redemptive leap into a nonmediated Otherness.

Laclau and Mouffe, on the contrary, propose a new version of the old Edouard Bernstein's archrevisionist motto "goal is nothing, movement is all": the true danger, the temptation to be resisted, is the very notion of a radical cut by means of which the basic social antagonism will be dissolved and the new era of a self-transparent, nonalienated society will arrive. For Laclau and Mouffe, such a notion disavows not only the political as such, the space of antagonisms and struggle for hegemony, but the fundamental ontological finitude of the human condition as such— which is why, any attempt to actualize such a leap has to end up in a totalitarian disaster. This means the only way to elaborate and practice livable particular political solutions is to admit the global a priori deadlock: we can solve particular problems only against the background of the irreducible global deadlock. Of course, this in no way entails that political agents should limit themselves to solving particular problems, abandoning the topic of universality: for Laclau and Mouffe, universality is impossible and at the same time necessary. There is no direct "true" universality; every universality is always already caught into the hegemonic struggle, it is an empty form hegemonized (filled in) by some particular content that, at a given moment and in a given conjuncture, functions as its stand-in.

Are, however, these two approaches really as radically opposed as it may appear? Does Laclau and Mouffe's edifice not also imply its own utopian point, the point at which political battles would be fought without remainders of "essentialism," all sides fully accepting the radically contingent character of their endeavors and the irreducible character of social antagonisms? On the other hand, Agamben's position is also not without its secret advantages: since, with today's biopolitics, the space of political struggle is closed and any democratic-emancipatory movements are meaningless, we cannot do anything but comfortably wait for the miraculous explosion of the "divine violence." As for Hardt and Negri, they bring us back to the Marxist confidence that "history is on our side," that historical development is already generating the form of the Communist future.

If anything, the problem with Hardt and Negri is that they are *too much* Marxists, taking over the underlying Marxist scheme of historical progress: like Marx, they celebrate the "deterritorializing" revolutionary potential of capitalism; like Marx, they locate the contradiction within capitalism, in the gap between this potential and the form of capital, of the private-property appropriation of the surplus. In short, they rehabilitate the old Marxist notion of the tension between productive forces and the relations of production: capitalism already generates the "germs of the future new form of life," it incessantly produces the new "common," so that, in a revolutionary explosion, this New should just be liberated from the old social form. However, precisely as Marxists, on behalf of our fidelity to Marx's work, we should discern the mistake of Marx. On the one hand, he perceived how capitalism unleashed the breathtaking dynamics of self-enhancing productivity—see his fascinated descriptions of how, in capitalism, "all that is solid melts into air," of how capitalism is the greatest revolutionizing force in the entire history of humanity. On the other hand, he also clearly perceived how this capitalist dynamic is propelled by its own inner obstacle or antagonism, so that the ultimate limit of capitalism (of the capitalist self-propelling productivity) is capital itself. The incessant development and revolutionizing of capitalism's own material conditions, the mad dance of its unconditional spiral of productivity, is ultimately nothing but a desperate flight forward to escape its own debilitating inherent contradiction.

Marx's fundamental mistake was to conclude, from these insights, that a new, higher social order (communism) is possible, an order that would not only maintain, but even raise to a higher degree and effectively fully release the potential of the self-increasing spiral of productivity which, in capitalism, on account of its inherent obstacle ("contradiction"), is again and again thwarted by socially destructive economic crises. In short, what Marx overlooked is that, to put it in the standard Derridean terms, this inherent obstacle/antagonism as the "condition of impossibility" of the full deployment of the productive forces is simultaneously its "condition of possibility": if we abolish the obstacle, the inherent contradiction of capitalism, we do not get the fully unleashed drive to productivity finally delivered of its impediment, but we lose precisely this productivity that seemed to be generated and simultaneously thwarted by capitalism. If we take away the obstacle, the very potential thwarted by this obstacle dissipates. (Therein would reside a possible Lacanian critique of Marx, focusing on the ambiguous overlapping between surplus value and surplus enjoyment.) So the critics of communism were in a way right when they claimed that Marxian communism is an impossible fantasy—what they did not perceive is that Marxian communism, this notion of a society of pure unleashed productivity outside the frame of capital, was a fantasy inherent to capitalism itself, the capitalist inherent transgression at its purest, a strictly ideological fantasy of maintaining the thrust to productivity generated by capitalism, while getting rid of the "obstacles" and antagonisms that were—as the sad experience of "really existing capitalism" demonstrates—the only possible framework of the effective material existence of a society of permanent self-enhancing productivity.

So where, precisely, did Marx go wrong with regard to surplus value? One is tempted to search for an answer in the key Lacanian distinction between the object of desire and the surplus enjoyment as its cause. Recall the curl of the blond hair, this fatal detail of Madeleine in Alfred Hitchcock's *Vertigo*. When, in the love scene in the barn toward the end of the film, Scottie passionately embraces Judy (who has been refashioned into the dead Madeleine) during their famous 360-degree kiss, he stops kissing her and withdraws just long enough to steal a look at her newly blond hair, as if to reassure himself that the particular feature that makes her into the object of desire is still there. So there is always a gap between the object of desire itself and its cause, the mediating feature or element that makes this object desirable. Back to Marx: what if his mistake was also to assume that the object of desire (unconstrained expanding productivity) would remain even when deprived of the cause that propels it (surplus value)? The same holds even more for Deleuze, since he develops his theory of desire in direct opposition to the Lacanian one. Deleuze asserts the priority of desire over its objects: desire is a positive productive force that exceeds its objects, a living flow proliferating through the multitude of objects, penetrating them and passing through them, with no need for any fundamental lack or "castration" that would serve as its foundation. For Lacan, however, desire has to be sustained by an object cause: not some primordial incestuous lost object on which desire remains forever transfixed and whose unsatisfying substitutes all other objects are, but a purely formal object that causes us to desire objects that we encounter in reality. This object cause of desire is thus not transcendent, an inaccessible excess forever eluding our grasp, but behind the subject's back, something that directs desiring from within. As is the case with Marx, Deleuze's failure to take into account this object cause sustains the illusory vision of unconstrained productivity of desire—or, in the case of Hardt and Negri, the illusory vision of multitude ruling itself, no longer constrained by any totalizing One. We can observe here the catastrophic political consequences of the failure to develop what may appear a purely "academic," philosophical, notional distinction.

Notes

1 See Jacques-Alain Miller, "La passe: Conférence de Jacques-Alain Miller," paper presented at the fourth Congrès de l'AMP, Comandatuba—Bahia, Brazil, August 9–12, 2004.
2 See Giorgio Agamben, *The State of Exception* (Chicago: University of Chicago Press, 2004).
3 See Jacques-Alain Miller, "Le nom-du-père, s'en passer, s'en servir," available at www.lacan.com. It is interesting to note how, in his very polemics against the Hegelian Aufhebung, Miller repeats its operation. That is to say, when Miller deploys the concept of anxiety as the affect which signals the proximity of the Real, he opposes it to the central role of the Name-of-the-Father, of the paternal Law, in Lacan's previous thought: the paternal Law functions as the operator of Aufhebung, of the "significantization," symbolic mediation/integration, of the real, while anxiety enters as a remainder of the Real that resists its symbolic Aufhebung. However, when Miller asks the question of what happens with the paternal Law after this introduction of anxiety as the signal of

the Real, he strangely reproduces the very terms of Aufhebung. Of course, the Name-of-the-Father continues to play a function, but a subordinate function within a new theoretical context. In short, the Name-of-the-Father is maintained, negated, and elevated to a higher level—the very three features of the Hegelian Aufhebung.

4   Michael Hardt and Antonio Negri, *Multitude* (New York: Penguin, 2004), xvi. All parenthetical citations refer to this edition.
5   G. W. F. Hegel, *The Phenomenology of Spirit*, trans. A. V. Miller, with analysis and foreword by J. N. Findlay (Oxford: Oxford University Press, 1977), 332.
6   This is also why Hardt and Negri's reference to Bakhtin's notion of carnival as the model for the protest movement of the multitude—they are carnivalesque not only in their form and atmosphere (theatrical performances, chants, humorous songs), but also in their noncentralized organization (208–11)—is deeply problematic. Is late capitalist social reality itself not already carnivalesque? Furthermore, is "carnival" not also the name for the obscene underside of power—from gang rapes to mass lynchings? Let us not forget that Mikhail Bakhtin developed the notion of carnival in his book on Rabelais written in the 1930s, as a direct reply to the carnival of the Stalinist purges.
7   Giorgio Agamben, *The Coming Community*, trans. M. Hardt (Minneapolis: University of Minnesota Press, 1993), 5–6.
8   Ibid., 6–7.

7

Hegel as the Other Side of Psychoanalysis

Mladen Dolar

It is obvious at first sight that wherever one opens Lacan's *Seminar XVII, The Other Side of Psychoanalysis*, one finds Hegel. He is one of the principal interlocutors, one of the reference points, on equal footing with Freud and Marx, with whom he forms a strange tripod on which the whole argument is based. It is clear that the very notion of the master's discourse, the basic type of discourse as a social bond, the discourse that is actually the hero of the title, that is, what constitutes the reverse side of psychoanalysis,[1] stems from a certain reading of Hegel's dialectic of lord and bondsman—or master and slave in the old parlance, which I will retain here for the sake of simplicity, despite its inaccuracy, since this is an inaccuracy constantly committed by Lacan himself, following Alexandre Kojève. On the one hand, for Hegel this dialectic inaugurates the realm of self-consciousness, which he emphatically describes as "the native realm of truth" where "being-in-itself and being-for-another are one and the same."[2] On the other hand, it presents in the same gesture Hegel's own theory of a minimal social bond: there is no self-consciousness, no self-reflexivity of consciousness, without at the same time the establishment of a social structure in a nutshell, the establishment of an " 'I' that is 'We' and 'We' that is 'I' " (110), the minimal constitution of a "We" that will be the subject of what Hegel calls spirit (and will get its full deployment in a subsequent chapter 150 pages later).

The social bond that underlies self-consciousness implies as its consequence a certain division of labor, or rather a division into labor and enjoyment, a scission between the two. So the elements that Lacan needs and uses are all there: master, slave, subjectivity, work, enjoyment. Giving the Hegelian account a little twist, one can disengage from there the four Lacanian entities: the concept of the master signifier, S_1, for the master is the master only by virtue of representing "the fear of death, the absolute Lord,"[3] the signifier of pure negativity that acquires its authority from its connection with death; he is the master only as the sign of the master. One can also, with some interpretative liberty, extricate the element of knowledge, S_2, as the know-how implicit in the slave's work; the slave has to possess a certain knowledge in order to be able to deal with things, to crack their obstinacy. S_1, S_2, $\$$, a—the elements are all there, their minimal and necessary connection appears to be there, but are they there in the right order? Is the connection the right one? Is Hegel a proto-Lacan, a Lacan who doesn't know yet that he is Lacan, a figure of knowledge that does not know itself? An unconscious Lacan? Or is Lacan the ultimate Hegelian, even though he doesn't quite announce his coming out? (Rather, anything but.) What is the status of Hegel's discourse here? It obviously serves as a source and a backdrop against which the theory of the four discourses can be established; it is its necessary condition but not at all its sufficient condition. For at the same time that theory can be put in place only if proper distances are taken in regard to Hegel. Let us start with the simple question: Where is Hegel's own discourse to be placed in relation to the theory of the four discourses? Lacan's answer, in *The Other Side of Psychoanalysis*, appears to be surprisingly inconsistent: he comes up with three different claims in three different sessions, such that Hegel seems to occupy all the places—well, almost all. What are we to make of this, what is its logic? Is this Lacan's symptom?

In the fifth lecture we can read the following: "It is clear that his truth is hidden from [the master, in the master's discourse], and a certain Hegel stated that it is delivered to him by the work of the slave. There you have it; however, it is a master's discourse, this discourse of Hegel's, which relies on substituting the State for the master through the long pathway of culture, culminating in absolute knowledge" (90). In a first reading, Hegel's discourse would thus ultimately be an instance of the master's discourse. In this account Hegel is not taken as someone who debunks

Hegel as the Other Side of Psychoanalysis 131

and lays bare the figure of mastery and domination at its very source, but as someone who, through exposing it, is already taking sides; he takes the side of the master, and he himself perpetuates what he is describing and analyzing. He is not the man scrutinizing the evidence, he is part of the story, a participant, an accomplice before and after the fact.[4] The proof of this is that the master-slave story is but a nutshell, a bud from which a political theory is to be developed, and the consequences to be drawn. The structural inequality that the master-slave relation was based upon has to be overcome, superseded by recognition among equals (*Anerkennung*), by the ethical substance of community and by the rule of universal law—the rule, that is, of an ideal abstract common master in relation to which all are treated as equals. The master had to become disembodied, or rather, in a further step, he acquired a new and rather massive body, for he is incarnated in the State. And Hegel, notoriously, was the Prussian State philosopher, or so the story goes. So we have the slide leading from the master to the State, the substitution of the State for the master, as Lacan compresses the story, which seems to be Hegel's way of endorsing the master. The pathway of culture (*Bildung*) is the long process of education leading from the enforced obedience to the master to the freely chosen obedience to the State as the incarnation of Reason.

Yet it is true that at the same time Hegel is telling another and seemingly different story in which the hero is the slave, not the master, for the truth of this scenario is on the side of the slave. The slave is the one who can work his way to emancipation, while the master abandons himself to pleasure and thus squanders all the prestige which he initially gained by fearlessly defying death. This other story, the historic defeat of the master and the victory of the slave, had a lot of popularity in leftist discourse (though curiously Marx himself never mentions it, not in any explicit way) and was particularly credited by Kojève, who was Lacan's subject supposed to know about Hegel. Yet Lacan always maintained that this part of the story was a hoax. As early as *Ecrits* we can read the following: "The work, Hegel tells us, to which the slave submits is giving up jouissance out of fear of death, is precisely the path by which he achieves freedom. There can be no more obvious lure than this, politically or psychologically. *Jouissance* comes easily to the slave, and leaves work in serfdom. [*La jouissance est facile à l'esclave et elle laissera le travail serf.*]"[5]

So Hegel's model opposes the master's enjoyment to the slave's work. The master can shuffle all the burdens onto the slave's shoulders and abandon himself to pleasure, while the work, pertaining to the slave, is based on the renunciation of enjoyment, and hence *Bildiung*, the formation of outer and inner nature. "Work is desire held in check [*gehemmte Begierde*, inhibited desire], the fleetingness staved off [*aufgehaltenes Verschwinden*, restrained disappearance]; in other words, work forms and shapes the thing [*sie bildet*—not just the thing, but also the subject]" (118). But this is precisely the lure, says Lacan: the problem is not the master's enjoyment, as this enjoyment may well be just the hypothesis of the slave, the figment of his imagination, the projection of the slave's own impasse, which is the impasse of his desire, and his inner blockage is presented as the external impediment.[6] The problem is quite the opposite: it is the slave's enjoyment that comes surprisingly easily, and which presents an obstacle to the slave's liberation.

One can understand this in the immediate sense, namely that the renunciation of enjoyment itself produces enjoyment; the very act of renouncing is always ambiguous, and there is never a subtraction of enjoyment that wouldn't be at the same time an addition, in the very same gesture. Fighting the enjoyment, advocating the suppression of enjoyment, always turns into a remodeling of enjoyment, offering new ways of enjoyment rather than of getting rid of enjoyment. Indeed, enjoyment appears as the one thing that one can never be rid of. It is recalcitrant to negation, and its negation produces a surplus. A and non-A don't cancel each other out but produce more A, or rather a different sort of A, an A'. This is already implied in the very ambiguity of Lacan's concept plus-de-jouir: it can be read as surplus enjoyment, but at the same time it can also mean no more enjoyment; it has the contours of an imperative, something like "Stop enjoying!" or "Cut it off!" So the very same gesture that prohibits, inhibits, and stops enjoyment produces a surplus, something one gets in place of the cut-off enjoyment.

All ascetic practices testify to this, most notably those described by Hegel in *The Phenomenology of Spirit* under the heading of the unhappy consciousness, which is consciousness that is ultimately prepared to give up all its worldly possessions and corporeal enjoyment, all its autonomy, and treat itself like a thing. However, the more the subject does this, the more there emerges a residue, a bit of the substance that cannot be

Hegel as the Other Side of Psychoanalysis   133

quite turned into the subject, and which is precisely the bit of enjoyment, the surplus enjoyment that has unexpectedly emerged in the operation — and the subject, the subject of self-consciousness, emerges precisely as correlative to that bit.

So, to cut a long story short, the slave is enslaved by his own enjoyment and not by the master's, he is paid off with bits of enjoyment, and the surplus enjoyment is what his work produces and what makes him work. The slave would thus get both the work *and* the enjoyment, while the poor master is lost in mere pleasure and withers away. Or so it would seem from the account given in *Ecrits*.

But in *Seminar XVII* the figure of the slave takes on a more complex and precise shape, and its economy is perhaps reversed: "I call this slave S_2, but you can also identify him here with the term 'jouissance,' which, first, he didn't want to renounce, and second, he did indeed want to, since he substitutes work for it, which is not at all its equivalent" (198). The slave didn't want to renounce enjoyment and so clings to his bare life, in the opening scene of domination, while the master was, supposedly, able to put his life at stake, to disentangle himself from his substantial bonds. But in the second step the very clinging to enjoyment implied the renunciation of enjoyment, its substitution with work. This work, now says Lacan, is not at all equivalent to jouissance. Or rather, it may well produce jouissance, for it produces surplus enjoyment, but this moment of surplus enjoyment is intercepted by the master. The slave pays the master with surplus enjoyment, and the master is the one who is able to collect the surplus enjoyment (in return for wages?). In a further turn, the master will ultimately be able to turn the surplus enjoyment into surplus value and accumulate it, make it circulate, count it, and measure it. So it is no longer simply a question of the slave easily obtaining enjoyment, recuperating the bits of enjoyment that hold him enslaved. The question is rather the theft of enjoyment, the spoliation of the slave's enjoyment by the master. This is what makes the master's discourse go round, and what makes it work.

For the moment we are just pursuing one simple thread, namely that the supposed historic victory of the slave over the master has not, and will not, take place.

It is quite evident, in effect, that not for a single instant can one hold that we are in anyway approaching the ascendancy of the slave. This unbelievable way of giving him the credit—giving his work the credit—for any kind of progress, as we say, of knowledge is, truly, extraordinarily futile (199).

So the ascendancy of the slave is a hoax, and the progression toward absolute knowledge—"that the slave ends up, at the end of history, at this point called absolute knowledge" (198)—is a mirage, the very name of the Hegelian fallacy. On this first account, Hegel appears to be the agent of the master, while the absolute knowledge appears as an expression of the position of the master, the gesture of mastery par excellence, its lure—all the more a lure since it is presented as the spoils waiting for the slave, the reward for his work and renunciation, his revenge on the master, and the promise of the path by which he would eventually become the master himself. Despite the revolutionary rhetoric that seems to oppose it, this is the lure that helps to maintain the master's discourse in place, through that very rhetoric. The supposed victory of the slave is really the ultimate victory of the master, his revenge.

But Hegel cannot be completely confined to that role, and the *dispositif* of the master-slave story offers more points of entry than one. So far I haven't considered the problem of knowledge, the slave's knowledge, since what gives the slave his status is a certain dialectic, a tension between knowledge and enjoyment, epitomized by what we can call the matheme of the slave, S_2/a, on the right-hand side in the master's discourse.

What kind of knowledge is this? In the twelfth session of the seminar, we are surprised to read the following:

> Hegel is the sublime representative of the discourse of knowledge [*savoir*], and of university knowledge.
>
> We others in France only ever have as philosophers people who travel the highways and byways, little members of provincial societies, such as Maine de Biran, or else characters like Descartes, who wander all over Europe. . . . Here in France, you won't find the philosophers in the universities. We can claim this as an advantage. But in Germany they are in the university. (200)

Hegel is now seemingly cast in another role—has Lacan changed his mind between February and June 1970?

Hegel as the Other Side of Psychoanalysis 135

First of all, what is at stake is not only the fact that Hegel happened to be a university professor by profession. The problem is that the university is already inscribed in the position from which he speaks, for as a philosopher he places himself in the paradigmatic place of the representative of the university. According to his habitus, his fundamental bearing, he couldn't possibly be anything else, for example a lens grinder, a cosmopolitan traveler, a persecuted sage, or an eccentric genius. The formative place of expression of his knowledge is the university, which, historically, at this point really appears in its modern sense for the first time. This is the time when Wilhelm von Humboldt, Hegel's friend, introduced major reforms into the organization and into the very conception of what a university is—he was the one who founded Berlin University in 1810, where Hegel would go to teach eight years later, and which bears his name to this day, the Humboldt University.

But this is not all: one could also say that Hegel universalizes the University, he turns the whole of the world, all regions of existence, logic, nature and culture alike, all philosophical attitudes and theories, all subject positions—he turns all this into a single, progressive path of knowledge, the self-development of a universal system of knowledge, the most massive University imaginable. The world is a part of the University, not the other way round; all of our activity is caught up in university discourse. In the Hegelian system we are all students (including and in the first place Hegel himself), we are always studying for exams, taking more and more advanced courses and acquiring more and more grades; we are trapped in a program of "permanent education," until the ultimate grade, absolute knowledge, the PhD to finish all PhDs. World history is the world university!

Is Hegel then the "most sublime university professor"? It seems that he fits this role as well as, or rather better than, the first one, that of the master. Rather, the two roles are not really in contradiction; he can appear as an ideal agent of the master precisely insofar as he is an agent of universal knowledge. The ideal Professor has, for the first and last time, succeeded in resolving the universality of knowledge into an all-encompassing system in which he can construe authority and the State as an embodiment of philosophy, an incarnation of Reason. In the university discourse knowledge is in the position of the agent and in a quid pro quo it can appear that authority, along with all institutions of power, stems from knowledge as its consequence. It is knowledge that institutes power as a moment of its own internal self-development that can posit all its presuppositions and thus abolish them. It is mastery universalized to the degree that the master himself can be reduced to the mere impotent figure of the monarch.

But the whole point of Lacan's construction of the university discourse is that this is another lure, that the seemingly autonomous and self-propelling knowledge has a secret clause, and that its truth is detained by the master under the bar. Historically, it is not just that Hegel is placed precisely at the juncture of the inauguration of the modern university, it is also that this is the juncture at which capitalism was established as the ruling discourse, after the French Revolution, that event which inspired so much enthusiasm in Hegel. Capitalism is instated in conjunction with the university discourse, its twin and double. Couldn't one see in Hegel precisely the figure of the transition from the revolution to the capitalist normalization, where knowledge appears precisely as the ideal medium of both? After all, the University is, among other things, also the best neutralizer of revolutions; it receives them happily into its bosom and turns them into an affair of knowledge—the best example is May 1968. The University particularly adores the label of "subversive knowledge," which alleviates its bad conscience.

Historically—and this is just an aside—it would be interesting to explore the vagaries of the fates of German and French philosophy and the University that Lacan briefly mentions in our quote. Most significantly, the philosophers one cannot find in the German University, this otherwise ideal place for philosophers, are Marx and Nietzsche in the nineteenth century, and Freud and Wittgenstein in the twentieth. A most paradoxical place would have to be reserved for Heidegger: to be brief, one could say that his project was a thought that would be recalcitrant to the university discourse, a way of thinking which would retain the symbolic efficacy of knowledge that university discourse has thwarted. Yet, from the outside, this project produced its most catastrophic moment precisely in its intersection with University, in the *Rektoratsrede*, which one can read as a program for a University not based on university discourse—a moment where thinking opposed to the university discourse was to become, in a highly political gesture, the starting point of a proposal to reform the university that was inextricably mixed with a new form of domination. Anyway, after Hegel, philosophers were actually not so easy to find in German universities. The greatest moments of German philosophy were perhaps produced outside of it, and then eventually recuperated by the university.[7]

In France, it seems that in many respects the situation is the reverse of the German one: there is, to be sure, a whole tradition of grand philosophical figures outside the university, including Sartre and Lacan (along with Georges Bataille, Maurice Blanchot, and many others), but the more interesting thing is that even philosophers in the university, often holding senior positions, actually see themselves as, are generally perceived as, and behave like outsiders. They present themselves as an underground movement inside the university, a bunch of guerrilla fighters who have to take on a temporary disguise, an alias—consider the cases of Althusser, Foucault, Derrida, Deleuze, Badiou, and others. Is this to be read as a disavowal of their position, so that the ideal proponents of university discourse are ultimately those who present its inner opposition, or are they really introducing something else than university discourse, offering a way out of its impasses? I will leave this question suspended.

To return to the main thread, on closer inspection the two roles attributed to Hegel in the first two accounts, that of the master and of the professor, actually do not fit him as well as it may seem if one looks at the historical evidence of his posterity. In spite of rumors to the contrary, it is obvious that neither the state nor the university ever followed Hegel's footsteps, as their subsequent development took a completely non-Hegelian, or even anti-Hegelian course. Hegelianism as a state philosophy and Hegelianism as a model of university knowledge have rather acquired the status of a fantasy, or even of a horror show, an object of dread, a nightmare, a figure against which it was deemed necessary to establish fundamentally different models of politics and knowledge. Hegel's ghost, in the disguise of the Master and the Professor, served as a warning, not as a model to follow.

Obviously, the subsequently prevailing liberal political theory, in its assumptions about the nature of state and political power, is at the opposite end of Hegel and it took an incredible feat of imagination, an intellectual somersault, a masterpiece of conjuring, to see the triumph of liberal democracy as the Hegelian end of history. If we cast a superficial glance at the entire development of post-Hegelian philosophy, if I may take the liberty of simplifying the general thrust, we can easily see that it basically defined itself as a farewell to Hegel, a way out of the Hegelian trap, whether in its Marxist or Nietzschean variety, in the whole analytical tradition, in the theory of science, the phenomenological, the Heideggerian tradition, down to structuralism, poststructuralism and postmodernism. The slogan of "the end of metaphysics," shared in one way or another by all these extremely varied traditions (even if understood in radically different ways), always meant, in the most immediate sense, the departure from the last, from the paramount and most notorious, of all metaphysicians. If an ultimate proof was needed of the untenable nature of Hegel's position, one could always produce the exhibit always most ready at hand, absolute knowledge. The mere mention of these words was enough and, unfortunately, it looks like Lacan was following the general thrust in this respect.

But at this point I want to argue only the simple thesis that while Hegel may well appear to be the paradigmatic case of the master's discourse and the university discourse, the modern forms of domination and knowledge never followed his footsteps. Quite the opposite, he was taken as the model opponent (or was it rather a model straw man?) against which they established themselves. Hegel may well have stood at the origin of university discourse, but it is also clear that someone who raises a claim to absolute knowledge cannot possibly be placed within the framework of university discourse, so that this extreme point had to be repressed and abandoned in order for the modern university discourse to be established.

Is Hegel's a master's discourse or a university discourse, and does one have to decide one way or another? The link between the two concerns the question of the status of knowledge. Lacan's claim is that Hegel stands at the end of a long philosophical tradition, that is, of a particular kind of knowledge that established itself by an act of dispossession. The knowledge was originally, from the outset, on the side of the slave, and philosophy emerged when the master dispossessed the slave of his knowledge. This is the claim that Lacan doesn't tire of repeating throughout the seminar:

> What does philosophy designate over its entire evolution? It's this —theft, abduction, stealing slavery of its knowledge, through the

Hegel as the Other Side of Psychoanalysis 139

maneuvers of the master. . . . The entire function of the episteme in so far as it is specified as transmissible knowledge . . . is always borrowed from the techniques of craftsmen, that is to say of serfs. It is a matter of extracting the essence of this knowledge in order for it to become the master's knowledge. (21)

Philosophy in its historical function is this extraction, I would almost say this betrayal, of the slave's knowledge, in order to obtain its transmutation into the master's knowledge. (22)

The transference, . . . the plundering, the spoliation, of what, at the beginning of knowledge, was inscribed, hidden in the slave's world. . . . If we look at it more closely, subtracting the slave's knowledge from him is the entire history whose stages Hegel follows step by step. (91)

The slave . . . was knowledge at the outset. The evolution of the master's discourse is here. Philosophy has played the role of constituting a master's knowledge, extracted [*soustrait*] from the slave's knowledge. Science . . . consists in this transmutation of the function, if one can put it like that. . . .
 Be that as it may, there is certainly a difficulty in knowledge, which resides in the opposition between know-how [*savoir-faire*] and what is *episteme* in the strict sense. The *episteme* was constituted out of an interrogation, a purification of knowledge. (173-74)

So there is an opposition: on the one hand we have the slave's knowledge, which is the starting point of knowledge, since knowledge stems from the slave, but it is a practical knowledge, a know-how, a savoir faire, a knowledge pertaining to handcraft, to the crafts. It is craft knowledge, knowledge involved in work that makes work possible, for there is no work without knowledge. On the other hand we have the episteme, the epistemological knowledge, the purified knowledge, the theoretical knowledge, which is knowledge to be transmitted and which appears on the side of the master—and indeed philosophy was, from the outset, the pastime of the masters.
 In order to get from the first to the second, a transmutation had to take place, a change of function, which involved an act of theft, of plun-

dering. The famous scene from Plato's *Meno*, the questioning of the slave, to which Lacan refers several times, can be taken as emblematic: the slave is shown to possess the knowledge, an intricate piece of geometrical knowledge, but only by being questioned by the master, by being asked the right questions and led by the hand. So the demonstration that even the slave knows actually reduces the slave even more to his status of the slave. The knowledge originally spoliated from the slave is given back to him, in a quid pro quo, as a theorem, but this is the final act of spoliation. This also shows that universal theoretical knowledge is of an entirely different kind from its origins, the know-how, and by getting that knowledge back from the master, as it were, the slave's dispossession is completed. Sharing the universal episteme demonstrates his subjection.

If this is the birthplace of philosophy, then philosophy, as the discourse of pure universal knowledge, can be seen as the agent linking the master's discourse and the university discourse, the transition between the two. Academia, after all, started its career as Plato's Academy, from which it got the name it bears to this day.

In the first lecture Lacan opposes two faces of knowledge, the articulated face (episteme) and know-how, that is "so akin to animal knowledge, but which, in the slave, is not totally devoid of the apparatus that transforms it into one of the most articulated network of language" (21). There is an almost animal know-how, a knowing how to deal with things, but the slave is "the speaking tool," according to Aristotle, the signifier is there, the articulation is there, and since there is no knowledge without a signifier, there is no work without a signifier, so the two faces are always already there, although the articulation hasn't yet taken the form of episteme. The question turns around the precise nature of the signifying articulation of knowledge, and this is where Lacan somewhat mysteriously introduces thermodynamics, with the twin notions of entropy—that is, the loss of energy—and conservation of energy. What is the energy of the signifier? What makes it tick, what propels it? Lacan insists at quite some length on what is actually the title of his third lecture, namely that knowledge is the means of jouissance ("Savoir, moyen de jouissance"), that the secret of its status is to be sought in its dialectics with enjoyment.

This is where thermodynamics comes into play, a theory that aims at the conjunction of energy and machines. The signifier is the machine, jouissance is the energy ("the signifier as . . . an apparatus of enjoyment" [54]), but their conjunction is extraordinary: the starting point is that the very incidence of the signifier entails an entropy, that is, a loss of energy, a loss of jouissance. The signifier mortifies jouissance, it mortifies the body, but that very loss is at the same time something that produces a residue, a surplus, a surplus jouissance ("the lost object . . . by which enjoyment is introduced into the dimension of the subject's being" [55]). The signifier is the obstruction of jouissance, but it is propelled by what it obstructs.[8] The thermodynamics of jouissance is a process in which the loss is compensated, as it were, by something that comes into its place, which is not the same as what was lost, since one never gets that back, but something instead of it, a by-product of the operation, and which is enough to keep the machine turning. What is lost of jouissance is recuperated as the surplus, and the problem of discourse as a social bond is how to allocate this surplus. The strange thermodynamics of jouissance revolves around the fact that the loss of energy becomes itself the source of another kind of energy, that there is no way simply to lose or be rid of jouissance. Here is a key passage:

> In fact, it is only through this effect of entropy, through this wasting, that enjoyment acquires a status, that it shows itself. This is why I initially introduced it by the term *Mehrlust*, surplus enjoyment. It is precisely through being perceived in the dimension of loss—something necessitates compensation, if I can put it like this, for what is initially a negative number—that this something that has come and struck, resonated on, the walls of the bell, has created enjoyment, enjoyment that is to be repeated. Only the dimension of entropy gives body to this fact, that there is surplus pleasure to be recovered. (56)

The emergence of the master's discourse, the elementary type of discourse, is based on an operation where the residue is recuperated, reinscribed by a signifier, S_1. The incidence of the signifier (the first S_1) is like a dam that blocks jouissance, it produces a residue, and this residue is the backdrop for the emergence of S_1 (the second S_1), the residue that propels the repetition of S_1, the conservation of lost energy.

In an obscure passage, Lacan says that "the signifier [is] repeated at two levels, S_1, S_1 again. S_1 is the dam. The second S_1, down below, is the pond that receives it and turns the turbine. There is no other meaning to the conservation of energy than this mark of an instrumentation that signifies the power of the master. What is collected in the fall has to be conserved" (91–92). The first S_1 is the incidence of the signifier, that which makes knowledge (as know-how) and work possible and which dams jouissance. The second S_1, seemingly a mere repetition of the first, is separated from the first by the residue that was produced by entropy, the loss of jouissance entailed by the signifier. In the gesture of repetition it deals with that residue, it puts it to use, it turns it into an instrument, it intercepts it in a seeming tautology, it conserves its energy. The repetition of S_1 is propelled by the production of the by-product and has to be repeated over and over again to deal with the surplus.[9] This is also the operation in which S_2 comes into place, as the element of slave's knowledge, that is knowledge inscribed in the master's discourse: the tautology of S_1 frames the slave's knowledge, it assigns it a place, it becomes the knowledge in the service of the master, and this also means that the master doesn't have to know anything, he is not the master through his knowledge. Knowledge is left to the slave—or at least until the advent of philosophy.

Philosophy conjures the figure of a knowing master, and the "real" master would supposedly be the one who would obtain that privilege by his knowledge alone—hence Plato's dream of the philosopher-king. The theft of knowledge, the inaugurating act of philosophy, would thus mean that the master would appropriate S_2 and make it one with S_1; the fantasy of philosophy is an amalgamation of S_1 and S_2, a knowledge-power, a power-knowledge (in Foucault's parlance). But the knowledge that has been thus extracted from the slave's knowledge has also been neutralized in the process. It was at the same time extricated from its dialectics with jouissance, it became "academic knowledge," and that extrication implies that it has become knowledge deprived of truth: "When in the master's discourse S_2 was put in the slave's place, and when in the discourse of the modernized master [i.e., university discourse] it was then put in the master's place—. . . that knowledge [is] not the same" (38). It has been universalized and neutered, and "the philosophical tradition has some responsibility for this transmutation" (34). The end of this process is accomplished by Hegel with his monster concept of absolute knowledge, the knowledge that, at the end of the grand metaphysical tradition, has severed all its ties with its origins in a self-grasp of a *causa sui*. So philosophy would thus be, by its very nature, the incipient form of the university discourse, the birth of the university discourse from out of the spirit of the master's discourse, and Hegel would thus be the ideal proponent of both.

But enough of Hegel bashing; it's perhaps time for some Hegel praising. It is clear that in the first two accounts, Hegel as master's discourse or university discourse, Lacan is but following the general thrust, and despite the lucid insights and the intricate web of the four elements, he is not saying anything surprising as far as Hegel is concerned, but embroidering the generally received image of Hegel. In the second lecture, however, we find his most famous claim about Hegel, which does sound surprising after what has been said so far: "Hegel, the most sublime of hysterics" (38). There is something counterintuitive in this qualification; one can hardly imagine anyone less hysterical than Hegel. Apart from that, to qualify his hysteria as sublime can perhaps hardly be seen as an asset (we can remember that he was already qualified as "the sublime representative of the discourse of university knowledge" [200]).

In the hysteric's discourse, which is now assigned to Hegel, the place of the agent is occupied by a very different kind of entity, by $, which in Lacan's algebra designates the barred subject, the subject of desire, the subject of the unconscious. As the subject which is on the side of lack, not on the side of the signifier of either mastery or knowledge, it is divorced from both mastery and knowledge, although implicated in both. One of Lacan's basic tenets is that the impact of the signifier also entails the subject, that this subject of the signifier is by its nature hysterical, and that hysteria is a "universal" trait of the speaking being, the consequence of the assumption of speech. Language hystericizes the subject. It produces a subject always in deficit in relation to what he or she is saying, always somewhere else, a subject impossible to pin down to the signifier which tries to fix it, name it, assign it a place, as well as the subject irreducible to the meaning and to the signifiers he or she produces. This follows from the very basic formula, the definition of the signifier, namely that the signifier represents the subject for another signifier, which also implies that there is no signifier of the subject, so that this is a process of an always failing representation. This impossibility to be pinned down presents a problem for both the master and knowledge, which cannot capture and entrap the hysterical subject in their network. This is a subject recalcitrant to being captured, and hence a subject that undermines the authority of both master and knowledge. Placing Hegel on the side of the hysteric's discourse is placing him on the side of subversion of the first two models, although the hysterical gesture is always ambiguous. We can venture a hypothesis that Hegel was perhaps the first philosopher to take into account the hysterical subject, and it is perhaps here that the novelty of *The Phenomenology of Spirit* and the source of its peculiar and enduring fascination lie.

What is the nature of subjectivity that underlies the progress of *The Phenomenology of Spirit*?

We cannot say, in effect, that *The Phenomenology of Spirit* consists of starting from the so-called *Selbstbewusstsein* (self-consciousness) grasped at the most immediate level of sensation, thus implying that all knowledge is known from the outset. What would be the point of all this phenomenology if it were not a question of something else (38)?

So the subject of *The Phenomenology of Spirit* is not the subject of a knowledge that knows itself. Its self-consciousness correlates to knowledge that escapes it; it cannot grasp itself in a self-transparency, and the desire that propels it undermines all the different figures of knowledge. It always displays, time and time again, that they cannot be justified. The hysterical nature of this subject bores a hole into knowledge, into all different types of knowledge (and Hegel's wager is to establish the complete "all-inclusive" list of all possible attitudes of knowledge, theoretical and practical, individual and social, abstract and historical). It is propelled by a desire that can find no rest and satisfaction in any particular figure of knowledge. But in this permanent dissatisfaction it is a subject that produces knowledge, and in the hysteric's discourse knowledge, S_2, is situated in the place of the product. "The desire to know is not what leads to knowledge. What leads to knowledge . . . is the hysteric's discourse" (23).

A knowledge that doesn't know itself, a subjectivity that eludes self-grasp, a desire that cannot find a hold: all this qualifies the hysterical subject as the very opposite of philosophy. Hence couldn't one claim that hysteria was always the other of philosophy—its reverse, its other

Hegel as the Other Side of Psychoanalysis 145

side? It is something to be excluded from the philosophical field, in order for it to constitute itself as such. At the very beginning of the philosophical treatment of hysteria—seen as an ailment connected with femininity and sexuality—there stands no less an authority than Plato, who actually provided the canonical piece that was the major reference for the millennia to come.[10] *Hysteria* originates in the Greek word for the womb, and Plato's theory saw its source in the "traveling womb," which could wander around the body, settle itself in any place, and demand satisfaction—a theory that had its adherents up to the nineteenth century. Throughout the Middle Ages and into the beginning of modernity it appeared in the frightful images of demonology and was behind the persecution of witchcraft; it presented the image of a radical evil, the connections between the woman and the devil.[11] Then, with the emergence of modern medical sciences, it was seen as an especially stubborn and nonlocalizable symptom that could not be defined, isolated, or cured. The history of hysteria is a long one, and it largely coincides with the particularly poignant aspect of treating femininity, the woman's desire and its incomprehensible nature. Whenever the philosophical discourse stumbled upon hysteria as this obscure unfathomable figure of desire that defies knowledge, it always produced most indicative symptoms, a swarm of follies the most prominent philosophers were prepared to utter on the subject.[12] Hysteria was always seen as a nonphilosophical, antiphilosophical stance to be excluded if we are to remain philosophers. Philosophy seemed to be based on the elimination of hysteria.[13]

It is true that with Hegel the problem of the hysterical subject appears in an abstract form, torn from any immediate connection with sexuality and femininity and considered only in its elementary traits, but its basic structure is nonetheless in place. We could say that Hegel's great feat was in turning the hysterical subject, which was the other of philosophy—the subject which is structurally incapable of knowing itself—into the subject of philosophy, the agent of the concept. There is a paradoxical and delicate step that places his approach outside the register of the master's discourse and its modern avatar, the university discourse, the discourse of universal knowledge.

One can object at this point that it is not Hegel who is hysterical here, but his hero, the consciousness making its slow progress from sense certainty to absolute knowledge. Hegel can be seen as the one who supervises this process, defines its rules, and sees to it that it is going in the right direction. He can perceive the truth of it that escapes the subject, so in his very neutrality, in his nonintervention, he is all the more the master (or the Professor). Still, this frequent criticism doesn't quite work. A crack is opened in the discourse that cannot be quite closed once it has appeared, and the external sign of it is perhaps the fact that things obviously got out of hand, out of Hegel's hand. One needs only to consider the structure of *Phenomenology*, which doesn't correspond to its initial plan, where it looks like the development is going in curious directions and taking unexpected turns, every chapter growing out of proportions, and it looks like Hegel is struggling to keep the discipline of the concept in the midst of an impending chaos. The production of knowledge, animated by the (hysterical) subject, cannot be quite contained in the framework of the master's discourse and the university discourse. There is something like an excess of the hysterical gesture—but this is what makes the position of absolute knowledge utterly ambiguous: is it the gesture by which the master and the professor finally eliminate the hysterical excess, the crack in the knowledge, or is it the gesture that reflects this excess itself and endorses it? We will come back to this.

The subject that cannot know itself, that cannot self-reflexively grasp itself, the nonphilosophical consciousness that wants to grasp the truth with its knowledge, but that perpetually fails to do so, becomes the protagonist of philosophy. The subject constantly tries to justify its knowledge before a big Other, but a big Other that it has itself instituted or unwittingly brought about. The wager of *The Phenomenology of Spirit* is that knowledge is measured by the standards it itself proposes and implies, and it always falls short. The attempt to grasp the truth by means of knowledge—the minimal initial requirement for the subject—is always insufficient. Each figure of knowledge fails, but through this series of failures knowledge is actually produced—but not a knowledge within the subject's grasp. It is rather a knowledge that escapes him, a knowledge "hinter dem Rücken des Bewußtseins," as Hegel puts it, "behind the back of consciousness" (56). The inability to satisfy its own standards produces a constant hysterization of the subject, it has to make ever-renewed attempts, and this is the spring that generates knowledge. The irreducibility of $\$$ to S_1 and S_2 is the key to the progress of consciousness and the constant production of S_2. Bear in mind that knowledge, *das Wissen*, *le savoir*, is something other than understanding, comprehension, *das Erkenntnis*, *la connaissance* (a distinction somewhat difficult to maintain in English).[14] Lacan insists on this: "What we discover in even the slightest bit of psychoanalytic experience is, indeed, of the order of knowledge and not of acquaintance [*connaissance*] or representation" (32). Even more: "No, there is nothing in common between the subject of *connaissance* and the subject of the signifier" (53).

Knowledge is not a matter of understanding. Understanding would be that knowledge which knows itself, which grasps itself and finds itself in objects, the knowledge of representation and correspondence, of *adaequatio*, and hence prey to fantasy. "On ne comprend que ses fantasmes," says Lacan in one of his famous slogans, one understands only one's own fantasies. Understanding is fatally entwined with recognition, cognition falls into the trap of re-cognition, reducing the unknown and the foreign to the well-known, known since times immemorial, finding what one always already knew, with the effect of "yes, this is it," or, which is the same, "yes, this is me." Understanding is finding oneself in fantasy, reestablishing its framework to accommodate more and more, enlarging it, not dissipating it, not traversing it—but traversing the fantasy is the point psychoanalysis should lead to, in a process that is contrary to understanding, a dissipation of understanding, and hence an affair of knowledge.

Knowledge that doesn't know itself, and which is assigned to the place of production, the product of the hysteric's discourse, will acquire a key function in the process of analysis, for this knowledge accomplishes the work in analysis. The knowledge does the work. "How could saying no-matter-what lead anywhere, unless it was determined that there is nothing in the random production of signifiers that, simply because it involves signifiers, does not bear upon this knowledge that is not known [*qui ne se sait pas*], and which is really what is doing the work?" asks Lacan (37). The work of this knowledge can produce truth, and the initial move of analysis always implies the hysterization of the subject, it reminds him or her of the hysteria he or she might have forgotten.

Since the hysterical subject, with its irreducible negativity, is the principle and the driving force of dialectical progress, the lack of correspondence of the subject to itself and to its own criteria produces a constant sense of "this is not it," that any particular configuration of objectivity and knowledge is inadequate—and this is precisely the formula with which Lacan defines hysterical desire as inherently unsatisfied or even as the desire for dissatisfaction, a desire to remain desire. Hegel actually treats this attitude with a gesture analogous to that of the analyst, that is, by insisting that "this is in fact it," that the very failure to find "it" is "it." This enables not only the placement of *The Phenomenology of Spirit* under the banner of hysteria, but also, inversely, the clarification of hysteria with Hegelian concepts. In his account of the analysis of Dora, the paramount case of hysteria, Lacan directly employs Hegel's dialectic of the "beautiful soul": "Look at your own involvement . . . in the disorder you bemoan."[15] "You yourself are a part of the reality you resist, you are complicit in bringing it about." The moment of negativity, by which the (hysterical) subject is irreducible to any positivity, has a counterpart in a movement where positivity is engendered by this negativity and which serves to prolong the very dissatisfaction. This is the part where the hysterical position is ambiguous, not merely subversive in its ability to shake the master and to bore holes in knowledge, but also an accomplice in the world that represents its unhappy fate.

Here we can see how the basic structure of hysteria can be described with the Hegelian logic of reflexive determination: the subject's other is nothing other than the subject in its "oppositional determination," *gegensätzliche Bestimmung*. Every positive term may well betray subjectivity—"this is not it"—yet subjectivity persists only through the series of these betrayals, through the impossibility of finding its true "expression" or equivalent. There is a double meaning to *betray*, it can mean both to present and to misrepresent, and both meanings coincide here. The very failure to find itself is the locus of the subject. In this pulsation between the perpetual "this is not it" and "this is it," the Hegelian subject maintains itself as hysterical.

The parallel with hysteria can be seen on yet another level, which one can see at several points in *Phenomenology*, most clearly in the figure of unhappy consciousness: the deadlock, the impasse of a certain position of knowledge, is staged and inscribed in the body. Hysteria always appears as a bodily symptom, as a conversion of a signifying deadlock into a bodily symptom, as a staging of that deadlock in the hysterical theater. (Lacan speaks of the law as "called into question as a symptom" (48), that is, as a hysterical symptom that stages its impasse.) One can see this mechanism at work when the unhappy consciousness translates the impasse of its position into a practice, a practice of doing away with its corporeal enjoyment, an incessant, desperate, and futile attempt to be rid of bodily functions, to dispossess itself of the body, in order to join *das Unwandelbare*, the unchangeable beyond, only to experience that it never can and thus to reproduce its unhappiness. So the "theoretical" position is refuted not in theoretical terms, but through staging its truth in bodily terms that undermine the theory. This is the line that Slavoj Žižek has convincingly argued in one of his books.[16] This can be seen as the way in which the subject, $, displays its connection with the *a* under the bar, on the left side of the hysteric's discourse, the moment that detains its truth, the hidden cause of its split, the reminder of the impossible tie between philosophy and enjoyment, enjoyment as the limit of subjectivity and the edge of knowledge.

We have seen how Lacan proposes to locate Hegel in three different discourses: he presents him as the paramount Master, the paramount Professor, and somewhat astonishingly the paramount hysteric (I suppose in each case as the most sublime of all). The curious thing is that he seems to fit perfectly all three roles; he obligingly always offers good reasons for such a placement, as if this multifaceted man who endeavored to encompass totality in his system would indeed produce such a comprehensive discourse that could happily accommodate all imaginable discourses and receive them into its bosom, as if he would offer a metadiscourse in which all types can find their place and congregate. All? There is one that is conspicuously missing. Let me finish with an attempt to envisage a link between Hegel and the analyst's discourse.

What I am aiming at is not so much the question of how Hegel's own discourse functions by its immanent logic, but that of the place he has come to occupy for us. First, we can see in Hegel the figure of a subject supposed to know, the figure against which the subsequent development of philosophy has to be measured and before which it has to justify itself. (After all, who could be better suited for the role of the subject supposed to know than someone who raised the claim to absolute knowledge?) Adorno opens the first of his *Three Studies on Hegel* with the statement that it is wrong to ask what Hegel is for us today, the problem is rather what we are for him—can we measure up to him?[17] Are we worthy of him—whether as his heirs or his buriers? It is we who have to justify ourselves, let ourselves be judged, and not put ourselves in a position of someone who can dispense easy judgments. Of course, the subject supposed to know is also a hated figure, just like the analyst, and the measure of transference can be both love and hatred (or, rather, it easily shifts from one to the other), so that those who hate him, and who by far outnumber his adherents, are equally prey to transference. Negative transference has taken the upper hand, given that everybody wants to escape metaphysics and strike a blow at the last metaphysician, but this is still a variation of transference, fuelled by a hope to get out of his long shadow, to be cured of transference. He inspires many reactions, most often rage and awe, almost never indifference. There can be the feigned indifference of someone like Deleuze, with his famous slogan *oublier Hegel*: one should forget Hegel and not try to criticize him or surpass him. But then again, he needs Hegel as a straw man, the construction of a monster as a backdrop against which he can be Deleuze. There can be the sudden resuscitation of Hegel as the subject supposed to know in a tradition that seemed to have forgotten him, with the mixed blessing of the appearance of Kojève in France, and the storm to follow. There can be the posthumous revenge of Hegel on the analytical tradition, with the emergence of the problem of self-reference and self-reflexivity, although this tradition has always treated him as some indecipherable monstrosity. This can take many forms. Hegel, the philosopher who promoted reconciliation as the highest philosophical aim, ended up at the very opposite of representing reconciliation—he is the figure of harsh division. There is a universal admiration and general acceptance of Kant, whatever the critical misgivings may be, but with Hegel one is constantly in the line of fire.

At the same time as the subject supposed to know, Hegel has functioned as refuse, a discarded residue, a cast-off of the grand metaphysical tradition, a figure of the opaque and ungraspable other, a waste that cannot be disposed of. One hates him for having imposed on us some of the most obscure and difficult texts of the philosophical tradition—nobody reads Hegel, but everybody knows he is a monster. One cannot grasp him, assign him a neat place; any attempt to surpass him seems

Hegel as the Other Side of Psychoanalysis 151

to get stuck in something he has already foreseen, a trap he has already laid for us, as if the very refusal to follow him is already forestalled and inscribed in what one wants to refute, as if he always places us when we want to place him. But the paradox is that he occupies this position of the residue and the waste precisely in the extreme claim to universality, to universal knowledge, or even more, to absolute knowledge. It is as if the very excess of universality starts to function as the residue, as a moment recalcitrant to universality; the extreme claim to reason is what appears unreasonable in Hegel; the excess of reason defies post-Hegelian reason. The extreme figure of universal knowledge is refractory to knowledge, the claim to all-encompassing system cannot be quite encompassed. This is the point where the slogan of absolute knowledge starts functioning as its very opposite: the refuse of knowledge, the repellent residue, something to be excluded and disposed of in order to continue with philosophy, an outrage, a scandal, the universal and absolute monster. Lacan keeps coming back to it throughout this seminar, following the general course of indignation. His argument is that absolute knowledge "would only be to mark the annulment, the failure, the disappearance at the conclusion of the only thing that motivates the function of knowledge—its dialectic with enjoyment. Absolute knowledge is supposed to be the abolition of this conclusion, purely and simply" (38). It would be *un tout-savoir*, a knowledge forming a whole in its own self-transparency and self-sufficiency, the ultimate incarnation of S_2, or, rather, of S_2/S_1 on the left-hand side of the university discourse, the union of knowledge and mastery, the knowledge relying on the ultimate gesture of the master.

But couldn't one argue that this figure which was supposed to abolish the dialectic of S_2 and *a*, abolish the *a* of surplus enjoyment, started to function precisely as an incarnation of *a*? The leftover, the surplus produced by philosophy, not in some murky depths which one would have to dig into in order to unearth the obscure object of philosophical desire, but at the very height, in full light, in the light of the midday sun (*der Mittag der Wahrheit*, says Hegel, the noon of truth, in a figure that anticipates Nietzsche, and which Lacan, on the level of his task, renders with a pun, *le mi-dit de la vérité*, the half-said of truth). The refuse, the residue emerging in the form of universality and absoluteness, the universality gone a bit too far, the universality run amok, the residue of the all-encompassing totality, not as something that this totality would be unable to cover, but in the very gesture of its totalization. Absolute knowledge is thus a symptom of post-Hegelian philosophy, its monster, its impossible—should one recall here Lacan's dictum that the real is the impossible?

Rather than seeing in absolute knowledge the ideal embodiment of S_2/S_1 on the left-hand side of the university discourse, we could propose to read it as a/S_2 on the left-hand side of the analyst's discourse, to give it another twist, another quarter turn. It would be the conjunction of a as refuse and the leftover of knowledge, the place of the analyst as the agent of the analyst's discourse, and under the bar knowledge in the position of truth. As for us, we are on the other side, occupying the position of $, struck with rage and awe or the attempts at dismissal, trying to come up with a web of signifiers that could get us out of this impasse.

Lacan refuses absolute knowledge as a monstrosity, but couldn't one argue that he adopts it in another way? For couldn't one see *la passe*, this Lacanian ending of analysis, the end of something that looks like an infinite process ("Analysis terminable and interminable," as Freud formulated the problem), the passage from the position of the patient to the position of the analyst, the pass out of impasse—couldn't one conceive it as Lacan's own version of absolute knowledge?[18] Lacan's formulas to conceptualize the end of analysis have a strangely Hegelian echo: couldn't one read *The Phenomenology of Spirit* precisely as a process of traversing the fantasy, *la traversée du fantasme*, of working our way through the fundamental fantasies that have organized our modes of being? And isn't the point of the process to put a stop to interminable blah-blah, to achieve a subjective destitution, the abandonment of the underlying assumptions that underpinned the subject and its world, the realization that the failed attempts of knowledge to grasp the truth circumscribe the very locus of truth, the pass in the very impasse? The knowledge that works and in the process produces the truth? The analogy has its boundaries, which are not difficult to establish; of course, it all happens on a different level, yet it seems that what matters more than the limits of an analogy is the moment where we can see the reenactment of the same gesture. If it seemed that absolute knowledge was the point that condenses the Master and the Professor, it now appears that at the very same point one can see an exit, the pass which leads to the analyst: Lacan, our Hegel?[19]

Notes

1 Jacques Lacan, *Le séminaire, livre XVII: L'envers de la psychanalyse*, ed. J.-A. Miller (Paris: Seuil, 1991), 99.
2 G. W. F. Hegel, *The Phenomenology of Spirit*, trans. A. V. Miller (Oxford: Oxford University Press, 1977), 104. All further references in the body of the text are to this edition.
3 Ibid., 117.
4 "One doesn't see at all why there would be a master as an outcome of the struggle to death for pure prestige. And this despite Hegel who says that this would result from this strange state of affairs at the outset" (Lacan, *Le séminaire, livre XVII*, 198).
5 Jacques Lacan, "The Subversion of the Subject and the Dialectic of Desire," in *Ecrits*, trans. B. Fink (New York: Norton, 2002), 296; published in French as *Ecrits* (Paris: Seuil, 1966), 811. All further references to *Écrits* will be to both the English version and the French original. Already in the "Rome Discourse" we can read the following: "In fact the obsessional subject manifests one of the attitudes that Hegel did not develop in his dialectic of the master and the slave. The slave has given way in face of the risk of death in which mastery was being offered to him in a struggle of pure prestige. But since he knows that he is mortal, he also knows that the master can die. From this moment on he is able to accept his labouring for the master and his renunciation of pleasure in the meantime; and, in the uncertainty of the moment when the master will die, he waits. . . . he is anticipated in the moment of master's death, the moment from which he will start to live, but in the meantime he identifies with the master as dead, and through this he is himself already dead," Lacan, *Ecrits*, 96/314.
6 Slavoj Žižek returns to this point on several occasions. For example, "That would be the last lesson of the famous Hegelian dialectics of the Lord and the Bondsman . . . : the Lord is ultimately an invention of the Bondsman, a way for the Bondsman to 'give way as to his desire,' to evade the blockage of his own desire by projecting its reason into the external repression of the Lord" ("Beyond Discourse-Analysis," in *New Reflections on the Revolution of Our Time*, ed. E. Laclau [London: Verso, 1990], 252).
7 The case of the Frankfurt School is also indicative: people who started outside the university and continued in exile were eventually recuperated as the grand figures of the German University.
8 In a further reversal, it is then the surplus that obstructs the signifying machinery and its smooth running; it is the spanner in the works of the signifying machinery.
9 In the first lecture, Lacan speaks about "the exteriority of S_1" (*Le séminaire: livre XVII*, 11) in relation to the signifiers which are already there (and which he designates by S_2)—"S_1 is the one which has to be seen as intervening," and this intervention is what actually constitutes a discourse, it makes the discourse out of signifiers already there. Here the description is more subtle: one can designate the "initial" signifiers as the first S_1, the designation of the very incidence of the signifier, and then the master signifier as the second S_1, which then retroactively turns the initial signifiers into S_2. It totalizes them and assigns them a function, turns them into instruments.
10 *Timaeus*, 91 b–c. Plato, in a completely psychoanalytic fashion, sees the distinction

masculine/feminine as a distinction between localization and nonlocalization: masculine enjoyment is localized in a particular organ (and is thus circumscribed with a "phallic" signifier, castration, etc.), while feminine enjoyment is omnipresent and thus dangerous; it opens up a dimension beyond phallic enjoyment. But Plato's ways part with psychoanalysis with his commonsense advice that sexual satisfaction is the way to cure hysteria.

11 If it was true that for the ancients (not only for Plato, but also for Hippocrates, Galen, etc.) hysteria originated from the "lack of sex, lack of children" (lack of what a woman wants) and that "sex and children" would magically cure it, the medieval perspective presented the opposite picture: the difficulties of hysteria were rooted precisely in intemperance, connections with demons, copulation with the devil, the secret orgies, unbounded jouissance, and the cure was to be sought in Christian virtue, celibacy, refraining, and so on. Too much enjoyment or the lack of enjoyment? The trouble is that there is no proper measure of enjoyment.

12 A good compendium of various follies uttered by philosophers, from the pre-Socratic times up to Russell, on the subject of women, is to be found in Annegret Stopczyk, ed., *Was die Philosophen über Frauen denken?* (Munich: Matthes and Seitz, 1980).

13 In her first book, *Subjects of Desire* (New York: Columbia University Press, 1987)—a book she should be reminded of—Judith Butler argues a similar point: desire is something philosophy has traditionally either tried to get rid of in order to arrive at pure knowledge, or else something that had to be reduced to philosophical thought and incorporated into its progression. Her close reading of French interpretations of Hegel (Kojève, Hyppolite, Sartre, Lacan, Foucault) tries to isolate a gradual detachment from Hegel, for whom desire was subsumed to a unitary philosophical project and served to determine a subject's self-reflexivity in it. But the gradual departure from Hegel in those readings brought desire to light as something irreducibly heterogeneous and dislocated, a process in which its subject lost the ground of self-reflexive conceptuality. Yet her very title shows a mistaken perspective: the problem with desire is not so much its subject as its object. The object presents the nonreflexive heterogeneous moment; this is what brings about an unsurpassable dislocation of the subject, its bar, and this is the point of Lacan's *objet a*. Subject and desire form a dialectics ("Subversion of the subject and dialectics of desire," says Lacan), while the object is recalcitrant to dialectics and reflexivity.

14 The distinction between *Erkenntnis* and *Wissen* is actually crucial to Hegel as well. One can read the "Introduction" to the *Phenomenology* precisely as a passage from the structures of Erkenntnis to those of Wissen (and its relation to truth).

15 Lacan, "Intervention on Transference," in *Feminine Sexuality*, ed. J. Mitchell and J. Rose, trans. J. Rose (London: Macmillan, 1982), 65.

16 See Slavoj Žižek, *For They Know Not What They Do* (London: Verso, 1991), 142–46.

17 Theodor Adorno, *Drei Studien zu Hegel* (Frankfurt am Main: Suhrkamp, 1971), 9.

18 I owe this suggestion to Jacques-Alain Miller.

19 The formula was proposed by Alain Badiou.

8

**When Surplus
Enjoyment Meets**

Alenka Zupančič   **Surplus Value**

Lacan's theory of discourses (or social bonds) is among other things a monumental and in many respects a groundbreaking answer to the question of the relationship between signifier and enjoyment. This point has already been made by Jacques-Alain Miller: before *The Other Side of Psychoanalysis*, Lacan's conceptual elaborations were based on a fundamental antinomy between signifier and enjoyment.[1] These two terms were either radically opposed (as in *The Ethics of Psychoanalysis*) or else posited as two heterogeneous elements qualified by a certain structural homology (as in *The Four Fundamental Concepts of Psychoanalysis*, where Lacan claims, a propos of the drive, that "something in the apparatus of the body is structured in the same way as the unconscious"—and we know that "the unconscious is structured like speech." We thus have a structural analogy between enjoyment and signifier: the two elements are heterogeneous and remain apart, yet they are related by this structural analogy).

The theory of discourses is something else: it articulates the enjoyment together with the signifier and posits it as an essential element of every discursivity. Moreover, this recognition of the discursive dimension of enjoyment brings forward the political dimension of psychoanalysis: "These reminders are absolutely essential to make at a time when, in talking of the other side of psychoanalysis, the question arises of the place of psychoanalysis in politics. The intrusion into politics can only be made by recognising that the only discourse there is, and not just analytic discourse, is the discourse of *jouissance*, at least when one is hoping for the work of truth from it."[2]

The question of how enjoyment articulates with the signifier, and the fact that it does so, is thus the very point where psychoanalysis intervenes in, "intrudes" into, the political. Lacan makes a point of the fact that enjoyment is (or has become) a political factor, be it in the form of promise ("make another effort, work a little harder, show a little more patience, and you will finally get it!"), or in the form of the imperative "Enjoy!" which often weighs down our contemporary existence in a rather suffocating manner.

But first—how does Lacan, in *Seminar XVII*, succeed in conceptually linking enjoyment with the signifier? Via the following suggestion which he repeats, in different forms, all through the seminar: the loss of the object, the loss of satisfaction, and the emergence of a surplus satisfaction or surplus enjoyment are situated, topologically speaking, in one and the same point: in the intervention of the signifier. Lacan develops this in reference to the notion that Freud introduces in his essay on *Group Psychology*, that is to say, in the work that constitutes precisely an inaugural attempt by Freudian psychoanalysis to think some essential aspects of the social (and the political). The notion at stake is that of the "unary trait" (*einziger Zug*) with which Freud points out a peculiar characteristics of (symbolic) identification. The latter is very different from imaginary imitation of different aspects of the person with which one identifies: in it, the unary trait itself takes over the whole dimension of identification. For example, the person with whom we identify has a peculiar way of pronouncing the letter *r*, and we start to pronounce it in the same way. That's all: there need be no other attempts to behave, dress like this other person, do what she does. Freud himself provides several interesting examples of this kind of identification—for instance, taking up a characteristic cough of another person. Or there is the famous example from a girl's boarding school: one of the girls gets a letter from her secret lover which upsets her and fills her with jealousy, which then takes the form of an hysterical attack. Following this, several other girls in the boarding school succumb to the same hysterical attack: they have known about her secret liaison, envied her her love, and wanted to be like her. Yet, the identification with her took this extraordinary form of identifying with the trait that emerged, in the girl in question, at the moment of the crisis in her relationship.

This example is indeed most instructive. It circumscribes two essential points that Lacan takes up in relation to this Freudian notion. First, although the unary trait can be absolutely arbitrary, its significance for the subject that "picks it up" as the point of identification is of course not arbitrary at all. The uniqueness of the trait springs from the fact that it marks the relation of the subject to satisfaction or enjoyment, that is to say, it marks the point (or the trace) of their conjunction. This is quite apparent in the boarding school example. Something else is also obvious in this example: the hysterical attack of the first girl is the trait (in this case, already a symptom) that commemorates her love affair at the precise point where there is an imminent danger of the girl losing the (beloved) object; hence her jealousy. This is the second important point of emphasis that Lacan picks up from Freud, and which concerns the link between loss, the unary trait, and a supplementary satisfaction. According to Freud, in the event of the loss of the object the investment is transferred to the unary trait that marks this loss; the identification with a unary trait thus occupies the (structural) place of the lost object. Yet, at the same time, this identification (and with it the repeating and reenacting of that trait) becomes itself the source of a supplementary satisfaction.

Lacan transposes this into his conceptual framework by interpreting the unary trait as "the simplest form of mark, which properly speaking is the origin of the signifier" (52). He links the Freudian unary trait to what he writes as S_1. Furthermore, he delinearizes and condenses the moments of loss and supplementary satisfaction or enjoyment into one single moment, moving away from the notion of an original loss (of an object), to a notion of loss which is closer to the notion of *waste*, of a useless surplus or remainder, which is inherent in and essential to jouissance as such. This thinking of loss in terms of "waste" is also what leads him to introduce the reference to the thermodynamic concept of entropy, to which we return below. So, jouissance *is* waste (or loss); it incarnates the very entropy produced by the working of the apparatus of the signifiers. However, precisely as waste, this loss is not simply a lack, an absence, something missing. It is very much there (as waste always is), something to be added to the signifying operations and equations, and to be reckoned with as such. In *Seminar XX*, Lacan will sum up this status of enjoyment as loss-waste by the following canonical definition: "jouissance is what serves no purpose [*La jouissance, c'est ce qui ne sert a rien*]."[3] This is precisely what distinguishes waste from lack: something is there, yet it serves no purpose. What it does, on the other hand, is necessitate repetition, the repetition of the very signifier to which this waste is attached in the form of an essential by-product. "*Jouissance* is what necessitates repetition," says Lacan, and he goes on to show how it is precisely on account of this that jouissance goes against life, beyond the pleasure principle, and takes the form of what Freud called the death drive.

This is indeed a very significant shift in Lacan's conceptualization of jouissance. There is an immediate link between signifier and jouissance: it is by means of the repetition of a certain signifier that we have access to jouissance, and not by means of going beyond the signifier and the symbolic, by transgressing the laws and the boundaries of the signifier. Lacan makes a point of stressing several times that "we are not dealing with a transgression" (56). Let me quote the most significant passage:

> [Enjoyment] only comes into play by chance, an initial contingency, an accident. The living being that turns over normally purrs along with pleasure. If *jouissance* is unusual, and if it is ratified by having the sanction of the unary trait and repetition, which henceforth institutes it as a mark—if this happens, it can only originate in a very minor variation in the sense of *jouissance*. These variations, after all, will never be extreme, not even in the practices I raised before [masochism and sadism]. (56)

So, what do we have here? First an accident, an initial contingency in which a subject encounters a surplus pleasure, that is to say jouissance; this encounter might be unusual in respect to the pleasure principle as norm, yet this does not mean that it is in any way spectacular or colossal. It is unusual, since it represents a deviation from the usual path of pleasure in the direction of jouissance, yet this deviation or divergence is never extreme, not even in what seem to be the most extravagant practices of enjoyment. It is bound to the repetition of the signifier that institutes it as a mark, and in this sense it always remains within the realm of the signifier. The status of jouissance (and of the death drive) is thus essentially that of something intersignifying, so to speak: it takes place, or gives body to, a gap or deviation that is internal to the field of signifiers.

One could say that for the Lacan of *Seminar XVII* jouissance is nothing but the inadequacy of the signifier to itself, that is to say, its inability to function "purely," without producing a useless surplus. More precisely, this inadequacy of the signifier to itself has two names, appears in two different entities, so to speak, which are precisely the two nonsignifying elements in Lacan's schemas of the discourses: the subject and the *objet a*. To put it simply: the subject is the gap as negative magnitude or negative number, in the precise sense in which the Lacanian definition of the signifier puts it. Instead of being something that represents an object for the subject, a signifier is what represents the subject for another signifier. That is to say that subject is the inner gap of the signifier, that which sustains its referential movement. The *objet a*, on the other hand, is a positive waste that gets produced in this movement and that Lacan calls the surplus enjoyment, making it clear that there is no other enjoyment but surplus enjoyment, that is to say that enjoyment as such essentially appears as entropy.

Let us now first take a look at how all this can be seen in the functioning of the master's discourse as a fundamental form of discursivity.

The Master's Discourse

$$\frac{S_1}{\$} \rightarrow \frac{S_2}{a}$$

In reading the master's discourse, as well as in reading all the other discourses, we must start from what constitutes its fundamental impossibility. All four discourses revolve around a central impossibility: mastery, education, analysis—the famous "impossible professions," characterized as such already by Freud (and Lacan adds to this list of impossible professions also "inciting desire," which relates to the hysteric's discourse). Lacan circumscribes the fundamental impossibility that determines the master's discourse by pointing out that it is strictly impossible for the master as subject to *faire marcher son monde* (make the world around him run). To make people work, he says, is even more exhausting than it is to do the work oneself. And the master never does this. Instead, he gives a sign (master signifier), and everybody starts running.

$$\frac{S_1}{\$} \rightarrow \frac{S_2}{}$$

This part of the schema is thus the very formula of a "signifier represents the subject for another signifier." In sociopolitical terms it could be also read as: it is impossible to establish any sufficient reason for a master to be the master. There is always a gap or a leap involved here (which is precisely where the hysteric attacks the master), an arbitrariness on account of which a concrete subject-master is instituted by the signifier, and draws its power not from any of his or her inner abilities, but solely from this signifier itself. We know that in the context of new (democratic) masters, it is precisely this leap that is under the imperative of disintegrating into something linear and, above all, accountable (counting the votes, knowledge, skill, wealth), as well as being filled in with the question of merit, substituted for the chain of reasons. The modern form of the social bond is largely determined by the imperative (call it unattainable ideal) of commensurability between the (master) signifier and the subject.

What about the other part of the schema, which concerns the relationship between the signifiers and surplus enjoyment?

$$\frac{S_1}{} \rightarrow \frac{S_2}{a}$$

Lacan illustrates this part by introducing the thermodynamic notion of entropy. In a famous passage, he invites us to imagine the following scene. We are invited to descend 500 meters with a weight of 80 kilos on our back and, once we have descended, to go back up. It is clear that while performing this operation we will sweat our guts out and will be under the impression that we have performed some serious work. Yet, if we overlay signifiers of the theory of energetics on this exercise, we'll get an astonishing result: namely, that no work was done, that the performed work equals zero. For Lacan, entropy names this fact of loss, waste, or, considered from another angle, pure surplus, which he designates as small *a*.

However, we must be very careful in understanding this example. The idea we might get from it is that we have, on the one hand, real physical work and, on the other, the signifiers that fail to account for this work, the loss (or entropy) being the amount of physical work not accounted for. Yet, this kind of duality (which might indeed be found in earlier Lacan) is emphatically not what he aims at here. There is no pure physical work at the outset of this process, the only pure work is precisely the element of entropy *produced* by it. In order to see this more clearly, we must remember that what we have at the outset is a signifying knowledge (S_2), propelled to work by the master-signifier.

$S_1 \rightarrow S_2$

In other words, what we have is savoir faire, know-how, or, more precisely, knowing-how-to-do, knowledge at work, (signifying) knowledge and work as originally bound together (S_2). We could also formulate this Lacanian claim by saying that work is originally structured as a signifying network.

In the master's discourse, the master signifier induces something similar to the process of the distillation of knowledge (as savoir faire): knowledge becomes detached from the work with which it is bound up upon entering this discourse and is attached instead to the master signifier.

> It is here that you have the entire effort to isolate what is called *episteme*. It's a funny word, I don't know if you've ever given it much thought—"putting oneself in the right position", in short it's the same word as "*Verstehen*". It is all about finding the position that makes it possible for knowledge to become the master's knowledge. The entire function of the *episteme* in so far as it is specified as transmissible knowledge—see Plato's dialogues—is always borrowed from the techniques of craftsmen, that is to say of serfs. It is a matter of extracting the essence of this knowledge in order for it to become the master's knowledge. (21)

Lacan lays great emphasis on this point: a knowledge that "does not know itself" and that works passes into articulated knowledge that can be written down and thought independently of the work which it is bound up with at the outset. This is why Lacan can go on to make the rather surprising claim that what is thus being stolen from the slave (and appropriated by the master) is not the slave's work, but his knowledge.

This, for Lacan, is the real spoliation and alienation at work in this discourse. On the other hand work as such, "pure work," is strictly speaking the result, the product, the fall-out of this operation. The product of the master's discourse is surplus work, work as surplus (and, at the same time, as "pure work"). Surplus work is the element of entropy that appears as the positive correlate of a subject who appears as a negative magnitude of the symbolic.

$$\$ \quad a$$

The lower level of the master's discourse displays precisely this: there is a (non)relationship between the negative magnitude brought about by the intervention of the signifier ($\$$), and that other negativity that this system produces as a waste or surplus (a), on account of which the whole of the system never exactly equals the sum of its parts. The a, the surplus enjoyment, can thus also be read as work that seems to go to waste and that nobody knows what to do with—except for trying to regulate it through the science of ethics.[4]

The pure work is the entropy of this system (of the master's discourse), its point of loss, something that wouldn't be there were the result equal to the sum of its elements, something that wouldn't be there if the self-referential work of the signifiers were to function perfectly, without that negative magnitude ($\$$) on account of which the apparatus of signifiers is also the apparatus of enjoyment.

This brings us to another crucial point that I would like to stress before leaving the master's discourse: in this seminar Lacan often poses (and presupposes) a certain equivalence between work and enjoyment, and this is what makes it possible for him to directly relate his theory of the discourses to some aspects of Marxian theory. There is something in the status of work (or labor) which is identical to the status of enjoyment, namely, that it essentially appears as entropy, as loss, or as an unaccounted-for surplus (by-product) of signifying operations. (It is needless to stress that this structural link between work and enjoyment has absolutely nothing to do with "enjoying one's work" or "enjoying working," which presuppose the work to be the means of enjoyment. Lacan's point, on the contrary, is that signifying knowledge is the means of work and/or of enjoyment.)[5] Lacan's further point is that in the master's discourse this entropic surplus element incarnates its inherent obstacle or impossibility and calls for repetition.

To recapitulate the four fundamental features of the master's discourse:

1. We have the prima facie dimension of symbolic castration—power is bestowed upon the subject by a master signifier; it comes and determines him from the outside, quite independently of the question of his "real being."
2. We therefore have a pure negative magnitude (or incommensurability) as the truth of this discourse, in other words, not only that the subject is but that which the master signifier represents for another signifier; at the same time, the truth (or essence) of the master signifier is nothing else than this internal gap, its inadequacy to itself, the fact that it can be what it is only via a minimal difference toward itself.
3. In the place of the other we have the signifying knowledge at work, subjected to what I am calling the distillation of knowledge from work. Knowledge binds with the master signifiers, thus:
4. We have, as product of this discourse, a pure surplus work or surplus enjoyment, a positive waste, which is not exactly the unaccounted-for work, but rather the result of the knowledge-at-work being accounted for and articulated. This is the point of the coincidence of loss and surplus, a coincidence that is essential to the Lacanian notion of the *objet a*.

The Hysteric's Discourse

$$\frac{\$}{a} \rightarrow \frac{S_1}{S_2}$$

The hysteric's discourse could perhaps best be described as a sort of "objection of conscience"—a reminder (often in the form of a symptom) that the apparatus $S_1 \rightarrow S_2$ does not exhaust the integrity of the discourse, that, in the end, it does not come out without a remainder or surplus, and that it is blind to its own truth. The hysteric's discourse is the discourse of the subject (as agent) who bases her revolt on the following grand narrative, which is also a perspectival illusion: the master signifier pushes the subject under the bar, suppresses it, conceals it, and builds its mastery on that concealment. The perspectival illusion involved here concerns the fact that both terms actually appear simultaneously, and that the subject itself (precisely as embodiment of the inherent gap of the signifier) is more a result of the inaugural signifying gesture than of something that simply exists before it or independently of it.

We saw before that the starting point of the master's discourse is precisely the impossibility for anything like a subject to actually run or propel discursive reality. It is this very impossibility that seems, in the hysteric's discourse, to suddenly become a possibility, for the subject now appears as the agent of the discourse. However, what is at stake in this discourse, which is very much a *reaction* to the master's discourse, is rather that the subject is affirmed as an (otherwise) secret agent of the agent, its cause (or the cause of the cause), as the real motivation of the motivation, that is to say of S_1.

$$\$ \rightarrow S_1$$

Here the essential impossibility related to this discourse comes into play (namely that of "inciting desire"), for if the subject is to function as the cause of the cause, it is by becoming the cause of the (other's) desire.

According to Lacan, the hysteric's discourse is the only discourse that actually produces knowledge. On a slightly different level, one could also say that the hysteric usually puts forward a few fundamental theses, which I propose to sum up as follows: "An injustice is being done to the subject," "the Master is incompetent," "The signifier always fails to account for the truth," and "Satisfaction is always a false satisfaction." Let us take a closer look at these theses.

Half jokingly one might say that hysteria is an allergy to S_1, and that it appears in the name of its repressed truth. The hysteric's discourse often appears as discourse about injustice, and enthusiastically pleads for the rights of that which remains outside or at the edge of the signifier as symbolic. The complaint about injustice is of course usually formulated as an empirical claim, and as such, it could be "true" or "false." Yet, and more importantly, with the hysteric this is also always a structural complaint (this is why it often seems that hysteric subjects can find something to complain about in every situation); it is structural because it is based upon, and points at, a constitutive fact of every signifying discursivity: namely the incommensurability between the signifier and the subject which I pointed out when discussing the master's discourse (to put it simply: the incommensurability between what I am personally and my symbolic role or function). This gap, this negative magnitude, constitutive of the signifier and the symbolic order, is, as it were, the transcendental incommensurability (or "injustice") on which the hysteric relies when making her empirical complaints and accusations, and from which these latter draw their discursive power. For, false as these accusations might be empirically, on the transcendental level they are always true; they point toward an essential feature of symbolic discursivity as such.

This is why, here we come to the second thesis, the hysteric likes to point out that the emperor is naked. The master, this respected S_1, admired and obeyed by everyone, is in reality a poor, rather impotent chap, who in no way lives up to his symbolic function. He is weak, he often doesn't even know what is going on around him, and he indulges in "disgusting" secret enjoyment; he (as a person) is unable to control himself or anybody else.

In popular jargon, this attitude of attacking and undermining the masters, pointing at their weaknesses, is usually said to be castrating. Yet, although it does indeed have to do with the question of castration, it is much more ambiguous than this popular wisdom implies. The hysteric's indignation about the master really being just this miserable human being, full of faults and flaws, does not aim at displaying how castrated he is; on the contrary, it is a complaint about the fact that the master is precisely *not castrated enough*—if he were, he would utterly coincide with his symbolic function, but as it is, he nevertheless also enjoys, and it is this enjoyment that weakens his symbolic power and irritates the hysteric. In this sense, the hysteric is much more revolted by the weakness of power than by power itself, and the truth of her or his basic complaint about the master is usually that the master is not master enough. In the person of a master, the hysteric thus attacks precisely those rights she is otherwise so eager to protect, namely what remains or exists of the master besides the master signifier. In other words, the target of the attack on the master is his surplus enjoyment, *a*. This is what is superfluous, what should not be there, and what, on the obverse side of the same coin, represents the point where the master is accused of enjoying at the subject's expense.

The next thesis of the hysteric's is that the signifier always fails to account for the truth. There is an important and massive affinity between the hysteric's discourse and the mistrust of the symbolic (of language) as medium of truth. This failure extends from the classical hysterical question, "This is what you are saying to me, but what is it that you really want?" via a rejection of symbolic power as ungrounded in (subjective) truth, proclaiming symbolic forms and rituals as empty, to a direct wager on truth as the real that evades all of the symbolic. The question why the hysteric insists so much on the claim that the signifier always betrays the "true truth," that it misses the truth in the very act of formulating it, is an interesting one. It seems that the hysteric places the whole truth precisely in that Lacanian "other half" of truth that is never covered by the signifier.

In *Seminar XVII*, Lacan formulates this notorious and persistent theme of his teaching: "The only way in which to evoke the truth is by indicating that it is only accessible through a half-saying [*mi-dire*], that it cannot be said completely, for the reason that beyond this half there is nothing to say. That is all that can be said. . . . One is not speaking of the unsayable, whatever the pleasure this seems to give certain people" (57–58). The way Lacan conceptualizes this claim in *Seminar XVII* could perhaps be most simply summed up as follows. If truth is accessible only through a half-saying, this is because of its specific topology, because truth is essentially a place: the place, to be precise, where the signifier touches, or holds on to, castration (and vice versa), the place of their constitutive conjunction, the lack (or the negative magnitude) being the very pillar of the signifier. In other words, the whole truth would be the signifier + castration/lack. Yet, since the latter is constitutive of and inherent to the signifier, and not something existing beside it, the truth is never "whole." At the same time, this inherent lack is precisely the gap that enables the "deviations" in the direction of (surplus) jouissance, which I have referred to above, to take place; it is, as Lacan puts it, when something strikes on the walls of this lack, or gap, that enjoyment is created. In this perspective, the other half of truth could simply be said to be jouissance. Yet, again, not in the sense of the whole truth being something like "the signifier + jouissance," but in the sense of jouissance being the inherent impasse or impossibility of the signifier itself. These remarks can perhaps shed some light on the hysteric's position concerning the question of truth and signifiers.

The hysteric loves truth and wants to have it whole. To this end, the hysteric subject tends to disjoin the conjunction of the signifier and the lack, to situate them on two different levels, and to declare the castration/lack to be the truth of truth. The truth of truth—and thus what reveals symbolic truths as "lies"—is the lack as *real*. The other variant of this thesis is that surplus enjoyment (or indeed any kind of enjoyment) is by definition false, which simply means that it is never capable of utterly compensating, or covering, the real of the lack. The hysteric places the whole truth precisely in that half, where there is nothing (more) to say. At the same time, he or she goes to great lengths to make it speak. The hysteric often offers herself as articulation of truth and, instead of speaking it out, enacts it in her own being, by lending it her body in the form of a symptom.

This brings us to the hysteric's fourth thesis, which concerns the question of satisfaction: the latter is always false, inadequate; that is, it is disproportionate in respect to the negative magnitude that founds any discourse. "That is not it!" is the well-known motto of hysterics when it comes to matters of satisfaction, and the other notorious feature is the emphasis on renunciation, loss, nonsatisfaction, sacrifice. The hysteric is the guardian of the negative, of the incommensurable and the impossible. The well-known problem of this stance is that it fails to see that this renunciation and sacrifice themselves very quickly become a source of surplus enjoyment or satisfaction. The hysteric is satisfied with nothing, in both possible meanings of this expression. It is not only that nothing can satisfy him or her, but that the nothing itself can be an important source of satisfaction. This is why, in Lacan's schema of the discourse, surplus enjoyment (*a*) is in the place of truth.

Consequently, one of the important things that the hysteric's discourse bears witness to is that surplus enjoyment cannot be eliminated from discourse, however hard one tries; that a "not enough" always meets its "too much," which only further complicates things; that the problem is not only a lost, inaccessible enjoyment, but also a surplus enjoyment that we cannot exactly get rid of. On a certain level, the dreams or, more precisely, the ethical ideal of the hysteric is that a discursive system would work by relying only on its constitutive negative magnitude or loss: this way, things would be clean, and truth would immediately coincide with the real as impossible. However, a discourse does not only lean upon an impossible, but also constantly produces the impossible in the form of surplus enjoyment, which it often doesn't know what to do with.

The University Discourse

$$\frac{S_2}{S_1} \rightarrow \frac{a}{\$}$$

Let us now move on to the university discourse, which could be understood as the predominant social bond that we live in today, following some of Lacan's own indications that point, among other things, to a fundamental affinity between the university discourse and the capitalist economy. I will thus proceed by comparing what Lacan refers to as the discourses of "the old and the new masters."

What Lacan recognizes in the university discourse is a new and reformed discourse of the master. In its elementary form, it is a discourse that is pronounced from the place of supposedly neutral knowledge, the truth of which (hidden below the bar) is Power, that is, the master signifier. The constitutive lie of this discourse is that it disavows its performative dimension: it always presents, for example, that which leads to a political decision, founded on power, as a simple insight into the factual state of things (or public polls, objective reports, and so on).

Jean-Léon Beauvois provides a good example of this in his discussion of a series of sociopsychological experiments, which involve precisely this paradigm of the authority camouflaging itself behind what is presented as a free, objective choice.[6] We confront the other from a position of a certain (social) authority, with a choice between two actions, one of which he is most reluctant to do, while making it known, at the same time, that this is precisely the action we expect from him. Second, we keep repeating that the choice is entirely his. Given these two circumstances, the following will happen: he will do exactly what we want him to do, which is contrary to his (previously tested) convictions. Furthermore, because of the configuration of free choice, he will rationalize his action by altering these very convictions. In other words, instead of viewing the action that was so perfidiously imposed upon him as something bad that he had to do (since the authority demanded it), he will convince himself that the bad thing is actually *good*, since this is the only way for him to justify the fact that he has freely (and rationally) chosen his course of action.

This is one face of the university discourse. I will concentrate here on another face, which is more directly economic and links it, as suggested before, to the logic of capitalism and to its specific way of dealing with enjoyment. Several authors have already pointed out that we live in a "society of enjoyment." Not simply in the sense that we massively indulge in all sorts of enjoyment while neglecting or bypassing social duties and responsibilities, but rather in the sense that enjoyment itself has become our most prominent and inexorable duty.[7] I propose to explore this thesis from a specific angle: through a reading of the university discourse—following Lacan's suggestion—in the light of how it modifies the nature and the status of enjoyment (in relation to the master's discourse).

In discussing the master's discourse, we've seen that a distillation of knowledge (as know-how) is central to it: knowledge becomes a pure signifying knowledge, while pure work is produced by this discourse as its "indivisible remainder"—as waste or loss, something that is not covered by the signifier, something that does not count (but can, precisely because of this, appear as pure sign of the prestige of the master—prestige in the sense that it is prestigious to take on something that serves no purpose and is not immediately involved in the economy of exchange).

Now, how does this change on the ground of the economy of the reformed discourse of the master, of modern capitalism? To put it simply —and as Marx has already pointed out—this pure work, work as such, itself has to appear on the market as a commodity for sale. The very existence of capital hinges on this point. Capital emerges only when the possessor of the means of production finds, on the market, a *free* worker selling his labor power as object.[8] This is something new, something that emerges only in a specific historico-economic stage. In other words, labor power as *pure* (labor) is already a result of a complex signifying operation: in itself and before that operation, pure work is never *pure* work, but is something closer to the slave's "knowledge at work." Pure work is not what is originally given, and then lost when one lays the apparatus of signifiers over it: it is a product of this operation. Labor as commodity is labor as object. But this also means that the entropic element (*a*) changes its place in the social bond. It now—and only now—appears in the place of the Other, which Lacan describes as "the place of more or less tolerable exploitation."

A very significant implication of this shift is that, in order for capitalist exploitation to function, the entropy or loss, the amount of work not accounted for, or simply not counted, has, precisely, to start to be counted (and "valued"). This is the whole point of the surplus value that Marx conceives as the core and driving force of capitalism. The fact that labor-power appears as commodity or object is what makes this possible. The revolution related to capitalism is none other than this: it founds the means of making the waste count. Surplus value is nothing else but the waste or loss that counts, and the value of which is constantly being added to or included in the mass of capital.

$$S_2 \rightarrow a$$

The shift to this new discourse is founded upon two major changes that characterize it. The first is that we are no longer dealing with a configuration where everything adds up (or should add up) to the same total (plus, of course, the element of entropy). The total is increasing, and this is called accumulation of capital. What makes this accumulation possible is, as Lacan himself puts it, that the surplus enjoyment starts to be counted.[9] The entropic element is itself transformed into value and added as supplement. The second point is that we are no longer dealing with the form of repetition characteristic of the master's discourse. Instead, we have an endless movement where the otherness linked to the surplus (enjoyment) is smoothly and constantly reintegrated into the mass of capital, which needs this constant differentiation and reappropriation of the differential as a condition of its increasing power. Marx summarizes this in terms of the value becoming the subject (we could say the agent) of the process.[10] It is operating and accumulating at the place of S_2 by appropriating what is working at the place of *a*.

Lacan formulates this shift as follows: "Once a higher level has been passed, surplus *jouissance* is no longer surplus *jouissance* but is inscribed simply as a value to be inscribed in or deducted from the totality of whatever it is that is accumulating—what is accumulating from out of an essentially transformed nature" (92). In this passage from the level below to the level above, jouissance changes its nature, and Lacan goes so far as to call it now "an imitation surplus *jouissance*" (or "a semblance surplus *jouissance*").

What does this expression mean? It means that the valorization of surplus enjoyment eliminates or neutralizes the element of obstruction at work in surplus jouissance, the element that, in the master's discourse, binds enjoyment with repetition. Repetition is, in its essence, the repetition of enjoyment as impossible (which is not to say as nonexisting: enjoyment exists precisely as "impossible"). I would say that this is what Lacan has in mind when he says that the master's discourse grapples with a fundamental impotence concerning the creation of a joint or link between surplus enjoyment and the master's truth (the split subject). Repetition could be seen precisely as a symptom of this difficulty. Lacan goes on to claim that with the passage to the university discourse (and to the logic of capital) "the impotence [*impuissance*] of this conjunction is all of a sudden emptied. Surplus value combines with capital—not a problem, they are homogeneous, we are in the field of values. Moreover, we are all up to our necks in it, in these blessed times in which we live" (207).

The problem at the very core of surplus enjoyment is thus "emptied"; everything runs smoothly, we are enjoying and having the time of our life. Except that this is not exactly the case. Feelings of frustration grow, and the imperative of enjoyment becomes more and more suffocating.

Capitalism, in its junction with the university discourse, is above all the discourse of the possible. Its fundamental slogan could be expressed in these terms: "Impossible is not possible." Just think of how companies like to advertise themselves with the motto: "Impossible is not in our vocabulary." Yet the psychical counterpart of this—on the side of the subjects falling out of this discourse as its products—is either a general ennui, or alternation of apathy and frenetic activity. Why? It is not enough to say that desire is awakened only by an obstacle and sustained by an element of the impossible. What is at stake is the problem of the framework of enjoyment, which collapses in upon itself. Lacan speaks of imitation surplus jouissance. Does this imply an opposition between authentic and nonauthentic enjoyment? No, at least not in the sense in which an authentic enjoyment is also being sold to us as yet another form of the possible, as some supposedly lost original state of harmony where all things added up perfectly.

One of the central points of psychoanalysis is the following discovery: jouissance, the practice of enjoyment, is what gives form to some fundamental impossibility—this is what distinguishes jouissance from pleasure. And what is "imitation (of) enjoyment"? In Lacan's time, the products that so clearly and directly answer this question were not yet as omnipresent as they are today (and I will come to this in a moment). What was present was a slogan that appeared in the name of freedom and in which Lacan immediately saw something of a deadlock: *Jouir sans entraves!* (Enjoy without hindrance!) He saw this so quickly because in his theory (and practice) he'd already come to the insight that jouissance as such *is* a hindrance, and that "to enjoy without hindrance" amounts to nothing else but "enjoyment without enjoyment," that is, without that which is constitutive of enjoyment. And is not "enjoyment without enjoyment" precisely the formula prescribed to enjoyment in our societies? Sweets without sugar, fat-free pork roasts, coffee without caffeine—these are all excellent examples of imitation surplus enjoyment in the most literal sense of the term. They are also very good examples of a short circuit between enjoyment and abstinence, so characteristic of capitalist economies. Just think of how to spend is to save, and to save is to spend. If I want to save, say, $100, I have to buy this computer (instead of that one); on the other hand, if I don't buy anything and just keep the money, I save nothing.

If we come to perceive this kind of enjoyment more and more as being "empty," the reason is not that it is deprived of its full substance, since the image of enjoyment as something full and substantial is in itself fantasmatic, and the will to aim directly at the pure substance of enjoyment is the obverse side of the same coin that I was describing above. The problem is that this kind of enjoyment without enjoyment is deprived of the very impossibility that structures the enjoyment and gives it its form (also its social form). Removed from the above-mentioned products is what binds them to what Freud called the death drive— their (potential) danger, the limit that they set to pleasure or, to put it in another way, the fact that enjoyment is precisely the inherent limit of pleasure.

The inexorable imperative "Enjoy!" is being systematically accompanied by the warning (well known, for example, to the smokers): "Enjoyment will kill you. Enjoyment is damaging to your health"—that is to say, by the reminder of the obstructive element at work in any enjoyment. And this double bind is then followed by the promise of salvation which will separate these two facets: we produce and offer harmless enjoyment, enjoyment without the element of obstruction, *jouissance sans entraves* or, to put it yet another way, entropy-free enjoyment, enjoyment as pure value.

The valorization of enjoyment is part of a new process of what I previously called distillation. In this discourse, it is no longer knowledge that is being detached from the entropic element of work/enjoyment, it is this very entropic element itself that is being detached, in the name of knowledge and value, from its own entropy or negativity. What is being exploited and squeezed in every imaginable way is now precisely our enjoyment as an immediate source of surplus value. For if—as I argued before and to put it simply—contemporary exploitation of enjoyment and excess operates by eliminating the obstructive element in it, this by no means signifies that this obstructive element simply disappears from the face of the earth. It means only that it keeps reappearing in new, unexpected configurations, which can then in turn be subjected to the extrication of surplus value. Drives are plastic; just let them come up with another symbolic (or imaginary) configuration of enjoyment that can then be detached from enjoyment per se, cashed in as "positive value," and of course sold back to us as "life-style" (of enjoyment). Yet what at the same time drops out below is precisely a pure negativity: the death drive as incarnated in the subject who is in no way the master of knowledge and value accumulated in this discourse, and even less the master of enjoyment, but who is their fall-off, excrement, the refuse of his or her own (ideological) value, refuse of the very value so generously attributed to the subject in this discourse (I am referring of course to the ideological celebration of free subjectivity).

$$\frac{a}{\$}$$

If we now go a step further (or rather a step backward, to the left side of the university discourse), we will be able to see how this emptied impossibility and impotence (or, from another perspective, this omnipresent possibility) goes hand in hand with an even more massive and striking impotence and impossibility, indicated by the position of the master signifier in this discourse.

$$\frac{S_2}{S_1}$$

In Lacan's words: "What is striking, and what no one seems to see, is that from that moment on, by virtue of the fact that the clouds of impotence have been aired, the master signifier only appears even more unassailable, precisely in its impossibility. Where is it? How can it be named? How can it be located—other than through its murderous effects, of course. Denounce imperialism? But how can this little mechanism be stopped?" (207). Is this double bind not the most striking figure of today's so-called world order? There is certainly no shortage of unsatisfied people, also ready to show this nonsatisfaction in a number of various ways. But there is also a general feeling of utter impotence, not only as to the effect of this demonstration of nonsatisfaction, but also as to the question of whom exactly to attack. Who, for instance, is globalism?

The capitalist production (also in its social dimension) is a constant production of otherness, and a constant valorization of this otherness, of its transformation into a value. Capitalism is a major producer of differences, as well as a major leveler or equalizer of these same differences. This is what makes it the greatest promoter of liberalism and of all kinds of liberties and rights (especially the right to be different), and the greatest deactivator of any real liberating or subversive potential of these differences. Let me again resort to a quote, this time from Brian Massumi, who formulated this very well.

> The more varied, and even erratic, the better. Normalcy starts to lose its hold. The regularities start to loosen. This loosening of normalcy is part of capitalism's dynamic. It's not a simple liberation. It's capitalism's own form of power. It's no longer disciplinary institutional power that defines everything, it's capitalism's power to produce variety—because markets get saturated. Produce variety and you produce a niche market. The oddest of affective tendencies are okay—as long as they pay. Capitalism starts intensifying or diversifying affect, but only in order to extract surplus-value. It

hijacks affect in order to intensify profit potential. It literally valorizes affect. The capitalist logic of surplus-value production starts to take over the relational field that is also the domain of political ecology, the ethical field of resistance to identity and predictable paths. It's very troubling and confusing, because it seems to me that there's been a certain kind of convergence between the dynamic of capitalist power and the dynamic of resistance.[11]

This insightful passage condenses very well the two basic points that, following Lacan, I think qualify the now predominant social bond.

1. The hijacking, diversifying and exploiting of what Massumi calls the affect and what Lacan calls (surplus) jouissance, by valorizing it or recognizing it as a potentially infinite source of surplus value.
2. The paradoxical convergence of power and resistance, the growing impossibility of delimiting them, the unassailability of the master signifier, which account for the frustrating impotence of any resistance.

Let us stop briefly at some recent modifications that have affected the prevalent postmodern imperative of happiness, and which function as the ideological means of exploitation of (surplus) enjoyment.

First of all, one should point out that happiness is a weighty duty, much weightier perhaps than any patriotic duty. Consider the following striking passage that comes from one of the promoters of the importance of happiness, Dennis Prager: "We tend to think that we owe it to ourselves to be as happy as we can be. And this is true. But happiness is far more than personal concern. It is also a moral obligation. . . . We owe it to our husband or wife, our fellow workers, our children, our friends, indeed to everyone who comes into our lives, to be as happy as we can be."[12] Instead of mocking this passage or taking it as a perverse attempt to justify a selfish pursuit of personal happiness and satisfaction by presenting it as emanating from a universal moral duty, we would do better to take it quite literally. What does it say? That it is our social duty to be happy, and that this is far from easy. It is hard to be happy. Which is very true. Something runs persistently against it. The moment our social duty largely coincides with what we are supposed to want anyway (happiness), it becomes abundantly clear that it is far from clear what we actually want. Be happy, it's only up to you, nobody stands in your way any longer. As subjects, we are brutally and massively confronted with the impasse of our enjoyment (and desire), almost as in a gigantic, world-scale burlesque psychoanalysis. Before you come around complaining about anything, try to resolve your personal problems, since it is they, and only they, that stand in the way of your happiness! This is a very powerful and ingenious ideological maneuver which, in the first move, makes the traditionally personal issue of happiness a public, social, and political concern, makes it an inseparable part of these concerns, and then, in a second move, pushes it back to our personal lives precisely as inseparable from these concerns. That is to say, in a caricature, that the global economic problems will be resolved when we all resolve our personal problems and frustrations.

However, it is also a fact that this burlesque social psychoanalysis was at least partly interrupted by September 11 or, more precisely, by what was made of it. On the ideological level, terrorism (as "our common" and dangerous enemy) shifted the logic of happiness into a new form of a more traditional configuration: there is something objective that stands in the way of our happiness; personal sacrifices will have to be made (economic as well as the sacrifice of some of our acquired social and private liberties); duty no longer directly coincides with happiness, and nobody is asking us to think positive about terrorism and to make the best of it. To be sure, what we have now is hardly a move forward. Yet something that one might call a repoliticization of the political is emerging. Political struggles and antagonisms are forced to come forward as political struggles and antagonisms, and as much as they still try to hide behind supposedly neutral laws of economy or intelligence reports, this is less and less successful. The political resistance that is also emerging and building up, especially since the beginning of the war in Iraq, will soon face an imminently political decision. Will it rest content with forcing the "democratic masters" to start (again) playing by the rules of the university discourse, demanding that all political decisions be grounded in objective knowledge and follow only from an insight into the factual state of things, and then punishing them when the gap between political decisions and the objective arguments leading to them becomes too apparent, or when the reports on the basis of which political decisions are made turn out to be fabrications? In other words, and to put it in Lacanian terms, will it rest content with pointing out the gap between S_2 (the chain of reasons) and S_1, demanding that it disappear (or become less obvious, i.e., that S_1 be properly hidden under the bar), or will it recognize that it is precisely this gap, on account of which no political decision can ever be *fully* absorbed into the chain of reasons, that is also the condition of possibility of any alternative politics? To put this in the present context: if the reports about Iraqi nuclear weapons had in fact been true, would the decision to attack Iraq have been any less political? No, it would still be a political decision, and precisely as such it could be countered by a different political decision or will. Thus, by pointing up the irreducibility of the gap between S_2 and S_1 in all the forms of discursivity, I don't mean to imply that since no political decision or project can ever be fully justified by or grounded in what precedes it (or in its circumstances), we might as well stop complaining about it and pointing at dirty interests behind it. Or that it doesn't really matter what we do (politically), since whatever we do, this gap will always be there and all political decisions will ultimately always be decisions of Power. On the contrary, it is precisely because of this that it matters very much what we do.

Notes

1 Cf. Jacques-Alain Miller, "Paradigms of *Jouissance*," *Lacanian Ink* 17 (2000): 10–47.
2 Jacques Lacan, *Le séminaire, livre XVII: L'envers de la psychanalyse*, ed. J.-A. Miller (Paris: Seuil, 1991), 90. Parenthetical citations in the text list page numbers in the French edition.
3 Lacan, *The Seminar of Jacques Lacan, Book XX: Encore or On Feminine Sexuality, the Limits of Love and Knowledge*, ed. J.-A. Miller, trans. B. Fink (New York: Norton, 1998), 10.
4 Lacan says, "When we read Aristotle we have the suspicion that the master's relation to the slave really presented him with a problem. . . . We can see clearly what is at stake, it is what, in the name of surplus jouissance, the master receives from the slave's work. . . . The problems of ethics here, suddenly, start to abound—the *Nicomachean Ethics*, the *Eudemian Ethics*, and several other works of moral reflection. It is irresolvable. Nobody knows what to do with this surplus *jouissance*. In order to successfully place a sovereign good at the heart of the world, you need to be as embarrassed as a fish with an apple" (204).
5 Lacan says, "The *a*, as such, is strictly speaking what follows from the fact that, at

its origin, knowledge is reduced to an articulation of signifiers. This knowledge is a means of *jouissance*. And, I repeat, when it is at work, what it produces is entropy. This entropy, this point of loss, is the sole point, the sole regular point at which we have access to the nature of *jouissance*" (56–57).

6   Jean-Léon Beauvois, *Traité de la servitude libérale: Analyse de la soumission* (Paris: Dunod, 1994).
7   See Todd McGowan, *The End of Dissatisfaction? Jacques Lacan and the Emerging Society of Enjoyment* (Albany: SUNY Press, 2004).
8   In *Capital* (Harmondsworth: Penguin, 1990), Marx writes, "Labor-power can appear on the market as a commodity only if, and in so far as, its possessor, the individual whose labor-power it is, offers it for sale or sells it as commodity. In order that its possessor may sell it as a commodity, he must have it at his disposal, he must be the free proprietor of his own labor-capacity, hence of his person" (171).
9   According to Lacan, "Something changed in the master's discourse at a certain point in history. We are not going to break our backs finding out if it was because of Luther, or Calvin, or some unknown traffic of ships around Genoa, or in the Mediterranean Sea, or anywhere else, for the important point is that on a certain day surplus pleasure became calculable, could be counted" (207).
10 Marx writes, "In truth, however, value is here the subject of a process in which, while constantly assuming the form in turn of money and commodities, it changes its own magnitude, throws off surplus value from itself considered as original value, and thus valorizes itself independently. For the movement in the course of which it adds surplus value is its own movement, its valorization is therefore self-valorization. By virtue of being value, it has acquired the occult ability to add value to itself" (*Capital*, 255).
11 Brian Massumi, "Navigating Movements," in *Hope*, ed. M. Zournazi (New York: Routledge, 2003), 224.
12 Dennis Prager, *Happiness Is a Serious Problem* (New York: HarperCollins, 1998), 3.

9

Enjoy Your Stay: Structural Change in *Seminar XVII*

Oliver Feltham

The whole of Nature is one sole Individual whose parts, that is, all bodies, vary in an infinity of modes, without any change of the whole Individual. — Spinoza

There is a problem in Lacan's *Seminar XVII*. It runs as follows:

— Lacan distinguishes four different discourses which implicate the speaking being; together, they structure the social field and determine everything that can be said, practiced, and instituted. Lacan claims that they form the arches of reality.[1]
— These discourses are said to consist of the relationships between four terms — the split subject $, the master signifier S_1, the treasury of other signifiers S_2, and enjoyment a, which occupy four distinct places — "agent," "other," "production," and "truth."
— These discourses, although they may coexist, are said to emerge at different points throughout history.

The first question raised by this conceptual construction is, quite simply, What determines the emergence of these discourses, given that they can each be analyzed as constituted from the same combinatory of terms in the same order? That is, the formal restraint on Lacan's structural analysis is double: not only must the same four terms occur, but also in the same order. Without the latter restraint one can generate twenty-four combinations with four variables and four places. What then determines the emergence of these ordered discourses such that there are four of them and four alone?[2]

Here lies the problem: Lacan has two if not three different answers to this question: in one he sounds like Hegel (whom he continually criticizes), in the other he sounds like Freud (whom he criticizes for his mythical geneses of structure), and very occasionally he sounds like Thomas Kuhn (whom he never mentions), or an early Alain Badiou (which is anachronistic). What then is the correct or, rather, Lacanian answer?

In at least one stratum of his thought Lacan is a structuralist, insofar as he recognizes the following (and this will be a minimal definition):

— The *ontological priority* of structure; that is, speech acts and subject positions depend on and inscribe themselves within these four structures or discourses.[3]
— The *immanent self-determination* of structure—these structures in turn do not depend on or inscribe themselves within anything higher; there is no englobing metastructure.
— The *total coverage* of structure; every speech act and subject position is inscribed in these structures.[4]
— The *exclusion of genetic explanations* of phenomena; that is, if a social phenomenon or institution is determined by one of the four structures, then there is no sense in trying to identify its historical origin.[5]

This last point leads us to the question of history. According to the structuralist, a series of facts can only be assigned an origin, a meaning and an orientation, and thus be presented as a "history," insofar as they are already inscribed within a structure. Well before the development of structuralism as a distinct method, Freud had already laid the foundations for such a conception of history in his analysis of the Wolf Man. In this case, Freud discovers the possibility of a retroactive projection of a primal scene—the patient's own intimate history, originating in this primal scene, is thus coordinated by a structure, that of fantasy. In other words, for the structuralist, structure is ontologically prior to history. The fundamental consequence of this principle is that history as the supposition of meaning—or even merely of sequence— within a multiplicity of facts is, in Lacan's words, "a futile search for meaning" (18).

However,

1. if more than one discursive structure can be discerned, and
2. if these structures have not existed from the beginning of time (contingency), and
3. if it is said that one of the structures leads in some manner to another structure, then
4. history as change occurs; that is, there has been structural change.

Our problem can then be reframed: How is it possible to think such structural change without any recourse to a notion of history as sequence? Lacan recognizes the emergence of this problem when he says, "There is not the slightest idea of progress" (122) in what I am articulating here, and "this is not in any sense to be viewed as a series of historical emergences."[6] Moreover, Lacan continually inveighs against Hegel's conception of history—to the point that one suspects it is the very notion of history itself, for Lacan, which is Hegelian.

If the recourse to history as a sequence or external ground for these structures is ruled out, how then can a structure immanently determine its own dissolution and the emergence of a new discourse? In Lacan's own terms, the master's discourse has mutated into its capitalist style. "Why," he asks, "good heavens, is this taking place, and why is it not taking place by chance?" (195).

Of course, Lacan is not alone in having this problem with structural change. If we understand it as the problem of what remains the same across change, and if that change is to have both motivation and destination, then it is an explicit problem of both Marxism and structuralism, of the philosophy of science and aesthetics, of political science and systems theory. It is one of the problems of contemporary philosophy: How is it possible that everything change place and yet some kind of coherency ensue? In the end, it is the problem of history because if we can't answer it, then we have to ask ourselves "Has anything changed?" or "Is there anything new under the sun?"

So, there is a multiplicity of heterogeneous discourses.[7] This multiplicity has not always existed. When it comes to explaining this multiplicity, one cannot admit an external context (such as those that go under the names of "ecosphere" or "complexity" nowadays), because structure is self-sufficient, and one cannot admit a metastructure—one of Lacan's principles being that there is no metalanguage.[8]

What can be done? This problem is intrinsic to the theory of the discourses. Lacan, of course, is quite aware of it: he proposes three different solutions. Our task is then made simpler; it will be a matter of working out whether there is some form of compatibility between the different solutions, or rather a case of kettle logic.

The first solution is that of structural evolution: there is an operation or mechanism internal to each discourse that always tends to produce another discourse. The root of one discourse is thus found in the characteristics of another. This solution itself occurs in several different versions in the seminar: there is the theory of the "quarter turn" via the agent-other operation; there is the theory of "inversion" via production; and then there is the theory of "perpetual dynamism."

The second solution is that of the contingent encounter of discourses; it is just such an encounter, for example, between the master's discourse and the hysteric's discourse (in the form of philosophy), that produces another discourse, that of the university.

The third solution offered by Lacan to this problem of structural change—and it is rare—is the theory of the cut: there is an absolute cut between each discourse such that each emerges as a novelty.[9]

I shall examine each of these solutions as they occur in the seminar.

Solution I: Structural Evolution

First, there is the solution of structural evolution, which comes in three versions.

Type A: The Theory of the Operational Quarter Turn

The theory of the operational quarter turn states that there is an operation internal to one discourse that produces another discourse. In his initial explanations of the master's discourse, Lacan argues that it can be found structuring the speech acts and writings usually grouped together under the name "philosophy." He argues that the constitutive operation of philosophy is the theft or expropriation of the slave's knowledge, such as Socrates's interrogation of a slave boy in the *Meno* (20–21, 24, 34, 91, 173). This extraction of the slave's knowledge causes a change to occur in the status of knowledge, a "purification," in Lacan's terms. Lacan later reveals that this operation is actually a transitional operation which produces the university discourse—which he also terms the "modernized" master's discourse. The university discourse is held to structure science, bureaucracy, and state socialism. The operation responsible for the university discourse is a transitional operation because a true master, of course, does not want to know anything about it; all he does is issue commands and demand that, whatever production is at stake, it work.

Lacan begins by employing this theory of the operational quarter turn to support a kind of "historical novel" or even "historical romance" that he unfolds during the seminar: he tells a fascinating story about the development of the "modern" master's discourse. Lacan explicitly recognizes the complications and the risks involved in telling such a story; they lead him to develop alternative solutions to the problem of structural change. But before I go into these complications, let me try to tell you the story.

In the beginning, there was Yahweh, the Old Testament God, pronouncing anathemas through the prophets. Yahweh's condemnations—the S_1 as command or imperative—instituted the master's discourse (158, 179). How? By denouncing something that existed before his arrival—and we can already see that this beginning is complicated in a Derridean sense. Yahweh intervenes against a kind of generalized prostitution of humanity that resided in its myths and rites, in its worshipping of a mixture of the divine and the earthly in a kind of promiscuous cosmic harmony.[10] Lacan translates this into Yahweh's "ferocious ignorance of sexual knowledge."

Then along came philosophy, which caused the master to want to know something about the slave's technical knowledge, to extract this knowledge and so to generate the episteme, or a master's knowledge, and concomitantly its distinction from mere technical knowledge. Philosophy grounds this distinction by arguing that the slave's knowledge is unreflective while the philosopher's is reflective. This suits Lacan, since the master's discourse also schematizes the primordial structure of the speaking being (or the paternal metaphor), whereby the S_2 figures unconscious knowledge, as "knowledge that does not know itself." In terms of philosophy, one can only agree that this extractive institution of reflexivity is one of its fundamental operations; another example is found in the very beginning of Aristotle's *Metaphysics*, where the philosopher is placed in the position of an architect directing workers in a building site—workers who "know not what they do, as fire burns."

After philosophy—our historical novel continues—comes the stage of science. The emergence of science is marked by a further purification of knowledge operated by the setting into doubt of all theoria: that is, by Descartes's cogito (23, 178).[11] Scientific knowledge is not the same thing as Aristotle's theoria, since the former unfolds within a finite centered cosmos, the other within a decentered infinite universe (Lacan's reference is Alexandre Koyré). Once we reach the stage of science, the master's discourse has fully evolved into the university discourse.

This leads me to a parallel strand of the story whereby philosophy, by expropriating the slave's knowledge, anticipates the development of capitalism—Socrates begat Bill Gates (it's in the eyes)—and in *Seminar XVII* at least, Lacan thinks of capitalism as a master's discourse. However, the emergence of capitalism requires that the product of the slave's work—the surplus enjoyment owed to the master—be one day counted and totalized, thus becoming surplus value (92).[12] Note that science is not innocent in this rise of accounting under the reign of number.[13] Lacan then claims—and this is part of his polemic against the Marxist-Leninist view of history—that the capitalist master's discourse can also produce the university discourse via an operational quarter turn. Instead of going under the name of the cogito, the operation goes under that of revolution. You want a revolution?, he says, Voila! You'll get it, things revolve just so, and you get a new form of master, state socialism (34, 37).[14] And everyone lived happily ever after.

Here ends the historical novel as supported by the operational quarter turn. What is the consequence for our problem of history and structure? It's simple: history has a structure; history as a sequence is reinstated insofar as there is an order to the emergence of the discourses—first the master's discourse, then university discourse, then, via the theorem added in "Radiophonie" that both "progressive" and "regressive" quarter turns are possible, the hysteric's discourse, which is followed by and implies the analyst's discourse.

Obviously there are a few gaps here. In Jim Hopkins's terms, the theory is not "epistemically good," because it doesn't explain everything —notably the emergence of the hysteric's discourse. The good news is that Lacan does have an answer: he posits that the hysteric's discourse is there in the first place and produces the master. It does so because, and I quote, "What the hysteric wants . . . is a master . . . so much so that you have to wonder whether this isn't where the invention of the master began from. That would elegantly bring to a close what we are in the process of tracing out" (150). This is quite clear, but it leaves open the question of why the hysteric's discourse comes first. Elsewhere Lacan remarks that it exists whether psychoanalysis exists or not, due to the signifier's inauguration of the absence of a sexual relation. One could think that he thus renders the hysteric's discourse eternal; moreover, this solution becomes problematic because the master's discourse is supposed to schematize the absence of a sexual relation, so it should come first.

However, Lacan saves himself from the arduous task of plugging up the gaps in this theory of the quarter turn by recognizing that there is a far more serious problem at stake: he is running an enormous risk, and that risk goes under the name of Hegel. Since it is an operation internal to each discourse that supposedly necessitates the emergence of the next discourse, one is perilously close to Hegel's *The Phenomenology of Spirit* with its dialectical progress from one figure of spirit to another, a progress that ends up constituting a totality. Lacan continually recognizes the Hegelian risk in the modes of polemic, denial, and acknowledgment, yet he does not follow such recognition with a decisive distinction between his theory of change and that of Hegel. In terms of polemic, he sideswipes *The Phenomenology of Spirit* for being a history of schools of thought or a "school history" rather than a history of any absolute. He also argues that Hegel misrecognized the mechanism at work in the relation between the master and the slave, that his account of the struggle for prestige via risking death is a myth (178). Finally, he argues that it is absurd to think that the slave's work results in a true knowledge (91, 199). In terms of denial, he states, "There is not the slightest idea of progress" in what I articulate (122). Finally, in terms of acknowledgment, after explaining the quarter turn that produces science, he says, "One is always more or less led at some moment to grasp at an archaic theme, and, as you know, I incite you to be prudent" (91). However, this prudence does not give rise to any operation designed to exclude archaism, at least not immediately.

Quite apart from this risk of reinstating Hegel, Lacan introduces his own complication into the theory of the quarter turn. He realizes that the expropriation of the slave's knowledge by the master presupposes the introduction of a desire for knowledge; if the master doesn't want to know anything, he asks, how does philosophy get him to desire knowledge, the famous desire for knowledge assigned to all men in the first line of the *Metaphysics*? The answer lies in Socrates's hysteria. It is the hysteric's discourse that lies behind any desire for knowledge (24, 36–37, 41, 120, 122).[15] This complication whereby the master's discourse + the hysteric's discourse = the university discourse leads to the second main solution to structural change, that of contingent implication. Before we get to that, let's examine another theory of immanent and thus necessary structural evolution, which I will term the theory of production via inversion.

Type B: The Theory of Production via Inversion

This theory states that if each discourse is determined by a dominant element found in the position of the agent, in the top left corner, and if, in the bottom right corner, there is an element that is the product of the discourse, then each discourse produces another discourse in the form of its dominant element. In short, a discourse produces the discourse whose dominant element is found in its place of production. For example, in the university discourse the barred S is in the bottom right corner, which implies that it produces the hysteric's discourse, in that the latter's dominant element is the barred S, the split subject.[16]

I term this the theory of production via inversion because the positions of the four terms are inverted between the two discourses in question. Moreover, this theory lies behind the very title of the seminar, which could be also translated as the inverse, the obverse, or the underside of psychoanalysis: that is, the very same type of productive inversion occurs between the master's discourse and the analyst's discourse — each produces the other. Lacan says, "The master's discourse has only one counterpoint, the analytic discourse" (99). Later on, he claims, "the analytic practice is strictly initiated by this master's discourse," and, toward the very end of the seminar, he remarks, "It is fairly curious that what [the analyst's discourse] produces is nothing other than the master's discourse, since it's S_1 that comes to occupy the place of production. Perhaps another style of S_1 might emerge from the analyst's discourse" (177, 205).

Enjoy Your Stay: Structural Change in *Seminar XVII*   187

Again, the problem with this theory is that it is incomplete. With such dual pairing—the master's discourse + the university discourse, and the university discourse + the hysteric's discourse—one cannot account for the emergence of each pair. One is constrained to claim that members of the pairs mutually produce each other, but that each pair has existed eternally.

Type C: Dynamism via Impotence

Let's turn to the last theory of structural evolution Lacan offers in *Seminar XVII*. I call it the theory of dynamism via impotence, which itself is an interesting mutation of the Aristotelian definition of movement, "the actualization of the potential [*dynamis*] *qua* potential." Structural change for Lacan requires the actualization of potential *qua impotence*.

In the second-to-last session of the year, Lacan pursues the question of what makes the agent act when it comes to these discourses. In my eyes, it is another way in which he entertains the question of history by posing the question of the genesis or origin of these discourses. He continues, "What inaugurates this agent, what bring him into play?" (199). He answers by saying that these discourses contain their own driving mechanism—there is no agent external to them—and the driving mechanism does not lie simply in the position of the agent. Indeed, as he says, "The agent is not at all necessarily someone who does, but someone who is caused to act" (197).

The driving mechanism lies at the level of two relationships: one of impossibility and one of impotence. The relation of impossibility is said to lie between the place of the agent and the place of the other. Lacan's example is what happens when a master issues commands so that people —others—work; he remarks that making people work is more tiring than working itself. However, to explain "impossibility" it would be more to the point to remark that ultimately it is not commands that get people to work, but rather their pay, the promise of some enjoyment. The relation of impotence, on the other hand, consists of a barrier that lies between a discourse's production and its truth. This is Lacan's most concise response to Hegel—and, one might add, to ecological politics— there is no chance that production can coincide with truth (203). Lacan's example is that of the university discourse's supposed production of subjects of knowledge or thinking beings. He says, "There is no question of a subject of this production being able to see itself for a single instant as the master of knowledge" (203). I would also interpret this barrier of impotence as that faced by students when confronted with the injunction to produce original work, to transform themselves into what Lacan calls the myth of the author, the self-identical "I" that signs the proper name. Interestingly enough, the barrier itself is constituted of jouissance, and perhaps this would go some of the way to explaining why writing a PhD is so painful; one has to relinquish the enjoyment inherent in the position of the student and become a professional academic—in other words, enter into the master's discourse (202–8).

Lacan does not explicitly develop an account of why these relations of impossibility and impotence would lead to structural change in general, much less to any particular structure. Rather he suggests that the inscription of a perpetual dynamism and a perpetual instability grounds either a kind of tendency toward structural change or a perpetual structural change:

> If it's one's wish that something turn—of course, ultimately *no one can ever turn, as I have emphasized enough*—it is certainly not by being progressive, it is simply because it can't prevent itself from turning. If it doesn't turn, it will squeak away, there where things raise questions, that is, at the level of putting something into place that can be written as *a*. Has that ever existed? Yes, no doubt, it is the Ancients who, in the end, give us the strongest proof. (208)

This passage constitutes an astonishingly rich development of his thought; formally, however, it is quite predictable—one solves the problem of structural change by claiming that these discourses have always existed and that they are always changing. Such is the Heraclitean or even Bergsonian solution: "All is flux." The problem, however, with the paradigm of permanent change is that it always presumes totality—all is flux—a presupposition marked in the epigraph from Spinoza, a presupposition that Lacan explicitly rejects.

In any case, we have an incomplete theory again: there is no account of the generation of these particular structures as a result of such permanent change. To be more precise, Lacan can think the change of structure, but he can't account for the multiplicity of these structures. It's a kind of *vel* like "your money or your life": you can think change or multiplicity within this structuralist paradigm, but not both.

But before moving on to the next solution, it is important to note that Lacan is not alone in taking up the solution of perpetual dynamism; where he is alone is in how quickly he realizes that it's a dead end. Alain Badiou once adopted a similar position and wrote an entire book on it, *Théorie du sujet*, in which he unwraps a Lacanian-Maoist reformulation of structuralist dialectics.[17] Deleuze and Guattari, even slower, wrote two books together on the basis of a similar position—*Anti-Oedipus* and *A Thousand Plateaus*—in which they develop accounts of the permanent instability of structure and the permanent possibility of its dissolution.[18]

Three theories of structural evolution—the operation of the quarter turn, inversion via production, and perpetual dynamism—and none of them work. Yes, philosophy is—in part—a master's discourse, and theories have to work. Lacan has a problem, and it is not going away.

In his continuing struggle with this problem, specifically in the complications that arise in the quarter-turn theory, Lacan develops an entirely different type of solution to the problem of structural change: the solution of contingent implication.

Solution II: Contingent Implication

The solution of contingent implication holds that it is the contingent encounter of discourses that produces another discourse. For example, Lacan says quite clearly that the encounter between the hysteria of philosophy in Socrates's interrogations of *doxa* and the mastery present in Greek society eventually produces the university discourse in the form of science. The relay for this production is the philosophical tradition that itself consists of a cementing of this encounter between the hysteric's discourse and the master's discourse. The result is that Descartes, at the outset of modern science, can repeat Socrates's philosophical operation of interrogation, but this time choosing a different target, that of theoretical knowledge itself.

Another example occurs when Lacan speaks directly of the cogito; he does so immediately after asserting that the master's discourse leads to the analyst's discourse, suggesting that by way of Descartes's inauguration of the university discourse in the form of science, psychoanalysis is rendered possible (178). This is a very familiar claim to readers of Lacan, not the least among them Jean-Claude Milner, who concentrates an entire chapter on the equivalence established between the subject of the unconscious and the subject of science. What we then end up with is the following: the master's discourse, within its transformation into the university discourse via the cogito, encounters a momentary emergence of the hysteric's discourse insofar as the cogito both presents and sutures the split between the subject of enunciation and the subject of the statement. This mix renders possible the analyst's discourse.

So how does this solution fare? It seems to be on the right track, as far as avoiding Hegel goes: the replacement of structural necessity by contingency and encounter prevents one from rewriting *The Phenomenology of Spirit*. Moreover, the consequence for history is that one does not generate an ordered historical series; there is no global sense to history.

However, one pays the price of still employing some theory of the production of discourses; this particular mix of discourses will produce that particular discourse. In other words, there is a local sense to change — what, then, one is entitled to ask, produces this multiplicity of discourses in the first place? The multiplicity/change vel strikes again: we can think change but not multiplicity. So we have another incomplete theory, but at least we are no longer in the position of Hegel's bastards, repeating his legacy without the name.

The third and ultimate solution provided by Lacan for the problem of structural change is quite simple. He says there is no structural change. This solution, quite appropriately, is called the theory of cuts.

Solution III: The Theory of Cuts

According to this theory, there is an absolute cut between each discourse, or, in other words, each discourse emerges, unique, and the emergence of the discourses is absolutely contingent. The consequence, as Milner puts it, is that there is no transformation internal to a system, only transformations between systems.[19] This formulation can be reinforced and clarified by adding that any such transformation between systems is asystemic or astructural: there is no structural change.

That, despite such contingency, every discourse that has emerged involves the same terms is due to the fact that they always implicate the speaking being.

What examples of this theory can be found in *Seminar XVII*? The best example is when Lacan speaks of the inauguration of the master's discourse in the anathemas pronounced by Yahweh (158, 179). Here you have not the death of God as inaugurating an era, but the birth of a God, not the melancholic flight of the Gods as sung by Hölderlin, but the ferocious entrance of a God, as reported by Hosea. Another example occurs when Lacan asserts that it is nothing other than the practice of psychoanalysis itself that opens up the discourse of analysis (177).

It is not in *Seminar XVII* but in *Seminar XX*, three years later, that Lacan punctuates his theory of the four discourses by explicitly adopting the theory of cuts.[20] Moreover, he theorizes the moment of the cut itself, of the occurrence of a new discourse, as a brief emergence of the analyst's discourse. I take this to mean that, in the moment of emergence, the *objet a* is in the dominant position without any fantasy blocking it with a semblance; thus the symbolic order is devoid of necessity, and contingency reigns briefly at the level of what can be done. Again Lacan is not alone, since this, I take it, was the solution adopted by Slavoj Žižek under the name of the "vanishing mediator" in his attempt to think the possibility of new structures in the field of politics.

What is the consequence for history? Again, with the adoption of contingency, there can be no order to the emergence of discourses. Lacan marks this in *Seminar XX* by saying, "This is not in any sense to be viewed as a series of historical emergences."[21] So history as a sequence with a sense does not exist, but neither does history as global change: all history is immanent to the emergence of a discourse, and each emergence marks an epoch. Moreover, without such emergences there would be no history whatsoever, since literally nothing new would happen under the sun.[22]

So with the theory of cuts we seem to have an account of the multiplicity of discourses that does not need a theory of structural change and does not break with Lacan's injunction against metalanguage and history as an imaginary totality.[23] Does this theory hold up?

The problem one encounters with any such account of the unconditioned emergence of structure is that one must presume that these structures are self-movers in Aristotle's terms, that is, that they are sovereign insofar as they are self-generating or *auto-poietic*. Again Lacan is not alone in employing this solution: he is joined by the advocates of general systems theory—I'm thinking of Niklas Luhmann, Humberto Maturana, and Francisco J. Varela, even Ilya Prigogine and Isabelle Stengers—who think the genesis of structure by saying "a cut opens a universe." The problem is that what we thus have are four "mini" absolutes—again we have become Hegel's bastards, or, since that is a little rough, a bunch of Hegelettes.

The problem of structural change—along with the problem of singularity and multiplicity—is what motivates the exit from structuralism in contemporary French philosophy. Whether this exit has been achieved is far from certain. I take the frenzied bandying of the moniker *poststructuralism* to be a sure sign of this uncertainty. The value of Lacan's theory of discourses for philosophy lies not so much in its rapid exhaustion of the various options for thinking either change between structures or the multiplicity of structures, but rather in the challenge it lays at philosophy's door; that of thinking the role of jouissance, a challenge that Lacan renders explicit in *Seminar XX*.

In my view, contemporary philosophy in the form of Alain Badiou's work can provide a theory of both the multiplicity of structures and contingent astructural change.[24] What Badiou's philosophy adds is basically:

1. The contingency of structural incompleteness or instability: not every structure permits global change.
2. The possibility of anomalous events that occur in the register of the real, outside structure (they are not grounded in any external reality/context), and which can initiate change if there are.
3. The elaboration of structural preconditions for transformation—someone recognizes and names the event as belonging to the situation—this means that the process of change is not sovereign, it does not start with a blank slate, and so one has no Hegelettes. Finally,
4. A new way of thinking subjects of change, subjects who, over time, participate in the invention of a new symbolic order by means of hypotheses and enquiries concerning the belonging of the anomalous event to a structure.

However, I am not yet convinced that Badiou's philosophy can account for the role of jouissance in such change. Such is the challenge.

Notes

1. Jacques Lacan, *Le séminaire, livre XVII: L'envers de la psychanalyse*, ed. J.-A. Miller (Paris: Seuil, 1992), 13. Further citations appear parenthetically in the text.
2. As Lorenzo Chiesa has remarked in an unpublished communication, there are hints at the possibility of a fifth discourse, the discourse of capitalism, in both *Seminar XVII* and *Seminar XVIII*. However, the problem of structural change remains whether there are four or five discourses.
3. Lacan says, "[This] arrangement . . . is already inscribed in what functions as this reality I was speaking about before, the reality of a discourse that is already in the world and that underpins it, at least the one we are familiar with. Not only is it already inscribed in it, but it is one of its arches" (13).
4. Consider: "The discourses in question are nothing other than the signifying articulation, the apparatus whose presence alone, whose existing status, dominates and governs anything that at any given moment is capable of emerging as speech. They are discourses without speech, which comes and lodges itself within them" (194).
5. Lacan says, " 'That will do!' I hear you say. Do we really need to explain everything? And, why not, the origin of language too? We all know that to structure knowledge correctly one needs to abandon the question of origins. What we are doing, by spelling this out, is superfluous with respect to what we have to develop this year, which is situated at the level of structures. It is a futile search for meaning" (18). See also: "Our first rule is never to seek the origins of language, if only because they are demonstrated well enough through their effects" (181).
6. Jacques Lacan, *The Seminar of Jacques Lacan, Book XX: Encore, or On Feminine Sexuality, the Limits of Love and Knowledge*, ed. J.-A. Miller, trans. with notes by B. Fink (New York: Norton, 1998), 16.
7. See Jean-Claude Milner's reading of Lacan's discourse mathemes in *L'oeuvre claire: Lacan, la science, la philosophie* (Paris: Seuil, 1995). In Milner's eyes, multiplicity and heterogeneity are intrinsic to Lacan's definition of the discourses, and the discourses are nonsynchronous: statements made under one discourse cannot coincide with statements made under another.
8. Lacan remarks to this effect in "Radiophonie," precisely concerning what he calls "Hegelian formalism." See *Autres Ecrits* (Paris: Seuil, 2001), 412.
9. This is the solution that Jean-Claude Milner seizes upon as the correct solution for the theory of discourses. We shall see.
10. Lacan says, "If there were something necessary here to make present some ocean of mythical knowledge regulating the life of men . . . the best reference could well be what Yahweh condemns . . . with the term 'prostitution' " (179).
11. In session 11, Lacan is able to show that the cogito itself is structured by the master's discourse, whereby the subject of enunciation is produced as an unattainable effect. He observes that when Descartes asserts his "I am thinking therefore I am," it is via a questioning of this knowledge that has already been trafficked and mixed with the master-signifier via philosophy (178).

12 Lacan paraphrases and adopts Hegel's own historical narrative here, saying that the surplus enjoyment is owed to the master because the latter appears to have initially risked his own jouissance (123, 198): "Something changed in the master's discourse at a certain point in history. We are not going to break our backs finding out whether this was due to Luther, or Calvin, or some unknown traffic of ships around Genoa, or in the Mediterranean Sea, or anywhere else [Braudel], for the important point is that on a certain day surplus-enjoyment became calculable, could be counted, totalized. This is where the accumulation of capital begins" (207).
13 According to Lacan, the emergence of science requires the cogito, and the manipulation of number, and the placing of the guarantee of truth with God (186). On the role of mathematics as algebra, see 103, and as thermodynamics, see 92.
14 As Lacan remarks, the master's discourse structures capitalism insofar as the place of the proletariat in the master's discourse is the slave (173).
15 This is the question of the origins of the "epistemological drive," and Lacan's answer, at least here, is the hysteric's discourse.
16 According to Lacan, the university discourse maps the evaporation of the subject of science, and so the hysteric's discourse, placing the effaced subject in first place, can evidently be understood as a type of protest to this operation. At an empirical level, one can allow that universities produce a certain current of hysteria. But one would also have to admit, following the theory of production via inversion, that the hysteric's discourse produces the university discourse since the hysteric's discourse produces S_2, knowledge. Lacan explicitly adopts this implication in the shape of recognizing that psychoanalytic knowledge ultimately owes its source to the discourse of Dora and the other hysterics to whom Freud listened.
17 Alain Badiou, *Théorie du sujet* (Paris: Seuil, 1982). Badiou argues therein that every element of a structure is both statically fixed and placed by an algebraic logic *and* dis-placed according to a topology that renders it open to change.
18 Gilles Deleuze and Félix Guattari, *A Thousand Plateaus: Capitalism and Schizophrenia*, trans. and foreword B. Massumi (Minneapolis: University of Minnesota Press, 1987).
19 For Milner, the function of the four discourse mathemes is to develop an ahistorical theory of the cut between different structures.
20 Jacques Lacan, *The Seminar of Jacques Lacan, Book XX*, 16.
21 Ibid.
22 The four discourses allow a repunctuation of history according to modifications of the terms and the relationship between the terms (see 23).
23 Lacan says, "In the world of discourse, nothing is everything, as I say—or better . . . 'everything' as such is self-refuting" (61).
24 See Badiou's *L'être et l'événement* (Paris: Seuil, 1988), forthcoming in English as *Being and Event*, trans. O. Feltham (London: Continuum, 2005).

10

More Thoughts for the Times on War and Death: The Discourse of Capitalism in Seminar XVII

Juliet Flower MacCannell

In the discourse of the master the *a* is precisely identifiable with what a laborious thought, Marx's, produced, namely what was, symbolically and really, the function of surplus-value.

We have logical needs. . . . We are beings born of surplus-pleasure, as a result of the use of language. . . . It is language that uses us. Language employs us, and that is how it enjoys.
—Jacques Lacan

A reading is displaced when it is torn away from a classroom guided by a teacher (*maître*) with "a role, with a place to occupy, which is, undeniably, a place that has a certain prestige."[1] But the master's discourse is no longer what it once was. Only a dislocated reading can register the significance for us, here and now, of Lacan's 1969 *Seminar*. We must read it with an ear for linguistic nuance—a literary ear—so as not to miss the echo of the political, economic, and cultural traumas in which it was embedded. By traumas I chiefly mean the Vietnam War. For many years it was unacceptable to read Lacan with history and politics in view, at least in the United States, and these lines of mine evoked a negative reaction in 1986: "[Lacan] distinguishes his effort from the limited political and economic one by drawing attention to the parallel . . . between his notion of the surplus enjoyment (*plus-de-jouir*, surplus joy/also no more enjoyment) and Marx's surplus value: he claims his notion is 'much more radical.' "[2] Of course, 1986 was the peak of Reaganomics, the heyday of recovering from "Vietnam syndrome": it was "morning once again in

America." Analytical discussion of alternative economies or the subjective costs of capitalist economy was unwelcome—even in literary circles. Today, with war once more the horizon (and limit) of our desire to know, *Seminar XVII* brings important clarification to surplus enjoyment's crucial function in the capital transformation in discourse it investigates. I will argue that Lacan's surplus enjoyment holds astonishing explanatory power regarding the question "Why war?" As Lacan lays it out (46–94), the affinities between his surplus enjoyment and Marx's surplus value will also appear: each marks the value added to or subtracted from the totality of work accomplished on behalf of a symbolic economy, bringing to light how economy/discourse generates its excess and lack from within.

Surplus Enjoyment: "Treating" Jouissance

Discourses ("forms of the social tie") are the means culture employs to expel troublesome jouissance from its subjects—and then to "treat" that jouissance once it inevitably and hauntingly returns. Lacan marks the second coming of jouissance as the half-real, half-fantasized *objet a*, the representative of surplus enjoyment. Why jouissance's ghostly return? Because it is as crucial to discourse as the signifier is. The *a* designates the constitutive impossibility within a discursive system as if it were possible. It is offered up as discourse's hidden truth, its objective or subjective reality, purveying its secret deficit as if it were a plus. The *a* stands for the aura that lends value and prestige to all the elements in a discourse.

$$\frac{S_1}{\$} \rightarrow \frac{S_2}{a}$$

Master's discourse

Let us look briefly at how the master's discourse classically treats jouissance. It places jouissance under official ban for everyone, except for the slave who alone enjoys. Masterly discourse designates the slave as the site of superabundant jouissance; however, it also locates the system's absolute lack in this same slave—the lack (of knowledge) the whole discourse is designed to make up for. The discursive system organizes itself around the possibility of turning the slave's unknowing enjoyment into *work* that produces profit for the whole. Gain, in this system, is derived exclusively from subtracting what the slave has (jouissance), transforming it into work, and transfiguring it yet again into a symbolic addition (an addition to the symbolic). Through the alchemy of symbolic signification the extraction of the slave's jouissance as work is counted as no loss; the discourse figures the slave's privation only as profiting the whole.

Marx would say that the real source of profit is simply the slave's work; what accrues to the system from its expropriation of that work is surplus value. Lacan, however, points out that Marx doesn't realize "that its secret lies in knowledge itself, just as the secret of the worker himself is to be reduced to being no longer anything but a value" (93). As Lacan translates Marx's surplus value under capitalism into the surplus value in a linguistic economy (the master's discourse), he discovers what is new to its subsequent cultural history. Marking what accrues to the system (through the restrictions it places on jouissance) as its total knowledge, or S_2, Lacan designates the cultural profit achieved by these limits "surplus enjoyment," represented as the (a).

Although the slave's work is absolutely essential to the profit of the whole, it is just as essential that the master (the slave's contradictory in the algorithm) do no work. If knowledge is to expand in the master's regime, the master himself must be under no necessity to inject his own energy or his own labor into the field. Profit must come to him at no loss—without his having to lift a little finger, Lacan says.

Lacan formulates the discourse of mastery as one that puts the signifier S_1 at the head or in the capital position: the upper-left-hand side of the algorithm. Because the signifier S_1 accomplishes the transformation of real into symbolic power (surplus enjoyment), it is the "dominant" (the position of power). The signifier's discursive power comes from the way it limits and expels real jouissance. It gains ascendancy over the whole, however, by becoming its master signifier, a unique word that organizes throughout the discourse's entire universe of meaning: its *mot d'ordre*, enunciated by the master.

The master's word exploits the lack it installs (in the real, in the subject, in the slave) as a way of reproducing the jouissance originally lost as if it were value added to the whole. A purely metaphorical achievement:

the master's word is, Lacan says, a "creative" word. In reality, of course, the master himself only *represents* the supreme signifying power of the master signifier. True, he enunciates the system's overall command, but the very thing that empowers the signifier is also fundamentally what empowers the master: a limit to jouissance. (Phallic jouissance is thinkable only as excluded, for Lacan.)

Still, a system that can balance out the totality of its expenditures and losses only by the legerdemain of turning loss into profit forgets that its initial costs are never really compensated. There has to be some slippage. Work, after all, remains a real loss of energy, even where it results in overall accrued knowledge, S_2. In truth, the entire system of valuing knowledge, Lacan reminds us, constantly bleeds away energy and is destined to entropy: "When the signifier is introduced as an apparatus of jouissance, we should thus not be surprised to see something related to entropy appear, since entropy is defined precisely once one has started to lay this apparatus of signifiers over the physical probe" (54).[3]

Entropy is unavoidable in a discursive system because of the mechanism of repetition (S_1 S_1 S_1 S_1 S_1) that implements its meaning-making. Lacan uses a thermodynamic analogy to demonstrate: "S_1 is the dam. The second S_1, down below, is the pond that receives it and turns the turbine. There is no other meaning to the conservation of energy than this mark of an instrumentation that signifies the power of the master. What is collected in the fall has to be conserved. This is the first of the laws." However, "there is unfortunately something that disappears in the interval, or more exactly does not lend itself to a return to, to restoring, the starting point" (92).

The first jouissance excluded from discourse (Freud calls it the lost object) is comparable to the initial absolute loss of energy in thermodynamics: it is never really made up for, no matter how elaborately the system of signifiers tries to gild the deficit. The loss only grows incrementally until it finally dooms the system to winding down at the end of history, where total knowledge and symbolic energy become completely commensurate: "Knowledge implies an equivalence between this entropy and information" (94).

Just as energetics laminates the physical world with signifiers to mask an original loss of jouissance, energy, the master's discourse also obscures the terminal loss of its dynamism by misrecognizing the nature of work. If the thermodynamic laws of conservation of energy seem to balance out, this is only because they don't recognize work for the absolute loss it is (real energy expended): "I defy you to prove in any way that descending 500 metres with a weight of 80 kilos on your back and, once you have descended, going back up the 500 metres with it is zero, no work. Try it, have a go yourself, and you will find that you have proof of the contrary. But if you overlay signifiers, that is, if you enter the path of energetics, it is absolutely certain that there has been no work" (54). The master cannot afford to count actual work done as a real expenditure—not the work of the slave, nor his own spent to set the system of signification in motion (the trouble he himself took to enunciate its commanding word).

"Something necessitates compensation . . . for what is initially a negative number," Lacan says (56). So, in the interval between the signifiers something else emerges, a counterentropic force field outside the play of signifiers: the *a*, or surplus enjoyment. "There is a loss of jouissance. And it is in the place of this loss introduced by repetition that we see the function of the lost object emerge, of what I am calling the *a*" (54). "In fact, it is only through this effect of entropy, through this wasting, that enjoyment acquires a status and shows itself. This is why I initially introduced it by the term *Mehrlust*, surplus enjoyment" (56).

The master's discourse makes loss appear adequately recuperated—as "excess." Nonetheless, it is really not sufficient unto itself. Without the slippage (introduced by the *a*) that skews the inexorably congealing destiny of jouissance, all social and linguistic exchange would finally, slowly wind down to zero. In *Beyond the Pleasure Principle*, Freud found that repetition leads to inertia. The motivating force behind the entire system of signifying repetition is the lost object, which returns as a death drive that announces the second coming of the lost jouissance—a death drive that disrupts the entropic destiny of signification. While the death drive is only a mental representative of the lost object (lost energy or jouissance), it still injects a new energy into the field of the pleasure principle constituted by the value—the surplus value (Lacan's *a*)—of the lost object. Breaking into the pleasure principle that dooms all signifying acts to inertia, the death drive fortuitously spurs us to the mental labor required to prevent organized life from declining to zero.

In the master's discourse, surplus enjoyment is thus the practical, quasi-mechanical source of the swerve from terminal entropy; it alone makes jouissance energy (apparently lost to the signifier) return, greater than ever: "Only the dimension of entropy gives body to the fact that there is surplus jouissance there to be recovered" (56). Surplus enjoyment is the energizing aftereffect of the signifier.[4]

When Lacan, justly, links the repetition inhering in the pleasure principle to the repetition required for signification (S_1 S_1 S_1—the chain that retroactively produces knowledge, S_2), his Freud joins hands with Marx. For if "on the side of surplus enjoyment there is something else," it requires a science other than Newtonian laws of conservation (of energy and matter): economics. Mechanics limited the universitarian Hegel's conception of the end of history—wherein absolute knowledge would prevail—for mechanics grants "primacy to everything at the beginning and at the end and neglects everything in between, which may be of the order of something arising from knowledge, placing these pure numerical truths, that which is countable, on the horizon of a new world. [Doesn't] this signify, all by itself, something completely different from the increasing role of absolute knowledge?" (92).

The "horizon" Hegel overlooked and Marx had an imperfect inkling of is that of a brave new universe of accounting: "Isn't this very ideal of a formalization in which henceforth everything is only to be counted—where energy itself is nothing other than what is counted, than what, if you manipulate the formulas in a certain way, always turns out to add up to the same total—the rotation, the quarter turn here? Doesn't this make it the case that in the place of the master an articulation of completely new knowledge, completely reducible formally, is established?" (92). The basic laws of conservation of knowledge are affected: "Something changed in the master's discourse at a certain point in history" (207), a shift that openly appears first in the sixteenth or seventeenth centuries. Here, the master's apparatus of value creation gets turned inside out and, unburied, becomes both visible and computable: "We are not going to break our backs finding out whether this was due to Luther, or Calvin, or some unknown traffic of ships around Genoa, or in the Mediterranean sea, or anywhere else, for the important point is that on a certain day surplus pleasure became calculable, could be counted, totalized. This is where what is called the accumulation of capital begins" (207).

What prevails henceforward is a discourse that relegates the slave and the master to relatively minor discursive importance. They existed only for the sake of generating a whole system of knowledge. But now knowledge is itself the productive force: "In the place of the master an articulation of completely new knowledge, completely reducible formally, is established, and . . . in the slave's place there emerges, not something that might be inserted in no particular way into this order of knowledge, but something which is its product instead" (92).[5]

The function of surplus enjoyment changes fundamentally as the master's discourse yields to the university discourse (Hegel's and capitalism's). The *objet a* secreted in the master's discourse (as its hidden source of value) is openly declared as what produces value: "Surplus value combines with capital—not a problem, they are homogeneous, we are in the field of values. Moreover, we are all up to our necks in it, in these blessed times in which we live" (207). "We are up to our necks in it": a fantastic immersion in a substance that is nothing other than accumulated jouissance—unspent, and at a safe remove from the whole apparatus that actually produced surplus enjoyment: the signifier, metaphor, and castration (the excluding of jouissance).

A social revolution has taken place. The worth of an individual is no longer defined by his condition, but by his market value, free as he now is to sell his labor. He does not realize, however, that he is also selling out his know-how (*savoir-faire*), which has inhered in his work all along, despite the master's designating its genesis in his slave's absolute absence of knowledge. Now what gets systematically expropriated is not simply the slave's (ignorant) jouissance (transubstantiated into knowledge by the alchemy of signification). It is also the conversion of the producer's unknown knowledge into a formal value to be recuperated by (and accumulated in) the system. How? By the accounting of surplus enjoyment:[6] "Rather than progress having been made through the work of the slave . . . it is a matter of the transference, plundering, spoliation of what, at the beginning of knowledge, was inscribed, hidden, in the slave's world. . . . what subtracts the slave's knowledge from him is the entire history whose stages Hegel follows step by step" (91). The secret of the worker himself is to be reduced to no longer being anything but a value. Once a higher level has been passed, surplus jouissance is no longer surplus jouissance but is inscribed simply as a value to be inscribed in or deduced from the totality of whatever it is that is accumulating (92). However, the brave new universe of accounting that formalizes surplus enjoyment (by adding it up) devalues what produces knowledge: "In the process, what you lose is your knowledge, which gave you your status" (80).[7]

As discourse trades in (and economizes on) the formalization of surplus enjoyment, its significance undergoes a tectonic shift: it is now the *agent* of the discursive dominant (accumulated knowledge or wealth). S_2 does not merely give university discourse a crucial (supplementary) prestige; it is its *dominant* (in the upper left hand of the algorithm). Surplus enjoyment *a* is what confirms the discourse's total value.

A discursive revolution, a "quarter turn," changes everything within. With S_2 as its dominant, university discourse does not produce, but is headed up by cumulative knowledge, a wealth of know-how ("capital," Lacan says) tied directly to surplus enjoyment.[8] This shift reflects a primary change from what prevails in the master's affairs, in the way the system compensates for its expropriations (here, of knowledge). The producer of knowledge is now repaid not with ignorant jouissance (like the slave) but with *identity*: he now *identifies himself* with *wealth*, the new *dominant*: "Why does one let oneself be bought by the wealthy? Because what they give you stems from their essence of wealth" (95). In reality this loss, like the slave's, remains unrepaid: "The wealthy acquire this knowledge on top of everything else. It's simply that, precisely, they don't pay for it."

Only economics ("this other field of energetics . . . which is the field of jouissance" [93]) can assess how lack and excess (necessary to discourse's functioning) are installed in a revolutionized discourse governed by accumulated surplus enjoyment. Once surplus enjoyment is reforged as rigorously countable and accountable surplus value, it also begins functioning the way Marx understood it to: as a scam, as a sham —simulated jouissance. It fraudulently claims to make up for the absolute loss integral to the origination of its economy. "What Marx denounces in surplus value is the spoliation of *jouissance*. And yet, this surplus value is a memorial to surplus *jouissance*, its equivalent of surplus *jouissance*" (92).

Compare the differing roles of surplus enjoyment in the master's discourse and in its successor: the unseen purpose of the first is to order, collect, conserve, and regulate jouissance for the profit of the whole. A mere discursive quarter turn, however, changes surplus enjoyment from the discourse's hidden motive force to what *officially* implements it. Surplus enjoyment then is entirely analogous to capital—or in current terms, "wealth-creation."

Lacan muses: no one, not even Marx or Adam Smith, ever thought to ask, "What is wealth?" "Ever since there have been economists nobody, up till now, has—not even for an instant . . . —ever made this remark that wealth is the property of the wealthy. Just like psychoanalysis which . . . is done by psychoanalysts . . . why not, concerning wealth, begin with the wealthy?" (94). Because its answer is tautological: "Wealth is an attribute of the wealthy." The tautological-as-theological (the "I am that I am") puts us in the neighborhood of the discursive "dominant":

> The wealthy have property. They buy, they buy everything, in short —well, they buy a lot. But I would like you to meditate on this fact, which is that they do not pay for it.
>
> One imagines that they pay, for reasons of accounting that stem from the transformation of surplus *jouissance* into surplus value. But first, everyone knows that they very regularly add surplus value on. There is no circulation of surplus value. And very much in particular, there is one thing that they never pay for, and that is knowledge. (94)

Capitalism (formally indistinguishable from the university discourse) makes it abundantly clear that wealth accumulation dictates the distribution of value (as sham jouissance) throughout its entire discursive system, dominating every relation, intimate to global, by providing the pattern for every mark of worth. True, Max Weber had already said that for capitalism to function everything must be assigned a monetary value, and every single thing must be made *accountable*. But Lacan is after something different in *Seminar XVII*: the social and psychical implications of this brave new world of accounting.

Unbalanced Psychical Accounts: Fathers and Leaders

In the position of discursive product (in the master's discourse), surplus enjoyment (loss-turned-to-profit) could never bear too much exposure. In the world of accounting, it is no longer the mysterious product of a system's lack and excess, but its very face. Consider the consequences. With surplus enjoyment as its head and accumulated surplus value assuming the discursively dominant position, the figure that will correspond to or exemplify its preeminence is neither master nor father, but what Freud's *Group Psychology* names "the leader."

This reveals why Lacan takes pains in *Seminar XVII* to distinguish masters and fathers from *leaders*; his constant, if minor, theme is how (really, whether) the master signifier (S_1) and its social representative (the master) are rendered formally invalid by the capital(ist) shift. In capitalist discourse, the leader does not metaphorically represent total social value; he is defined by being identical to the discursive dominant (accumulated knowledge or wealth). He is its metonym, incarnating the surplus enjoyment in the system and thus making it appear as if it had never been produced at all. He is what guarantees that its surplus enjoyment has neither been fathered nor created. The leader, that is, far from symbolizing the cumulative value that conditions the whole system, is part and parcel of it and refuses all responsibility for any of the losses a meaning system based on repetition requires.

What are the subjective sources and consequences of the tropological shift in representing the discursive dominant? The psychical root of capitalist discourse, according to Lacan, is a child's identification with (or wish to substitute itself for) the *impotent* father (109). The helpless infant feels itself drowning in a pool of cumulated libidinal capital because it is incapable (due to its prematurity) of enjoying outright:

> [Do you recall what I said concerning] the relationship between capitalism and the function of the master—concerning the altogether distinct nature of what can be done with the process of accumulation in the presence of surplus *jouissance*—in the very presence of this surplus *jouissance*, to the exclusion of the big fat *jouissance*, plain *jouissance*, *jouissance* that is realised in copulation in the raw? Isn't this precisely where infantile desire gets its force from, its force of accumulation with respect to this object that constitutes the cause of desire, namely that which is accumulated as libido capital by virtue, precisely, of infantile non-maturity, the exclusion of *jouissance* that others will call normal? (111–12)

Capitalism would develop childlike leaders who dispense with the masterly/paternal engines of value- and meaning-creation (the signifier and the castration that produce the ability to father) in favor of what is already accumulated as surplus enjoyment—already capital. This is because this discourse's leader has a personal relation to jouissance that differs entirely from the master's. The master is a priori excluded from jouissance: he can't hoard it as the primal father did, for he may accrue it only surreptitiously as a symbolic value—and then only as surplus enjoyment recuperated for his people's sake. In capitalist discourse, by contrast, the leader is neither the castrated father of original creation, nor the fearsome, all-enjoying father of prehistory. He merely husbands always already cumulated surplus enjoyment; or, more exactly, he both husbands it and really *is* surplus enjoyment himself.

Wealth is the discursive quilting point (*point de capiton*) the leader automatically embodies. His identification with collective wealth makes his powers seem as if they were not created by the father's restrictions on jouissance (or by the master's creative-metaphoric word). His jouissance appears endless and without origination because, as Freud notes, the leader draws all libidinal investment into himself, returning it in equal measure to each of the group's members as echoes and mirrorings, multiplied infinitely because "imaginarily."[9] A mesmerizing figure, the leader embodies the aggregate assets of the community without having actively to acquire or produce them.

Nonetheless, Lacan reminds us, the image of a painlessly accumulated jouissance remains a fake: phony jouissance ("jouissance en toc" [95]). In the master's discourse, surplus enjoyment is the mysterious source of reflected value, and metaphor is the mechanism that alchemically transforms its minus into a plus. In capitalist discourse, surplus enjoyment is an absolute value that radiates its aura without needing metaphor to amplify it.[10] Consequently the leader is a discursive, if auratic, disavowal of the master's discourse—disavowal that its wealth originates in pulsations of lack and excess. A purely imaginary—openly counterfeit—surplus enjoyment becomes the official, true coin of the realm, because no real energy was expended minting it. Formed of this sham substance, the leader is very much the Golden Calf in Hosea that so intrigues Lacan in *Seminar XVII*; a Golden Calf of which Ronald Reagan is perhaps the first outstanding example. Reagan's fiction of a postscarcity society based on a trickle-down, supply-side economy denied anyone ever had to pay: budget cuts would simply force more growth; tax cuts would do the same. Under Reaganomics, at the neo-Hegelian end of history everyone basks in boundless, endless riches.

Despite Reagan's disclaimers, however, even the wealthy must have paid—once. Surplus enjoyment cannot actually persist without a signifying repetition, which necessitates loss. To analyze capitalist discourse properly therefore requires locating precisely where its discursive loss gets mobilized into profit. Of course, since its collective wealth is not symbolized but incarnated in its leader, it is extremely difficult to discover who pays. Indeed, the loss is transferred out: Freud says in modern groups the violence internal to all discourse is simply deported—directed against other groups. Exporting essential loss makes it always someone else who pays. (Which is perhaps why Western media fetishize Third World hunger.)

Moreover, there are actual losses for the subject internal to capitalist discourse. If in the master's discourse the subject is divided from jouissance by the signifier (that is, castrated by language), his jouissance loss is at least prized as a libidinal gift to society. In the discursive quarter turn or revolution that succeeds the master's, however, Lacan shows the subject "divided" not by the signifier but "by jouissance" (73). Divided from what? From knowledge. From the accumulated surplus enjoyment that knowledge represents. Consider carefully the changed position of the subject, $, in hysteria and university discourse:

$$\frac{S_2}{S_1} \rightarrow \frac{a}{\$}$$

University discourse

$$\frac{\$}{a} \rightarrow \frac{S_1}{S_2}$$

Hysteric's discourse

In classical order, the subject's libidinal sacrifice (castration) is deemed "holy" (Freud) for producing a store of knowledge made doubly precious by the *objet a* the secret source of all value. In the two subsequent quarter turns, *a* shifts position: the subject's division is now *by* the jouissance everyone has a right to, and *from* all knowledge of it.

In university discourse subjective division is written:

$$\frac{a}{\$}$$

In hysteria, it is written:

$$\frac{\$}{a}$$

Putting these two discourses together is an unusual move on my part, yet economically, they are structural kin. In hysteria, the subject, $\$$, gains the dominant position—at the cost of having its truth (the a) completely divorced from its only half-spoken (*mi-dit*) signifier (S_1).[11] The hysteric subject's loss of knowledge (S_2) is no longer paid out with the truth of the system, because the place of truth is occupied by a (sham) surplus enjoyment cut off from the signifier that originally produced it.

In university discourse, a different though equally divisive displacement appears. The role of work, no longer recognized as the energized element of the discourse, puts the subject in the position of discursive product (lower right, the position of loss). S_2, the total accumulation of knowledge, is in the dominant position, granted supreme social power through the agency of surplus enjoyment, a.

The effects of the shift are not limited to those taking place in the individual subject. We need only glance, Lacan writes, at the emergence of "consumer society" (92) to grasp that surplus enjoyment has gone from being an internal source of evaluation to being just one more measure of equivalent value: "'Consumer society' derives its meaning from the fact that what makes it the 'element' . . . described as human is made the homogeneous equivalent of whatever surplus *jouissance* is produced by our industry—an imitation surplus *jouissance*, in a word. Moreover, that can catch on. One can do a semblance of surplus *jouissance*—it draws quite a crowd" (92–93).

More Thoughts on War and Death

The intrusion into politics can only be made by recognising that the only discourse there is, and not just analytic discourse, is about jouissance.—Jacques Lacan

With our new century, Lacan's 1969 evocation of the leader's jouissance in the evolving discourse of capitalism is prescient. Ignorance and nonknowledge—the dialectical other of S_2—are valued while simple-minded juvenility characterizes our political and cultural leaders: consider the proud "gentleman's C−" President W. clowns around, mispronouncing words while insisting his favorite reading is a child's nursery book. Any critique emphasizing such a leader's stupidity only strengthens him, for his very role is to embody the innocence and the ignorance that is undivided bliss (jouissance).[12]

Late capitalist discourse is at constant war with whatever threatens to divide its substance; "divisive" is now its worst pejorative. If capitalism's first move was "getting rid of sex"[13] (castration, division by signifiers), the demand for wholeness untouched by the signifier is tellingly indexed by the Freudian slip of (accidentally) murdering (with friendly fire) a fair number of wordsmiths—journalists in Iraq.

But why approach these alterations of the master's discourse and the hyperinflating of surplus enjoyment "literarily," and why evoke "war"? Like modern consumer society and the calculus of pleasure in the Reformation, Kant's *Third Critique* left art swimming in (simulated) jouissance. For Paul de Man "something happened" in the *Third Critique* that forever changed the relation of art to culture and social life (and, troubled by this, he counseled keeping distance from "aesthetic ideology"). Lacan's similarly phatic pronouncement that there is something that exists only in literature and nowhere else implies to the contrary that literary language's surplus value, brought to full dominance in university/capitalist discourse,[14] provides unique access to it. As for war in this discourse: it is unavoidable. While universities undergo decade-long "culture wars," late capitalism stages its wars as awesome spectacles or simulations.

Lacan gave *Seminar XVII* in 1969–70, a time primed for thoughts on war and death.[15] The utterly unintelligible Vietnam War raged on, interminably, intolerably, inexplicably; it became the new fixed horizon of all our youthful aspirations, the final depository of all projected future work, a noncredible war, whose purpose and rationale were blatantly formal and artificially posed as game playing: "the domino theory." Before Vietnam, no one imagined how dehumanizing a war fought under no convincing ideology could be. Devoid of ideological consistency, this war nonetheless dominated all intellectual efforts, its dominion exercised chiefly through figures: "body counts" and "kill ratios." American war planners believed that expending x numbers of bullets per day would guarantee victory. The media made available an overwhelming flood of information that utterly occluded any real reflection on the true cause of this hapless enterprise. Knowledge lost self-confidence: the "need-to-know basis" appeared for the first time, along with euphemisms such as "terminate with extreme prejudice." Norman Mailer's response to everyone's question, "Why Are We in Vietnam?" was as cryptic as that of the CIA agent who answered me with, "Well, those peasants are sittin' on a lot of valuable real estate." Such reasoning is now normalized: the April 9, 2003, *New York Times* editorial begins, "As allied forces seize more and more of Iraqi real estate every day," betraying indifference to the fate of soldiers and civilians and alarm at the potential loss of Iraqi oilfields. The relative revaluing of property over lives was first noted (with sheer, shocked horror) during Vietnam.

Political anxiety logically followed. Every nation tied to the common horizon of this bizarre new type of war suffered anxiety of leadership, whose known modalities were so obviously faltering. The psychical correlate was anxiety about deposing the "father-master" as chief representative of symbolic power. In favor of what? Some looked to Freud's *Totem and Taboo*, a cautionary political allegory of Enlightenment regicides where sons resent and murder a hated primal, privative father; then, poised to enjoy what he had forbidden (sexual enjoyment of mothers and sisters), they deny it for themselves (in a Kantian/superegoic, postrevolutionary parallel of depriving themselves of their own best "Thing.") Pandemic envy of each other's free enjoyment threatens all order. By self-limiting jouissance the brothers convert mutual envy into "fraternal or group feeling" (universal brotherly love); the would-be Hobbesian struggle over possession of goods is turned instead to the profit of the whole.

Totem and Taboo is not, however, the proper allegory for capitalist discourse and its wars. Lacan looked beyond its primitive scene to the modern discourse analyzed by Freud's *Group Psychology and the Analysis of the Ego*, where the group's primordial envy does not disappear but is transformed into a love that forges a union out of what otherwise fractures it. Group life after the patriarchy, "brotherly" *social gain* conceals all losses through the structure of its leadership. The leader is no longer formed in the image of a father.[16] Rather, Freud pictures the new representative of social gain as radiating, reflecting, and refracting the whole group's binding love. The displacement (of the prohibiting father) works by identifying the leader with jouissance itself. Identification transforms ego love by supplanting it: the leader substitutes himself for each individual's ego ideal. Held thus in common, he *becomes* the commonwealth.

Accordingly, any privation of jouissance due to the new social order is repaid with a "universality" echoed endlessly among the members, relayed through the leader, whose full-flowing magnetic love holds them in bonds of a peculiarly asexual type (i.e., with no division by the signifier). Spread evenly among all, there can be no gap between the representation of total group love and its representative (contrast this with the gap or "interval" that empowers classical mastery). Freud thus explores a new discourse, a frankly "libidinal" social tie without (sexual) division, which piques Lacan's interest.[17]

Lacan's painstaking algorithmic alteration of the master's discourse at the formal level tallies with Freud's *Group Psychology*, which challenges Freud's own earlier representations of the father in *Totem and Taboo*, the Oedipus myth, and later *Moses and Monotheism*. Reviewing Freud's fathers/leaders, Lacan remarks how passing strange it is that in most text-myths the father is murdered for preventing his son, unconsciously or not, from enjoying his own mother. But the exception, *Group Psychology*, says it all; it shows that the real burning question is not the son's enjoyment of the mother but, "How can and does a group survive the death of the father?" When Oedipus solves the riddle of the Sphinx, his success puts a halt to the decimating tribute (of their "best and brightest") the Sphinx was exacting of the Thebans. It also ends the mysterious plague spreading death and destruction throughout all the Theban people. The result is, yes, Oedipus's provisional enjoyment of his mother; but, ultimately, Oedipus's symbolic castration results (he loses his eyes, needs his daughter for support, and so on), and it saves the city. Only once the son is castrated does the riddle of how the group survives the primal father's death get answered. Similarly, in *Totem and Taboo* what creates social solidarity after the father's murder is the brothers' communally shared guilt and regret for the loss of the father's *protection for the whole horde*: self-castration by the brothers salvages the community. Finally, Lacan notes that in *Moses and Monotheism* (the text that intrigues Lacan in *Seminar XVII*) Freud voices the suspicion that Moses was murdered after transmitting God's laws to his people,[18] placing a parricide (restriction on paternal enjoyment) as what preserves the group.

But not in *Group Psychology*. Although he makes comparatively little of it, Lacan is surprised by the complete absence of hatred for the leader—and no evident desire to murder him (a wish the father ordinarily provokes). The leader is beloved; no murderousness shapes his group; and the remarkable absence of malice toward him indexes the singular depth of the discursive shift. Denial of murderous wishes, like taming the violence of language (castration, metaphoric cuts, etc.) is a way of stating that the group no longer feels threatened by death; like the ego, it "knows" itself immortal. This is ego-logical: the group ego essentially lives on in or as the afterlife—the surplus enjoyment—of what the master/father created.

Where does war figure in? I again point to Vietnam—more precisely, to those who protested it. They sadly reappeared, distorted and larger than ever, in the new leader who emerged full-blown on the American political stage. Is there any doubt that Ronald Reagan, blustering about getting government off our backs, also transformed our image of cultural leadership from a masterly one to that of a leader imbued with harmless, painless, imitation jouissance? Was any leader ever less patriarchal than Reagan? Any earlier president could be a "father"—leaders as different as Lincoln, Johnson, Teddy Roosevelt, or Kennedy were masterful and patriarchal. But Reagan a *father* figure? Hardly! The media made it abundantly clear Reagan enjoyed a terrible relation to his children.

The "Teflon president" instead conveyed, by image and gesture, that auratic power derives solely from that higher stage of surplus enjoyment Lacan explains in *Seminar XVII*: the sham, but expansive puissance of jouissance "en toc." Reagan identified with, and did not merely represent, the wealth of the nation;[19] under his regime, everyone would effortlessly "grow wealth." (This soon proved a wealth only deficits, credit spending, and manipulated accounting could produce.) Although Reaganomics economically ravaged several social classes, Reagan transformed the presidency with lasting impact on all forms of leadership today.

Ultimately the group constituted by this leader exacts its own price. Even if sexual division (castration) is displaced as the primary mechanism of social organization, the new form of its division (by jouissance)

Lacan discovered requires an even greater privation, a deeper loss than any the master's discourse imposed. After all, surplus enjoyment must still really add to the group's fortunes—there is no way to dispense with this—but it cannot afford to do so by exploiting its members from within. (To avoid deadly rivalry is presumed necessary.) It must therefore seek its energy source outside the group—for example, in Iraq. But late capitalist discourse masks the privations it necessarily exacts to turn a painless profit. It no longer openly engages in this colonial takeover (although there are new apologists for colonialism, like Niall Fergusson and Dinesh D'Souza).

Instead, our discourse obscures the privations imposed to increase its wealth through a device I can only call "reverse envy": you identify with those you are exploiting for your economy's functioning. Capitalism, that is, extends the mechanisms of group-leader identification well beyond its borders to include even the aliens and enemies exploited for its sake. Such Adam Smithian sympathy for the enemy-brother finally proves different from what Freud expected. With mutual hostility foresworn within the fraternal group, Freud thought it would be necessary to displace it as violence against other groups (intergang warfare). However, a secondary remodeling (the first is envy into equality and hatred into brotherly love) appears in the late capitalist discourse. It still requires real destruction and loss to generate its surplus jouissance, but now hostility—even open hostilities, war itself—must be absorbed in the aura of universal love. War is now a means of radiating love—this is how the Iraq war is posed—no matter how lethal.

Iraq. A war with such self-contradictory rationales that it goes Vietnam one better: liberation from without; liberal democracy installed there, while the same is beaten bloody in the talk shows at home. Waving like a banner overall are the same endless restrictions on knowledge. War demands knowledge as ignorance, as represented perfectly by the televisual stream of unintelligible battlefield reports from embedded reporters. Caught in the same (formal) discourse of late capitalism, reporters, war protesters, soldiers, and congressmen cannot escape how it twists hate into love. Where a passion for the signifier outweighs the countervailing passion for ignorance, it erupts in the streets to raise a symbolic word against the new regime of stupidity. But "die-ins" (like the "tea-and-rice sympathy diets" of the Vietnam era) partake of the same crucial identification process internal to the "modern" group: so that surplus enjoyment can remain the free agent of the dominant, we must lovingly embrace those we need to destroy. Even our wounds have to be self-inflicted; our casualties are not from enemy blows, but from "friendly fire," "blue on blue."

Iraq is the world's first war ("a war unlike any other," a TV general intones) fought as a form of militant accounting: a "businesslike" war, with employee costs kept down and instant payoffs for victims of the death it deals. (Soldiers who "accidentally" kill or wound civilians have sacks of money to compensate families immediately.) Humanitarian aid rains down, along with the bombs, each packaged (inadvertently) to resemble the other. The war's stated goal? To establish a businesslike government for Iraq through pairing bureaucratic chiefs of each new Iraqi government department with an American counterpart—installing there the bureaucracy reviled here. Bureaucracy: a system now structured not by Weberian rationality but by the discursive dominant of innocent ignorance, with CEO leaders who "didn't know" or "can't recall" (and are cheered on for their ignorance). A discourse, then, where war's loss and death (the real, jouissance) are denied even more cravenly than Freud, in "Thoughts on War and Death," remarked of World War I.

The balance sheet of Iraqi casualties, civilian and military, merits those mythical accountings that were the hallmark of Vietnam. Why? To lay claim to the historical end to history, to a system without gaps or flaws that refuses to concede to the real of jouissance the power to disrupt (or even energize) it. A system that appears not to create what it gains (Reagan's "rising tide" floats all boats—jouissance aplenty, indivisible jouissance for all). Once the manufactured value of accumulated surplus enjoyment becomes surplus value *in itself*, accounting will never be anything any longer but a pure, unreadable fiction. All losses can be made up for by creative accounting, deficit spending, or outright fraud: all "problems" that economic growth will, by itself, remedy—at no cost.

Absolute loss. Death. Only real destruction, rather than symbolic expropriation, seems capable now of generating the crucial lack that energizes our kind of economy and prevents its decline into depression. For accumulated wealth to remain our dominant, the be-all and end-all of our discourse, we must criminalize poverty and insist the wealthy never have to pay. War is the *only* drive, the only slippage in the system: "The rich man doesn't pay"; the poor do.

Notes

An earlier version of this essay was published in Slovenia as "Nekai âasu Primernih Mislio Vojni In Smrti," trans. Alenka Zupančič, *Razpol* 13 (2003): 157–91.

1   Jacques Lacan, *Le séminaire, livre XVII: L'envers de la psychanalyse*, ed. Jacques-Alain Miller (Paris: Seuil, 1991), 46. All further references to this volume will be given in the body of the text.
2   Juliet Flower MacCannell, *Figuring Lacan: Criticism and the Cultural Unconscious* (Lincoln: University of Nebraska Press, 1986). I liked the literary ambiguity of *plus-de-jouir*: no more—by colloquially dropping the *ne* in *ne plus*, for example, "plus de pain" ("out of bread"); and, also, just "more." It resonated with the French for Marx's surplus value (*plus-value*).
3   Further, "When you construct a factory somewhere, naturally you draw energy, you can even accumulate it. Well then, the apparatuses that have been installed so that these sorts of turbines function to the point where you can put the energy in a bottle are built according to this same logic I'm speaking about, namely the function of the signifier" (54–55).
4   "This is the dimension in which work, knowledge at work becomes necessary insofar as it initially stems from . . . everything that can possibly be articulated as signifier" (56).
5   Hegel anticipated that, at the end of cultural development, the master would transform into the figure of the State (90). Lacan says this is "definitively refuted by some discoveries made by Marx" (90).
6   The slave's concrete knowledge about jouissance is a contradiction, since jouissance excludes knowledge. Marx grasped the hidden labor value in what the slave produces: Lacan saw it was actually knowledge the master expropriates.
7   Marx underestimated the function of knowledge and overestimated work as the ultimate producer of surplus enjoyment. The master excluded jouissance to gain in knowledge. Even though this is the ostensible aim, the master's system had to keep gaining in overall jouissance-energy to prevent winding down. This jouissance-gain, subtracted from the slave, gets surreptitiously offset by increasing the slave's knowledge (know-how; *savoir-faire*): his potential for education and enlightenment.
8   Lacan's Parisian audience would know the opening of Marx's *Capital*, where the wealth of the Western nations presents itself as a vast accumulation of commodities.
9   Sigmund Freud, *Group Psychology and the Analysis of the Ego* (1921), in *The Standard Edition of the Complete Psychological Works of Sigmund Freud*, ed. J. Strachey (London: Hogarth, 1955), 18:65–143.
10 Lacan alludes to Diderot's scoundrel, Rameau's nephew, who educates his son by dangling a gold coin for him to idolize (222).

11 A propositional truth never fully excludes the position of the speaker who enunciates it; Lacan says this of Freud's urtext on perversion ("A Child Is Being Beaten"): "This proposition has the effect of being sustained by a subject divided by *jouissance*" (73).
12 Universities are quite complicit with innocence/ignorance as the dominant; many now account the overall value of their education as quite apart from student achievement. One leading Ivy League university grants 90 percent of its graduates honors.
13 Jacques Lacan, *Television: A Challenge to the Psychoanalytic Establishment*, trans. D. Hollier et al. (New York: Norton, 1990), 30.
14 "Reading" is Lacan's response to his own question, "How to behave in the face of culture?" (208) when the Neolithic had *langue, parole, savoir*; but no reading (218).
15 I shared the same wartime horizon in the same city as Lacan's *Seminar XVII*—but not the same year. In 1968 I knew nothing of him. *Seminar XVII* nonetheless evokes memories: of mingling with Parisian students similar in political posturing and critical attitude to those Lacan engages in the direct-action seminars.
16 Lacan says the work of sexual positioning done by language must be recalled at the moment when, "in talking of the other side of psychoanalysis, the question arises of the place of psychoanalysis in politics" (90). In *The Regime of the Brother: After the Patriarchy* (London: Routledge, 1991), to worry through the problematic of the politics of sexual positioning "after the father" I too turned to *Group Psychology*. My "the regime of the brother" is what Lacan had already called "fraternity": its social outcome is always "segregation" (132). But *Seminar XVII* was first published in 1991: the times—of war and death—had surely urged these questions on us.
17 Comparing President Clinton to George W. Bush illustrates the discursive shift away from sexual division. Clinton made, not inherited, his money and he was frankly sexual in manner (a sexuality exposed by Kenneth Starr). Bush identifies himself wholly with (1) the unearned wealth Lacan calls dammed-up libido (capital); (2) the ignorance that is bliss; and (3) innocence—his sex life (unlike Clinton's) is never mentioned.
18 Lacan calls on Biblical experts and scours Europe for a copy of Eric Sellin's *Moses*, Freud's textual authority for the "murder" of Moses.
19 A recent study shows, surprisingly, that Hitler was highly enamored of "wealth"—abstract and real. Steven Erlanger, "Hitler, It Seems, Loved Money and Died Rich," *New York Times*, August 7, 2002.

11

Dominique Hecq

The Impossible Power
of Psychoanalysis

The Other Side of Psychoanalysis is Lacan's most political seminar, beginning as it does during the student unrest following the disappointing contestation of May 1968. Moreover, although Lacan seems to desperately cling to the symbolic, one feels the pull of the real in his discourse. This is most obvious in his discussion of jouissance and the function of the father. Here, one finds a shift in Lacan's theory of *objet a* and a break with what he now presents as Freud's doubling of the myth of the Oedipus complex. I would argue, however, that the truth of the matter is not only correlated with the "place of psychoanalysis in politics," as Lacan would have it, but also with the place of politics in psychoanalysis, and hence, with the (im)possible power of psychoanalysis itself.[1]

Indeed, after May 1968, this question of the (im)possible power of psychoanalysis looms higher than ever in Lacan's discourse, that is, both at the formal level of the structure of this discourse and at the narrative level. More particularly, power, impossibility, and impotence are notions that pervade Lacan's discussion of the psychoanalyst's act, jouissance, *objet a*, real and symbolic fathers, and truth, moving on to "a discourse that would not be a *semblant*," which testifies to his distancing himself from the father as agent of castration.[2] This question of power prompts him to elaborate his theory of the four discourses in an attempt to subvert the make-believe of a social bond commonly attributed to the discourses of philosophy, politics, and science—including medicine.

Interconnected through the derivation and permutation of their components, these four discourses allegedly reveal the structure of a social bond whose definition remains, strangely enough, taken for granted: following Hegel's dialectic of the master and slave, Lacan seems to conceive of it in terms of relations of power and domination.[3] Similarly, it is only in terms of power and domination that he uses concepts or signifiers which he borrows from Freud, Marx, and Bataille to substantiate some of his own conceptions. Consequently, the question I wish to ask here is not so much about "the place of psychoanalysis in politics" as about the relationship between power and psychoanalysis.

While one of my aims is to briefly historicize and problematize the concept of power, I also wish to draw attention to some intertextual inferences that highlight points of (im)possibilities in Lacan's four paradigmatic discourses. I will address four subthemes: Freud's notion of the impossible and the psychoanalytic act, the four discourses and jouissance as the impossible, Oedipus and the return of the dead father and, finally, the equivocation of jouissance. This is because "the intrusion into politics can only be made by recognizing that the only discourse there is . . . is the discourse of *jouissance*, at least when one is hoping for the work of truth from it" (90).

Psychoanalysis does not purport to exert any power. Nonetheless, psychoanalysis is interested in the genesis of power as that which produces change. I am thinking of the act of the analyst, on the one hand, and of that which exerts authority or control over others, on the other; for example, in forms of aggressivity and dominance, including political influence or ascendancy. In point of fact, Freud has shown not only that there is interplay between these two aspects of power, but also that dominance implies an unconscious submission to the source of power.

Now, somewhat ironically, psychoanalysis was born of impossible power, notably, the requirement to use no power. This came at the request of Frau Emmy von N.: "Don't move, say nothing, don't touch me," she told Freud at the beginning of the treatment.[4] Freud abandoned hypnosis and inverted the injunction to establish the setting for the talking cure with its famous rule, the prerequisite of its own (im)possibility.

But where does one situate the analytical act, the possibility of it succeeding in a technical field which is delimited by impossibilities such as the uselessness of any active or suggestive intervention, or the impossibility of saying everything? Freud set limits to psychoanalysis, of course, but these had little to do with the constraints of praxis. Rather, these were brought to bear on inner constraints: the rock of castration for men and masculine protest of penis envy for women. Understandably, it didn't take Freud long to rank analyzing as the third impossible task alongside governing and educating. In his usual linguistically picky fashion, Lacan reminds us of this in chapter 12 of *Seminar XVII* (201).

Often compelling the subject to a need for punishment, the superego has, Freud suggests in *Civilization and Its Discontents*, its origin in some subjection to power through fear of losing the love of the love object.[5] Once the prohibition is interiorized, the subject never fails to experience anxiety in the face of the superego. Because the origin and energy of this superego are located in the unconscious, it is particularly ferocious. Yet, as an heir to the parental superego, it might also happen to be its inverted image. This is the kernel upon which reason has no grip, which explains the impossibility of educating.

Why should Freud be so pessimistic when it comes to the possible success of the treatment? At the risk of simplifying Freud's reasoning, I would suggest that this is because the drives cannot be educated. Drives change object or register—as in sublimation or desexualization—but they never give up. Besides, as Freud discovered, unconscious processes know nothing about either contradiction or time. On the other hand, the compulsion to repeat, negative transference, and the death drive are important resistances to the cure. Love sweeps everything away, it would seem.

Perhaps here is the navel of the impossible power of psychoanalysis for Freud. The treatment aims at reactivating the subject's infantile neurosis rather than at treating only identifiable symptoms. Yet, although the analytic situation produces some transference neurosis, it does not merely replicate an infantile neurosis. According to Freud, the analyst's power over symptoms can be compared with sexual potency: the most powerful man, capable of creating a whole child, could not possibly produce in the female organism a head, an arm, or a leg only; he is not even capable of choosing the sex of the child.[6] The words Freud uses are *Macht* and *Potenz*, that is, power and sexual potency. Thus here is the space allocated to the act of the analyst: the analyst's power is nothing but a power he or she has no control over; the best he or she can do is to trigger the transference and sustain it. As to interpretation, here is what Françoise Dolto said twenty years ago: "L'analyste, c'est le patient, c'est lui qui interprète"—the analyst *is* the patient, it is the patient who interprets.[7]

Of course, psychoanalysis does not seek to educate. Nor does it seek to moralize or normalize. At stake in an analysis is reconciling the subject with her desire and this desire with the law, that is, the law of castration, of the prohibition of incest, which does not mean submitting to the social state of affairs, the political state, or fashionable mores. As Freud said somewhere, psychoanalysis does not purport to have a vision of the world.

What can one say about politics? In "Group Psychology and the Analysis of the Ego," Freud distinguishes between two "artificial crowds," namely, those originating from some external constraint aiming at preventing their dissolution in the army and the church.[8] This kind of sociological perspective highlights the figure of the father and the bond between a people and its leader, a bond of an identificatory and hypnotic nature—identification being the most archaic mode of love, since one identifies with the lost object. Identification with the leader is allegedly more complex. What the crowd puts in place of its ego ideal is the same object; this is not to say an external object, but the object of fantasy, the cause of desire, the fetish. The leader thus becomes invested with an ideal function that might, in a Kleinian register, be compared with the projection of the crowd's internal objects. All individual members of the crowd have "identified with others in their own egos."[9] One might say that they have renounced their own ego ideal at the expense of some other, imparting to this agency some part of their superego and relinquishing their moral exigencies in the name of their charismatic leader. Since the exceptional being has become their foundation, what they entertain with this figure is, however, a quasi-hypnotic relationship, with all the dependencies this implies due, for instance, to some overestimation of the love object.

Lacan revisits these three famous impossibilities through the four discourses. He will not make the impossible into a dead end as that which can necessarily not be done, but rather makes it the foundation of all discourse, "for each impossibility . . . is always linked to . . . impotence" (203). In this sense Lacan's framework for modal operators in *Seminar XVII* is not an Aristotelian one: necessity (impossibility) and contingency (impotence) are not opposed to each other, but rather interrelated. The impossible here is at the intersection between the symbolic and the real, which testifies to a collapsing between symbolic and real in Lacan's thought.

But why, one might like to ask first, *this* term of discourse?

First, because a discourse establishes the social bond by articulating subjects not only to the imaginary—and to ideology, but also to the symbolic—to language. Second, because a discourse aims at truth: as Freud made clear, the analytic relationship is predicated upon the love of truth and on the distrust of make-believe and lure, a proposition that Lacan reiterates here as well. The truth of unconscious desire, indeed, reveals itself only through speech. Moreover, there are neither true nor false concepts except in language. Thus the question of being, for instance, entails neither truth nor lie: being is. This is also what Lacan suggests, albeit more radically, when he says the following about his elaboration of the four discourses in the contingent situation of 1968:

> The discourses in question are nothing other than the signifying articulation, the apparatus whose presence, whose existing status alone dominates and governs anything that at any given moment is capable of emerging as speech. They are discourses without speech, which subsequently comes and lodges itself within them. Thus I can say to myself, concerning this intoxicating phenomenon called beginning to speak, that certain reference points in the discourse in which this is inserted would perhaps be of such a nature that, occasionally, one does not start to speak without knowing what one is doing. (194)

In the wake of Foucault's work, it would appear in 1968 that some disciplines have to do with truth without quite deserving to be called sciences: these are what Francophones have become used to calling *sciences humaines*, the human sciences.[10] In 1966, Foucault claims these sciences humaines to be "knowledges" or "discursive practices." In 1968, Lacan, who, like Freud, attempted to rethink psychoanalysis according to a scientific paradigm, now turns it into the matrix of these knowledges. It follows that truth becomes a decisive, albeit somewhat confusing, concept in *The Other Side of Psychoanalysis*, much of the discussion being beyond the scope of this essay.

Psychoanalysis and medicine are radically opposed in that psychoanalysis does not use knowledge to cure a symptom. Labeling symptoms means nothing in psychoanalysis. As we know, the hysterical symptom defies medical knowledge just as it defies medical discourse—it might be useful here just to recall that knowledge has different acceptations for medicine and psychoanalysis, of course. Thus for Lacan, knowledge (*connaissance*) and truth are at opposite ends of the spectrum in the discourse of science, while knowledge (*savoir*) and truth are interrelated in the psychoanalytic setting, since knowledge is "something spoken, something that is said . . . that speaks all by itself—that is the unconscious" (90).[11] In other words, the truth of the symptom cannot be read in terms of medical knowledge, or data. Hence Lacan's categorical imperative to analysts that they forget what they know.[12] As the clinic shows, faced with the hysteric and her question, medical discourse is impotent. In "Radiophonie," Lacan suggests that this partly explains why "educating is doomed to failure."[13] Thus impotence is the sister of truth as well as the sister of the symptom, whereas jouissance is the impossible.

Now, to arrive at the articulation of the master's discourse, Lacan twists Hegel's dialectic of the master and the slave: like Heidegger, Lacan observes that the struggle unto death is not real in this conflict, for there is a preexisting pact that prevents the death of the slave. This pact is a symbolic one, which means that language preexists rivalry. Thus, far from being master in his own house, the master in *Seminar XVII* only occupies a place in a structure.

Lacan examines three versions of the master's discourse: the philosopher's version, the capitalist's version, and the physician's version. The agent is the master himself, the one who commands.

It follows that Descartes's cogito is the master signifier of this system. But the real question now arises as to where the subject of such discourse might be: nowhere. The subject is repressed in the universality of the discourse itself.

Philosophy, Lacan suggests, erases the subject in favor of universal knowledge. Truth, the impetus of discourse, is repressed. The subject hides his own division from himself through identifying with the transparency of self-awareness.

As for the capitalist, though he does not seem to know what he wants, he nonetheless requires that everything run smoothly. He wants efficient professionalism — today, one might say efficient strategies, as in publish or perish/pay or perish. Such are the masters of a society where the blind are leading the blind on the pretext that it is for the good of the other. If one wanted to be flippant, one might sum up the discourse of the capitalist as "Work because I need you to."

For Lacan, the university discourse is akin to the master's discourse. But here, knowledge — that which is being passed on from generation to generation — fails to suppose that there is a subject in the equation: authors are but names tagged onto laws in the great capital of knowledge.

At this point in the seminar, not without demagogy, Lacan tells a crowd of students that they are in the position of other with regard to those who teach them, just like slaves or proletarians with regard to their masters: "In the articulation that I describe as the university discourse, the *a* is in the place of what? In the place, let's say, of the exploited in the university discourse, who are easy to recognize — they are students" (172). Without spelling it out, he is saying that these students are conditioning the jouissance of academics who produce only a fantasy: the hope that knowledge might produce jouissance, or truth. But in the light of what has been said before, this is impossible. Such knowledge produces no more truth than psychiatry does.

In a way, *The Other Side of Psychoanalysis* is an occasional discourse, particularly in the sense that Lacan attempts to seduce students by offering them the position of the exploited in the university discourse. It is, however, somewhat ironic that he should derive his most significant concept, that is, *objet a*, from Marx's concept of surplus value, with *a* as the excess jouissance that has no use — no use value — and yet persists by definition for the sake of its own "spending," for the sake of jouissance. For this is a part of jouissance that has nothing to do with pleasure: this is "the accursed part" (*la part maudite*), as Georges Bataille would have said, the part that one acquires in order to spend.[14] This excess jouissance is power of pure loss.

But what is jouissance in *Seminar XVII*?

In *Totem and Taboo*, Freud posits two hypotheses: the tyrannical father of the primal horde who owns all the women has been killed and eaten by his sons, for they wished to appropriate his power. Once dead, the father radically incarnates the prohibition, for in death, "the dead father became stronger than the living one had been—for events took the course we so often see them follow in human affairs to this day."[15] The movement from life to death parallels the movement from prevention to prohibition: prevention requires only physical force, whereas prohibition presupposes speech. The effect of force is specific; the power of speech is universal. Thus the death of the father takes the place of a signifier insofar as it is endowed with universal value and insofar as the Name of the Father substitutes itself for it. Lacan's move here establishes the connection between death and language.

Here, jouissance no longer signifies the impossible return to the mother, the Thing, the unnameable. Jouissance is here the father's jouissance, which is prohibited to the son. Like Freud's death of the father of the primal horde, this jouissance is a mythical invention. Although Lacan denounces its mythical status, he turns it into the very principle of what he calls the real father who "carries out the work of the master agency" as pure effect of the signifier (146).

That Freud could not steer away from a myth, Lacan interprets as the very index of the real, a "logical obstacle of what, in the symbolic, declares itself to be impossible" (143). He then makes it clear that the real father is a "structural operator." The real father, then, is the agent of castration—which has nothing to do with the fantasy of the castrating father, the imaginary father. The real father is reduced to his very function, that is, to symbolize castration: if he is the guardian of jouissance, it is by dint of the fact that the father is dead that they "do not enjoy what is there for them to enjoy" (143). Hence, it is only because he is called a father. He is but a name. Thus, for Lacan, the impossible of the Freudian myth lies in that one cannot kill a name: "A name can also be used to plug something up. I am astounded," says Lacan, "that it is possible to associate the idea that at this level there can be some murder or other, with this plug of a name of the father, whatever it may be." Further: "One is not the father of signifiers, at the very most one is 'because of'" (150–51).

Seminar XVII, however, does not resolve the question of the real father. The question underlying all others floats away, one might say, with one sentence about Lacan's interpretation of Freud's myth of the dead father—or is it a dream? "Even for the child, whatever one might think, the father is he who knows nothing about truth" (151). Here is the truth about castration. The father knows nothing of truth because, like King Lear, I would suggest, he "didn't know that he was dead" (142). With this in mind, one might argue that writing *The Interpretation of Dreams* was Freud's own way of performing symbolic self-castration following the death of his father. As if to metaphorically enact the dream of the dissection of his own pelvis, as a performing artist might do, Freud proceeded to his dissecting himself symbolically.

In *The Other Side of Psychoanalysis*, the father is a creditor, "what one simply calls 'my agent.' You can see what that means in general: 'I pay him for that.' Not even 'I compensate him for having nothing else to do'" (146). Lacan, it seems to me, eludes the distinction between real father and symbolic father, both being "effects of language," both being "structural operators." The real father, though, articulates the two terms of a logical contradiction: he is castrated and not castrated; he is an impossible, or the one who prevents access to the impossible of jouissance. Hence the accepted conception of the father as one who is not doing much: the father intervenes as little as possible, provided he occupies his position. However, like the psychoanalyst who plays dead, he must be paid for being there.

More than anything else, *The Other Side of Psychoanalysis* marks a shift in the signification of castration through an interpretation of the dream of the dead father. True, Lacan maintains that "castration is a real operation that is introduced through the incidence of a signifier, no matter which, into the sexual relationship. And it goes without saying that it determines the father as this impossible real" (149). Far from being a fantasy, castration partly generates desire, but it is impossible to reduce it to the prohibition, for castration does not entirely consist in the operation of a privation, with its reference to the law and to a father. Castration has become that which is affiliated to the dead father as guardian of jouissance, not knowledge. The Other—that is, the Other as lacking— becomes the foundation of castration.

Although Freud acknowledges that *a* prohibition might cause desires, he does not claim that *the* prohibition—and thus, language, generates desire. Lacan, on the other hand, posits that it is the prohibition that produces desire, or, as he puts it, "castration . . . leaves something to be desired." In this sense, he is close to Bataille: "If psychoanalysis makes sex present for us, and death as a dependency," excess jouissance is a modality of frustration (150).[16]

Lacan examines the concept of jouissance within various parameters such as social ascendancy, work, politics, and libidinal economy. Following Freud's thesis in *Beyond the Pleasure Principle*, Lacan locates jouissance in repetition, thus in the drive: "The path towards death is nothing other than what is called *jouissance*" (18). The repetitive character of the drive, of trauma, the timeless effect of the mythical object—or rather the part object as cause of desire—are predicated upon a jouissance that entails a reunion with the lost object. Not only is this jouissance impossible, it is also prohibited since the subject relinquishes it upon acceding to speech, marked as it is by the law of language and linked as it is to the dead father. However, the impossible is not the prohibition. While the father circumscribes the impossible, it is the mother who is prohibited. In order to eschew this difficulty, Lacan alters the signification of *objet a*: while *objet a* remains the index of jouissance, the cause of desire, and as such the sacrificial object one finds in the work of Bataille, *objet a* becomes the means of access to being, to the absolute, to jouissance and death.[17] It is as though *objet a* now both stands for jouissance and serves as proxy for it in the field of desire and language—the spoiled sign of jouissance, the impossible excess of discourse itself.

Finally, one might like to ask what the place of truth is in the four discourses, for it is striking that it occupies a privileged position in discourse itself. The truth of the master-slave relationship is produced neither by the master nor by the slave. The truth of a scientific proposition is inherent in the formula: the truth of the hysteric can only be spoken in analysis, thus in relation to the analyst's discourse. Yet the subject can accede to the truth of his desire only through his relationship with the Other, that is, the Other of analysis, and not the Other of knowledge. Is this because truth "makes the master signifier of death manifest" (200)? This would suggest that truth, rather than being an index of impotence, is one of impossibility. It is, at any rate, accessible only "through a half-saying" and cannot therefore be said wholly "for the reason that beyond this half there is nothing to say" (200).

At this point of impotence on this author's part, I hope that by identifying points of impossibility in Lacan's discourses I have conveyed his conceptualizing of paradoxes inherent in society as a series of practices whereby everything is reduced to speech and its effects, thereby highlighting the place and function of the subject's jouissance.

Notes

1. Jacques Lacan, *Le séminaire, livre XVII: L'envers de la psychanalyse*, ed. J.-A. Miller (Paris: Seuil, 1991), 90. All further references to this volume will appear in the body of the text.
2. Jacques Lacan, *Le séminaire, livre XVIII: D'un discours qui ne serait pas du semblant*. Unpublished.
3. See Mladen Dolar's essay in this volume, "Hegel as the Other Side of Psychoanalysis," for a reading of *Seminar XVII* based on Lacan's inconsistent treatment of Hegel, a philosopher who is "omnipresent in this seminar and whose dialectic of master and slave presents the background for the very introduction of the discourse of the master."
4. Sigmund Freud, *Studies on Hysteria* (1893–1895), in *The Standard Edition of the Complete Psychological Works of Sigmund Freud*, ed. J. Strachey (London: Hogarth, 1955), 2:49.
5. Sigmund Freud, *Civilization and Its Discontents* (1930), in *The Standard Edition*, 21:59.
6. Sigmund Freud, "On Beginning the Treatment" (1913), in *The Standard Edition*, 12:130.
7. Françoise Dolto, *Séminaire de psychanalyse d'enfants, 2: Édition réalisée avec la collaboration de J. F. de Sauverzac* (Paris: Seuil, 1985), 19.
8. Sigmund Freud, *Group Psychology and the Analysis of the Ego* (1921), in *The Standard Edition* 18:79.
9. Freud, *Group Psychology*, 94.
10. Michel Foucault's book *Les mots et les choses: Une archéologie des sciences humaines* was published in 1966 by Gallimard, determining the foundation of the subsection Bibliothèque des Sciences Humaines.
11. There are two possible translations for the term *knowledge* in French: *savoir* and *connaissance*. The point of making the difference is that *savoir* is expressed in prepositional clauses introduced by the verb *savoir*, as in *je sais que*, "I know that . . . ," whereas the verb *connaître* expresses knowledge in a transitive way, as in *je connais madame X*, "I know Mrs. X."
12. Jacques Lacan, "The Function and Field of Speech and Language in Psychoanalysis," in *Ecrits: A Selection*, trans. B. Fink (New York: Norton, 2002), 57.
13. Jacques Lacan, "Radiophonie," *Scilicet* 2–3 (1970): 97.
14. See Georges Bataille, *La part maudite, précédé de la notion de dépense* (Paris: Minuit, 1990).
15. Sigmund Freud, "Totem and Taboo," in *The Standard Edition*, 13:143.
16. See also Georges Bataille, *L'érotisme* (Paris: Minuit, 1957).
17. See ibid.

PART III **Discourses of Contemporary Life**

12

Éric Laurent   **Symptom and Discourse**

Lacan, in the classical phase of his teaching, insists that we must not forget the "tragic sense" or the "tragic experience" at the heart of psychoanalytic treatment. The political experience, as formulated by Marcel Gauchet, is also the experience of an irreducible division.[1] In classical terms it is an experience of "stasis," of conflict. Or, in the terms of Carl Schmitt, it can be defined in terms of friend and enemy.[2] In all these cases, it is the experience of a pulling apart that is tragic because without remedy. In turn, psychoanalysis is an experience of the bar over the subject and a bar over the Other. This is above all our own version of the "tragic experience," as it is lived out in the treatment itself. When psychoanalysis neglects this initial rupture it collapses into psychotherapy.

The mass diffusion of psychotherapies is accompanied by a therapeutic posture in politics. This has been described by one author in the following terms: "Groups and institutions increasingly adopt the posture they believe to be that of the psychoanalyst: listening to suffering. This triumph of the psychotherapist has disastrous effects: the abandonment of autonomy, depression, regression."[3]

How can we adopt a psychoanalytic position whose effects are different from these? How do we address the collectivity? In his "Theory of Turin," Jacques-Alain Miller has reintroduced the sometimes neglected distinction between the subject and the individual: "What is individual is a body, it is me. The subject-effect that is produced within the individual, and which disturbs its functions, is articulated with the Other, the big Other."[4] The collectivity is a collectivity of subjects. Miller deduces two interpretative practices from this. One reinforces alienation on a massive scale; the other refers each of the members of the community to their own solitude, which is the solitude of their relationship to an ideal.

We could, in the same vein, analyze Lacan's intervention in 1970 when on two separate occasions he addressed the public at his seminar and the students at the University of Paris at Vincennes with the avowed intention of "shaming" them. The final sentence of *Seminar XVII* reads: "I happen to make you ashamed, not too much, but just enough." From the good-enough mother to the analyst who makes one ashamed enough—now that's a detour Winnicott would have never predicted!

Two Attitudes in the Face of Guilt: To Shame and to Forgive

Strange intervention! How psychoanalytic is it to shame people? As if there weren't already enough shame to go around! As if the shame of living was not the nucleus of what subtends the demand addressed to the psychoanalyst in the register of neurosis! Lacan stresses it himself in this seminar. How are we to conceive of the position of the psychoanalyst as adding to this shame? Is it a matter of a "moralist of the masses," or even of an "immoralist," as André Gide said, who refers each person to the solitude of his or her jouissance in their relationship to the master signifier?

This same *Seminar XVII* includes an appendix, an "impromptu" that took place at Vincennes on December 3, 1969, under the heading "Analyticon." The reference of this title is quite precise. The mention of Petronius's *Satiricon* is explicit in February 1970. Lacan refers to this satire in order to distinguish between the wealthy and the master. The occasion arose for him with the appearance of Fellini's film by the name of *Satyricon*, with its "spelling mistake." The Roman comedies, like the satires, constitute an original genre, particular to the Republic, and then to the Empire, distinct from the Greek models that inspired them.

This "shaming" comes on the heels of Lacan's reflection on the mainspring of the psychoanalyst's action, as seen by Freud. For Freud, it is a question above all of an action that is founded on the "love of truth."

This is psychoanalytic frankness. In its name Freud sweeps aside the niceties of social communication in order to bring about the recognition of a real. Lacan thus draws an opposition between the limits of action in the name of the love of truth, and action that bears upon shame, which relates to a different field.

Shame is an eminently psychoanalytic affect that belongs in the same series as guilt. One of the reference points for psychoanalytic action is never to alleviate guilt. When the subject says to you that he feels guilty, he will have excellent reasons for saying so and, as it happens, he is always right. This, in any case, is what the hypothesis about unconscious guilt feelings holds. Contrary to psychotherapies, psychoanalysis recognizes and admits this guilt. The phrase "making ashamed" is inscribed in the Freudian tradition, and it is a constant clinical position throughout Lacan's work.

When Lacan makes a political action out of the way one handles this register, he is in advance of the "moral" phase that the forgetting of politics was to soon engender. The importance of moral language in exchanges in the public sphere was not so obvious in 1970 when the final echoes of the politics of that century were still resonating. As soon as we became as one after the collapse of the Berlin Wall, we began to encounter the language of morality. We experienced an unfolding of the demand for apologies, for regrets, for forgiveness, for repentance, all terms borrowed from the language of morality; "being ashamed" has become a worldwide symptom.

Contrary to "making ashamed," the master's discourse seeks to treat guilt through the act of forgiving. But this "moral vocabulary" was only a symptom, as Gauchet notes, of what the "rights of man" would come to assume with respect to politics. We have gone some distance further in the collapse of political discourse and are now at a point at which politics has been reduced to a discourse about legal redress for individual harm: "Approaching the problem from a different angle, we live in societies that have integrated their own critique as a means of self-constitution. . . . The rights of man come as a simultaneous response to these needs and these questions. . . . they define what is wished for without the interminable disputes over what moves history and over what its course foreshadows."[5]

Foreseeing the moral phase of political language, Hannah Arendt, in

1958, placed forgiveness and the promise at the center of her reflections in *The Human Condition*, which has been translated into French with the title *Condition de l'homme moderne*, in reference to André Malraux. She makes forgiveness and promising two fundamental forms of the bond that transports human action into the dimension of language, two founding acts of the new moral discourse, the sole regulator of action and its faculty for triggering new processes without end.[6] But are we still in a perspective in which the world of rules now seeks to be regulated by forgiveness and the promise, rather than by the death penalty and its administration? Jacques Derrida took this question up in his seminar at the École des Hautes Études between 1996 and 1999, which was devoted to the question of forgiving. Since 1999, his seminar has been devoted to the death penalty.[7]

Derrida makes forgiveness an altogether central question in what he singles out as a new religiosity. In a sense, the return of the religious, more so than a return of belief, is a renewal of the request for forgiveness. Derrida notes that the request for forgiveness is carried out in an Abrahamic language around the entire world, and that this has something artificial about it. It may very well have no significance in the language of the religion or in the dominant forms of wisdom in the society in which this demand appears. The contrast between East and West is very interesting in this respect. Is this something the East has borrowed, like the discourse of science, from the Abrahamic discourse? Derrida raises this question by pushing the logic of forgiveness beyond the "request for forgiveness," beyond the question of its address. He wishes to explain forgiveness purely in terms of reason and its failure. We would say that he is questioning it beyond the Name-of-the-Father. He formulates a strange paradox: absolute forgiveness would be to forgive the unforgivable to someone who has not asked for forgiveness. It is for him a way to "explode human reason, or at least the principle of reason interpreted in terms of calculability. . . . The impossible is at work in the idea of unconditional forgiveness."[8]

The horizon of generalized forgiveness combines with the question of knowledge. Generalizing forgiveness with a global movement that seeks reconciliation can be approximated to the function, in Hegel, of absolute knowledge. Moreover, Derrida describes Hegel as a "great conciliator." Forgiveness, like absolute knowledge, delivers us from the question of truth. It assures the homogeneity of the world, that all the bad jouissance could be reintegrated by means of forgiveness.

Not for one second does Lacan believe in the State deduced from absolute knowledge, from reconciliation, or from regulation. He believes not in absolute knowledge but in incompleteness. He said as much at Vincennes in December 1969.[9] On the basis of incompleteness, all dimensions of the interpretation of the political unconscious can be located, knowledge cut off from its tragic sense and from its meaning as truth, but which, however, enables human action to be accompanied. Lacan's making ashamed does not presume any forgiveness. It is a making ashamed that contrasts with identificatory fixation. Lacan concluded his intervention at Vincennes by saying to his audience, "The regime is looking at you, it is saying, 'Look at them enjoying!'" (240). The master puts on display those who do not make themselves responsible for their own jouissance. Not being responsible for one's own jouissance was not sexual liberation, and all the stupidities that were then beginning were rather a fixation on a regime of jouissance. Lacan thus predicted the rise in power of "communities of enjoyment" under the universalizing language of "liberation." The fascination with the "enjoying class," including the young, has reinforced the system: "There are people who enjoy! Yet another effort, you are not there yet!" The effect of fascination and repulsion was guaranteed, as was the indication of the effort that needed to be made in order to attain this point of jouissance for which everybody had to work even harder, which just reinforces the system of the master: back to work! Frenchmen and Frenchwomen, yet another effort in order to enjoy as they do!

Confronted by this, the position of "making ashamed" does not consist in *fixing* the subject to, but in *dissociating* the subject from, the master signifier and thereby bringing out the jouissance that the subject derives from the master signifier. There, where the master signifier displays obscenity with an absence of modesty, psychoanalysis on the contrary reinstates the veil and evokes this demon in the form of shame. With this "Look at them enjoying!" Lacan announced the regime of fascination with reality shows, which are a declension of enjoyment and its demonstration.

The Mode of Enjoyment as a Symptom: Interpreting *Rameau's Nephew*

Lacan discussed this issue in 1967. A discourse attempting to reconcile the subject with truth is not the same thing as one trying to reconcile a subject with his shame. He notes that one fights in the name of truth, and one could even say that one dies in the name of truth. This is the whole value of the beginning of chapter 13: "It does have to be said that it is unusual to die of shame." This resonates like a *Witz* and immediately manifests the difference between dying for the truth, which traverses all of History, and dying of shame, which is rather rare (209). Lacan adds, "Yet it is the one sign . . . whose genealogy one can be certain of, namely that it is descended from a signifier." In effect, there have not been any "dead from shame" among beings who do not have language. They live and die without it being possible for their existence to be glorious or shameful, servile or noble. Lacan compares this relationship of the living with the powerful contrast Hegel makes between noble consciousness and vile consciousness. He speaks of Hegel and his cold humor (197). We could say that Hegel builds a work out of this cold humor, in his reference to the function of the living being's vile mode of enjoyment.[10]

Let's see how Hegel contrasts noble consciousness with vile consciousness. He states that the heroism of serving the nobility has been transformed into the heroism of flattering the monarch. The subject pursues his action of renunciation toward the absolute monarch, but to the point of sacrificing his life. In order for the heroism of flattery to take up the lead and assure the monarch's being, it was necessary that not every member of the nobility die. As a result, to Hegel's delight, in the passage from the heroism of silent service to the heroism of flattery, culture will encounter a new development: the values of death will be continued in life by passing into language.

It is therefore fortunate that we have had the heroism of flattery, since it enabled civilization to take a leap forward. The elevation of flattery to heroism was a step in the direction of a new organization. Here you have a point of view that stems from cold humor, if one compares for example these pages from Hegel with the rhetoric of authenticity. The inauthenticity of the language of flattery is not a problem for Hegel, because there is no psychology at work, there is only the entry of the heroic posture into language.

In order to grasp what is at stake in a mode of enjoyment, Lacan refers in his Seminar to the grand figure of *Rameau's Nephew*, who for Hegel incarnates the culmination of the moral impasse of the Enlightenment. This reference has to be understood as a "You have been preceded by this great man." *Rameau's Nephew* is a great work of French literature, but it became one quite late, not during Diderot's lifetime: none of his masterpieces, none of those considered his masterpieces today, were published during his lifetime. Neither *Rameau's Nephew* nor *Jacques the Fatalist* saw the light of day during his lifetime. *Rameau's Nephew* was really something quite contingent, an unforeseen event. It lay unknown at the bottom of a drawer, a fact to which Lacan is referring when he says:

> A character called Diderot published *Le Neveu de Rameau*, let it fall from his pocket. Someone else took it to Schiller, who knew very well it was by Diderot. Diderot never worried about it. In 1804 Schiller passed it on to Goethe, who immediately translated it and, up until 1891—I can tell you this, because here is the tome, which I brought from my own library—we only had a French retranslation of the German translation by Goethe, who, moreover, had completely forgotten about it one year after it appeared, and who perhaps never saw it, for they were in the midst of that Franco-Prussian brawl. . . . Goethe himself was no doubt unaware that it had appeared. (222)

Lacan is emphasizing the contingency in order to show that things like that, unsigned, unpublished, forgotten at the bottom of a drawer, can still have an impact.

Satire and Symptom

In the *Phenomenology*, in his analysis of the Enlightenment, Hegel goes so far as to say that *Rameau's Nephew* is "culture in its pure state."[11] He says it in the sense in which the work describes the social semblant in a direct way. "There are lots of beggars in this world, and I can't think of anybody who doesn't know a few steps of your dance"—the dance of seduction, of enjoyment. The nephew replies, "You are right. There is only one man in the whole of a realm who walks, and that is the sovereign. Everybody else takes up positions." Even the master signifier does not escape.

> Do you think he doesn't find himself from time to time in the vicinity of a dainty foot, a little lock of hair, a little nose that makes him put on a bit of an act? Whoever needs somebody else is necessitous and so takes up a position. The king takes up a position with his mistress and with God; he performs his pantomime step. The minister executes the movements of courtier, flatterer, flunkey or beggar in front of his king.[12]

Describing it as pure culture means that one is using words that mean nothing, nothing effective in Hegel's sense—that is, cut off from the capacity to do anything.

This is the point of view that Kojève develops, when he aligns Rameau's nephew, in Hegel, with the beautiful soul. Rameau's nephew is, apparently, the figure who is the antithesis of the beautiful soul; there is nothing pure about him, and yet the two are the same. The beautiful soul is the one who criticizes and is indignant, who is the man of the republic of letters. For Hegel, it is Voltaire. In the indignant man of letters lies a "critique of society." According to Kojève, "It is a purely verbal critique but it is already an action since it is negative. [The critic] is more active or more true than the man of pleasure."[13] The tenderhearted man is someone who, unlike the man of pleasure, refuses to enjoy the world as if he were a pig: "He wants to realize himself as an isolated individual, unique in the world, but he only thinks he has value through his critique of society. In order to preserve his own value, he therefore wants to preserve the society that he criticizes. It is a purely verbal critique, he does not want to act."[14] The tenderhearted man contrasts a utopia with the given world, for, as Kojève says, "He has no need to know what link exists between the ideal and reality," that is, how one might realize the ideal.[15] This is where Lacan took this point from Hegel, whom he cites in "Proposal on Psychical Causality," where one finds the famous remark, "Utopia ends in madness because it is in permanent disharmony with the real."[16] For the tenderhearted man, "it is nevertheless through his utopian critique that he becomes more real," as Kojève says. "The tender-hearted man finally becomes conscious of the reality of the society that consists of individuals such as the man of pleasure and the tender-hearted man. And he becomes a man of virtue. He aligns himself, not with the order that he criticizes but with other criticisms. He thereby founds a party."[17] He joins with the party of the virtuous. The man of virtue not only forms a party but also wishes, according to Kojève, "to suppress individuality, egoism, by subjecting it to a discipline of education. This is his mistake. He believes that the ideal society will automatically result from the reform of all the particulars. Fortified with the real *Aufhebung*, that of particularity, the one that can unite it with the universal is not a personal sacrifice; yet it is this sort of sacrifice that virtue is seeking."[18]

This is the pathway that leads to the man of the Enlightenment. First, the emergence of the isolated man of letters, the tender-hearted man: the language of the *Aufklärung* is essentially different from that of the intellectual because it lays the ground for an effective revolution. "In *Rameau's Nephew* Diderot, an 'honest man,' can say nothing new in comparison with what Rameau's nephew says to him because the latter is perfectly conscious of himself."[19] In a sense he is the perfect scoundrel. When Kojève says that Diderot has nothing to say to anyone who is perfectly conscious of himself, one sees the root of what Lacan denounces as one of the ailments of psychoanalysis: producing scoundrels. If the subject becomes perfectly aware of himself, maintaining the strict discourse of Rameau's nephew would be drive-based cynicism. One could emerge from an analysis like Rameau's nephew, thinking moreover that one was a genius. At least Rameau's nephew knew that he was a failure. But there is something of the perfect scoundrel in this becoming conscious of oneself, in being at the level of his turpitude, of his jouissance, not having to give an account of himself. Lacan has called into question the relations between this and genius by enquiring into the relations between the scoundrel and stupidity. He did not say that if one gives Rameau's nephew an analysis he will lose all his genius, but that if you take a scoundrel he will become stupid. These questions are similar, even homologous. But, Kojève says, Diderot "transcribes the language of Rameau's nephew and renders it universal, legible to all. Rameau's nephew is at the extremity of individualism. He is not concerned about others. Diderot suffers and wants the whole world to know. If everybody speaks like Rameau's nephew then this will change the world." Kojève ends by saying, "The *Aufklärung* is Rameau's nephew universalized."[20]

In this universalization of the discourse that Kojève produces or imagines, in which everybody speaks this way, as a will to change the world, one sees the hallmark of a discourse that changes the world: a certain type of relationship with the master's discourse that touches upon semblances; the world of the Enlightenment as coming to the end of semblances by identifying everybody as scoundrels. Good scoundrels: he doesn't say that one has to kill everyone, one's neighbor, and so on. Rameau's nephew is a good dog. What is striking is that, at base, within the horizon in which everybody is speaking like this, it would be, Hegel adds, pure culture after all: it wouldn't be effective in any way. In order for it to be effective, sooner or later all this is important only if the semblances are reconstructed. The *Aufklärung* is the reign of propaganda, that is, of reason as propaganda that allows for the defamation of society. This is how Kojève translates an Enlightenment reflection on society. He adds, concerning the revolutionary agitator who slanders the existing order: "The revolutionary is therefore a liar. Through him society slanders itself. Because he denounces a lie, he is a liar himself."[21] This is a strange way to be a man of truth. Yet it is what Lacan takes up in his *Ecrits* when he presents the revolutionary as a *man of truth*.

In his generalized lie, in this denunciation of semblances by means of a lie, the revolutionary lie which announces an order that will be superior to an existing order and that denounces all semblances, Kojève introduces a dialectical shift: once the revolution has taken place, there will be a new order dependent on absolute knowledge, the State of absolute knowledge. From that point on, truth will no longer have any purchase, because truth will from now on only be able to say what is. And this no longer carries any force, because it will not be able to negate anything.

The analytic discourse allows us to set up the moral-immoral debate of Rameau's nephew in a different way. The cynical exit from discourse brought about by the nephew is defeated by its own ineffectiveness. Psychoanalysis is required if the effectiveness of drives, of jouissance, is to manage to recreate semblances that work, and not an order that falls apart. Only in psychoanalysis can the relations between truth and knowledge illuminate the semblances that render a human order possible, even though it subverts the order of things installed by the master.

Guilt, Shame, and Self-Hatred

One must remark that the forms of the push to enjoy have reintegrated the formula of "look at them enjoying." We live in an age of the generalized reality show. Anyone can become the slave of today's regime of voyeurism. For fifteen minutes of ephemeral celebrity, anyone can occupy the place of the person that one watches enjoying. What the screen of the reality show ultimately refers to is the mortifying dimension of the mirror stage in relation to the superego. In any *Big Brother* or *Kohl-Lanta*, the other has been eliminated, and, on the horizon, so has the self. Shame is in the last instance "the shame of living," from which the master signifier may occasionally give some relief.

Lacan never forgot that the mirror stage allows us to situate the depressive position. At the end of *Seminar V*, concerning a clinical case of a depressed subject that could have been interpreted in relation to a castrating woman, Lacan instead situates the subject in terms of privation and loss of the maternal love object, commenting on the "depressive position that Freud teaches us to recognize as determined by a death-wish focused on oneself."[22] Lacan follows Melanie Klein in considering that, in his description of melancholy, Freud is describing the subject's relations with the Other of jouissance, which he fails to recognize. The depressive position states a truer relation than the first identification with the all-loving father. What is at stake in depression, what Lacan in *Seminar V* calls the "demand for death," is this very relation articulated in language, that is, in the Other of which I make my demand.

Inversely, this relation to the Other situates the zone of the superego and the commandment, addressed to me by the Other and summarized by the commandment "Love thy neighbor." For Freud, it is the world outside that comes first; for Lacan it is the Other that starts speaking commandments, this Other that sends me back to that part of myself I reject. "The Christian commandment then reveals its value in being extended: 'As yourself you are, at the level of speech, the one you hate in the demand for death; because you are unaware of it.' "[23] This is Lacan's reprise of Freud's remarks in *The Ego and the Id* that hate comes first in relation to love and that hate originates in the primordial refusal that the *lust-Ich* opposes to the external world. This is why in *Encore* Lacan considers that Freud invented *hateloving*.

This is also why the question posed to us by murder-suicides is not elucidated by an appeal to the psychology of despair alone. Whenever the motive of despair is evoked, one has to be careful. Anything can always be explained by despair, any social catastrophe, any rupture of ties, any act of nihilism, any suicide. It is a suspect causality that Lacan, on occasion, inverts. He notes, in *Television*, that it is rather hope that leads to suicide. At the time, it was the hope for a rosy future. When the Ideal enters into a contradiction with somber reality, crushing it, the subject is found to have no recourse under the speech of the Ideal. He thus commits suicide in an appeal to the Ideal of hope. Hope is a virtue, but virtue does not have solely positive aspects. One must clearly distinguish between different types of despair and relate them to the self-hatred that leads a subject to certain forms of suicide: murder-suicide, altruistic suicide, or assassination suicide.

Self-hatred can manage to inscribe itself in the Other, in a spectacular manner, via the suicidal assassination or attack. Bernard Henri-Lévy has recently reminded us of the systematic use of human bombs in the Sri Lankan civil war for a generation now. But there are many varieties of suicidal assassination. It is a spectacular mode that has been privatized. Recall the one who called himself HB, human bomb, at Neuilly. This paranoid subject wrapped himself in explosives and threatened to blow up a kindergarten class in order to have an obscure fraud linked to his professional activity recognized. We almost never learned about this because the incident was terminated by HB's brutal death. The memory of this incident is alive today because it is said that the conduct of the mayor of Neuilly, who himself engaged in direct negotiations despite the risks involved, plus the discrete political management he then set in motion, were not without their effect in his appointment as minister of the interior. We also know of murder-suicides in the offices of American companies that have been made more murderous by the circulation of weapons benefiting from considerable technological advances. From the paranoid-schizophrenic employee to the frank paranoiacs, those excluded from the job market have taken their revenge, testifying in their manner to the privatization of the Other. Since then, there have been the high school massacres involving American adolescents, which demonstrate that it is not material misery that provokes this taste for suicide in a generation. Columbine High, scene of the school shootings on

April 20, 1999, remains the name associated with these facts. Columbine was followed by the most contemporary wave of bomb suicides, those inspired by religious fanaticism, especially throughout the Muslim world, which are inscribed in a secular tradition that the complicated East has never abandoned.

The idea behind this juxtaposition of different suicides is that it shows us how the regression at stake goes far further than that of an identification with an ideal. It concerns our first link to the external world; the connection between religion and this point is no doubt secondary.

Moreover, Lacan criticizes Freud for having wanted to diffuse religion by highlighting the place of the father, even as he founds the necessity for the first identification to an all-loving father. The opposition is clear. One conceptualizes the first identification either through love, on the basis of the father, or on the basis of the worst, of the rejection of the lost and nonrecognizable part of jouissance. We are thus brought back to the evil God who demands a death and commands the sacrifice of one's most precious object, which then comes to occupy the position of lost object. This is the God whose very existence leads to the question of murder. Murder-suicides raise the question of *a* that harborer of jouissance, the question, in other words, of that God which is one name for the superego (113).

The discourse of the rights of man, which is "a new discourse of the explanation of self and of conviction concerning the self, is not only multiple and contradictory."[24] It must also know that it has at its horizon an impossibility other than that of forgiving the unforgivable, or a right to conquer other than that of the abolition of being condemned for life, as Jacques Derrida concludes from his examination of the death penalty. It must include the limit of the calculability of the distribution of jouissance that self-hatred introduces into the calculus. If we distinguish what is a right and what is a fact, it is a fact about humans that they hate the Other in themselves. In order to distance this hatred of the Other within ourselves, it is better to distance oneself from one's neighbor in the right way, than to lump everything together and treat it all as the same.

Can it be said, concerning such a description of the fascination with self-hatred, a hate without forgiveness that is administered outside any law, a death penalty that is extremely difficult to eradicate in actuality, that we have formulated an interpretation? It depends on the address and the place it is accorded. It is clear that the community of subjects who have taken the unfathomable decision to pass to an act, to cut themselves off from the Other, this genuinely unavowable community, will not understand anything. It is a community radically separate from the community of those who endlessly go over the scene of their death in their thought, as Maurice Blanchot and Jacques Derrida have said and written. If it is not entirely vain to evoke this, it is by addressing oneself to "enlightened opinion," which is also a psychotherapized opinion sensitive to subjective pain. The exigency of "asking for forgiveness," an ethical moment to which a certain number of authors are attached, appears, as such, to be a demand to forget the disappearance of shame. This is a demand of the contemporary superego, which bears inside itself the seeds of its own destruction.

The End of Shame and Political Death

One cannot forget the effects of jouissance even if one is no longer ashamed of them, especially in politics. Shame and guilt are not articulated with the superego in the same way. "The only thing one can be guilty of, at least from the psychoanalytic point of view, is of having given up on one's desire."[25] Lacan's "having given up on one's desire," "avoir cédé sur son désir," translates and transposes Freud's *Triebversicht*. What is the consequence of the drive's functioning in our permissive civilization, in which no one ever hears the voice that incites them to give way on their jouissance? This is where the chasm lies that Jacques-Alain Miller has brought to light. On the one hand, permissive society authorizes jouissance; on the other, it denounces desire. I would say that the permissive society leaves us with as much dignity as the particularity of our drives. It simply pushes us to express them. This is the post-romantic morality whose fallout Charles Taylor sees in the concern for self-expression in the well-named "free time," precious to the citizens of Western democracies. As Taylor says,

> The notion that the life of production and reproduction, of work and the family, is the main locus of the good life flies in the face of what were originally the dominant distinctions of our civilization. ... The affirmation of ordinary life ... involves a polemical stance

towards these traditional views.... This was true of the Reformation theologies....

It is this polemical stance, carried over and transposed in secular guise, which powers the reductive views like utilitarianism which want to denounce all qualitative distinctions....

The key point is that the higher is to be found not outside of but as a *manner of living* ordinary life.[26]

In this way of living an ordinary life, valid for everyone, the concern for particularity finds its place in the lineage of the romantic preoccupation with the particularity of peoples beyond a universal relationship to reason. This is now encountered in the concern for self-expression, where everyone has to succeed in locating that part which escapes the production/reproduction process. In this sense the aesthetic care for the self, thought by Foucault as a form of neo-Stoicism, is also inscribed within this neoromantic dimension. Foucault put it in these terms: "What preoccupied [the Ancients] the most, their grand theme, was the constitution of a type of morality that would be an aesthetics of existence. Well I wonder whether our problem today is not, in a certain manner, the same as theirs."[27] This can be summarized in the form of an imperative Taylor takes from the Californian injunction: "Do your own thing."

Ordinary Life and the Sciences

The distinction between ordinary life and the instance that transcends it is mobilized, at further costs, by the advances of the life sciences, which contribute to a powerful renewal of the ordinary. They radicalize the questions that Hans Jonas has been raising in the public domain from 1968 onward in his work *The Phenomenon of Life: Towards a Philosophical Biology*, and in *Das Prinzip Verantwortung* (1979), with its beautiful title meaning "the responsibility principle," in which he attempts to render us responsible for a subject of the living as such, modeled on the Kantian subject. Peter Sloterdijk announced the dramatic change in register of this question in a lecture published in 2000 with the ironic title, "The Domestication of Being": "A part of the human race, with its entrance into the highly technological era, has brought a case about itself and against itself where what is at stake is a new definition of the human being."[28] He does not hesitate to group together biotechnology and the techniques of atomic physics over their potential to destroy the species: "Collective memory is thus right to mark the month of August 1945 with its two atomic explosions on Japanese cities as the date of the physical apocalypse and the month of February 1997, in which the existence of the cloned sheep was rendered public, as the date of a biological apocalypse. . . . These are actually two key dates in the human being's case against itself."[29]

Francis Fukuyama adopts similar views, though in a less boring way, in *Our Posthuman Future*.[30] As he comes from the English-speaking world, he is obliged not only to warn of the dangers, but also to offer remedies. He sees only one, which is that of preserving "human nature." This term actually covers two completely heterogeneous notions: on the one hand, that of human nature as originating in natural law, which deduces the nature of Man from God; and on the other hand, a human nature deduced from the living being—the corporeal and genetic integrity of man as defined by biological science. He deliberately runs the two together and thus formulates the undertaking that democracies must adopt: "We do not want to disturb the unity or continuity of human nature, and by that, the rights of man based upon it."

In fact, biotechnology already makes it possible to upset quite a number of things by combining what is currently achievable with various fantasies. One can situate its action in three essential domains. First, the techniques of biotechnology allow us to better control our moods and our personality, even if the results are insufficient. They allow the establishment of a new average personality. The example Fukuyama takes to illustrate this point is the use of medication to remove the inequality of moods between the sexes. He compares the use of Ritalin with that of Prozac. Prozac is prescribed more often to women, in order to combat the depression that affects them unequally by raising their serotonin level to levels that occur in men. Ritalin is frequently prescribed to young men to calm them and to adjust for their higher levels of hypomania. In this sense one can say, if one relates Fukuyama to Taylor, that prescription permits the subject to approach a mean and, moreover, to experience that "ordinary life" that is now the experiential frame of our civilization. From this perspective, a true appreciation of "self-worth," of depression, can be made. Guilt and shame are now useless virtues. Whatever the feelings of shame might be, there is always the hope of treatment. From this point of view, shame and guilt are indistinguishable.

Second, we can expect an accentuation of the impact of biotechnologies on life expectancy, which, combined with the decline in the birth rate, has affected retirement schemes and altered the balance of electoral age groups. Again, advances could worsen the situation. The question could be formulated in this way: What will be the consequence of living for forty more years, if there is no remedy for Alzheimer's? More profoundly, this technology changes the meaning of death. There is no longer anything but old age, in its most ordinary manifestation, with its procession of dysfunctions. Here again, biotechnology appears in the service of "ordinary life"; it obliterates the asperities as well as the dramatic meaning of existence. But, from another point of view, they inscribe themselves perfectly well in the more or less hallucinatory project of "the aesthetic amelioration of self," the infernal race with that piece of jouissance that is lost forever. Postromantic or not, it is a chase after the flight of *objet a*.

Whatever one thinks should become reality or remain fantasy, these "improvements" of the species pose a fundamental question. The impact of hopes for genetic treatments makes the shadow of a renewed eugenics reappear. We are no longer in the context of the 1930s, when Franklin Roosevelt wished for the sterilization of mental patients in order not to weaken the democracies in the face of the mounting perils. Today we are confronted with budgetary choices. Will the so-called genetic therapy for intelligence be reserved for the rich, or will it be reimbursable by Social Security? Will this reach the point of creating new, unequal races of humans? Acquired genetic knowledge overturns the juridical fiction of equality between subjects and permits, at least fantasmatically, a tendency toward the parents' preformed ideal. How can we organize a public debate, one that is worthy of the name, on all these questions and not let the markets act blindly? The robber barons of the past century, American and others, have expended fortunes to construct mausoleum-palaces that we continue to visit, such as the Frick or Pierpont Morgan collection in New York and Jacquemart-André in Paris. The rich today, born of industry, finance, or show business, spend as much to make both their own and their children's bodies improved, living mausoleums.

Fukuyama counts on a barrier of "human nature," a fiction to be installed through regulation, in order to construct a barrier against the unobserved developments of biotechnology, when they operate, like the death drive, in silence. Crossing the barrier would require that one speak about it. The scientists and the liberals in the English-speaking world hesitate to do so. One notes that in the United States, the partisans of human nature predominantly come out of religious fundamentalism and the Catholic Church, where, according to the doctrine established by the pope in 1996, human nature depends on the soul, introduced by God in an "ontological leap" at a certain moment in evolution. Gregory Stock, director of the Department of Medicine, Technology, and Society at the University of California and former advisor to President Clinton, is not one for grand laws or for new grand national agencies. He prefers to delegate the choices to parents where their children are concerned and otherwise use the existing agencies that oversee public health. Geoff Mulgan, for Blair's cabinet, is not favorable to new regulations and is satisfied with an agency conceived on the model of the current HFEA (Human Fertilisation and Embryology Authority) that makes England the most permissive country in Europe for biotechnology research, allowing it to maintain its incontestable industrial advantage. The French, like the Germans, are very happy to oppose pursuing research on stem cells extracted from human embryos. On these questions, a debate was recently organized by the Blairists between Fukuyama and Stock in London. These questions, which will have great importance for our lives, are not the object in France of any important public debate. The Cité des Sciences tries its best but to limited effect. The Swiss pharmaceutical giant Novartis's planned withdrawal from the United States, which heralds other developments in European industry, has been the object of only a handful of commentaries.

"Human Nature" and the Habitat of the Subject

What does this fiction of "human nature" presuppose? In its approach to nature and the human, doesn't it assume that man could inhabit nature harmoniously? Is this not one of those myths that psychoanalysis has contributed to displacing? This is a point Lacan discusses in his 1969 "Allocution on Child Psychoses." He first examines the myth that psychosis has a link with freedom in its universalizing function, to which he opposes the real of segregation, then moves on to the myth of "the supposed ease" that the experience of psychoanalysts is said to give in regards to sexual questions. He seriously deflates their pretension to be heralds of the liberation of mores, noting rather that they content themselves with their fine speeches on morality after psychoanalysis. The real that this myth of sexual "liberation" by the psychoanalyst covers is that psychoanalysis operates on fantasy.

Lacan discusses the question of child psychoses on the basis of the child's implication in the mother's fantasy: "The child, susceptible to being implicated in any fantasy, becomes the mother's 'object' and henceforth has the sole function of revealing this object's truth. The child realizes the presence of what Jacques Lacan designates as *objet a* in fantasy. By substituting himself for this object, he saturates the mode of lack in which (the mother's) desire specifies itself."[31]

Let's pause on the lesson Lacan draws from this advance in contemporary psychoanalysis, which for him begins with Winnicott, but of which, he says, he "alone [has] seen the precise import." That Winnicott had isolated the fact that an inanimate object could be considered as a piece of the mother's body, a *doudou*, is not as reassuring as this gentle [*doux*] name implies:

> The important thing nevertheless is not that the transitional object preserves the child's autonomy, but whether or not the child serves as a transitional object for the mother. And this suspension will only yield its reason at the same time as the object yields its structure—which is, namely, that of a condenser for jouissance, insofar as, by the regulation of pleasure, it is stolen from the body. It is because jouissance is out-of-body [*hors-corps*] that it can dream of itself as recuperated not only in another body but also in an inanimate object.[32]

This passage of Lacan's can be read as a direct commentary on chapter 3 of *Civilization and Its Discontents*. In his prejudice bound up with his immoderate love for his mother, Freud maintains a belief in a harmonious relation with the mother, which, ultimately, is covered by "primary narcissism." He deduces from it the relation to the body as a stable belief in an infrangible totality. For him, objects in the world are an extension of the human body to which they are added. He states that "by means of his instruments man is perfecting his own organs, both motor and sensory, or is considerably extending the limits of their power."[33] Nonetheless Freud reserves a place of nonhappiness for the subject of civilization: "Man has, as it were, become a kind of prosthetic God. When he puts on all his auxiliary organs he is truly magnificent; but those organs have not grown onto him and they still give him much trouble at times. . . . we will not forget that present-day man does not feel happy in his Godlike character."[34] The absence of happiness, the obstacle on the path to *Lustgewinn*, is approached in terms of *Kulturversagung*, civilization's refusal, as such, to satisfy the drives. Freud maintains this perspective, even as he supposes an initial complete satisfaction at the level of the ego. What Lacan emphasizes does away with this inaugural myth.

The Freudian prejudice of a harmonious maternal habitat is continued in his conception of a harmonious relation between mother and son constructed around phallic signification. Freud's uxorious character, as Lacan says, is deducible from his excessive attachment to this adored mother for whom he was, in return, her Siegfried. Freud would still say in 1933 in this regard that "a mother is only brought unlimited satisfaction by her relation to a son; this is altogether the most perfect, the most free from ambivalence of all human relationships. . . . Even a marriage is not made secure until the wife has succeeded in making her husband her child as well and in acting as a mother to him."[35]

In this affirmation of the "most perfect" of relations, Freud is clearly speaking of himself and his constitution as subject in the maternal fantasy, if one relates it to what we have learned from various biographies about the circumstances of his coming into the world. This prejudice could be enunciated only if one stops at the idea of desire as lack's being completed by phallic signification.

What psychoanalysis noticed first of all with Klein, then with Winnicott, and what Lacan theorized, is that the child is not all in phallic signification. The child is, rather, above all localizable on the basis of its place as object in the mother's fantasy, the cause of which is the *objet a*. We can easily see the consequences. The first is to situate the mother's desire in terms of fullness, and not of lack; in terms of causality and therefore of the production of effects, and not in terms of completion; and in terms of plenitude of jouissance, of relation to the "condenser," and not in terms of unlimited satisfaction.

The level of satisfaction at which the subject is "happy" is not that of a harmonious relation to the mother. It is that of the drive where, in order to recuperate jouissance, the subject makes the lost object the cause of his or her desire. The unnoticed correlate of this point is that the "happiness in fantasy"—just as one says "happiness in misfortune"— which is out of body returns to the body. Out-of-body jouissance increasingly removes itself from this body that is limited by pleasure. The object returns and shears up the body in a way that is different from that of the signifier. Each drive circuit makes increasing demands on the maltreated body. Multiple addictions, epidemics of anorexia/bulimia, and audiovisual hypnosis are there to demonstrate the uncertainty of the hold that phallic signification maintains and the limits that it implies. As inanimate objects animated by fantasy, we are an appendage to these condensers of jouissance that carve up the body.

Inversely, from the point of view of the circuit emanating from the Other we are at a point where we have become the Other's "transitional object"; that is, we have become objects that have passed into the "transition" of generalized exchange. The experience of psychoanalysis indicates that the self-evidence of the "total body" is not at all obvious. By becoming the cause of desire, the body is like an inanimate object that is susceptible to being produced, exchanged, and industrialized. When Lacan expressed this in 1969 the industrialization of the body was in its infancy, yet it was enough for him to raise the question of the future of the body as object: "The question is whether, by virtue of the ignorance about where this body is held by the subject of science, one will come to the point, by law, of cutting up this body for the purposes of exchange."[36] In the name of analytic experience, Lacan perceived the breach that the biological industry would come to occupy. Similarly, he refers to this carving up of bodies by jouissance in a contemporaneous text, "Radiophonie" (1969), where he displaces the question of the sepulchre, so dear to the existential perspective of "being for death." On the basis of jouissance, he relates this question to a logical structure: "The empty set of bones is the irreducible element by which other elements, the instruments of jouissance, necklaces, goblets, arms, are organized: there are more sub-elements to enumerate jouissance than there are to make it reenter the body."[37] The bones, the remains of the body, and the instruments of jouissance outside the body find themselves taken together as elements of the apparatus for enjoying.

Enjoying the Unconscious or Condensing One's Jouissance

For the Lacan of the 1970s, we are never contented with organ objects. The necklaces, goblets, and arms are always in excess relative to drive borders. In our societies of abundance, bodies no longer simply plug themselves into trinkets; they plug into objects produced by scientific activity. The new improvements to the body—medicines, gene therapies, anti-aging treatments, production of organs by stem cells, even the production of bodies through cloning—are only extensions. The habitat of language is also a habitat of a world encumbered by these objects produced by the pharmaceutical industry. The psychoanalytic experience does not plead the case for our being able to count on a love of "human nature" among our citizens, strong enough to resist promises of jouissance.

The problem is therefore not that the power or the place of the other is as either a mother or a grandmother, and that one is promised mountains and marvels of biologically improved happiness. What is important is that we are not treated as an object of exchange that can be cut up, detailed beyond all our hopes. The present powers in China do not refrain from taking without consent the organs of those condemned to death. The power in democratic societies proposes inserting into the body every improvement of which science, with its own powers of derealization, can dream. Parents will want the best for their children, they will want it all: the child and his genetic improvement, one that is more intelligent, more beautiful. The subject will want it all in order to be happy and will want to be used by technology to become a machine for self-discovery.

To be up to the challenge of such a promise, psychoanalysis should also remain a very sophisticated machine of technological experience for self-discovery. Psychoanalytic experience is also a way to displace "human nature" (which does not exist). If psychoanalysis has one fulcrum point, it's that it sees the fundamental futility to which the subject binds itself.

Psychoanalysis presents a manner of enjoying something that is not transcendent but which lies within the subject, though not hidden in its depths. Lacan could state that psychoanalysis is "a symptom," which we can retranslate, after Jacques-Alain Miller's work on the final teachings of Lacan, as "a way of enjoying the unconscious." There are many ways of enjoying something besides the Other's signifiers in me. Saying that psychoanalysis is a symptom is to give a very particular translation of the postromantic specificity of my jouissance. It is also to emphasize that each discourse is an apparatus of jouissance; that is, at one and the same time a brake upon it and a manner of getting by with it. If science is futile, it is because is does not indicate any means of enjoyment to us. However, it does not simply leave us adrift. Science does not anchor the subject to a discourse. It is, however, anchored to objects that have replaced what, until then, had been a product of art or the beautiful. What was initially perceived as commodity fetishism was a stopping point in generalized futility. Technical objects accumulate a particular *agalma* for us. Science has managed to make jouissance out of knowledge. Kant saw the celestial vault above our heads and the voice of conscience within as the limit of our experience. Shall we say that our experience is now that of the international space station above our heads, from which everything might fall down on top of us one day, and the voice of genetic modification within? These voices incessantly provoke us into a political debate over the public place. "Man is he to whom one addresses oneself"; this is all that remains for us. It is up to us to draw from it what we can. There is no other moral conscience than that of the examination of our follies and all our deregulating in order to isolate the consequences in the most explicit manner possible.

The effect of the ramification of the discourse of science is that it produces objects, on the one hand, and, on the other, abjects such as the psychoanalyst. The paradox of the ethics of analysis is that on the side of the analyst there is a "make oneself into the being of abjection," while on the side of the analysand the dignity of the signifier is set to work. The dignity of this place of the abject is that the ego is effaced. Psychoanalysts' "way of humility" brings them closest to the point of the real in language, which permits them to touch upon non-sense. Through the mediation of the analyst-object the analysand's work enables the deciphering of the unconscious to be attained as a result.

Notes

1. See, for instance, Marcel Gauchet, *La démocratie contre elle-même* (Paris: Gallimard, 2002).
2. See Carl Schmitt, *The Concept of the Political* (Chicago: University of Chicago Press, 1996).
3. M. Schneider, *Big Mother* (Paris: Editions Odile Jacob, 2002), 72.
4. Jacques-Alain Miller, "Théorie de Turin sur le sujet de l'École," *Aperçus du Congrès de l'AMP à Buenos Aires, juillet 2000* (Paris: EURL Huysmans, 2001), 62–63.
5. Gauchet, *La démocratie contre elle-même*, 346–47.
6. Hannah Arendt, *The Human Condition* (Chicago: University of Chicago Press, 1958). See, above all, chap. 5.
7. See Jacques Derrida and Elisabeth Roudinesco, *De quoi demain* . . . (Paris: Fayard/Galilée, 2001).
8. Ibid., 260.
9. Jacques Lacan, *Le séminaire, livre XVII: L'envers de la psychanalyse* (Paris: Seuil, 1991), 234. Further references to this edition appear parenthetically in the text.
10. See G. W. F. Hegel, "Virtue and the Way of the World" (sections 381–393), *The Phenomenology of Spirit*, trans. A. V. Miller, with analysis and foreword by J. N. Findlay (Oxford: Oxford University Press, 1977), 228–35.
11. Hegel, *The Phenomenology of Spirit*, 238.
12. Denis Diderot, *Rameau's Nephew/D'Alembert's Dream*, trans. with introduction by L. Tancock (Harmondsworth: Penguin, 1966), 121.
13. Alexandre Kojève, *Cours de l'année scolaire 1935–1936*, in *Introduction à la lecture de Hegel*, ed. R. Quenean (Paris: Gallimard, 1947), 87.
14. Ibid., 87.
15. Ibid., 88.
16. Ibid.
17. Ibid.
18. Ibid., 89.
19. Ibid., 135. And see *Cours de l'année scolaire 1936–1937, II Die Aufklärung*, 383.
20. Kojève, *Cours de l'année scolaire 1935–1936*, 135.
21. Ibid., 136.
22. Jacques Lacan, *Le séminaire, livre V: Les formations de l'inconscient*, ed. J.-A. Miller (Paris: Seuil, 1998), 502–3.
23. Ibid., 505.
24. Gauchet, *La démocratie contre elle-même*, 351.
25. Jacques Lacan, *Le séminaire, livre VII: L'éthique de la psychanalyse*, ed. J.-A. Miller (Paris: Seuil, 1986), 368.
26. Charles Taylor, *Sources of the Self* (London: Cambridge University Press, 1989), 23.
27. Hubert Dreyfus and Paul Rabinow, *Michel Foucault: Un parcours philosophique* (Paris: Gallimard, 1984), 325.
28. Peter Sloterdijk, *La domestication de l'être* (Paris: Mille et une nuits, 2000), 32.

29 Ibid., 34.
30 Francis Fukuyama, *Our Posthuman Future* (London: Profile, 2002).
31 Jacques Lacan, "Note sur l'enfant," *Autres écrits* (Paris: Seuil, 2001), 373–74.
32 Jacques Lacan, "Allocution sur les psychoses de l'enfant," in *Autres écrits*, 368.
33 Freud writes, "Motor power places gigantic forces at his disposal, which, like his muscles, he can employ in any direction; thanks to ships and aircraft neither water nor air can hinder his movements; by means of spectacles he corrects defects in the lens of his own eye; by means of the telescope he sees into the far distance; and by means of the microscope he overcomes the limits of visibility set by the structure of his retina. In the photographic camera he has created an instrument which retains the fleeting visual impressions, just as a gramophone disc retains the equally fleeting auditory ones; both are at bottom materializations of the power he possesses of recollection, his memory. With the help of the telephone he can hear at distances which would be respected as unattainable even in a fairy tale. Writing was in its origin the voice of an absent person; and the dwelling-house was a substitute for the mother's womb, the first lodging, for which in all likelihood man still longs, and in which he was safe and felt at ease." *Civilization and Its Discontents*, in *The Standard Edition of the Complete Psychological Works of Sigmund Freud*, ed. J. Strachey (London: Hogarth, 1961), 21:90–91.
34 Ibid., 21:91–92.
35 Sigmund Freud, *New Introductory Lectures on Psychoanalysis*, in *The Standard Edition*, ed. J. Strachey, 22:133–34.
36 Lacan, "Allocution sur les psychoses de l'enfant," 369.
37 Jacques Lacan, "Radiophonie," in *Autres écrits*, 410.

Marie-Hélène Brousse

13

Common Markets and Segregation

Let whoever cannot meet at its horizon the subjectivity of his time give up [the practice of analysis] then. For how could he who knows nothing of the dialectic that engages him in a symbolic movement with so many lives possibly make his being the axis of those lives? Let him be well acquainted with the whorl into which his era draws him in the ongoing enterprise of Babel, and let him be aware of his function as interpreter in the strife of languages.—Jacques Lacan

Lacan wrote this in 1953. The program traced for the analyst remains a necessity, since it is true that psychoanalysis, although taking place in a framework completely different from other social relationships, mobilizes—via the analysand's discourse—all the coordinates of an era: imaginary, symbolic, and real. But without doubt, today this discipline is even more essential, at the beginning of a new century, when society seems to escape the conceptual and theoretical readings that were formerly operational. The quantitative and qualitative consequences of these technological, economic, and political changes introduce a new real. Clinical practice finds itself structurally modified. If psychoanalysis is to continue and to progress in its orientation, the subject's cause, it must rest on a clear vision of the mechanisms of, and of what is at stake in, these changes.

A Modified Real

Some of these changes took place in the aftermath of the Second World War and the resulting new treatment of human beings. Others followed.

The regimes inspired by Marxism promised collective happiness on earth, no longer only in the afterlife, as monotheism had done in the past. Their fall has swept away—probably not once and for all, but at least for a while—this utopia and, at the same time, consecrated totalitarian domination of an economic system with its own logic. The ascent of religious fundamentalism as well as the modification of the very notion of war (through the development of terrorism) are novelties that have modified the political domain. Some of these changes, in the field of technique, are the consequence of the hegemony of the discourse of science in our societies. Not only has the real been definitively modified, but also among certain ways of thinking a scientism has imposed itself that, filtering into social practices, has become a form of power according to today's accepted principle that science has a monopoly on truth. The result is that science, outside its own domain, has become a system of belief.

These economic, political, and technical changes share a common direction: they aim at the universal. This is true of capitalism, the single market; it is also true of those technical revolutions that aim at universal diffusion; and it is most especially true of science. This is no longer a time for parochialism, for small groups, for autarchy. The world tends to impose the same truth for all, as a real.

In 1947, just after the Second World War, in a text called "British Psychiatry and the War," Lacan described the epoch that had just begun. First, he showed that the psychoanalyst, in order to advance in his discipline, must accept projecting himself into politics. Saluting Great Britain, which, during the war, maintained the status of "conscientious objector," he wrote, "This war has, I think, shown well enough that in the future the dangers for humanity will not come from the excessive unruliness of individuals. It is now clear that the dark powers of the superego coalesce with the most spineless abandonment of conscience to drive men to a death that is accepted for the least humane of causes, and that not everything that appears as a sacrifice is necessarily heroic."[1] Faced with the horrors committed by the masses and by fascinated and fanatical groups, the "unruliness" of conscientious objectors seems more like a guarantee than a peril. The expression "dark powers of the superego" evokes, in the context of the first years of this century, the rise of all fanaticism. Terrorists' sacrifices do not imply any heroism, but rather a wager on jouissance in heaven, an idea that dies hard. As for "the most spineless abandonment of conscience to drive men to a death that is accepted for the least humane of causes," we will have no trouble finding contemporary examples of this position of appeasement. The following visionary sentence of the same text is a portrait of our epoch: "In this century, the increasing development of means to act on the psyche, a concerted manipulation of images and passions that has already served successfully against our own judgment, our resolution, our moral unity, will bring on new abuses of power."[2] This is precisely where we are now. What are the new forms of the abuse of power?

The rise of universals of all kinds is provoking fundamental modifications in the domain of ethics. The sudden appearance of ethics committees linked to the forward march of science that Jacques-Alain Miller and Éric Laurent have analyzed, the development on a national and international level of recourse to the law, is not, in its very nature, an answer to the question, because the singularity of psychoanalysis is located precisely in the domains of ethics and judgment. Since its invention by Freud, the link of psychoanalysis to ethics is manifested in the abandonment of all suggestion, of all social and moral judgment on the part of the analyst, and by the fact that a subject's symptom is constructed in the treatment by her own speech, just as the solution will only be one if she invents it herself. The analyst directs the treatment, not the life choices of the patient.

Nevertheless, as Lacan has shown, psychoanalysis itself came into being as a consequence of the discourse of science. Without the development of a scientific medicine that labeled as fakers those hysteric patients who did not fit into the framework of truth as described by biology (therefore excluding them), Freud would not have discovered unconscious phenomena. Psychoanalysis retains this singular place, borne by the advances of science but treating what science had revealed and abandoned at one and the same time. Psychoanalysis treats, in a rational way, through ethics, those excluded from the universal. Psychoanalysis banks on subverting the dark powers of the superego and the renunciation of conscience through unconscious desire.

The Therapeutic, a Contemporary Universal

What is excluded today from the ambient universal that determines the clinical real with which we are confronted? Let us name it: the therapeutic. In fact, any human phenomenon, from the most exceptional (various traumas) to the most common (ordinary events in professional, love, or family life), has become a potential aim of therapeutic care. In *Civilization and Its Discontents*, Freud wrote: "[Ethics] does in fact deal with a subject which can easily be recognized as the sorest spot in every civilization. Ethics is thus to be regarded as a therapeutic attempt—as an endeavor to achieve, by means of a command of the super-ego—something which has so far not been achieved by means of any other cultural activities."[3] Freud drew a functional equivalence between morals and the therapeutic. Today we could say that, in Western societies at least, the therapeutic perspective has replaced the moral and religious perspective in the management of the "sorest spot" that Freud spoke of. It follows from this that the category of mental illness is disrupted and in crisis. If, every time a subject wagers his or her desire, if, every time a subject's mode of satisfaction is shaken, she needs therapy, then how does one delineate the field of illness, and mental illness in particular? Jean-Claude Maleval has pointed out the proliferation of categories of mental problems in the various versions of the *Diagnostic and Statistical Manual of Mental Disorders* (DSM).[4]

Two things must be noted. First, the successes of scientific medicine have promoted the therapeutic, care, and healing to the level of universal value. We have begun to think that ingurgitating the appropriate molecules can heal all the pains of living; we have begun believing in happiness through pills and surgery. But, second, when medicine is scientific, it precisely delineates the domain of its intervention.

A great many human processes have therefore been excluded from the strictly scientific field of intervention. However, through the transformation of the therapeutic into a universal value, these processes have been torn from the domains that traditionally managed and controlled them. The result of this twofold movement is that the therapeutic has dissociated itself from the fields of medicine and illness, and it has been thus demedicalized, in the scientific sense, by departing from the field of health and illness in order to ensure a regulating function in the social field by medicalizing it in a completely ideological sense. Jacques-Alain Miller has pointed out that psychotherapies constitute a cushion of compassion that our societies depend on for their security. In other words, the therapeutic perspective serves the discourse of the contemporary master.

The Fulcrum of the Matheme of Discourses

Starting in 1968, Lacan, in his continued movement toward reaching the subjectivity of his time, again uses linguistics, proposing the category of discourse to formalize the structure of the social link. This small, four-part matheme, by means of which he reduces all social links in which the subject is taken to four forms: the master's discourse, the university discourse, the hysteric's discourse, and the analyst's discourse.[5]

The master's discourse is characterized by putting a signifier that commands in the position of agent.[6] Think of Balzac's time and the imperative attributed to François Guizot: "Get rich!" Or, following Lacan, think of another signifier that shows the tight link between the master and the police: "Move on!" The master signifier is written S_1. It is obvious that it changes with the times and the type of social organization. Since the advent of the hegemony of capitalism as the economic model of human societies, our hypothesis has been that this S_1 is "market"—more precisely, "common market." As Lacan states in "Proposition of 9 October 1967 on the Psychoanalyst of the School," "Our future [is] as common markets."[7] Today, in 2004, this is no longer the future but a political and economic reality that, beyond a Europe having difficulty constituting itself, is global. One term, globalization, has unveiled it as the empire, *Impero*—that is to say, as unique and not, for all that, common. Nothing can or should stop the circulation of products and profits.

What is the knowledge, written by Lacan as S_2, that corresponds to the master signifier? Let us take, as a hypothesis, that it is what in the specialized literature is called "procedures" or "protocols." All the major capitalist companies, and many public or private institutions, in order to rationalize their way of functioning, use a manual, or code, of procedure that describes and computerizes the actions and behavior necessary for executing tasks. From companies like McDonald's or Gap to the treatment of cancer in France, in piloting planes or the way the police functions, people follow the procedures whose ancestor, ridiculed by Charles Chaplin in *Modern Times*, was Taylorism, which is to procedure and protocol as a Stone Age tool is to a precision instrument. The envisaged modes of functioning through research protocols, quantitatively (through statistics and calculus), and qualitatively (through the subjects' words), are torn from their agents and then reinjected in the form of universal procedures, generating knowledge acquired free of charge. These universal procedures enable management of the market, that is, management of the world, since nothing today escapes the logic of the market. All human activity is therefore destined to be calibrated in terms of maximum profit and minimum cost. The S_2 is therefore the knowledge that corresponds to market management.

S_1 and S_2 constitute the totality of the structure of the modern master. As we can see, this modern master ceased being hierarchical by becoming universal. He counts on the universality of scientific knowledge, from which he differs, however, in his relation to the real. Jacques-Alain Miller, in his two articles "Milanese Intuitions," contrasted the authoritarian master with the liberal master.[8] The authoritarian master constitutes himself on the model of the father, the chief; he is a paternalistic master based on a vertical structure of power and on sanction. The modern master comes out of the globalizing logic of the market and procedures: the structure is horizontal.

How does the modern master exercise power under these conditions? How does he survey or punish? The resulting control comes from a mutual functioning that is either communitarian or corporate. Instead of the notations and inspections that the war in Iraq has shown to be obsolete, it is—as Jacques-Alain Miller has recently remarked—evaluation that has taken over. Evaluation does not supply any superior hierarchical position; it could even, ideally, be done by a machine, just as, ideally, a diagnosis could be made just by using the *DSM*. With the help of an adequate manual for evaluation, individuals should, under the guidance of their peers, be able to make their own diagnoses.

As Miller pointed out, this situation profoundly modifies contemporary clinical practice.

> Classical clinical practice, as we learned it and taught it, had as its pivot the Name-of-the-Father and was directed with consideration for the positions of the subject with respect to the Name-of-the-Father. It is in this practice that different modalities of desire or different modes of defense were distinguished. . . . Our classical clinical practice responded essentially to the structure of masculine sexuation, to the structure of the all and of the antinomian element. This is what enabled us to have these airtight, rigid, powerful clas-

sifications, which founded the notion of Lacanianism for generations.⁹

The clinic of an epoch corresponds to the master's discourse of that epoch. The transformation of the master's discourse, which is a setup that regulates and manages the jouissance of speaking beings by way of the passage of the Name-of-the-Father into the market, implies the modification of the subject's symptom as well as the modalities of transference. The function of surveillance and punishment corresponding to the Name-of-the-Father as S_1 is now assured by evaluations and procedures and no longer by prohibition and classification.

Let us now see what comes to locate itself under the bar of the matheme. First, what becomes of the subject? Our hypothesis is that what becomes the model for the subject of modernity is the subject in a system in which he is assigned a place by forms of circulation (of information, products, profits). Alone, he can connect with each and every one, with no limitation other than the technical. He is therefore an autarchic subject plugged into the instantly accessible universals of idle chatter and knowledge. He is less and less defined by a symbolic specific place in parenting structures, and therefore less and less determined by Oedipal coordinates. To this $ corresponds a new mode of jouissance.

In a short intervention at the Congress of the Ecole Freudienne de Paris in Strasbourg in 1968, published in the Italian magazine *La psicoanalisi*, Lacan said, about "context concerning the father" (*contexte regardant le père*), "I think that, in our epoch, the trace, the scar left by the evaporation of the father is what we can put under the general label of segregation. We think that universalism, that communication of our civilizations, homogenizes the relations among men. On the contrary, I believe that what characterizes our time—and this cannot escape us—is a ramified and reinforced segregation that produces intersections on all levels and only multiplies barriers."¹⁰ The segregation that is the regime of his satisfaction corresponds to the subject in a system. On the one hand, there is the "connected" subject; on the other, the speaking being reduced to a product.

In "Proposition of 9 October 1967 on the Psychoanalyst of the School," Lacan expresses the same idea: "Let us sum up by saying that what we have seen emerging, to our horror, represents the precursor's reaction to what is going to develop as a consequence of the reorgani-

Common Markets and Segregation   261

zation of social groups by science and, namely, the universality it introduces. Our future as common markets will find its equilibrium in a harsher extension of the processes of segregation."[11] The jouissance at stake in this new modality of the master's discourse, in which the S_1 is no longer correlated with the Name-of-the-Father, has to do with segregation. Some years ago I worked on James Ellroy's autobiography, showing how, in his own terms, Ellroy was constituted by what he called "parallel worlds," implying surplus jouissances and different signifiers, separated worlds that came together only in the mode of the passage to the act, in riots or crime. There, where the limit was unique, it multiplied and displayed, without embarrassment, its rapport to jouissance.

What we get, then, is the following model:

The places in each of the discourses

$$\frac{\text{agent} \quad \rightarrow \quad \text{work}}{\text{truth} \qquad \text{production}}$$

The formula of the master's discourse

$$\frac{S_1 \quad \rightarrow \quad S_2}{\$ \qquad a}$$

The hypothesis that we propose for an application of the formula to the postmodern master is therefore the following. Above are two elements having to do with the reorganization of human phenomena by science:

$$\frac{\text{global market} \quad \rightarrow \quad \text{procedures and protocols}}{(S_1, \text{master signifier}) \qquad (S_2, \text{knowledge})}$$

$$\frac{\text{subject in a system} \qquad \text{segregation}}{(\$, \text{the subject}) \qquad (a, \text{surplus jouissance})}$$

Below are two elements having to do with segregation: the autistic subject, to take one of Miller's formulas, and the virtual and isolated subject and the objects that give him a being of jouissance, objects destined to be rubbish. The result is a multiplication of communities: gay, lesbian, black, Latino, WASP, AA, NA, and so on, each with its own objects.

Such are the structural coordinates of modern clinical practice.

Notes

This article is translated from the French by Francesca Pollock and Sylvia Winter.
1. Jacques Lacan, "La psychiatrie anglaise et la guerre," in *Autres écrits* (Paris: Seuil, 2001), 120.
2. Lacan, "La psychiatrie anglaise," p. 120.
3. Sigmund Freud, *Civilization and Its Discontents*, in *Standard Edition of the Complete Psychological Works of Sigmund Freud*, ed. J. Strachey (London: Hogarth, 1961), 21: 142.
4. Jean-Claude Maleval, "Des vides juridiques aux évaluations," *Le nouvel âne* 1 (2003): 7.
5. Jacques Lacan, *Le séminaire, livre XVII: L'envers de la psychanalyse*, ed. J.-A. Miller (Paris: Seuil, 1991).
6. This is expressed as

$$\frac{S_1}{\$} \rightarrow \frac{S_2}{a}$$

7. Jacques Lacan, "Proposition of 9 October 1967 on the Psychoanalyst of the School," *Analysis* (Centre for Psychoanalytic Research, Melbourne) 6 (1995): 12.
8. Jacques-Alain Miller, "Milanese Intuitions," trans. Thelma Sowley, *Mental Online* 11 (2002): 9–16; 12 (2003): 5–14. Available at www.mental-nls.com.
9. Jacques-Alain Miller, "Milanese Intuitions [2]," *Mental Online* 12 (2003), 15.
10. Jacques Lacan, "Nota sul padre e l'universalismo," *La psicoanalisi* 33 (2003): 9.
11. Lacan, "Proposition of 9 October 1967," 257.

14

The Intimate, the Extimate, and Psychoanalytic Discourse

Pierre-Gilles Guéguen

The fashion of autobiography in literature has given the unveiling of intimacy a public and aesthetic value. Psychoanalysis is also an experience in which intimacy is convoked, but it is not treated in the same manner, and the "extimate," to use the concept invented by Lacan and developed by Jacques-Alain Miller, has a different status within it. Nevertheless, in whatever way intimacy or extimacy is treated, there can be no psychoanalysis without truth being brought into play. In his seminar *Encore*, Lacan commented, " 'The true aims at the real'—that statement is the fruit of a long reduction of pretensions to truth. . . . If analysis rests on a presumption, it is that knowledge about truth can be constituted on the basis of its experience."[1]

Literary Intimacy

Rousseau's *Confessions* and then his *Reveries of a Solitary Walker* brought the theme of intimacy into literature and, no doubt, into the realm of taste as well. This was accompanied in painting, in parallel, by family scenes or scenes of the likes of Jean-Baptiste Greuze that were intended to reveal the wonderful moments of family intimacy. This literary form can be contrasted with that of the "exemplary lives," adopted from antiquity, that marked the Grand Century. Moreover, as Jean Starobinski indicates, there is an "intimate," or, in any case, very unusual causality at work; and it was because persecution drove Rousseau to seek the "centre of gravity he lacked" that the attempt to expose the most intimate truth became, for him, such a "lived value." Jean-Jacques's "sadistic superego," he notes, "imposes relentless courage on him. Being exposed to a constantly harmful adversity for him warranted constant defiance in reply."[2]

In *Confessions* the proposition is not the same, moreover, as in *Reveries*, as his commentator has observed. In *Confessions* it is a question of saying everything, of invoking truth in the form of defiance but also in the form of reasoning, with the purpose of silencing the Other; it is a question of confiding what is purportedly beyond decorum and shame, in order to place oneself beyond judgment. Truth here takes on the appearance of a form of jouissance that allows one to be in the right and to prove a certainty to a real or imagined persecutory adversary. In *Reveries* we are transported beyond the reason that reasons. A new agreement is established between Jean-Jacques, his truth, and the world, founded on indifference to its solicitations and on a profound feeling of connivance with Nature, which does not fail to evoke the appeasement of a President Schreber.

Moreover, in describing the nature of this feeling, Rousseau discovers a formula that is remarkably clinically precise: "I enjoy myself despite them." The intimacy of the walker from now on rests upon an island of internal solitude that corresponds to a flight from the company of men and to a determined choice for a new form of enjoyment. "I only ever see animosity on the faces of men, and for me nature is always laughing," declares Jean-Jacques, at peace.

The culture of intimacy in the sense of calculated confidences, as measured by the writings of artists, extends into the nineteenth century with Henri Frédéric Amiel and the literary genre of the *journal intime*. From Amiel to Gide there is a concern for truth but there is also trafficking with the truth for the sake of the gaze of the universal reader who bears the name of posterity. The literature of the confession, again in our days, has its lovers and exegetes in a play with truth that at certain moments seeks transgression, and where the concern to *épater le bourgeois* can combine with a particular perversity or, at the least, a form of cynicism.[3]

It is, then, in all these cases a matter of a manipulation of truth that everywhere maintains a consistent Other as the addressee. Should I mention, in this regard, the "game of truth" made fashionable by the New Wave films of the 1960s, with their touch of sadism?

Another face of the taste for the intimate is the exaltation of the unhappy solitude in which an artist makes contact with that which is most profound in oneself. This is equally a grand theme of literary taste, both romantic (Baudelaire, Rimbaud) and modern (Conrad, but also Cendrars and, in a way, Céline). In this case, the taste for the true at times combines with the taste for happiness in evil evoked by Lacan in the first few lines of "Kant with Sade." On each occasion the relationship to the Other's or to one's own fault, that is, to jouissance, is invoked. In each case it is a question of making small accommodations to jouissance.

Thus, reference to the intimate resonates in the register of making use of truth in order to convince but also in that of using truth so as to make room for a new arrangement of the artist with human society, either by an exclusion that he agreed to or even wished for (outside the literary bond in which he opens himself up), or with the aim of attempting to authenticate a sense of oneself that would be the most profound and the most enduring in being.[4]

Literary intimacy therefore refers to the way in which truth is treated and to the use made of it in its transmission to others. But it is also valuable, if we examine it from another angle, as an effort to bear witness to what makes for the absolute singularity of a subject, a precious solitude populated by only one benevolent other: the reader. Undoubtedly, literature cannot do without that which founds all experience of sublimation and which opposes its being extracted from the sphere of narcissism: the consistency of an other.

What is above all striking in the origin of the popularity of the sentiment of intimacy in literature and in philosophy is effectively that it is willingly propagated more through the avenues of hysterical contagion than by logic, as the extraordinary success of *Confessions* and *Reveries* demonstrates. The literary intimate addresses us through our own hysterical identification with the true.

The intimate, through being taken for what is ordinarily hidden, is supposed to be more true when it is stated than whatever is given to public view in the most ordinary banality of daily life. The fascination with truth would thus be of a kind with the will to say everything, especially to say what shame and semblants requires to be hidden; ultimately, jouissance is at stake. Here one of those biases by which one aims to hunt down the key to an analysis manifests itself, but in my opinion this would not be the right path to take.

Analytic Uses of the Intimate

Analytic experience is, in effect, at least in a first approximation, for each subject who wishes to undertake it, a search for the truth. However, experience of the treatment quickly demonstrates to each person that truth shows itself delicate to handle, produces unexpected effects at the very least, and emerges as it wishes, as a surprise and when one expects it least.

In this matter it is necessary to give an important place to the opposition, taken from Heidegger—which Jean Beaufret indicated in his day—between truth that signals "adequation" and truth as unveiling, an opposition that Lacan does not fail to elaborate.[5]

There is even more, for, and this is putting it too briefly, today we are alert to the fact that Lacan, having made the unveiling of truth the aim of psychoanalysis (with some prudence, it is true),[6] ultimately states that truth can be only half said and that, all things considered, it is the "sister of jouissance."[7]

This point of view, which comes late in Lacan's teaching, would require a full discussion. In presenting this thesis Lacan is, effectively, not unaware that, as he indicates, he is thereby touching on the logic of psychoanalysis itself. As he asserts, "A logical system is consistent, however 'weak' it is, as they say, only by designating its force of effect of incompleteness, where its limit is marked" (76).

The objection could be made that in his time Freud had advocated the need for "analytic frankness." The patient is effectively expected to say everything and is particularly requested not to dismiss any thoughts that strike him as running counter to decency. It is not for nothing that the inventor of psychoanalysis took them to be "more true"; as early as "Project for a Scientific Psychology," he says that, in the unconscious, there are no "indications of reality," so that it is impossible to distinguish between truth and fiction invested with affect.[8]

Precisely because no fiction is indifferent to the construction brought about in analysis, the patient's effort must tend toward the true—not in the manner of Rousseau, who sits in his *Confessions* astride the true as if it were a weapon of combat, but rather as the subject's abandonment to the Other who speaks through him, like a "leaving be," *laisser être*. This, then, is the way that opens onto the discovery of how "the sexual impasse exudes the fictions that rationalize the impossible from which it stems," as Lacan puts it in *Television*.[9]

When, in "Direction of the Treatment and the Principles of Its Power," Lacan mentions the direction of conscience in reference to the analyst's task, he rejects it categorically.[10] But he does not renounce the tension in the direction of the true that activates the patient, even if he considers that at the outset it is at one with the prejudices that "cultural diffusion" has inspired in him concerning analytic experience. Thus, the analyzing use of the true contrasts with the confessional and with the avowal. It reveals itself to be necessary, however, if one is not to fail in the exploration of the sexual impasse.

The Use of the True and the Pass

If truth is a solid, as Lacan says, it can be approached from different directions. I will therefore distinguish an analyzing use of the true and another use that I will call the testimonial use—another facet of the relationship to truth in analytic experience, one that the subject deploys in his or her testimony on the pass.

This use takes into account the fact that in analysis the analysand discovers, bit by bit, truth effects that are not at one with his or her prejudices but which result from what he or she has been for the Other.

Lacan grasped this move from subjectivation to objectivation very early. He takes it into account in a letter he wrote July 14, 1953, to the person who had analyzed him, Rudolf Loewenstein, in these terms: "These pages have not been written in order to contribute to this file [the file on the split of 1953], but in order to give you, in the open tone that our special relationship allows, the lived testimony without which the history would not be able to be written. No objectivity can be attained in human affairs without this subjective foundation." In the apparatus of the pass, between the passand and the passers, unconscious knowledge extracted from the treatment is delivered up, always initially acquired in the analysis by a subjectivation of what comes as a surprise. The analysand's lines of destiny are thus revealed; the destiny that the unconscious has made for him is thereby organized. A new value of intimacy is in question. It is not the intimacy of the avowal, nor is it the intimacy obtained through the revelation of some primitive fact or the revelation of the hidden. It is rather the intimacy of the subject of the unconscious, intimacy that has nothing to do with the depths, but which was there, displayed on the surface like "a scab in the sun on a public holiday," according to the expression that Lacan uses. It was already there, visible, before the analysand had the means to subjectify it.

If it is true that in the pass the subject initially presents his case to his passers, and that it is one of the results of analysis to be able to have an effect upon this case before one faces others, this case is intimate only insofar as it disengages the signifying constellation that is particular to the subject and, in that respect, unparalleled. The passand's work, his or her relationship to the truth, consists in showing how this case, made up of signifying elements that are both discontinuous and yet organized, stems from their coherence, how unconscious knowledge is revealed there, made out of chains of letters arranged in such a way "that provided not one of them is left out, the un-known is arranged as the framework of knowledge."[11] This does not suppose saying everything—on the contrary, a reduction, in the philosophical sense of the term, is expected—but supposes saying everything that is necessary.

The intimacy that is here in question, the intimacy of the pass (it is a matter here of the pass in the procedure, in the account that is given to the passers) that we contrast with the intimacy of literature, or with the intimacy that comes into play in religious confession, consists in unflinchingly bringing a new form of knowledge, a new version of the relationship of a subject to the semblants, onto the scene of knowledge. It thereby modifies the set of semblants by adding a new element to them, and it produces a new version of them, a particular version that is nevertheless compatible with the old ones. The analyst is retained there as he who guarantees that the locus of the Other is barred, who retains the signifier that lacks and who, thereby, anchors the flight of meaning; it is the element outside the whole that enables the whole to establish its own limit. The analytically intimate in the institutional experience of the pass thus concerns both the desire for the Other and also the relationship with the Other that does not exist and to which the analyst in his "desert of being" [*desêtre*] is reduced.

Testimony and Truth

I will now distinguish a third type of relationship to truth, a new facet of this solid that is truth, following Lacan. It is the one that the appointed Analyst of the School produces for the larger analytic community, in what we call "the testimonial"—the public recounting of one's case and the work of investigation that goes with it, which, building on this case, comes to have the value of "teaching of the Analyst of the School."

The Analyst of the School's effort this time consists in passing the case from the singular to the paradigm by showing both the singularity of its construction and the power of generalization attached to it, the key that it contributes to opening the doors to clinical work. The truth is verified there once again on the basis of what the analyst's desire is supposed to be, a desire obtained on the basis of the pass in analysis, revealed in the pass, in the dispositive, and whose sound basis the Analyst of the School may or may not use in his participation in psychoanalytic research.

Here, too, and in a more or less direct way, according to the subject, the knowledge extracted from the treatment will become a contribution, but in a perspective that is no longer that of the effectuation of the pass, since in this exercise it is a matter of drawing the lessons that are valid for psychoanalysis as such. This is where the "new signifier" that Lacan called with his wishes will appear. In this third moment, where the analysis continues by way of the communication of its results, the truth of the intimate experience serves as a fulcrum, often discrete and yet nevertheless indispensable, in order to explain what an analysis is and to describe the problems the practice of psychoanalysis raises.

The Extimate and the Intimate

The term *extimacy* initially appeared as a neologism constructed by Lacan. It is therefore a signifier particular to psychoanalysis, but in the use that is frequently made of it, it is not always clearly distinguished from the significations generally given to that which is intimate.

However, the term *extimate* has not been forged in symmetry with that of intimacy. How can one grasp the fact that there is no comparison between intimacy and extimacy in terms of depth and dissimulation?[12]

That which is extimate is not the apotheosis of what would be the intimate, as is often thought.

But the two terms are not mutually exclusive, either. The extimate, like the intimate, is that which is the most hidden. Is it necessary to distinguish between what is hidden by the subject and what is unarticulable for the subject? I am inclined to adopt this binary contrast in the knowledge that in both cases this is also for the subject what is closest to him. While *intimate* always supposes that something has to be looked after and cannot be exposed clearly, even if only for reasons of modesty, so as to preserve semblants, *extimate* designates what could be said if one ever got to that point, for the extimate lies beyond semblants. It is an outcome that supposes that the barrier for semblants, the plane of identifications, has been breached. To attempt to grasp the extimacy of desire for a subject is also to attempt to approach the cause of one's desire. This is why the concept of extimacy is particularly suitable when touching on the nature of the drive, or on what Lacan calls the *objet a*, provided that one is alert to the fact, as Jacques-Alain Miller has pointed out on several occasions, that the *objet a* is itself also a semblant. As Miller notes, "There is in effect two interpretations of the barred A. There is its interpretation in terms of the Other's desire and there is its interpretation in terms of the Other's jouissance."[13] The relationship of extimacy concerns the latter.

Miller continues, "It is because there is a negative function at the heart of the dialectic of desire that one never says that the Other lacks desire. And it is precisely because of the impossible to negate where jouissance is concerned that one can assume that the Other lacks jouissance, this Other that does not exist." From this perspective, *extimacy* refers to the analyst after analysis, no longer as placeholder for the Other that lacks, but as a positive remainder of the analytic operation. In other words, *extimacy* refers to the manner in which the analyst has been the partner of the drive.

If one wanted to return to the distinction between *Confessions* and *Reveries*, the parallel would be made between the analytic intimacy and *Confessions* on the one hand, and on the other between extimacy and *Reveries*, though obviously on condition of transposing this opposition into the framework of the analysis of the neuroses.

Extimacy concerns, in effect, the cause of jouissance. I leave open here the question whether it can be said completely. I would be inclined to consider that it is transmitted, like truth, by the half saying (*mi-dire*), that it appears in the relationship of a case to the impossible that may on occasion be formulated as a paradox, a contradiction, a *Witz*, and that it results from the exposition without being completely included in it. It cannot be a question here of a mystagogy—although a mystery is appealed to here, one that touches on the subject's being. What is located through the methodical approach of making the signifier function in the analysand's subjective economy are occasional substances by means of which the drive has been brought into play. These substances have given their own coloration to the drive's demand, but the aim is Other. Lacan calls it *objet a*.

While the analytic intimacy of testimony is multiple, since it is extracted from an analysis that can only have been particular, the relationship of extimacy makes it possible to attain the One, but in a particular form of the One that cannot be collectivized.

The extimate, in effect, is that by which the analysand at the end of his trajectory attains the question of being, as well as the question of being analyst, through the initial bringing of the analyst's desire into focus that the extimate authorizes. Through the extimate, the analysand is introduced into analytic solitude and enters into the breach, where, since Lacan, he or she is supposed to remain with respect to the crucial problems raised by psychoanalytic knowledge. The analysand finds there his or her point of entry into what, in *Seminar XVII*, Lacan calls the analyst's discourse. This discourse, Lacan adds, is not to be confused with the analyzing discourse, and the analyst's solitude has nothing to do with Rousseauian withdrawal from the world (35).

The analyst's discourse is not a discourse of the expert who on the basis of constituted knowledge of psychoanalysis would have an opinion about everything. Nor is it the knowledge of the practitioner who finds the reason for his act in the effectiveness of his practice. Rather, the analyst's discourse presumes that the one who attempts to maintain it knows how to find what is analytic and what is not on each occasion, knows how to measure the relationship between the analytic and the social, and knows that there is no chance of rendering this calculation effective without passing through the singular pathways of a treatment directed in the proper manner.

272   Guéguen

The Analyst of the School, once appointed, sees an open door leading onto a tightrope: Will he be up to the task, or will he take a false step? Will he know how to tread the path? Here, experience is of no avail, but nothing can be done without having previously benefited from the accomplishment of an analysis and from the training that follows in its wake. How will he be able to walk the tightrope? As Lacan stressed, "It is not sufficient for a duty to be self-evident for it to be fulfilled."

Notes

1   Jacques Lacan, *The Seminar of Jacques Lacan, Book XX: Encore, or Feminine Sexuality, The Limits of Love and Knowledge*, ed. Jacques-Alain Miller, trans. with notes by B. Fink (New York: Norton, 1998), 91.
2   Jean Starobinski, *La transparence et l'obstacle* (Paris: Gallimard, 1971), 65.
3   Thus Philippe Lejeune is able to declare, on the back cover of his book *Pour l'autobiographie* (Paris: Seuil, 1998), "Personal papers also concern others. We unavoidably speak of them. From attacks on private life to defamation, from professional secrets to the freedom to write in prison, I will, then, explore the situations in which the law regulates the expression of intimacy. The autobiographical pact is a veritable engagement with one's duties and rights."
4   This is also how Maine de Biran perceives him at the beginning of the nineteenth century; he introduces into philosophy "the truly primitive fact of the intimate sense outside of the circle of affectation or blind determinism of instinct, which positively excludes this fact, rather than being its source" ("De l'apperception immédiate," *Oeuvres*, vol. 4 [Paris: Vrin, 1995], 109).
5   "When truth in the sense of adequation forgets that it is founded on truth in the sense of unveiling, it becomes the truth of subjugation and this is the death of truth. All that then remains is to venerate the yoke that weighs us down and elevate it to the dignity of the divine," Jean Beaufret, "De l'existentialisme à Heidegger," in *Martin Heidegger et le problème de la vérité* (Paris: Vrin, 1986), 97.
6   See the note with which Lacan concludes "The Freudian Thing," "For . . . truth proves to be complex in its essence, humble in its offices and foreign to reality, refractory to the choice of sex, akin to death and, on the whole, rather inhuman, Diana perhaps" (in *Ecrits: A Selection*, trans. B. Fink [New York: Norton, 2002], 137).
7   Jacques Lacan, *Le séminaire, livre XVII: L'envers de la psychanalyse*, ed. J.-A. Miller (Paris: Seuil, 1991), 76. Further references to this work are given in the body of the text.
8   Sigmund Freud, "Project for a Scientific Psychology," in *The Standard Edition of the Complete Psychological Works of Sigmund Freud*, ed. J. Strachey (London: Hogarth, 1966), 1:325.
9   Jacques Lacan, *Television*, trans. D. Hollier, R. Krauss, and A. Michelson (New York: Norton, 1990), 30. Translation modified.

10 Lacan, *Ecrits: A Selection*, 216.
11 Jacques Lacan, "Proposition of 9 October 1967 on the Psychoanalyst of the School," *Analysis* 6 (1995): 6.
12 On this point we refer to J.-A. Miller's course Extimacy, given in the Department of Psychoanalysis at the University of Paris VIII.
13 J.-A. Miller, course given in the Department of Psychoanalysis at the University of Paris VIII, unpublished lecture given February 5, 1986.

15

Bureaucratic Speech Acts and the University Discourse: Lacan's Theory of Modernity

Geoff Boucher

Bureaucratic Speech Acts and the Four Discourses

Lacan's diagnosis of modernity involves the displacement of the master by the bureaucrat. The decline of the master and the rise of the bureaucrat—including the totalitarian leader—implies a philosophy of history and a social theory. The problem that Lacan's historical theses address is that of bureaucratic rationalization and the impotence of hysterical protest (in the context of 1968). In considering this problem, Lacan's theory of the four discourses, elaborated in *Seminar XVII*, proposes that a structural matrix subtends the discursive practices that construct social reality. For Lacan, discourse is a "social link," implying that the various discourses determine institutional frameworks that mediate social antagonism in distinctive ways. Yet despite Lacan's hypothesis that the importance of knowledge in modernity implies the gradual displacement of politics by bureaucracy, the mastery of persons by the administration of things, this is not a philosophy of decline. Nor does Lacan advance a dialectical narrative that might culminate in the analyst's discourse instead of the master's discourse. Instead, Lacan postulates that the rotation of the positions in the four discourses is radically contingent —neither a circular theory of discourse, nor a teleology of liberation, but a theory of hegemonic articulations, linking discourse to power. In Lacan's thinking, the university discourse is linked to the ethical impasse of modernity: the forced either/or choice of the ethics of honor, the ethics of mastery, is replaced by an impossible neither/nor: neither utilitarianism nor fundamentalism. But the rise of the university discourse is connected with the mergence of analytic discourse, which is articulated to the ethics of psychoanalysis—Lacan's alternative to the utilitarianism/fundamentalism binary of modernity. Lacan proposes an ethical solution to the problems of modernity. Despite some sympathy for criticisms of capitalism, however, Lacan did not advocate a social revolution. Indeed, his interpretation of the movement of the radical students was that this represented a hysterical demand for a new master.

While the master's discourse is probably at its historical nadir today, it nonetheless retains a crucial function. Mastery is the discourse of self-identity and the control of others, which institutes the dominance of a master signifier, S_1, thereby organizing the field of knowledge, S_2, into conformity with the values promoted by this master signifier. At the same time, mastery conceals subjective division, $, while generating a fantasmatic object, a, as its by-product. The dominance of the master signifier orders the chain of discursive knowledge while repressing fantasy narration ($ ◊ a). The paradigm of the master's discourse is the master-slave dialectic, where the struggle to the death for recognition culminates in the enslavement of the one who gives way on desire. The slave is set to work for the master, but in this process the slave produces not only knowledge in the service of the master, but also the cultural universality that cannot be signified within the master's discourse and the alienated subjectivity of the slave. *Subjectivation* by the master signifier implies the lack of legitimacy of the subjectivity of the slave and the restriction of this surplus enjoyment to a nonvocalized excess. Nonetheless, the slave may transform the fantasy into a demand in the form of a hysterical revolt. The function of the master is not solely authoritarian repression, however, but also the foundation of new social links.[1] At the same time, the master's discourse is the discourse of the constitutive exception, and as such it is inherently connected to the drawing of distinctions between inclusion and exclusion, friend and enemy. For Lacan, the discipline of governance and the field of politics are the paradigms of the master's discourse. This field is dialectical, because mastery generates hysterical revolt as its form of inherent transgression, suggesting that mastery is inherently dialogical and political. This is exemplified by the discourse of the revolution, regarded by Lacan as a mere rotation of discursive positions rather than the elimination of mastery. Subversion, Lacan suggests, springs from consideration of the impossibility of mastery rather than the hysterical demand for a new master characteristic of political revolution.[2]

Derrida's analysis of speech acts endorses the modern *doxa* on the decline of the master. For Derrida, the event inaugurated by a speech act remains open because the play of difference cannot close the locution.[3] Speech acts are therefore plagued by "citationality," that is, by a generalized iterability that generates a play of repetition and difference. His analysis of inaugural declarations suggests that the conflict between the conventional nature of performatives and the inaugural function leads to the phenomena of repetition in history.[4] The "impossibility" of the declaration springs from the contradiction between its conventionality and its inaugural role. This is supported by historical analysis of declarations of independence, republics, and constitutions.[5]

The problem with Derrida's analysis is that it treats locution before—and independently of—illocution. Lacan proposes an alternative explanation of these phenomena based on a psychoanalytic grasp of illocution. The speech act is completed precisely through its inconsistency: the performative contradiction involved in inaugural declarations constitutes the master's discourse. The impossibility of this act, however, leads to a remainder that appears in fantasy narrations of the utopian social harmony to be expected from the new order. Unconsciously, mastery generates hysterical revolt as its inherent transgression, so that, for instance, the mass demand for *egaliberté* (to invoke Etienne Balibar's term) is the inherent reverse of the declaration of the Rights of Man. This eventually instigates a questioning of the master, leading to social rebellion. The master's discourse can be stabilized only when the social order inaugurated by the master's declaration is supported by a system of knowledge designed not to repress utopian fantasy, but to mobilize its elements as productive forces. Lacan can be interpreted as proposing that the decline of the master is the result of the rise of another discourse that initially supplemented and finally supplanted it.

From the thirteenth century onward, the discourse of mastery relied increasingly upon the university discourse for the elaboration of "disinterested knowledge" that actually served to legitimate the reigning master signifiers.[6] In the university discourse, where systematic knowledge is the dominant discursive factor, the recipients of the chain of knowledge must constitute themselves as formless objects to be shaped to the requirements of the educational process. Lacan aligns the discourses of science and technology with the university discourse, and he considers bureaucracy to be the perfect realization of the university discourse.[7] This should alert us to the thesis that the university discourse is a discourse of interpellation, that is, of the formation of subjects to serve a social order. Such interpellation is not a neutral description of facts but a performative act that generates the social relations required for the knowledge it purports to merely describe. Indeed, "historically, the university discourse . . . has effectively reversed the role of legitimating and rationalising the social, political and scientific practices that have grown up around it." So, despite the continued validity of the claim that "the hidden truth of the university discourse is that it is effectively a cover for the blind authority of the master's discourse," it nonetheless has become increasingly dominant in its own right.[8]

Foucault's analysis of the discourse of power inherent in institutional knowledge dissects the university discourse. Foucault claims that institutional knowledge deploys power at the level of the disciplinary locution, because institutional knowledge is a discourse that disposes of material bodies in order to interpellate an obedient "soul" into them. On the side of the interlocutor, the soul is the prison of the body, because material discipline involves the formation of a conscience that internalizes social norms. On the side of the speaker, the "neutral" discourse of knowledge conceals the operation of power operating in the name of these social norms. Four key claims can be derived from Foucault's analysis:

1. In disciplinary society, the discursive agency is systematic knowledge (of the offender, the offence and the law, for instance), which grounds a judgment in truth.[9] Foucault describes this systematic knowledge as "the disciplines" and defines them as "methods, which [have] made possible the meticulous control of the operations of the body, which assured the constant subjection of its forces and imposed upon them a relation of docility-utility" (137). He connects disciplinary knowledge with the entire complex of the human sciences, which he regards as a complex of "power-knowledge" because of its disposal of ma-

terial control over docile bodies (of the native, the inmate, the patient, the worker, the pupil, and so forth).
2. The object of the tables, prescriptions, exercises and tactics of disciplinary knowledge is the material (nonsignifying) body (131). Foucault makes it clear that the body is not a signifying element in the "carceral archipelago" of modern, disciplinary society, but something subjected to a material training regime. That is, discipline aims not at the reform of the juridical subject, but at the rendering docile of the individual anatomy. Hence the "anatomy of power," the modern "body politic," always places the body at issue. This is not a description of the material structure of human physique, but a performative that "invests it, marks it, trains it, tortures it, forces it to carry out tasks, to perform ceremonies, to emit signs" in a political technology of the body (25–26).
3. The truth of these disciplinary procedures is the inculcation of social norms. Their paradigmatic form is the examination, which in terms of speech acts means a procedure designed to legitimate the utterance of an evaluative judgment. "The examination combines the techniques of an observing hierarchy and those of a normalising judgement" (184). Yet this normalization is the opposite, the inversion of the power of the Prince, for the "domain of Panopticism is the whole lower region . . . of irregular bodies" (208). It is not that they are hidden—their invisibility derives from their ubiquity, from their character as infrastructure of the law, as "infra-law": "Disciplinary power . . . is exercised through its invisibility; at the same time, it imposes on those whom it subjects a principle of compulsory visibility" (187).
4. Finally, the product of the disciplinary operation is the soul, and "the soul is the prison of the body" (30). Indeed, the representations produced in the disciplined body—representations of pleasure and pain, linked to interests—are signifiers, whose signified is the "soul" (128). The soul is a by-product of the disciplinary operation, whose general formula had been discovered by Althusser: the subject is the result of material rituals in institutional contexts. But this soul is "repressed," not only because

it occupies the position of the signified of the signifier, but also because it is not accessible to discipline. The "theatre of punishment" of the Enlightenment accordingly ceded position to the "carceral archipelago" of modernity: discipline produces full, normalized *individuals* in the place where the empty, juridical *subject* was (307, 301).

Only with Lacan's theory can we grasp the relation between power and knowledge, on the one side, and the material body and "spiritual" subject, on the other. Because Foucault's analysis is focused on the locution—to the exclusion of illocution—he overlooks the indirect relation between power and knowledge. Knowledge is not immediately power (there is, for instance, knowledge in the real)—it is power because a subject *believes* that this knowledge is authorized by a convention. Hence the illocutionary force of an assertion relates the speaker to the authority of a consensus. Likewise, on the side of the interlocutor, Foucault regards the subject (the modern citizen) as an imaginary ruse, a symbolic fiction that conceals domination of the material body. This is connected to his famous rejection of the "repressive hypothesis." But Lacan's analysis leads us to conclude that the dominance of consciousness in the university discourse sutures the divided subject, excluding it from the field of knowledge. Foucault's analysis reproduces this exclusion without realizing that the Panopticon (the paradigmatic form of disciplinary power) depends on the real efficiency of symbolic fictions—precisely the characteristic of unconscious thinking that Foucault rejects.[10]

Speech Acts

These preliminary reflections indicate that a mobile equilibrium of coercion and consent might be distributed between the discourses of the master and the university. The social theory underlying Lacan's observations can be further explicated with reference to the fact that Lacan's discursive matrices are at once types of speech and forms of the social bond. According to speech act theory, it is the performative dimension of the speech act that institutes the social bond, as illocution has the power to cause the interpersonal relation to which it refers. To grasp the implications of the Lacanian theory of discourse, we therefore need to attend closely to the technical distinctions relevant to speech act theory. The well-known distinction between constative and performative speech acts corresponds to the difference between saying something and doing things with words. A constative utterance describes a state of affairs according to criteria of veracity (a statement of correspondence to reality that can be true or false), so semantics is the proper domain of the constative. By contrast, a performative utterance does something (alters the status of the referent) in the enunciation. For instance, "I do" in a marriage ceremony does not report that the person is married, but instead makes (does) the bond of marriage.[11] Unlike the constative statement, the performative utterance cannot be true or false—it can only misfire, can only be, in Émile Benveniste's terminology, "legitimate" or "illegitimate" (J. L. Austin uses the less politically suggestive terms "felicitous" and "infelicitous"). According to Austin's main stipulation, "there must exist an accepted conventional procedure having a certain conventional effect, that procedure to include the uttering of certain words by certain persons in certain circumstances."[12] John Searle, following Austin, refers to the institutional context within which the performance can be legitimate as the "conditions of satisfaction" of the performative aspect of the utterance.[13]

The psychoanalytic research of Shoshana Felman concentrated on the potential of the performative to misfire.[14] I propose that the link between misfires and the conditions of satisfaction can be explicated only once a third party is introduced into the loop that passes between speaker and hearer of a speech act. In this light, it is particularly significant that Austin abandoned the initial binary distinction between constative and performative for a ternary distinction between illocutionary force (performative dimension), locutionary act (constative dimension), and perlocutionary consequences (the ability of speech acts to engender consequences in partners in dialogue, for instance, persuasion or shock).[15] I suggest that the question of the uptake of the interlocutor is critical to the breakdown of Austin's binary distinction. Austin's explicit motivation for the shift, of course, is the radical instability of the division between two distinct classes of speech acts, which necessarily yields to an analysis of the different aspects of every speech act. Every speech act contains both a locutionary and an illocutionary component. This effectively subverts the true/false distinction as the criterion for the validity of the locutionary act. For the veracity of a statement now depends on the context implied by the utterance, and this context is determined by the "conditions of satisfaction" of the illocutionary act. As Austin notes, "the truth or falsity of a statement depends upon what you were performing in what circumstances."[16] Equally, however, the question of the uptake of the interlocutor becomes central as soon as we move from an ideal situation, where the speaker is fully authorized, to the social field, where the authority of the speaker to perform an institutional ritual is always open to interrogation, for the illocutionary force of the utterance now depends on the dialogical speech context that supplies the "conditions of satisfaction" for the performative legitimacy of the speech act. Without this consideration, it is impossible to explain the category of perlocution. Perlocution designates the singular by-product of speech acts, and where illocution is conventional, perlocution is unconventional. Perlocution depends on the uptake of the interlocutor, but this uptake is not purely personal. Indeed, perlocution depends on the emergence of a gap between the conventional requirements of the speech act and its actual execution — that is, perlocution emerges because of the presence in the utterance of an element of excess. In Lacanian terms, it is passed through the relay of the Other, which checks the "excessive" aspect of the utterance.

John Searle's typology of speech acts has the advantage of formalizing these "conditions of satisfaction" while advancing an exact classification of illocutionary forces. Searle's taxonomy is based upon the "essential condition" for the legitimacy of a performative speech act.[17] According to Searle's Ideal rule, "the speaker implies the satisfaction of the preparatory conditions, expresses the sincerity conditions and says the essential condition."[18] Searle holds that every speech act is defined by four components:

1. The illocutionary force indicator: the illocutionary point is that the speech act attempts to get the hearer or the speaker to do something, as opposed to a statement that represents a reality. Searle describes the illocutionary point as the "essential condition," which institutes a relation between speaker and hearer sanctioned by convention. In general, the essential condition specifies the rest of the conditions.[19]
2. The statement, or the "facts of the matter" relative to the action

performed, including the direction of fit, or relation between words and world, and the "preparatory conditions," such as knowledge required for belief formation.
3. The sincerity condition, which expresses the psychological state expressed in the speech act.
4. The "conditions of satisfaction" for the legitimacy of the speech act, including any extralinguistic institutional positioning required for their legitimacy.

I propose that Searle's analysis of speech acts can be mapped onto the basic matrix of discourse according to Lacan. Consider, for instance, the category of "declaratives." The formula for declaratives is:

$D\updownarrow\varnothing\ (p)$

D: the illocutionary force indicator for declaratives—the point is to institute a relation.
$\updownarrow$: the direction of fit is world-words, because "successful performance guarantees that the propositional content corresponds to the world."[20]
$\varnothing$: the sincerity condition is null, because declaratives are entirely conventional performances.
(p): the statement "that p," the relation to be instituted by the speech act.

The illocutionary force indicator, as Searle's analysis indicates, is something excessive to the statement, but it can be subtracted from the proposition "that p" without affecting its semantic content. It follows that the illocutionary force indicator can be identified with the Lacanian master signifier, S_1, which as a "signifier without signified" governs the enunciation through its exclusion from the statement. The illocutionary force indicator can be a verb such as "to declare," or an ideologeme authorizing a declaration, such as "in God's name." In a declaration, the illocutionary force indicator is the agency that performs the speech act.

The statement is analytically excluded from the illocutionary component and positioned as its other. In the declaration, the illocutionary force indicator positions the propositional statement "that p" as a chain of signification that is addressed by the enunciation. It follows that the statement can be identified with the Lacanian chain of knowledge, S_2, which in a declaration occupies the place of the other.

Bureaucratic Speech Acts and the University Discourse   283

The sincerity condition indicates, in Searle's terms, a null, or empty Intentionality. It is the place marker for the subjectivity of the agent that, in the declaration, is entirely subordinate to the conventional procedures of the performative ritual. I associate the sincerity condition in the declaration with the empty, divided subject, $, and locate this in the position of the truth of the declarative speech act.

Finally, the direction of fit in declarations is "words-world," indicating that the speech act causes the relation it purports to describe. This purporting to describe is precisely the key to the positioning of the direction of fit in this analysis, for the object of the speech act is systematically subordinated to the propositional content of the utterance, appearing only retroactively as the product of the performance. I therefore associate the direction of fit with the *objet a* and position it as the product of the declarative.

I realize that these last two points require some more justification.

I will first present my conclusions. The relation between these four conditions can be set out in a diagram:

AGENT: S_1	→	OTHER: S_2
D: The illocutionary force indicator and essential condition: the illocutionary point is that the speech act attempts to get the hearer or the speaker to do something		(p): The statement: the "facts of the matter" relative to the action performed, including the direction of fit, or relation between words, world and "preparatory conditions"
∅: The sincerity condition, which expresses the psychological state expressed in the speech act		↕: The "conditions of satisfaction" for the legitimacy of the speech act, including any extra-linguistic institutional positioning required for their legitimacy
TRUTH: $		PRODUCT: (*a*)

Lacanian analysis of declaratives as the master's discourse

A similar analysis can be applied to the category of assertives, whose formula is:

⊢ ↓ B(p)

An assertion consists of a chain of knowledge, expressed as a proposition, (p), whose form is "that p is the case," where? "In the world": ↓; the downward direction of fit indicates that words must conform to world. The agency is the proposition, addressed to the direction of fit, implying a form of verification. The illocutionary force indicator is the truth-value indicator, ⊢, which makes a claim regarding the adequacy of the propositional content, (p), expressed in the statement "that p." The truth of the assertion is, however, subordinated to the chain of knowledge. Indeed, that a *claim* has been made, as opposed to a mere registration of a preexisting fact, can be brought to light only by rephrasing the utterance to make explicit the position of enunciation. The sincerity condition is accordingly belief, because every locution is trivially also the illocution "I believe that p." Here we have a different arrangement of the four components of the speech act:

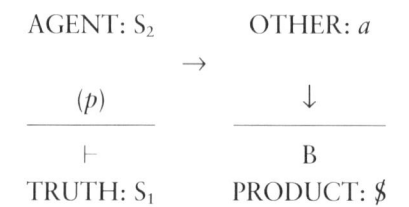

AGENT: S_2	OTHER: a
→	
(p)	↓
⊢	B
TRUTH: S_1	PRODUCT: $

Lacanian analysis of assertives as the university discourse

I shall now justify my association of the sincerity condition with the divided subject and the conditions of satisfaction with the *objet a*. Searle is frequently dismissed in cultural studies for reintroducing intentionality into speech act theory in defiance of Austin's stipulation that convention, not intention, defines the performative.[21] This defensive stance may insulate Austin from Derrida's celebrated deconstruction of speech act theory, but only at the cost of reducing Searle's insistence on the persistence of subjectivity to an amateur's mistake.[22] It therefore passes unnoticed that Searle's Intentionality is not mental but linguistic: "The Intentional state which constitutes the sincerity condition is expressed in the performance of the speech act."[23] Indeed, because insincere but

Bureaucratic Speech Acts and the University Discourse   285

legitimate performatives exist, Searle is forced to accept that "sincerity" is really the performance of the act. Better yet, Searle proposes that Intentionality is explained by a combination of belief and desire, which are distinct from the "conscious mental events" of psychological intentions and visual perceptions.[24] It follows that the sincerity condition expresses an empty, *unconscious* Intentionality that is constituted in language. The alignment of the sincerity condition with the divided subject is accordingly justified.

Nonetheless, the interlocutor retroactively imputes a "sincere intentionality" to the speaker as an ascribed psychological state. According to Searle, "it is the performance of the utterance act with a certain set of intentions that converts the utterance act into an illocutionary act and thus imposes Intentionality on the utterance."[25] From a Lacanian perspective, this is an inversion of the real relation. Searle then states that "for every speech act that has a direction of fit, the speech act will be satisfied if and only if the expressed psychological state is satisfied, and the condition of satisfaction of the speech act and expressed psychological state are identical."[26] Given that Searle believes that even speech acts with no "direction of fit" express beliefs, this means that every legitimate speech act depends on the coincidence of the sincerity condition with the conditions of satisfaction. In other words, every speech act raises, for the interlocutor, the question, What does the speaker *really* want? *Che vuoi?* In the strange temporality of this question, a gap opens between Intentionality and intentionality, making perlocution emerge. The distinction between a legitimate illocution generating a conventional sequel and an illegitimate illocution generating a perlocutionary consequence is precisely this alien Intentionality of a strange temporality—one of Lacan's definitions of the unconscious *objet a.*[27] As Felman notes, the speech act generates "a referential excess, an excess on the basis of which the real leaves its trace on meaning, and *this excess leads to power over others, i.e., perlocution* and the pleasure of the performative."[28] The alignment is justified.

Toward a Lacanian Theory of Reflexive Modernity

The key to grasping the articulation of the university discourse to that of the master in modernity is to recognize that the speech acts characteristic of bureaucracy are not claims, propositions, and so forth (i.e., assertives), but judgments, evaluations, summaries, and assessments. These correspond to a special class of declaratives, called "assertive declarations," whose principal difference with normative declarations is that the sincerity condition is full.[29] In other words, these are declaratives that suture the subject. What I describe as bureaucratic speech acts correspond to assertive speech acts deployed strategically (that is, with a perlocutionary aim) as assertive pseudo-declaratives. In terms of the matrix of the four discourses, these are declarations that conform to the matrix of assertives—that is, they are the result of the usurpation by the university discourse of the content (but not the form) of the master's discourse. Hence, I propose that we understand the modality of the hegemonization of the university discourse over the master's discourse in terms of the bureaucratic colonization of normative space. If we conceptualize modernity as characterized by the struggle of the modern (the university discourse) to supplant tradition (the master's discourse), then reflexive modernity is the moment in which the university discourse, having risen to the hegemonic position, begins to repress the master's discourse. I claim that reflexive modernity represents the hegemony of the university discourse, whose leading edge is the propagation of bureaucratic speech acts, as evidenced by the theoretical reflections and analysis of Third Way discourse. Indeed, the advent of a second, reflexive modernity intensifies the normative crisis of modernity, resulting in a generalized perversion. It can be postulated that the society of reflexive modernity is no longer a "disciplinary society," but a "society of control," where the mechanisms of discipline become at once ubiquitous and commodified. Intellectually, reflexive modernity is characterized by the turning of reflexive doubt on the structures of modernity itself. Sociologically, reflexive modernity is characterized by a heightened anxiety and by the prevalence of expert systems that take over the organization of everyday life.[30] The decline of the master implies the fragmentation of the social order into a multiplicity of social spaces governed by systems of guidelines and provisional rules. As Slavoj Žižek writes, "These (re)invented rules . . . endeavour to provide the viable frame of interaction for narcissistic post-Oedipal subjects. It is as if the lack of the 'big Other' is supplanted by 'ethical committees' as so many substitute 'small big Others' on to which the subject transposes his responsibility and from which he expects to receive a formula that will resolve his deadlock."[31]

The discourse of the Third Way represents a clear example of reflexive modernity in politics.[32] It is also a perfect illustration of what I am calling bureaucratic speech acts. Norman Fairclough's exhaustive analysis of the discourse of Tony Blair's New Labour is the crucial resource for my argument.[33] The agent in Third Way discourse is a chain of signifiers assembled according to the protocols of what might be called, with deference to Orwell, "list-speak." These are lists of antinomic terms assembled through the conjunctions "not only . . . but also." "New Labour political discourse is full of such lists," comments Fairclough, but "the elements in the lists are . . . connected only in the sense that they appear together" (28). We recognize this as the S_2 in Lacan's university discourse, the chain of signification lacking a master signifier. New Labour speeches exhibit a marked absence of polemical discourse (109). This is a discourse in the political field that systematically refuses to draw the friend/enemy distinction: "The political discourse of New Labour is inclusive and consensual—it tries to include everyone; there are no sharp divisions; no us versus them, no enemies" (34). Yet it manages to be sometimes "intolerant," "tough," "authoritarian," and even "draconian" (12, 105, 109, 110). How? Through the veiled reference to the reigning master signifiers of neoliberalism (66–94), introduced through the terms "community" and "one nation" (38). Hence, for instance, the discourse of globalization is presented in terms of the agency of a "knowledge economy," where "ghostly multinationals" remain a "shadowy presence" on the margins of this discourse (24). The New Labour message is explicitly formulated as a discourse of "education and training" through "cultural governance," exercised by means of the dominant ideological apparatuses of late modernity, the media (61, 123). The recipient of this message is positioned as an object in a discourse that operates on two levels: a formative discourse of social integration through work, combined with an implicit discourse of moral condemnation of social degeneracy of the marginal underclass (58). New Labour's explicit message, the subject of Blair's first speech as prime minister and the core term in subsequent communiqués, is all about inclusion (52). But "inclusion" means addressing "the British people" as the objectival consequence of static conditions, not as the subject of a process (54). At the same time, a second line of discourse replaces the concept of material poverty with the notion of moral marginalization, in order to criminalize and ultimately exclude this element (58). Hence the product of the discourse of inclusion is the training of the subjectivity of the citizen in terms of a normative distinction between productive citizens and criminalized underclasses.

It is not only that the discourse of New Labour corresponds precisely to Lacan's concept of university discourse. The means by which this discursive formation is produced is indicative of what I am describing as the bureaucratic colonization of normative space. The key characteristic of New Labour discourse is that it operates with passive sentences, lacking explicit subjects (24). Insofar as there are "agents," these are nominalized processes reified into static conditions (26–27). This enables a discourse that is "managerial and promotional," rather than "political and dialogical" (124). Preeminently, New Labour speech acts are sentences without subjects or objects, mere value-neutral descriptions of the steps to be taken toward "modernisation" (108–10). That is, New Labour discourse presents itself as a series of subjectless assertives. At the same time, New Labour discourse is characterized by "categorical, authoritative assertions" (100). The discourses of the "knowledge economy" and of "social inclusion"—New Labour's central policy foci—are composed of judgments, evaluations, recommendations, and summaries that have the force, as political statements, of declarations of government policy. Yet "the many declarative statements are overwhelmingly categorical assertions" (134)—that is, they are statements that, while they aspire to have the force of assertive declarations, have the form of normal assertives. In short, they are assertive pseudo-declarations, or bureaucratic speech acts.

The generalized fetishism of late modernity is a perlocutionary consequence of bureaucratic speech acts. The general Lacanian position—the "standard theory"—on the late modern "crisis of Oedipus" and the "decline of symbolic efficiency" is well known.[34] Its salient characteristics are that the decline of the paternal function, caused by the supplanting of social authority by forms of "therapeutic" bureaucracy, has generated a generalized weakening of the symbolic order. The "decline of symbolic efficiency" designates the collapse of the unity of the symbolic order, its fragmentation into a multiplicity of domains of signification, so that instead of a unified social order, we have now a dispersed network of lateral links between autonomous language games. The subject increasingly characteristic of this society of generalized perversion is the "pathological narcissist," whose relation to social norms is not internalized but remains an external relation to mere guidelines that can be manipulated. The pathological narcissist is dominated by the superego injunction to enjoy, where individuals fashion lifestyle choices through "lichettes" of jouissance. Consequently, the pathological narcissist expresses a cynical disbelief in symbolic efficiency, believing that instead of a singular universal Law, they exist within an inconsistent multiplicity of rules.

In this context, the hypothesis of an articulation between the master's discourse and the university discourse can explain the perverse situation of the decline of symbolic efficiency, where the subject simultaneously lays claim to and denies performative authority. The pervasive justification of power in terms of knowledge is not the end of the story in reflexive modernity; its inherent inverse is that the underside of this rationalized knowledge is legitimated, not by appeal to the institutional address of the speaker, but by means of their personal mastery. The characteristic contemporary politician relies not upon the authority of their office for the performative effect of their assertions, but upon their image, an amalgam of personal mystique and doctored charisma. This can be explained as follows. Modernity can be considered as that process within which the master's discourse is subordinated to the university discourse, in what I have described as a bureaucratic colonization of normative space. The master's discourse becomes relegated to those enclaves of privacy that remain unregulated by an otherwise pervasive corporate-bureaucratic domination of public discourse. Once this process is completed, however, modernity reflexively turns on itself: instead of the eclipse of the master's discourse, we have a pervasive privatization of public life, where the master returns as an uncanny double, at once our equal and something entirely other. It is not that the politician, for instance, is "one of us" elevated to high office; on the contrary, despite their studied aura of having a special access to the very substance of public opinion. In short, the politician is successful not because they openly identify with their symbolic mandate, but because this hidden identification, concealed behind the mask of imaginary dis-identification and the neutrality of the expert advice that they follow, lends them a sublime personal aura. This, I am suggesting, is the very form of appearance of the articulation between the hegemonic university discourse and the subordinated master's discourse in reflexive modernity. Bureaucratic speech acts—assertive pseudo-declarations—are the form that legitimation takes within this articulation of discourses.

Notes

1 Slavoj Žižek, "Four Discourses, Four Subjects," in *Cogito and the Unconscious*, ed. Slavoj Žižek (Durham, N.C.: Duke University Press, 1998), 77.
2 Jacques Lacan, cited in Mark Bracher, "On the Psychological and Social Functions of Language: Lacan's Theory of the Four Discourses," in *Lacanian Theory of Discourse: Subject, Structure and Society*, ed. M. Bracher, M. Alcorn, R. Corthell, and F. Massardier-Kennedy (New York: New York University Press, 1994), 218.
3 See Jacques Derrida, *Limited Inc.* (Evanston, Ill.: Northwestern University Press, 1988).
4 See Jacques Derrida, "Declarations of Independence," *New Political Science*, 15 (1986): 7–17.
5 See David Armitage, "The Declaration of Independence and International Law," *William and Mary Quarterly* 59.1 (2002): 1–32.
6 See Russell Grigg, "Discourse," in *A Compendium of Lacanian Terms*, ed. Hugette Glowinski, Zita Marks, and Sara Murphy (London: Free Association Books, 2001), 61–70.
7 Jacques Lacan, cited in Bracher, "On the Psychological and Social Functions of Language," 115.
8 Grigg, "Discourse," 69.
9 Michel Foucault, *Discipline and Punish: The Birth of the Prison* (Harmondsworth: Penguin, 1977), 19. All further references to this volume will be in the body of the text.
10 Miran Bozovic, "Introduction: An Utterly Dark Spot," in Jeremy Bentham, *Jeremy Bentham: The Panopticon Writings* (London: Verso, 1995), 1–28.
11 J. L. Austin, *How to Do Things with Words* (Cambridge: Harvard University Press, 1962), 13.
12 Ibid., 14.
13 See John Searle, *Speech Acts: An Essay in the Philosophy of Language* (Cambridge: Cambridge University Press, 1969).
14 See Shoshana Felman, *The Literary Speech Act: Don Juan with J. L. Austin, or, Seduction in Two Languages* (Ithaca, N.Y.: Cornell University Press, 1983).
15 Austin, *How to Do Things with Words*, 98–100.
16 Austin, *How to Do Things with Words*, 145.

17 John Searle, *Expression and Meaning: Studies in the Theory of Speech Acts* (Cambridge: Cambridge University Press, 1979), 1.
18 Ibid., 1.
19 See Searle, *Speech Acts*.
20 Ibid., 17.
21 See S. Petrey, *Speech Acts and Literary Theory* (New York: Routledge, 1990).
22 See Derrida, *Limited Inc*.
23 John Searle, *Intentionality: An Essay in the Philosophy of Mind* (Cambridge: Cambridge University Press, 1983), 9.
24 Ibid., 45.
25 Ibid., 20.
26 Ibid., 10.
27 Jacques Lacan, *The Seminar of Jacques Lacan, Book XI: The Four Fundamental Concepts of Psychoanalysis* (London: Norton, 1998), 25.
28 Felman, *The Literary Speech Act*, 80n.
29 Searle, *Expression and Meaning*, 17.
30 See Ulrich Beck et al., eds., *Reflexive Modernization* (Cambridge: Polity, 1994); Anthony Giddens, *The Consequences of Modernity* (Cambridge: Polity, 1990); and Anthony Giddens, *Runaway World* (London: Profile Books, 1999).
31 Slavoj Žižek, *The Ticklish Subject: The Absent Centre of Political Ontology* (London: Verso, 2000), 334.
32 See Anthony Giddens, *Beyond Left and Right—the Future of Radical Politics* (Cambridge: Polity, 1994); Anthony Giddens, *The Third Way—A Renewal of Social Democracy* (Cambridge: Polity, 1998); and Anthony Giddens, *The Third Way and Its Critics* (Cambridge: Polity, 2000).
33 See Niall Fairclough, *New Labour, New Language?* (London: Routledge, 2000). All further references to this work will appear in the body of the text.
34 See Paul Verhaeghe, "The Decline of the Function of the Father and Its Effect on Gender Roles," in *Sexuation*, ed. Renata Salecl (Durham, N.C.: Duke University Press, 2000), 131–56. See also Žižek, *The Ticklish Subject*, 313–92.

16

The "Revolution" in Advertising and University Discourse

Matthew Sharpe

Marketing should be an emancipator. It should unlock locks and cut bonds by suggesting and implying, by hinting and beckoning, not by defining. It should be the agent that frees, not the agent that imprisons us. In brief, we need more and more affirmative, plastic, humanistic, refreshing research, less and less scientific authoritarianism. Forward researchers! You have nothing to lose but your dogma. —Nicholas Samstag

Lacan's 1968 impromptu speech at Vincennes University is most famous for his retort to the student revolutionaries: "What you aspire to as revolutionaries is a master. You will get one."[1] Yet this "impromptu," which dates from the same period as his *Seminar XVII, The Other Side of Psychoanalysis*, also contains one further, incisive provocation. Pressed for time by an impatient audience, Lacan makes the striking claim—which is hardly irrelevant to his immediate surrounds—that in the contemporary world, "university discourse" is increasingly becoming the dominant form structure of social relations.

The master's discourse (1) versus university discourse (2)

(1) $\quad\quad\quad$ (2)

$$\frac{S_1}{\$} \rightarrow \frac{S_2}{a} \quad\quad \frac{S_2}{S_1} \rightarrow \frac{a}{\$}$$

Although what Lacan had immediately in mind were the societies of the now-former Soviet bloc, it is still surprising that there has not been more work that has taken the lead that this remark offers us, in order to also analyze the liberal-capitalist societies of the wealthy first world nations. In this essay, I want to do exactly this. By developing certain ideas that appear in more or less undeveloped form in Slavoj Žižek's work, I will contend that Lacan's notion of university discourse provides us with a vital theoretical resource for comprehending what is an increasingly ubiquitous element within our later capitalist conjuncture—what we might call "advertising discourse" or "advertising capital."

This article won't be the first to use Lacanian concepts in order to analyze advertising. Indeed, the figure of the Lacanian copywriter in the big ad firm is something of an academic's urban myth. In the first place, advertising is the element most uncontroversially identifiable as a *discourse* or *discursive apparatus* within the production-distribution-consumption complex of the capitalist system. In ads, words and images about something (usually the product, but see below) are enunciated by an agent (the advertiser) to a receiver (the consumer). The "raw material" that advertising is there to put to work—what economic theorists call "consumer demand"—is very obviously *near* to the "professional concern" of psychoanalysts. In the terms of Aristotle's *Rhetoric*, ads are a particular type of "deliberative speech": speech that aims to exhort or dissuade an audience regarding future courses of action.[2] For this reason, it literally "doesn't pay" for advertisers to be klutzes when it comes to the psychology, or psychoanalysis, of human desire. The second book of Aristotle's *Rhetoric*, itself a kind of guide for orators, contains a detailed psychology: what Heidegger called "the first systematic hermeneutic of the everydayness of being with one another."[3] Advertisers, similarly, are in the business of subjects' eros, and it behooves them to know how to position their products in the game of "hunt the slipper" that Lacan once described human desire to be.

If the possibility of using Lacanian psychoanalysis to analyze how advertisers "do things with words" (and images) is well established, however, we cannot say the same thing concerning either Lacan's later theory of the four discourses in general, or university discourse in particular. In the first section of this essay, I look at a recent attempt to use Lacanian theory to analyze the discourse of advertising, that of Yannis Stavrakakis in his article: "On the Critique of Advertising Discourse:

A Lacanian View." In line with Lacan's association of capitalism with the hysteric's discourse in *Seminar XVII*, Stavrakakis's article places advertising as a species of hysterical discourse. My contention, however, is that his argument is importantly flawed in two finally interrelated ways whose recognition points us in a different direction. First, Stavrakakis's piece is vitiated by its strikingly ahistorical character, only the most obvious index of which is his failure to produce a single example of an ad, beyond citing Lacan's 1967 reference to "Coca Cola" in his address at Baltimore. What Stavrakakis accordingly fails to trace, or indeed show any awareness of at all, are the quite striking changes, vocally celebrated by admen themselves, that have in fact become unquestionably hegemonic in advertising since the 1960s. Second, and more important, one crucial structural dimension of any Lacanian analysis is also conspicuously absent from Stavrakakis's text: namely, the dimension of social Law in its dialectical relationship with desire and enjoyment. However, as I will argue in the essay's second section, only when this dimension is considered can the "revolutionary" changes in advertising discourse initiated by Doyle Dane Bernbach (DDB)'s famous 1950s Volkswagen campaigns even appear on the theoretic map.

Advertising as "Mass Hysteria"? Stavrakakis's Lacanian Critique of Advertising Discourse

Stavrakakis begins "On the Critique of Advertising Discourse" by noting that "advertising constitutes one of the hegemonic discursive tropes in late modernity." By lamentable contrast, he continues, existing theoretical analyses of advertising have failed to "reach a degree of sophistication and rigour that would enhance its effectiveness and social relevance." Hitherto, these analyses have turned around three interrelated concerns, Stavrakakis argues:

1. advertising's imputed production and exploitation of "false needs," over and above real or "natural" human needs (as in Galbraith);
2. advertising's reputed use of manipulative psychological mechanisms scarcely differentiable from those of totalitarian propaganda (as in Huxley, or Marcuse); and
3. advertising's function within the wider capitalist system.[4]

The "Revolution" in Advertising and University Discourse 295

It is the said impotence of these approaches, Stavrakakis contends, that should animate a radical rethinking of the critique of advertising through Lacanian theory.

The starting point of any such Lacanian analysis of advertising, Stavrakakis says, has to be the distinction between need, demand, and desire articulated in "The Subversion of the Subject and the Dialectic of Desire" and "The Signification of the Phallus." The Lacanian notion of the absolute split between desire and need instituted by the subject's entry into the symbolic order allows critical reflection on advertising to forever forego the unproductive problematics of natural versus "false" needs, and the simple—and high-minded—complaint that advertising is a form of lying. Now, in its defense, classical economics has always recognized the insatiable nature of human desire. But, as Stavrakakis notes, the Lacanian understanding of desire not only provides us with a coherent explanation of this otherwise rather mysterious input into the wealth of nations. It also affords us a formidable lexicon with which to dissect the vicissitudes of desire, once it has become caught up in the defiles of the signifier, the dramatics of imaginary identification, and the dialectics of our unsociable sociability.

Stavrakakis's understanding of advertising can be illustrated precisely by considering a campaign of television advertisements that aired recently in Australia. The product was McDonald's new low-fat, "diet-friendly" salads and vegetarian meals. Its target demographic was young women and mothers who have to lug their kids to McDonald's. The ad starts with two young women ordering at the counter at a McDonald's store. The friendly staffer asks them the *che vuoi?* question directly: "What would you like?" At this moment, we cut to an imagined scene showing the girls indulging in some prohibited jouissance: "big strawberries, raspberries, cakes, porridge," if you like. In one ad, the two girls are pictured scoffing down nondietary McDonald's food—burgers, fries, milkshakes, sundaes. In a second variant, our heroine—a youngish mother—fantasizes about her doorbell sounding, and her opening the door to a muscle-bound pool cleaner. Having staged these forbidden, imagined satisfactions, the ads cut back to the reality of the women, who now cheerfully order their diet-conscious McDonald's salads. These products are then presented to us in a full-screen shot, accompanied by a young female voice explaining the products' caloric virtues.

In Lacanian terms, these ads operationalize an elementary metaphorization. The ad shows the impossible-forbidden Thing, and then the "reduced fat" product is offered as the substitute object in the place opened up by the proscription of this Thing:

Dietary salad

Prohibited Thing (high-fat food, illicit sexual encounter)

Notably, in the final image of the ad, the logo of the company appears—in this case the familiar "golden arches." I will return to the quilting functioning of the logo or brand signifier at the close of this article.

As Stavrakakis explains his position: "If advertising attempts to stimulate, to cause our desire, this can only mean that the whole mythological construction it articulates around the product is a social fantasy and, furthermore, that this product serves or functions as an object that causes our desire, in other words as an object-cause of desire, an *objet a* in the Lacanian vocabulary" (86). The game, that is, is to get your product into the place of *objet a*, the object cause of subjects' desire. As Stavrakakis continues: "In other words, in the advertising universe, every experience of lack is projected onto the lack of the product that is being advertised" (88). The "gain," or semblance of gain, that this elementary operation proffers to subjects is the promise that their constitutive lack as castrated social beings is in fact a contingent, removable one, "a lack that one simple move promises to eliminate: the purchase of the product." Stavrakakis quotes Baudrillard's remark on shopping malls in his groundbreaking 1970 work *The Consumer Society*, to elaborate upon this fantasmatic or "utopian" element in advertising: "The manifest presence of surplus, the magical, definitive negation of scarcity, the maternal, luxurious sense of being already in the land of Cockaigne . . . These [shopping malls] are our valleys of Canaan where, in a place of milk and honey, streams of neon flow down over ketchup and plastic" (88).

The downside to this advertising metaphorization is, however, that the maternal plenty that advertising sets up as the final signified of its signifiers is a lure. As Lacan argued in *Seminar XI*, drawing on Kant's notion of "negative magnitudes," the *objet petit a* as such is a "metonymy of nothing": an object there to hide from us the absence of any one Thing that could fully satisfy us. Hence, every time we purchase any of the objects that ads offer us, we undergo that desublimating experience of "That's not It!" described by Lacan in *Seminar XX* as "the very cry by which the *jouissance* obtained is distinguished from the *jouissance* expected."[5] The lack or gap the particular advertisement promised to fill is then reopened by the very act of consumption/consummation, and the whole process is set in chain again, with the consumer's desire, and his dissatisfaction, being solicited by the next advertisement, only to be similarly disappointed ad infinitum: "It is this particular economy of desire articulated around the advertised product qua objet petit a that guarantees, through its cumulative metonymic effect, the reproduction of the market economy system within a distinct 'promotional culture'" (89).

From this account, in terms of Lacan's theory of discourse, it seems Stavrakakis situates advertising as a version of the hysteric's discourse.

$$\frac{\$}{a} \rightarrow \frac{S_1}{S_2}$$

The undergirding fantasy of the pathological hysteria, Lacan stipulated, is the following:

$$\frac{a}{-\varphi} \lozenge A$$

As Julien Quackelbeen explains: "The hysteric, looking for an Other without lack [here, A], offers herself to him as a phallicised object [here, small *a*] to make him complete, to install him as [the] Other without flaw."[6] What is repressed in this operation is what is represented by the $-\varphi$ "witness of the non satisfaction of desire," or—put differently—the impossibility of a full sexual relationship that would reinstate the subject's unmediated access to jouissance. To quote Quackelbeen again, in words that might read as a précis of Stavrakakis's account of advertising: "The *objet a*, as pure obnubilation ... falsely promises that a sexual rapport can exist, from which the subject gains the illusory certainty of his having found the True, the Unique, until the approach of the object makes it fall back into the disappointing 'That wasn't it.'"[7]

How are we then to challenge Stavrakakis's identification of advertising discourse with the hysteric's discourse? And ought we then to attempt such a thing? Everything seems to fit. Does not Stavrakakis's position confirm, and reproduce, the veracity of Lacan's identification of the capitalist system, geared around the production of surplus value, with that of the hysteric in *Seminar XVII*?

The first thing to say here is that Stavrakakis's approach in "On the Critique of Advertising Discourse" is a markedly ahistorical one, given that he is approaching a discursive practice that he nevertheless acknowledges to be increasingly important in "late modernity." His failure to analyze any examples of "really existing" ads, however, is only one, and arguably the least important, index of this characteristic of his position. Stavrakakis also does not cite the voluminous literature in "marketing" that has emerged since the 1960s, as part of a process that now after all sees this practice sanctified as a sui generis field of knowledge in funded university departments in most of the first world. There are marketing textbooks to consider. Moreover, from shortly after 1945, we have, to inventory:

- novels that dramatize the lives of players in the industry (like Frederic Wakeman's 1946 *The Hucksters*);
- the autobiographical confessions of admen themselves (like Della Femina's 1969 *From Those Wonderful Folks Who Brought You Pearl Harbor* or George Lois's 1972 *George, Be Careful*);
- quasi-manifesto statements of first principles (such as Howard Gossage's 1967 *Is There Any Hope for Advertising?*);
- journals and magazines on the industry, like *Madison Avenue*;
- advertising art books like George Lois's coffee-table classic *The Art of Advertising* and, finally;
- the increasingly ubiquitous genre of firms' "mission statements," made famous in Tom Cruise's film *Jerry Maguire*.

What becomes evident when we look at this literature, however, is that the discourse and institution of advertising has been anything but stagnant in the fifty-year course of its ascension into sanctified academic legitimacy, not to mention increasing cultural ubiquity. Indeed, it is virtually universally maintained in this literature that there has been nothing short of a revolution within advertising, starting in the 1950s with Doyle, Dane, and Bernbach's radical new campaigns; culminating for a first time in the late 1960s with the meteoric rise of "new" firms like Wells, Rich, Greene; and then, in a neat illustration of Hegel's notion that every great event in history happens twice, coming into its own again from the 1990s until today.

It would of course be folly to argue, especially in a collection on Lacan, that Stavrakakis's failure to take a historical approach to advertising is by itself any argument at all against his position in "On the Critique of Advertising." His is a structural analysis of advertising discourse and, as such, it makes claims that could in principle be true despite such an omission. However, if Stavrakakis's "ahistoricism" sits beside, and so may have informed, a blindness to important structural features of advertising discourse, features that have become only more evident as a result of the historical changes in question, then this is a different issue altogether.

And this is in fact the case that I want to argue now.

The Bend in Madison Avenue:
The Rise and Rise of the New Marketing

The start of the second chapter of adman Jerry Della Femina's 1969 *From Those Wonderful Folks Who Gave You Pearl Harbor*, "Who Killed Speedy Alka Seltzer?" is categorical:

> In the beginning, there was Volkswagen. That's the first campaign which everyone can trace back and say: "This is where the changeover began." That was the day when the new advertising agency was born, and it all started with Doyle, Dane, Bernbach. They began as an agency around 1949 and they were known in the business as a good agency, but no one really got to see what they were doing until Volkswagen came around.
>
> Volkswagen was being handled in the United States by Fuller and Smith and Ross. Doyle, Dane took over the account in 1959. One of the first ads to come out for Volkswagen was the first ad that anyone can remember when the new agency style really came through with an entirely different look. That ad said simply: "Lemon." The copy for "Lemon" said that once in a while we turn out a car that's a lemon, in which case we get rid of it. We don't sell the lemons.

And we are careful as hell with our cars, we test them before we sell them, so the chances are you'll never get one of our lemons.⁸

DDB's campaign stood out so pointedly only against the background of the quite different approach to marketing predominant in the United States of the 1950s. This so-called Theory X approach, epitomized by the J. Walter Thompson agency,⁹ was animated by the solid Taylorist ambition to apply the results and values of modern technocracy—exactitude, objectivity, and order—to marketing. As the sobering title of Rosser Reeves's 1960 manifesto *Reality in Advertising* indicates, for this approach, due scientific process and method, undergirded by reams of statistical research, was everything.¹⁰ To quote Claude Hopkins's 1923 classic *Scientific Advertising*, which reemerged as a key industry resource in the 1950s: "The time has come when advertising has in some hands reached the status of a science. It is based on fixed principles and is reasonably exact. The cause and effects have been analyzed until they are well understood. The correct methods of procedure have been proved and established. We know what is most effective, and we act on basic laws."¹¹

Three features stand out in this "scientific" 1950s approach to advertising. The first is the importance of what Reeves called the USP, or "unique selling proposition." This was a proposition in the copy, repeated whenever possible, describing some feature about the product that differentiates it favorably from its rivals. Thomas Frank cites Reeves, detailing "ads for such accounts as Amacin ('fast, fast, fast relief'); Palmolive Soap ('You can have a lovelier complexion in 14 days with Palmolive Soap, doctors prove!'); and Viceroy cigarettes ('Only Viceroy gives you 20,000 filter traps in every filter tip to filter-filter-filter your smoke while the rich-rich flavor comes through')."¹²

The second feature is the use of sanctioned stereotypes from the lexicon of the hegemonic ideology of postwar "mass society": images of technological progress, material plenty, and the dramatis personae of the nuclear family. Frank writes,

> From its radiant tots, rosy-cheeked and grasping for frozen dinners, to its jolly workers, visibly joyous over the technological advances that their benevolent boss had made possible, the advertising of the period was fatuous in the extreme, and transparently so to much of

the audience. The accuracy of Michael Schudson's comparison of advertising to Soviet Socialist Realism is driven home forcefully by the 1950s advertisers' frequent use of Cold War Terminology and descriptions from the jet age military: here a car is posed next to a fighter plane, there a chemical company uses renderings of military hardware to solicit public goodwill.[13]

This leads us to the third feature of 1950s ad-making: the addressee of these ads was what critics designated sceptically as "mass man"—in the words of one, "a great anonymous dope"[14] who knew little about the science being used to sanction the products he was buying, and who could be persuaded en masse by the ads' transparent clichés. "Typically," Vance Packard complained in *The Hidden Persuaders* (1957), "they [the advertisers] see us as a bundle of daydreams, misty hidden yearnings. We annoy them with our seemingly senseless quirks, but we please them with our growing docility in responding to their manipulations of symbols that stir us to action."[15]

The change initiated by Doyle, Dane, Bernbach in this context is hard to overstate. As Frank argues in his landmark work, *The Conquest of Cool*,

> For all the sophistication of recent cultural theory, many of its practitioners still tend to identify the sins of consumer order as "homogeneity" or an obsessive logocentrism. In the advertising industry, that order's primary ideologist, however, these values were everywhere under attack by the mid-1960s. As a creative revolution followed in the wake of DDB's artistic and commercial success, the advertising industry began to recognize creativity, even more than science or organization or standardization or repetition or regulation, as a dynamic element of advertising and, ultimately, of the permanent revolution of capitalism itself.[16]

This "revolution" is evident in the emergence of the new type of 1960s adman, different in the extreme from the white-coated scientific authorities celebrated by Reeves and company. The archetypal adman of the 1960s was less scientist than artist and nonconformist. "If you are not a bad boy, if you're not a big pain in the ass, then what you are is mush, in this business," George Lois instructs prospective entrants to the trade in his 1972 memoirs. Rather than offering the type of post-Protestant examination of conscience one might have expected from a 1950s adman, Lois's *George, Be Careful* is littered with diverting tales of his "permanent revolution" against the "Prussian" order of the advertising agencies of the 1950s, including his petulant throwing over of the desk of a boss who had treated his "work" with insufficient respect, in an act in which — as he describes it — Pollockesque splotches of red ink were pitched onto the offender's office wall.[17] Lois spent much of his career coming and going from agencies, in order to "kick the curse of bigness," and to seek out environments more conducive to his creative approach to writing copy.[18] After a short period with DDB, he even left this father of all "creative" agencies in 1960 to found PKL (Papert, Koenig, Lois), one of the most successful agencies of the next decade. PKL resembled less the stifling Taylorist advertising agencies of the Madison Avenue of the 1950s, however, than the hip agencies of the 1990s analyzed in Naomi Klein's *No Logo* and in the pages of the *Baffler*: countercultural hotbeds peopled by "conduits of cool" who "can be seen . . . roaming the corridors of Fortune 500 companies dressed like club kids, skateboards in tow. They drop references to all night raves at the water cooler ('Memo to the boss: why not fill this thing with ginseng-laced herbal tea?'). The[se] CEOs of tomorrow aren't employees; they are, to use a term favoured by IBM, 'change agents.' "[19] As Lois remembers PKL: "The joint was unbefouled by mannerism, and nothing could stop us . . . we worked late because it was painful to leave its carefree atmosphere. . . . You start out by hiring people who are creative, then just give them room to do what they want. You just sit down and work with guys. Also we try to hire people who will disagree with us."[20]

Vitally, however, the changing of the guard in American advertising, from the organization man of the 1950s to the 1960s George Lois–style rebel, corresponded to the emergence of an entirely different style of advertising, which upset the Theory X modus operandi term for term. Just as "art" took over the place of "science" in the self-consciousness of admen, so what Frank dubs a "conquest of cool" replaced the use of staid stereotypes in the advertisements of the 1950s. If the formulaic 1950s ads addressed the faceless mass of organization men, their fawning wives and 2.3 kids, 1960s advertising increasingly began to embrace the values of individuality and singularity in a way that sometimes sounds uncannily familiar to those of us educated in the post-poststructuralist academy. As a 1970 column in *Madison Avenue* reflected on the changes in advertising in the last decade, if in "society" people might "strive for . . . acceptance, conformity, anonymity," advertising should appeal to people's drive to "stand out, to excel, to be idolized [and] adulated." We are far indeed from the encouragement of mindless conformism, as the text continues: "to be afraid to advertise in a way which talks about real problems and real differences is to be afraid to look in the mirror. To balk at communicating differently from competition is to balk at moving ahead of competitors."[21]

This very attitude has reemerged as the first principle of the advertising boom of the 1990s. In the wake of the opening up of the world to marketing, and the discovery of youth as a growing demographic, as Naomi Klein comments in *No Logo*, advertisers suddenly discovered the strictly dialectical possibility that "rather than creating advertising campaigns for different campaigns, campaigns could sell diversity itself, to all markets at once."[22]

According to *Rocking the Ages*, a 1997 work produced by Yankelovitch Partners, a leading U.S. consumer research agency, if "duty" was the "defining idea" of the 1950s, "individuality" had already taken this place for the "baby boomers," and

> [Generation] Xers are starting out with pluralistic attitudes that are the strongest we have ever measured. As we look forward to the next 25 years, it is clear that the acceptance of alternative lifestyles will become even stronger and more widespread as Xers grow up and become the dominant buying group in the consumer marketplace. . . . Diversity is the key fact of life for Xers, the core of the perspectives they bring to marketplace. Diversity in all its forms—cultural, political, sexual, racial, social—is the hallmark of the generation.[23]

What is at stake in this marked "changeover," to quote Della Femina, is what an adequate Lacanian critique of advertising discourse needs to chart.

From the Master to University Discourse: Charting the Revolution to the "New Marketing"

> We're young too.
> And we're on your side.
> We know it's a tough race.
> And we want you to win.
> —Advertisement for Love Cosmetics, 1969

What is essential about the much-touted new "creativity" in post-1960s advertising? Recalling the contention I announced in the introduction, doesn't it look pretty unlikely that we would want to use Lacan's university discourse to explain the newly emergent marketing orthodoxy, since its very practitioners themselves set their work up in explicit opposition to the scientistic, technocratic attitudes of the immediate postwar years? Differently, if the quasi-scientific USP about the product was among the key features of 1950s advertising, what might Lacan's theory of a discourse apparently modeled on the tertiary pedagogical process have to say about a new hegemony in advertising that increasingly has rejected this more or less educative rhetorical tool?

In addressing this question, I want to begin by noting (alongside Mark Bracher) that, against first appearances, modern science is not treated in *Seminar XVII* as an instance of university discourse. In the contemporary first world, Lacan agrees with the Frankfurt School theorists and others, science actually functions as a modality of the master's discourse, aiding and abetting the existing political powers-that-be at least ideologically, if not as a key means of production. For it is in something very like this vein that, while 1960s admen Bernbach, Femina, Lois, and others clearly challenged the postwar world's faith in science in their ads, what they pilloried and even openly spoofed (as we will see) was less science itself than what could be termed the ideological functioning of science as an unquestionable point of authority [S_1] within this historical conjuncture, and, as such, the technocratic contours of this conjuncture itself. On this point, Thomas Frank is adamant. Following 1959, he argues: "For ten years at least, the makers of American advertising would rank among the country's most visible critics of the mass society."[24] Moreover, by far the most powerful feature of the Volkswagen ads—and a feature which one can find throughout DDB's oeuvre—is their awareness of and deep sympathy with the mass society critique. Not only do the authors of these ads seem to have been reading *The Hidden Persuaders, The Waste Makers* and *The Insolent Chariots*, they are actively contributing to the discourse, composing cutting jibes against the chrome-plated monsters from Detroit and proffering up Volkswagens as badges of alienation from the ways of a society whose most prominent emblems were the tailfin and the tract home with a two-car garage.[25]

What is in play with the much-touted "creativity" in the new advertising, I want accordingly to argue, is something that concerns less any kind of emancipatory social moment, as George Lois's rhetoric might have us believing, than something structural that can be located at the level of elementary coordinates of discourse Lacan lays out for us in *Seminar XVII*. The so-called creativity of the post-1960s marketing in fact denotes a repositioning of advertising and advertisers in relation to the master's discourse, and—more broadly—to the structuring of authority in capitalist societies. Consider again the Bernbach Volkswagen advertisement celebrated by Della Femina. It is one of a string of campaigns wherein DDB flaunted the sacred "50s principle of the USP, describing its VW products as 'ugly,' 'monsters,' 'shoeboxes'; and even confided to the audience in one ad about an experimental model that was 'something awful. Take our word for it.'"[26] As with the apparently frank confession that Volkswagen occasionally turns out a lemon, then, you can see that what is taking place in these ads is importantly a new place itself. To be more precise, within these ads, the advertisers are resituating themselves as less on the side of the masters within the postwar technocratic capitalism, than as it were "with us," on *our* side of what Lacan wrote as S_1, the master signifier. In turn, these advertisements address us not as faceless, dumb "mass men," but as cool, savvy individuals, awake to the impotence of the postwar technocracy to deliver the absolute efficiency it promised, and to the insipidness of its stereotyped images of happiness.

A 1965 DDB advertisement allows us to place this change in the structure of the advertisers' enunciation perfectly. The ad stages directly the kind of ego ideal 1950s ads invariably recurred to: a suburban street with look-alike houses, lawns, and ordered shrubbery. However, in each driveway, incongruously, a Volkswagen Beetle sits. The copy addresses us frankly: "If the world looked like this, and you wanted to buy a car that sticks out a little, you probably wouldn't buy a Volkswagen. But in case you haven't noticed, the world doesn't look like this. So if you wanted to buy a car that sticks out a little, you know just what to do."[27]

Everything is here, as you can see, from the appeal to our desire to stand out and be nonconformist, to the critique of the old advertising and the recondite dreams to which it appeals, to the use of wit, all features that have since become marketing staples. In fact, I would argue that a recollection of Freud's position on wit in *Jokes and Their Relation to the Unconscious* is of the highest relevance here. Wit, for Freud, plays on the production of signifiers that can literally be heard or read in at least two ways. There is first the "normal" way: in jokes, what we are led to expect by the leading premises of the joke, when these are referred to the signifying conventions of our linguistic community. Then, in the punch line, as in the pun, a second way of hearing these signifiers opens up that allows a momentary *jouis-sens* or "enjoy-meant."[28] Even the Lacanian question to ask about this linguistic play is then this: if the sanctioned sense of the words refers us as addressees to the sanctioned big Other of our linguistic community, how does the witticism's second quasi-transgressive *jouis-sense* interpellate us, or to what agency does it refer us? Consider some examples: "Pick up weights, not blokes," an ad for an all-female gym quips; "Geelong Waterfront, must Sea," a banner recently addressed travelers arriving in that coastal town; "It is Mitsubishi," another campaign reads, which someone in marketing once confided to me that "once I understood that, I would understand everything." (We might well have referred this self-admitted autodidact to the *Traumdeutung*.)

In each of these advertising witticisms, I would ask, is it not as if there were a kind of double interpellation transpiring? On one hand, there is everyone else—those who literally won't "buy it," or the joke the advertiser is addressing to us. They are positioned as others supposed not to know or rather not to enjoy, as we will examine. On the other hand, though, in the flash of wit, such as it is, it is as if the advertiser had winked at us across a crowded room, bringing us into his antinomian confidence. "If the rest are the dupes, you and I, *we* are the ones who 'get the joke.' You can trust me": is it not something very like this that we hear time and time again in the new marketing's discourse? The advertisers, they are intimating to us, are *like us*. The advertisers understand us, and they too are sick of being had by the masters, and—as it turns out—also by the competition. As a 1966 DDB, Avis campaign stated baldly, in a way that anticipates the meta-advertising that has become more and more preeminent since: "People in this country don't believe anything they read in ads anymore. And with good reason. Most advertising these days is long on the big promise—a promise that the product doesn't always deliver."[29]

It is here, I agree with Stavrakakis, that we must recur to an insight in Jean Baudrillard's groundbreaking early work on consumerism, which —as we saw above—is a key resource for his Lacanian critique of advertising discourse. But it is a resource, I want to argue now, that Stavrakakis misreads, or reads in a partial manner. The venture of advertising, Baudrillard specified in *The System of Objects* of 1968 (a text Stavrakakis does not cite), is far from being a business that mobilizes desire outside of its relation to social law. It is, he specifies, "nothing more than a tremendous effort to materialize the superego.[30] However, if we follow Baudrillard on this, we need also to consider that, certainly in Lacan if not always in Freud, the superego is sharply distinguished from the symbolic moral law (or S_1) that demands our sacrifice of jouissance in the name of its more or less impersonal ideals and *regulae*. According to Lacan, the superego rather coincides with what he calls in *Seminar XVII* "knowledge as a means of enjoyment."[31] The superego's position of enunciation, if Lacan is right, is one of a kind of perverse, "malevolent neutrality."[32] On one hand, it always only, neutrally, speaks the truth, in the kind of more or less constant commentary on the subject's existence of which Lacan talks in *Seminar III*. This is why Lacan associates it primarily with knowledge, or S_2, rather than S_1. On the other hand, what the superego "objectively" knows of is nevertheless nothing less than the Truth of the subject's most intimate (or extimate) jouissance: what he or she desires "most deeply," as we say, or—in more precise structural terms—what he or she desires beneath the bar of sanctioned prohibitions, and what he or she might be able to consciously avow about him- or herself.

According to Lacan, the superego with which Baudrillard rightly associates the endeavor of advertising is—exactly like the point of enunciation of the creative, post-DDB advertising—precisely on "our" side of the authoritarian law [S_1] that prohibits unmediated access to jouissance. It is hence as far from demanding that we sacrifice enjoyment, and/or "wanting to know nothing about it," as Coca-Cola's famous slogan *Enjoy!*, which (albeit probably unknowingly) exactly reproduces what Lacan argues is the undergirding imperative of the superego.[33] Indeed, insofar as the new marketing has come more and more to mobilize the logics of the superego, I think we can explain the patent sense of obscenity that attaches to many of its exemplars, and which in part animates Naomi Klein's clear anxiety about this increasingly intrusive discourse in *No Logo*.[34] The fully legitimate response to a bank ad that tries to stage our most intimate wishes, or tells us to "give up our day job," can after all be nothing but an echo of an old Marx brothers line: "Why are you telling me that I should give up my day job, when in fact I deeply want to give up my day job!"

To draw in the threads tying us to *Seminar XVII* here, though, the only one of the four discourses within the seminar in which knowledge takes the "dominant" top left-hand position of agency, as you will know, is precisely that which Lacan dubbed the "university discourse."

University discourse

$$\frac{S_2}{S_1} \rightarrow \frac{a}{\$}$$

As Lacan explains this discourse, the S_2 of knowledge here addresses (→) individuals in the top right corner, not however as subjects but as real, more or less unformed objects [*a*: top right hand corner]. Whereas the master's discourse addresses us as knowing subjects for whom "ignorance is no excuse," as legal discourse has it, university discourse and pedagogy generally presumes a nonknowledge on the part of its addressees.[35] To paraphrase Louis Althusser, the knowledge embodied in the discourse is itself what, through the learning process, "makes these individuals into subjects." Hence, we are also pointed toward a first way of reading why it is that the divided subject [$\$$] appears in the bottom-right-hand corner of the grid, which Lacan designated as the place for what a discourse produces. However, as Slavoj Žižek rejoins: "'Production' (the fourth term in the matrix of discourses) does not stand simply for the result of the discursive operation, but rather for its 'indivisible remainder,' for the excess that resists being included in the discursive network."[36]

There is hence a second register to university discourse, within which what is produced by the agency of knowledge is not a fully formed subject, wholly identifiable with his or her place within the social system, as Michel Foucault was wont to imply about modern subjects in his more pessimistic moments. Žižek illustrates this second register of university discourse by reference to how medical discourse functions: "At the surface level, we are dealing with pure objective knowledge that desubjectivizes the subject-patient, reducing him to an object of research, of diagnoses and treatment; however, beneath it, one can easily discern a worried hystericized subject, obsessed with anxiety, addressing the doctor as his master and asking for reassurance from him."[37] In other words, the small *a* on the top right-hand corner of university discourse is not there simply insofar as the knowledge [S_2] in university discourse faces, and educates, a more or less unformed, ignorant individual. The *content* of the knowledge in question, as in the example of medical discourse, is knowledge of the individual considered as an object, in his or her Truth as a real suffering and enjoying Thing. As in DDB's confidences to us and its invitations to nonconformist jouissance, the sure mark that we have been interpellated by an instance of university discourse, is that we feel compelled by its terms to consider ourselves from a quasi-superegoic position of neutral self-observation, and to ask ourselves what we *really are* and *really want*, beneath whatever social masks and roles we may from time to time have taken up, and beyond whatever imprecise notions we might have previously entertained about our lives. At this point, then, an answer to the apparent problem that university discourse can hardly be used to explain a practice so avowedly antinomian as contemporary advertising also becomes evident. Whether the USP of 1950s ads described the object being advertised, differentiating it from other objects in "the system," by invoking "Instincts and Their Vicissitudes," we might say that the knowledge that was involved in advertising has not disappeared in the new marketing. It has just "turned around upon the subject."[38]

What is inevitably produced by this "turning around" of the new advertising, since one structurally can never as a subject ($\$$) fully know and assume what one is as real object a, is—in Žižek's words—"a worried hystericized subject, obsessed with [the] anxiety" that Lacanian theory reads as the unwavering index of the subject's having come too close to its primordially repressed Thing.[39] The questions that the subject always directs back at the locus of knowledge in university discourse hence bespeak exactly that sense of lack that, as Stavrakakis rightly points out in "A Lacanian Critique of Advertising Discourse," animates the next round of consumption in contemporary subjects: Is this really what I am? Am I enjoying enough, and could I enjoy more? Or, as a recent Australian mobile phone ad archly asked us to consider, is it always the other guy or the other girl that really enjoys?

Logos and/as the Quilting Point

My contention is that, against Stavrakakis, advertising discourse is a discourse enunciated from the perspective of a more or less directly intimate and/or obscene claim to knowledge (S_2) about us as Real objects, who enjoy and/or suffer (*Jouis!*). Advertisers invite us to take them into our confidence: like the Mystery Man in David Lynch's *Lost Highway*, they never go anywhere that they are not invited.[40] When we accept their invitation, we are encouraged to consider ourselves as objects of jouissance (*a*), and to respond, in our consuming passion, in the very name of the jouissance denied us by the master's discourse, which Freud held that we must forego as the price of acceding to civilization. This is why the "creative" advertising of the 1960s already integrated the critiques of "mass society" and "technocracy" at that time being produced within the radical academy, and why it is difficult not to hear echoes of the most gauche theory whenever one turns on commercial radio or television, let alone steps out into any public space, in wealthy first world countries. But why then does something strike us—or perhaps it does not—as patently unethical about all of this? Why does something strike us, perhaps, as being at best deeply inauthentic about the new advertising, and at worst more or less obnoxiously cynical?

The answer, of course, is simple. One does not need a mass of Lacanian theory to grasp that, if post-1960s marketing addresses us "sincerely" as enjoying Things (*a*) behind the veil of social masks and beneath the bar of older, more prudish social prohibitions, it nevertheless does so in order to animate the next round of consumption. This is the force of the retort: "Why are you telling me that I should give up my day job, when I deeply wish to give up my day job!" Even if you would not know it from the animated testimony of "creatives" like George Lois and company, advertisers are after all in the business of making money for themselves and for their clients, as Frank wryly observes in *The Conquest of Cool*. For all they pun and joke, confide in us, and use any means they are clever enough to think of to position themselves as "one of us," the whole operation remains a mode of exploitation in the properly premoral, Marxian sense. Marxist critiques of advertising, such as that of Dallas Smythe, that insist that advertising represents the expansion of the circuitry of commodification and commodity exchange into the nonproductive, private sphere, are in this way absolutely valid.[41]

In terms of Lacan's *Seminar XVII*, then, we can finally address the question of why the bottom-left-hand position in university discourse — which Lacan tells us is the position of Truth — is filled by S_1, the signifier of the master. In "Homo Sacer as the Object of University Discourse," Žižek specifies that, while the superego is primarily an agency of knowledge (S_2), it is "not directly S_2; it is rather the S_1 of the S_2 itself, the dimension of an unconditional injunction that is inherent to knowledge itself."[42] Lacan's alignment of the S_1 beneath the S_2 in university discourse hence indicates that what sustains the operation of this discourse is in fact the brute reality of extant social authority:

> The constitutive lie of the university discourse is that it disavows its performative dimension, presenting what effectively amounts to a political decision based on power into the factual state of things . . . suffice it to recall the market expert who advocates strong budgetary measures (cutting welfare expenses, etc.) as a necessity imposed by the neutral expertise devoid of any ideological biases: what he conceals is the series of power relations (from the active role of the state apparatuses to ideological beliefs) that sustain the "neutral" functioning of the market mechanism.[43]

Let me return one more time to the discourse of advertising, and in particular to the place of the logo or brand name that so provokes Klein in *No Logo*. In an age of decentralized production, Klein notes, the logo is increasingly becoming the only thing that brings together all the other components of given products. Tommy Hilfiger, like Hegel's monarch, does not himself, or through his company, directly produce anything, as Klein notes. He is in the business of signing his name. For, as Klein's *No Logo* documents, brands like Hilfiger's proper names or logos are nothing less than the most valuable form of hard equity these days, insofar as it is their presence and their presence alone on products that, like the proverbial Midas touch, can magically bump up the price that consumers will pay, sometimes exponentially.[44] It is, I would say, very hard to think of a more concrete and educative example than these logos of what Lacan called master signifiers (S_1), and his insistence that these signifiers were at once empty at the level of their content, and the most important "quilting" point within any discourse at all. Indeed, when you see a logo placed alongside, or after, the images that ads parade before us but which often have only the most tendentious relation to what they are there to sell, this is because logos function as pure master signifiers (S_1) within the advertisements. They are there merely to tie everything together, not to add anything new. To put it differently, they do not exist, they function. To get to the bottom of things, they function to guarantee that the signifiers of the ad do not float hopelessly but represent the company amid all the other signifiers with which advertising bombards us, thereby guaranteeing some return on the marketing investment. Putting it in a quip, as Lacan's placement of the S_1 beneath the bar on the left of university discourse in *Seminar XVII* would indicate, in advertising too, it remains all about the bottom line.

Notes

1 Jacques Lacan, *Le séminaire, livre XVII: L'envers de la psychanalyse* (Paris: Seuil, 1991), 239. Further references to this work are given in the body of the text.
2 Aristotle, *On Rhetoric: A Theory of Civic Discourse*, trans. with intro., notes, and appendices by G. Kennedy (New York: Oxford University Press, 1991), 15–16.
3 See Kennedy, "Prooemion," in Aristotle, *On Rhetoric*.
4 Yannis Stavrakakis, "On the Critique of Advertising Discourse: A Lacanian View," *Third Text* 15 (2001): 85. Further references to this work appear parenthetically in the text.
5 Cited in Ibid., 89.

6. Julien Quackelbeen, "Hysterical Discourse: Between the Belief in Man and the Cult of Woman," in *The Lacanian Theory of Discourse*, ed. M. Bracher, R. Cortell, and F. Massardier-Kenney (New York: New York University Press, 1994), 136.
7. Ibid., 134.
8. Jerry Della Femina, *From Those Wonderful Folks Who Gave You Pearl Harbor* (London: Sir Isaac Pittman and Sons, 1971), 24.
9. Thomas Frank, *The Conquest of Cool: Business Culture, Counterculture, and the Rise of Hip Consumerism* (Chicago: University of Chicago Press, 1997), 35–37.
10. Ibid., 42.
11. Ibid., 40.
12. Cited in ibid., 44.
13. Ibid., 48.
14. Whyte, cited in ibid., 49.
15. Cited in ibid., 41.
16. Ibid., 89.
17. Ibid., 81–82.
18. Ibid., 80–83.
19. Naomi Klein, *No Logo* (London: Flamingo, 2001), 71.
20. Frank, *The Conquest of Cool*, 82.
21. Cited in ibid., 90.
22. Klein, *No Logo*, 117.
23. Ibid., 110.
24. Frank, *The Conquest of Cool*, 76.
25. Ibid., 64.
26. Frank, *The Conquest of Cool*, 63.
27. Cited in ibid., 65–66.
28. Sigmund Freud, *Jokes and Their Relation to the Unconscious* (1905), in *The Standard Edition of the Complete Psychological Works of Sigmund Freud*, ed. J. Strachey (London: Hogarth, 1960), vol. 8, chap. 6.
29. Cited in Frank, *The Conquest of Cool*, 70.
30. Jean Baudrillard, "The System of Objects," in *Jean Baudrillard: Selected Writings*, ed. Mark Poster (Stanford, Calif.: Stanford University Press, 1988), 18.
31. Jacques Lacan, *Seminar XVII*.
32. See Slavoj Žižek, *Metastases of Enjoyment* (London: Verso, 1994), chap. 3.
33. What Freud called the "unconscious guilt" with which he associated the superego is strictly a function of this impartial knowledge of the subject's jouissance, according to Lacan. If Freud in *Civilization and Its Discontents* remarked the seeming mystery that it is the most moral individuals who are nevertheless most prey to this sense of unconscious guilt, on a Lacanian reading this becomes transparent as the result of the superego's referring of subjects' behaviors to the standard of this impossible, prohibited jouissance. It is indeed only the truth that each of these behaviors should be found wanting before this tribunal, and that accordingly the impartial knowledge of the superego should devolve into the concealed imperative *Jouis!*.

34 Witness the chapter titles: "No space," "No . . . ," "No . . . ," and so on.
35 See Renata Salecl, "Deference to the Great Other," in *The Lacanian Theory of Discourse*, R. Cortell, and F. Massardier-Kenney (New York: New York University Press, 1994).
36 Slavoj Žižek, "Four Discourses, Four Subjects," in *Cogito and the Unconscious*, ed. S. Žižek (Durham, N.C.: Duke University Press, 1998), 78.
37 Ibid., 78–79.
38 Sigmund Freud, "Instincts and Their Vicissitudes" (1915), in *The Standard Edition*, 14:126.
39 Žižek, "Four Discourses, Four Subjects," 78.
40 Slavoj Žižek, *The Art of the Ridiculous Sublime: On David Lynch's Lost Highway* (Seattle: University of Washington Press, 2000).
41 Dallas W. Smythe, "On the Audience Commodity and Its Work," in *Media and Cultural Studies: Key Works*, ed. M. G. Durham (London: Blackwell, 2002).
42 Slavoj Žižek, "Homo Sacer as Object of University Discourse." Available at www.lacan.com/hsacer.htm. Accessed May 2004.
43 Žižek, "Four Discourses, Four Subjects," 78–79.
44 Klein, *No Logo*, 24.

Contributors

Geoff Boucher completed his dissertation on postmarxian discourse theory at the University of Melbourne in 2003 and now works as a researcher for Deakin University's Centre for Psychoanalytic Studies. He spent 2003 in Germany, where he participated in the research seminar of the English Faculty of the Ludwig Maximillian Universität in Munich. He has articles forthcoming in *Philosophy Today* and *Telos*, and has coedited (with Matthew Sharpe) a forthcoming collection of critical essays on Slavoj Žižek.

Marie-Hélène Brousse practices psychoanalysis in Paris and is a professor in the Department of Psychoanalysis at the University of Paris VIII. She is a member of the World Association of Psychoanalysis and a member of its administrative committee. She is a member of the Ecole de la Cause Freudienne with the title of AME. She has published extensively in French and Spanish and has published in English in the *Psychoanalytical Notebook* and in *Reading Seminar XI* and *Reading Seminars I and II*. She is the former editor of *Mental*, a journal of applied psychoanalysis.

Justin Clemens teaches psychoanalytic studies at Deakin University, and is secretary of the Lacan Circle of Melbourne. His recent books include *The Mundiad* and *Avoiding the Subject*, co-written with Dominic Pettman. He is also the coeditor (with Oliver Feltham) of Alain Badiou's *Infinite Thought*.

Mladen Dolar taught for twenty years at the Department of Philosophy at the University of Ljubljana, Slovenia, where he now works as a Senior Research Fellow. He has published half a dozen books in Slovene and a great number of essays in journals and collective volumes in several languages, on subjects ranging from Hegel, Kant, psychoanalysis, fascism, and music to Foucault, Shakespeare, thrift, and love. He lectured at a number of European and American universities and most recently coauthored (with Slavoj Žižek) *Opera's Second Death*.

Oliver Feltham wrote his PhD on praxis, work, and ontology and has recently completed his translation of Alain Badiou's *Being and Event*, which is forthcoming. He currently teaches in the Department of Comparative Literature at the American University of Paris, the Paris Centre of the University of California, and Ecole Massillon. He is also a researcher at the Circle for Lacanian Ideology Critique at the Jan van Eyck Academie in Maastricht.

Contributors

Russell Grigg is a member of the Ecole de la Cause Freudienne, the New Lacanian School and the Lacan Circle of Melbourne. He lives in Melbourne where he practices psychoanalysis and teaches philosophy and psychoanalytic studies at Deakin University. He is the translator of Lacan's *Seminar XVII: The Other Side of Psychoanalysis*.

Pierre-Gilles Guéguen is a practicing psychoanalyst in Paris and a professor in the Department of Psychoanalysis at the University of Paris VIII. He is a member of the World Association of Psychoanalysis and the Ecole de la Cause Freudienne with the title of AME. He has published extensively in French and Spanish. In English he has published in *Psychoanalytical Notebooks* and in *Reading Seminar XI* and *Reading Seminars I and II*. He is the editor of the on-line journal, *Lacanian Praxis*.

Dominique Hecq is the author of the novel *The Book of Elsa*, two collections of stories (*Magic* and *Mythfits*), two books of poems (*The Gaze of Silence* and *Good Grief*), and two short plays (*One Eye Too Many* and *Cakes & Pains*). Her latest work, *Noisy Blood*, has just been published. She is the coauthor (with Russell Grigg and Craig Smith) of *Feminine Sexuality: Freud and the Early Controversies*. She currently teaches in the School of Creative Arts at the University of Melbourne.

Dominiek Hoens is a visiting professor at the Artevelde Hogeschool (Gent, Belgium) and founding member of the Jan van Eyck Circle for Lacanian Ideology Critique (Maastricht, Netherlands). As a philosopher he has published on psychoanalysis (affect, logical time, *sinthome*), Alain Badiou (subject, love) and literature (Musil, Duras). He is currently writing a book on "love" in Lacan's work.

Eric Laurent was analyzed by Jacques Lacan and practices psychoanalysis in Paris. He is a qualified psychologist and holds a doctorate in psychoanalysis. He is a former president of the Ecole de la Cause Freudienne and an executive member of the World Association of Psychoanalysis. He teaches in the Department of Psychoanalysis, particularly in its Clinical Section, at the University of Paris VIII. He has published widely, in several languages, on clinical and theoretical developments in contemporary psychoanalytic practice and on contemporary cultural issues. He has published ten books in Spanish and two in Portuguese.

Juliet Flower MacCannell is a scholar and writer who has devoted many years to elucidating Lacanian thought and its importance for the arts and humanities as well as for clinical work. She is Professor Emerita of Comparative Literature and English at the University of California, Irvine, and is currently co-chair of the California Psychoanalytic Circle. Her books include *The Hysteric's Guide to the Future Female Subject*, *The Regime of the Brother: After the Patriarchy*, and *Figuring Lacan: Criticism and the Cultural Unconscious*. Her recent research concerns are psychoanalysis and space, the democratic and religious subject, and the philosophers Jean-Jacques Rousseau and Alain Badiou.

Jacques-Alain Miller is a graduate of the École normale supérieure, member of the Ecole de la Cause Freudienne, and founder and former president of the World Association of Psychoanalysis. The editor of Jacques Lacan's *Seminar*, he has published several books under his own name, including *Lettres à l'opinion éclairée*, *Le Neveu de Lacan*, and (with Jean-Claude Milner) *Voulez-vous être évalué?* He is the director of the Department of Psychoanalysis at the University of Paris VIII.

Ellie Ragland is Frederick A. Middlebush Professor of English at the University of Missouri, Columbia. She is the author of *The Logic of Sexuation: From Aristotle to Lacan* and the coeditor of *Lacan: Topologically Speaking*. She has published and edited seven other books and more than one hundred articles. She lectures both nationally and internationally and is currently at work on *The Logic of Structure in Lacan*. She is the editor of *(Re)-Turn: A Journal of Lacanian Studies* and the former editor of *The Newsletter of the Freudian Field*. She is also a member of the European School of Psychoanalysis.

Matthew Sharpe lectures in philosophy and psychoanalytic studies at Deakin University, Australia. He is the author of *Slavoj Žižek: A Little Piece of the Real* and the coeditor (with Geoff Boucher) of the forthcoming collection of critical essays, *Slavoj Žižek: Critical Responses: Traversing the Fantasy*. He has written numerous articles in political philosophy, aesthetics, psychoanalysis, and Marxism.

Paul Verhaeghe is a professor of psychoanalysis at the University of Ghent, Belgium. His books include *Does the Woman Exist*, an academic study of hysteria and the construction of femininity in the work of Freud and Lacan; *Love in a Time of Loneliness*, on sex and desire; and, most recently, *On Being Normal and Other Disorders*.

Slavoj Žižek is a senior researcher in the Department of Philosophy at the University of Ljubljana and the codirector of the Center for Humanities at Birkbeck College, University of London. Among his recent publications are *Iraq: the Borrowed Kettle* and *The Puppet and the Dwarf* (2004).

Alenka Zupančič is a researcher at the Institute of Philosophy, Scientific Research Center of the Slovene Academy of Sciences and Arts, Ljubljana. She is the author of *Ethics of the Real: Kant, Lacan, Das Reale einer Illusion, Esthétique du désir, éthique de la jouissance*, and *The Shortest Shadow: Nietzsche's Philosophy of the Two*.

Index

Abraham: language of, 232
Academy (of Plato), 140
Adorno, Theodor, 109, 123-124, 149
advertising, 7, 292-308, 310
affect(s), 14, 25, 94-95, 101 n.27, 119, 174-175, 230-231, 266
Agamben, Giorgio, 5, 111, 114, 123
agency, 23, 84, 207, 282-284, 287, 306-308, 311; of master, 43, 60, 223
agent, 3, 66, 68 n.9, 121, 170, 179, 182, 187, 258-259, 261, 284, 286-287, 293; analyst and, 115, 152; capitalism and, 117, 121; of concept, 146; as dominant, 2, 186, 202, 212-213; father and, 43-44, 60, 84, 216, 223-224; hysteric and, 163-164; master and, 133-135, 140, 221-222, 258; as political, 124; as revolutionary, 110; subjectivity of, 282-283; superego of, 114
alienation, 38, 81-82, 161-162, 230, 275, 305; as primary, 36; as secondary, 36
"Allocution on Child Psychoses" (Lacan), 246-247
Althusser, Louis, 137, 278-279, 309
American(s), 24, 41, 80, 88, 195, 209, 211-213, 240, 246, 300, 302-303, 305
Amiel, Henri-Frédéric, 264-265
analysand's discourse, 254; matheme of, 3, 67

Analyst of the School, 269
analyst's discourse, 3, 6-7, 52, 67, 93, 99 n.8, 110, 115, 149, 152, 184-187, 189-190, 225, 271-272, 274
analytic discourse, 12, 91, 93-95, 97-98, 207, 238-239, 275
"Analyticon" (Lacan), 25, 230-231
Antigone, 19, 53
Anti-Oedipus (Deleuze and Guattari), 189
Arendt, Hannah, 120, 231-232
Aristotle, 4, 23, 99 n.6, 100 nn.20, 27, 120, 140, 177 n.4, 183-184, 187, 191-192, 220, 293
Art of Advertising, The (Lois), 298
ashamed, 14, 46; as being, 12, 231-232; as making, 11, 15, 19-20, 23, 26-27, 97-98, 230-233. *See also* Shame
Aufklärung (Enlightenment), 121, 209, 235, 237, 279-280
Austin, J.L., 280, 284
Australia, 63, 295

Babel, 254
Badiou, Alain, 1, 6, 88, 92, 99 n.2, 137, 180, 189, 192
Baffler, 302
Bakhtin, Mikhail, 128 n.6
Balibar, Étienne, 112, 276-277
Balzac, Honoré de, 258

barred Other, 270, 297
barred S ($), 4, 35, 70, 98–99, 130, 159–160, 179, 282–283; analyst and, 95, 97–98, 115, 152; capitalist and, 22; gaze and, 14; hysteric and, 72, 143, 146, 149, 163–164, 309–310; as ideological, 173; master and, 18, 91, 93, 161–162, 275; truth and, 73, 283–284; university and, 309. *See also* Four discourses; Matheme; Subject
Bataille, Georges, 137, 217, 222–225
Baudelaire, Charles, 264–265
Baudrillard, Jean, 296, 307–308
Beaufret, Jean, 266
Beauvois, Jean-Léon, 168–169
Being and Nothingness (Sartre), 14
Benjamin, Walter, 107, 111, 116–117, 123
Benveniste, Émile, 279–280
Bergson, Henri, 188
Berlin University, 135
Berlin Wall, 231–232
Bernstein, Edouard, 124
Beyond the Pleasure Principle (Freud), 199, 224–225
Big Brother, 15, 238–239
Biran, Main de, 134, 272 n.4
Blair, Tony, 246, 287
Blanchot, Maurice, 137, 242
Bracher, Mark, 304
"British Psychiatry and the War" (Lacan), 255
Bush, George W., 80, 208, 215 n.17
Butler, Judith, 154 n.13

Calvin, John, 200–201
capitalism, 6, 24, 46, 112, 118, 171–172, 212, 275, 293, 301–302; Bakhtin and, 128 n.6; castration and, 208; discourse of, 22, 182–184, 193 n.2, 195, 203, 206–207, 212–213; fantasy and, 121; as global, 113, 120–121, 123–124; hegemony of, 258; hysteric and, 109, 293–294; libidinial dynamics of, 121; Marx and, 119, 125, 170; master (discourse) and, 169, 183–184, 194 n.14, 196–197, 204–205, 305; production and, 174, 183–184; prohibition and, 4;

Puritanism and, 12; subject of, 206; university and, 108–109, 136, 168, 171, 200–201, 203. *See also* West(ern)
castration, 15, 79, 100 n.15, 108, 153 n.10, 165–166, 201–202, 212; avoidance of, 46; capitalism and, 208; as complex, 42–43, 58–59; as contingent, 296; Deleuze and, 127; Dora and, 63, 83; Herr K. and, 82–83; hysteric and, 75–79, 167; language and, 206–207, 211; law and, 218–219; love and, 66, 95; Oedipus and, 57, 210; Other and, 224–225; psychoanalysis and, 217–218; signifier and, 166; as symbolic, 43–44, 46, 50–51, 84, 163, 210; woman and, 71, 238–239. *See also* Father
Catholic Church, 245–246
Céline, Louis-Ferdinand, 264–265
Cendrars, Blaise, 264–265
Central Intelligence Agency (CIA), 80, 209
Chaplin, Charles, 258–259
Christ, Jesus, 111
Christianity, 48 n.13, 92–93, 97, 101 n.27, 154 n.11, 239; as bourgeois, 26. *See also* Kojève, Alexandre
Cité des Sciences, 246–247
Civilization and Its Discontents (Freud), 12, 57, 217–218, 247, 256–257, 313 n.33
Claudel, Paul, 96, 101 n.27
Clinton, Bill, 215 n.17, 245–246
Coca-Cola, 308; Lacan and, 293–294
Columbine High, 241
Coming Community, The (Agamben), 123
communism, 123–125
Confessions (Rousseau), 264, 266, 270
Congress of the École Freudienne de Paris in Strasbourg (Lacan), 260
Conquest of Cool, The (Frank), 301, 311
Consumer Society, The (Baudrillard), 296
Critique of Pure Reason (Kant), 21
Cruise, Tom, 298

Das Prinzip Verantwortung (Jonas), 243
death, 15–16, 24, 30–31, 101 n.24, 207, 211, 213, 234–235, 242, 245, 255–256, 272 n.5; being for, 224–225, 249–250;

demand for, 239, 241; enjoyment and, 37; existence and, 21; life and, 33, 111; master and, 153 n.4, 185, 220-221, 225; penalty and, 232. *See also* Father

death drive, 30, 37, 158, 172-173, 199, 218-219, 245-246

Debord, Guy, 16

defense, 37, 41, 259-260

Deleuze, Gilles, 1, 118, 127, 137, 150, 189

Della Demina, Jerry, 297-299, 303-305

demand, 38, 44, 46, 74-75, 83, 145, 230, 239, 241, 271, 275-276, 294-295

Depardieu, Gérard, 16

Derrida, Jacques, 7, 126, 137, 183, 232, 241, 275-276, 284

Descartes, René, 23, 134, 183-184, 189, 194 n.11, 221-222

desire, 12, 37, 73-74, 93-94, 100 n.20, 171-172, 175-176, 196, 218-219, 259-260, 285, 297, 305-307; analyst and, 95, 101 n.21, 108, 269, 271; ashamed of, 27; castration and, 224; cause and, 38-39, 46, 67, 76, 91, 93, 100 n.11, 112, 116-117, 126, 163-164, 219, 224-225, 249, 296; child and, 39-40, 42, 204-205, 248; democracy and, 118; Dora and, 62-63; giving way on, 153 n.6, 243, 275; guilt and, 12-13; as human, 293, 295; hysteric and, 38-39, 62-63, 72, 75-76, 81, 84, 101 n.29, 159-160, 186; as mother's, 36, 40, 48 n.9, 50, 57, 247, 249; of neurotic, 41; nobility of, 22, 97; Oedipus and, 60; of the Other, 115, 268-269, 270; perversion and, 98-99; philosophy and, 152, 154 n.13, 185; truth of, 73, 115, 225; unconscious and, 56-57, 75, 256-257

Diagnostic and Statistical Manual of Mental Disorders (DSM), 257, 259-260

dialectic, 120-121, 274, 295, 303; of desire, 154 n.13, 270, 293-294; form and, 120-121; Hegel and, 23-24, 108, 129, 185, 220-221, 226 n.3; hysteric and, 148; of knowledge and enjoyment, 133-134, 141-142, 151; Kojève and, 238; as structuralist, 188-189; of subject and other, 32, 34-35, 38, 207

Diderot, Denis, 24-25, 214 n.10, 234-235, 237

"Direction of the Treatment and the Principles of its Power" (Lacan), 267

Dolto, Françoise, 218-219

Domestication of Being, The (Sloterdijk), 243

Dora, 5, 39, 62-63, 69-70, 72, 74-79, 81-84, 148, 194 n.16

Doyle, Dane, Bernback (DDB), 294-295, 298-301, 304-306, 308

Dresden Madonna, 74, 83

drive(s), 30, 35, 37, 39, 116-117, 155, 187, 213, 218-219, 224-225, 238-239, 270-271. *See also* Death drive

D'Souza, Dinesh, 212

D'um discours qui ne serait pas du semblant (Lacan), 51

École des Hautes Études, 232

Écrits (Lacan), 131, 133, 238

ego, 21-22, 24-25, 34-36, 70, 73, 75-76, 92, 112, 121, 210, 219, 248, 251; psychology and, 26

Ego and the Id, The (Freud), 239

ego ideal, 70, 73, 77-78, 100 n.17, 209-210, 219, 224-225

Eitingon, Max, 88

Ellroy, James, 261

Empire (Hardt & Negri), 118

Encore (Lacan), 29, 58, 239, 263

enjoy(ing), 60, 114, 132, 171, 210, 238-239, 250; body and, 32, 35, 37; father and, 41-42, 59-60, 64, 66; gaze and, 15-16; imperative to, 171-172; Lacan and, 15-16, 233; master and, 100 n.19, 165-166, 196-197

enjoyment, 29-30, 96, 130, 132-133, 153 n.10, 154 n.11, 156-157, 159, 167, 179, 187-188, 199, 235, 251; being of, 37-39; capitalism and, 168-169; community of, 233; desire and, 293-294; discourse and, 69; exploitation and, 172-173; father and, 60, 64; imperative of, 172; as impossible, 29, 43, 168, 171-172, 175-176; knowledge and, 307-308; of master, 132, 164-165; mother and, 41,

enjoyment (*continued*)
210; philosophy and, 149, 151; prohibition on, 29, 38–39, 41; repetition and, 141, 171; repression of, 12; as satisfaction, 157; signifier and, 58–59, 115–116, 141, 155, 158, 161–162; of slave, 132, 196–197; surplus of, 110, 126, 132–133, 141, 151, 155, 158–159, 163, 165–167, 170–171, 175, 183–184, 194 n.12, 196, 197–208, 212, 214 n.7, 275–276; theft of, 133–134; as threat, 37, 41, 209–210. *See also* Jouissance; *Plus-de-jouir*

Ethics of Psychoanalysis, The (Lacan), 12, 16, 19, 24, 26, 29, 155

Fairclough, Norman, 286–287
fantasy, 52, 58–59, 81–82, 84, 93–94, 115, 172–173, 180–181, 190–191, 201–202, 223, 245, 249; academics and, 222–223; capitalism and, 121; communism and, 84; demand and, 275–276; desire and, 84–85; as fundamental, 41–42, 59–60; of hysteric, 78–79; and imaginary, 125; of mother, 246–248; myth and, 55–56; object of, 75, 219, 247; perversion and, 95, 97, 102 n.31 (*see also* Perversion); philosophy and, 137, 144; repression of, 275–277; traversal and, 116–117, 147, 152
father, 25, 36–37, 41–42, 46, 57, 67, 73, 81–82, 203–205, 211, 219, 239; as agent, 43–44; anxiety and, 40; castration and, 30, 37, 39–40, 43, 58–59, 60, 66, 70–71, 76, 83, 204–205, 217–218, 223–224; death of, 39, 64–65, 223–224, 258–259; desire and, 70–71, 74–75, 78–79; Dora and, 75–76, 81–83; function of, 30, 35, 42–43, 63, 67, 223; as idealized, 63, 67; as ill, 39, 63; imaginary and, 50–51, 60; as myth, 61, 65; as Oedipal, 40; phallus and, 63; as primal, 41, 44, 46, 58, 62, 64–66, 204–205, 209, 223 (*see also* Primal horde); as real, 50–51, 60–61, 84, 223–224; as symbolic, 82–84
Felman, Shoshana, 280, 285–286
Fergusson, Niall, 212

foreclosure, 60
Formations of the Unconscious (Lacan), 50
Fortune 500, 302
Foucault, Michel, 1, 7, 109, 137, 142, 220, 243, 278, 309
four discourses, 3–6, 29, 52, 58–59, 65, 93–94, 109, 130, 159, 179, 190–191, 217, 219–220, 225, 274, 285 286, 293–294, 308. *See also* Analyst's discourse; Hysteric's discourse; Master's discourse; University discourse
Four Fundamental Concepts of Psychoanalysis, The (Lacan), 29, 155
Frank, Thomas, 301–302, 305, 311
Frankfurt School, 153 n.7, 304
French Revolution, 136
Freud, Sigmund, 2, 5, 68 n.12, 71, 75, 79, 89–90, 91, 95, 98–99, 129, 152, 180, 200, 203–204, 208, 212, 215 n.11, 217, 239, 266, 310; castration and, 46, 206; Dora and, 75, 82–83, 194 n.16; drives and, 30–31, 157, 172–173, 242–243; father and, 25, 29, 40–41, 43–45, 48 n.13, 58–59, 73, 209–210, 223, 241; hysteria and, 62–63, 85–86; identification and, 65–66, 72, 77–78, 156–157; impossible professions and, 159; lost object and, 38, 198; mother and, 248; neurosis of, 64; Oedipus and, 5, 36–39, 41–42, 44–45, 48 n.13, 58–59, 73, 209–210, 223–224, 241; psychoanalysis and, 217–221, 230–231; repetition and, 35; structuralism and, 180–181; subject and, 256–257; superego and, 307, 313 n.33; university and, 136; wit and, 305–306. *See also* titles of specific works and names of patients
From Those Wonderful Folks Who Brought You Pearl Harbor (Della Femina), 298
Fukuyama, Francis, 113, 244, 246
Fuller and Smith and Ross, 299

Gauche, Marcel, 229, 231–232
gaze, 13–17, 46, 70, 73, 75, 76, 78–79, 81–82, 116–117, 264–265. *See also* Other
George Be Careful (Lois), 298, 301–302

Gide, André, 20-21, 230, 264-265
God, 17, 123-124, 183, 193 n.10, 194 n.13, 210, 236, 241, 244, 245-246, 248, 282-283; death of, 15-16, 190-191
Goethe, Johann Wolfgang von, 235
Gossage, Howard, 217-218
Greek, 92-93, 98-99, 101 n.27, 102 n.38, 145, 189, 230-231
Greuze, Jean-Baptiste, 263
Group Psychology and the Analysis of the Ego (Freud), 79, 156, 203-204, 209-210, 219
Guattari, Felix, 189
guilt, 6, 11-13, 14, 23, 27, 61, 99 n.5, 109-110, 123-124, 210, 231, 238-239, 242, 245, 313 n.33
Guizot, François, 258

Habermas, Jürgen, 120
Hamlet, 101 n.27
Hardt, Michael, 5, 118-125, 128 n.6
HB (human bomb), 240
Hegel, G. W. F., 2, 112, 121, 123-124, 153 n.4, 154 nn.13, 14, 180, 187-188, 214 n.5, 234-235, 312; absolute knowledge and, 142, 151, 200, 232; consciousness and, 23-24, 79, 132, 146, 234; Deleuze and, 150; democracy and, 120-121; dialectic and, 108, 129, 148, 185, 220-221; discovery of, 130, 135, 149-150; and Hegelettes, 191-192; history and, 180-181, 194 n.12, 201-202, 206, 298; as hysteric, 143-145, 148; as Lacan, 130, 152; master/slave and, 100 n.19, 131-134, 138; Rameau's nephew and, 236, 238; university and, 135-138, 200-201
Heigegger, Martin, 18, 21, 109, 136, 138, 220-221, 266, 293-294
Henri-Lévy, Bernard, 240
Heraclitus, 188
Hidden Persuaders, The (Packard), 301, 305
Hitchcock, Alfred, 126
Hobbes, Thomas, 24, 209-210
Hölderlin, Friederich, 190-191
Homo Sacer as the Object of University Discourse (Žižek), 190-191

Hopkins, Claude, 300
Hopkins, James, 184-185
Horkheimer, Max, 124
Hosea, 190-191, 205; Golden Calf and, 205
Hostage, The (Claudel), 96
Hucksters, The (Wakeman), 298
Human Condition, The (Arendt), 231-232
Humboldt, Wilhelm von, 135
hysteria, 5, 50, 81-82, 115, 153 n.10, 194 n.16, 206-207; analysis and, 110, 147; Hegel and, 143, 148; philosophy and, 145, 189; Socrates and, 186; suffering and, 85-86
hysteric, 5, 78-79, 84, 148, 220-221, 274, 297-298; demand of, 62-63, 67, 101 n.29, 156-157; father and, 63-64, 70, 76, 82-85, 93; jouissance and, 69, 71, 81; master and, 74-75, 80-82, 164-165; Oedipus and, 62, 67; phallus and, 75, 77, 79; symptom and, 83, 112-113, 148; truth and, 167-168, 225; young homosexual woman as, 69, 74-75, 77
hysteric's discourse, 5, 52, 72, 93, 109-110, 159-160, 183, 187, 190, 194 n.16, 258; advertising as, 293-294, 297-298; agent and, 163-164; Hegel and, 143-144; knowledge and, 145, 147, 186; master discourse and, 81-82, 143, 145-146, 189; matheme of, 3, 67, 80-81, 163, 206, 297; as other side of psychoanalysis, 84; truth and, 73, 75, 85-86, 148-149, 164-165

IBM, 302
Id-Evil, 112
identification, 49 n.17, 72, 83, 156, 205, 212-213, 241, 270, 297-298; of fanatic, 113; father and, 43, 65-66, 73-79, 239; as hidden, 289-290; hysteric and, 70-71, 76, 78-79, 84; as imaginary, 295; Lacan's theory of, 91-92, 100 n.15; object and, 73-74, 77-78, 219; unary trait and, 45, 157
imaginary, 6, 73, 92, 94-95, 115, 156, 205, 261; analysis and, 93, 115-116; ego and, 36; father and, 43, 50-51, 60, 84;

imaginary (continued)
  hysteric and, 69, 70–71, 78–79; identification and, 289–290, 295; myth and, 55–56; Other and, 35
impudence, 25–26
instinct, 31. See also Knowledge
"Instincts and Their Vicissitudes" (Freud), 309–310
International Psychoanalytic Association, 2, 88
Interpretation of Dreams, The (Freud), 57, 224
Iraq, 80, 177, 209, 213, 259–260
Is There Any Hope for Advertising? (Gossage), 298

Jerry Maguire, 298
Joffe, Roland, 28 n.6
Johnson, Lyndon, 211
Jokes and Their Relation to the Unconscious (Freud), 305–306
Jonas, Hans, 243
Jones, Ernest, 88
jouissance, 4–7, 30–32, 34, 38–39, 41–43, 70–71, 81–82, 84–85, 95, 98–99, 115, 142, 154 n.11, 187–188, 192, 216, 222–223, 237–239, 250–251, 264–265, 270, 289, 297, 309–310, 313 n.33; discourse of, 156; Dora and, 74, 83; extimacy and, 270–271, 307; giving way on, 242–243; heaven and, 255–256; hysteric and, 69–71, 80–83, 156; Id-Evil and, 112; as idiotic, 112–113; as imitation, 211; impossibility of, 38, 42–43, 46, 171–172; as infantile, 27, 204–205; as invasion, 29–34, 43, 46; libidinal economy of, 202–203, 224–225; loss and, 163, 177 n.5, 199, 206, 241, 245; master and, 80, 81–82, 196–197, 200, 205, 233, 261; Oedipus and, 36–37, 61–62; as out-of-body, 248–249; as phallic, 36, 70, 84, 197–198; prohibition of, 59–60, 66, 209–210, 223, 295, 308; road to, 31–32, 43; as Sadian, 13; science and, 251; signifier and, 30–31, 33, 42–44, 141, 158–159, 197–198, 206; slave and, 131, 133, 142,
201–202, 214 n.6; subject and, 12, 196, 225, 239, 260, 297–298, 313 n.33; truth and, 266. See also Enjoyment; Loss; Surplus jouissance
Joyce, James, 4
Jung, Carl, 112–113

Kant, Immanuel, 16, 111, 150, 208–210, 243, 251, 297
"Kant with Sade" (Lacan"), 13, 264–265
Kennedy, John, 77, 211
Kierkegaard, Søren, 107
King Lear, 19, 224
Klein, Melanie, 99 n.5, 112–113, 219, 239, 248
Klein, Naomi, 302–303, 307, 312
knowledge, 30, 79, 95, 119, 135, 147, 152, 154 n.13, 172–173, 203–204, 221–222, 282, 298, 308, 310; as absolute, 130, 133–134, 138, 142, 146, 150, 152, 200, 232–233, 238–239 (see also Hegel, G. W. F.); chain of, 283; as connaissance, 147, 220–221, 226 n.11; economy and, 287–288; hysteric and, 67, 81, 145, 148, 163–164, 186, 194 n.16, 207; as instinctive, 31–32, 38; jouissance and, 31, 33, 34, 43, 81–83, 141, 206, 222–225, 251, 307; loss and, 198; master and, 35–36, 80, 84–85, 139, 142, 144, 159–162, 196–197, 203, 214 n.6; master signifier and, 47 n.6, 115–116, 160–161, 163, 168, 194 n.11, 200–201, 258; Oedipus and, 67; Other and, 45–46; power and, 278–279, 289; of psychoanalysis, 271; as savior, 3, 135, 141, 146, 151, 160–161, 201–202, 214 n.7, 220–221, 226 n.11; science and, 183–184, 187–188; signifier and, 140, 162, 169, 177 n.5; of slave, 130, 133–134, 140–142, 169, 182–183, 185, 201–202, 214 n.6; subject of, 18, 188–189, 260, 269, 309–310; symbolic and, 136; truth and, 110, 115, 238–239, 263; types of, 139; of university, 2, 107, 135, 137, 309, 311; war and, 208–209, 212–213. See also S_2
Kohl-Lanta. See Big Brother

Index   325

Kojève, Alexandre, 23, 26, 92, 129, 131, 150, 237
Koyré, Alexandre, 92, 183–184
Kris, Ernst, 74
Kuhn, Thomas, 180

lack, 46, 58, 63, 71, 108, 117, 123–124, 126, 154 n.11, 205, 224–225, 248, 286–287, 296–297, 309–310; of being, 32, 35–36, 72, 75; as constitutive, 196; economy and, 166, 213; father and, 82–83; of jouissance, 270; of knowledge, 196–197; loss and, 33, 74–75; pass on, 44, 47; subject and, 73, 143, 148, 197–198; of truth, 16–17, 167; as waste, 157
Laclau, Ernesto, 123
lamella, 33
language, 57, 70, 81, 84–85, 90–91, 101 n.22, 140, 195, 208, 215 n.16, 224–225, 231–232, 234, 249–251, 254, 285; castration and, 58–60, 84, 206–207, 211; death and, 234–235, 239; Derrida and, 232; discourse and, 91, 100 n.9; origins of, 193 n.5; as political, 231–232; subject and, 3, 43, 143; symbolic and, 93–94, 165–166, 220, 221–222, 224
Laurent, Éric, 6, 11–13, 15–16, 18, 20, 27, 255–256
Leclaire, Serge, 1
Lefort, Claude, 120–121
Lenin, V. I., 123, 183–184
Le trio de mélo (Miller), 75
Lévi-Strauss, Claude, 52–57, 59
Lincoln, Abraham, 211
Little Hans, 39, 52, 57, 63; phallic experience of, 40
llanguage, 56–57; as motherly, 31–32
Loewenstein, Rudolf, 267
Lois, George, 298, 302, 304–305, 311
loss, 3, 202, 206, 239; death and, 213; as entropy, 162, 169, 177 n.5, 198; hysteric and, 81, 167, 207; of jouissance, 33, 38, 44, 141, 196–197, 198–199; master and, 169, 212; objet a and, 116–117, 163; as original, 33–34; of phallus, 77, 81; of satisfaction, 156–157; as surplus value, 170, 197–198, 203–204. See also Lack

Lost Highway (Lynch), 310
lost object, 38, 116–117, 156–157, 198–199, 219, 224–225, 241, 249
Louis XIV (Sun King), 109
Luhmann, Niklas, 191–192
Luther, Martin, 200–201
Lynch, David, 310
Lyotard, Jean-François, 1

Madison Avenue, 298, 302
Mailer, Norman, 209
Maleval, Jean-Claude, 257
Malraux, André, 231–232
Man, Paul de, 208
Marcuse, Herbert, 124, 294–295
Marx, Karl, 2, 119, 129, 131, 138, 162, 178 nn.8, 10, 181–182, 203–204, 214 nn.5–8, 217, 255, 311; capital and, 118–119, 169; Lacan and, 6, 183–184, 200; mistake of, 121, 125–126; surplus value of, 4, 34, 108–109, 170, 195, 202, 214 n.2, 222–223; university and, 136
Marx brothers, 308
Massumi, Brian, 174–175
master, 35, 46, 52, 65–66, 96, 109, 130, 159–160, 203–204, 230, 233, 238–239, 258–259, 275–276, 286–287, 292, 306; agent and, 133–135; castration and, 59–60, 82–83; Hegel and, 137, 145, 152, 194 n.12; hysteric and, 164–165, 184–185, 235; knowledge and, 67, 84–85, 136, 139, 143–144, 148, 151, 197–198, 200–202; power of, 141, 198; slave and, 93, 131, 133, 153 n.5, 177 n.4, 183, 185, 199, 201–202, 221–222; state and, 131, 214 n.5; subject as, 19, 35–36; worker and, 26, 159–160
master's discourse, 19–20, 91, 93, 99 n.8, 110, 141–142, 159–160, 170, 178 n.9, 183, 190–191, 195, 210, 221–222, 238, 258, 274, 276–277; advertising and, 305; capitalism and, 22, 169, 181–182, 194 n.14, 196–197, 200–201; as declarative, 283–284; as dominant, 3; enjoyment and, 134, 168–169, 171, 187–188, 202, 203–204, 205, 208; father and, 43, 70–71; Freud and, 58–

master's discourse (*continued*)
59, 65; Hegel and, 130, 138–139, 143, 145, 220–221; jouissance and, 81–82, 200, 259–260, 261, 310; knowledge and, 142, 160–161, 169, 183–184, 275; philosophy and, 140, 182, 189; politics and, 275–276, 287; science and, 304; students and, 26; subject and, 35, 93–94, 146, 164–165, 194 n.11, 206–207, 309; university and, 184–185, 186–187, 190, 277–279, 285–286, 289, 293. *See also* Matheme

master signifier, 3, 35, 47 n.6, 52, 79, 84–85, 92, 97–98, 100 n.17, 114, 153 n.9, 159–160, 179, 194 n.11, 197–198, 225, 261, 282, 312; body and, 35–36, 79; capitalism and, 46, 203–204, 224–225; castration and, 43–44, 59; Descartes and, 221–222; desire and, 21; Hegel and, 130, 235; hysteric and, 64, 67, 72, 74–75, 81–82, 85–86, 115, 165–166; knowledge and, 160–161, 168, 258, 275–277; shame and, 23, 26–27, 47, 230, 233, 238–239; *sinthome* and, 115–116; subject and, 18, 19–20, 22, 24, 36, 80, 110, 163; as unassailable, 173–174. *See also* S_1

matheme, 3, 4, 18, 194 n.17, 258, 260; of analyst, 3, 67; of hysteric, 3, 67, 80–81, 163, 207, 297; of master, 3, 52, 80, 159, 196–197, 262 n.6, 293; of slave, 135; of university, 3, 167, 206, 293, 308

Maturana, Humberto, 191–192

May 1978, 1, 136, 216, 220, 274; and Lacan, 18, 292

Meno (Plato), 140, 182

Metaphysics (Aristotle), 183–185

Milanese Institutions (Miller), 258–259

Miller, Jacques-Alain, 5, 72, 75, 79, 97–98, 111, 114, 116–117, 127 n.3, 155, 230, 242–243, 250–251, 255–257, 259, 261, 263, 270

Milner, Jean-Claude, 2, 189–190, 193 n.9

Modern Times (Chaplin), 258–259

modesty, 13–14, 270; absence of, 233

Monroe, Marilyn, 77

Morel, Geneviève, 60, 68 n.5

Moses, 210, 215 n.17

Moses and Monotheism (Freud), 41, 57, 65–66, 210

Moses (Sellin), 215 n.18

Mouffe, Chantal, 125

Mulgan, Geoff, 245–246

Multitude (Hardt & Negri), 118, 122

Muslim, 241

mytheme, 53

N., Frau Emmy von, 217–218

Name-of-the-Father, 30, 36, 40, 44, 48 n.9, 50, 51, 57, 61, 64, 70–71, 72, 100 n.17, 127 n.3, 223, 232, 259–261. *See also* Father

Narcissism, 265–266, 286–287, 289; as primary, 247

Negri, Antonio, 5, 118–123, 125, 128 n.6

neurosis, 50–51, 62, 64, 66, 76, 97–98, 218–219, 230, 270

neurotic(s), 41, 47, 52, 60, 75, 82–83

"Neurotic's Individual Myth, The" (Lacan), 52

New Labour, 287. *See also* Blair, Tony

New Wave, 264–265

Nicomachean Ethics, 177 n.4

Nietzsche, Friedrich, 23, 107, 136, 138, 151

No Logo (Klein), 302–303, 308, 312

Norvatis, 246–247

object loss, 117. *See also* Lost object

Object Relation, The (Lacan), 50

objet a, 3, 30, 33, 69, 73, 77–78, 91, 101 n.27, 107, 114, 130, 159, 177 n.5, 179, 188, 196, 216, 245, 270–271, 282–283, 285; advertising and, 296–297; ambiguity of, 116–117, 163, 224–225; analyst and, 95, 97–98, 110, 115, 152, 190–191; as fantasmatic, 275; fantasy and, 248; hysteric and, 69, 73, 75, 148–149, 206, 297–298, 309–310; ideological, 173; master and, 91, 93, 135, 161–162, 195; neurosis and, 76; perversion and, 96, 115; phallus and, 77; as product, 284; subject and, 77–78; as surplus, 160, 162, 165–167, 170, 197–199, 200, 202,

207, 241, 310; surplus jouissance and, 3, 45, 196; university and, 107, 221–222, 309; value and, 200–201, 206, 222–223; as woman, 45. *See also* Four discourses; Matheme; Other
obsessional neurosis, 52, 62, 64
Oedipus, 19, 32, 41, 50, 61, 210, 217; complex and, 2, 4, 34–40, 42–43, 48 n.9, 50–55, 57–62, 64–67, 76, 108, 211, 216, 260; crisis of, 288; as myth structure, 53
Old Testament, 183
On the Critique of Advertising Discourse: A Lacanian View (Stavrakakis), 294, 297–299, 309–310
Orwell, George, 286–287. *See also* New Labour
Other, 4, 15–16, 34–35, 73, 77–78, 99 n.5, 169, 240, 249–251, 281, 306–307; analyst and, 115–116, 267–269; demand and, 74–75, 239, 271; as *ganz Andre*, 124 (*see also* Gaze); gaze of, 15, 17, 70, 75; hate and, 242; hysteric and, 71, 79, 84, 297–298; jouissance and, 32, 36, 44–46, 95, 115, 270; shame and, 12–13; subject and, 13–14, 32, 37, 81, 146, 148, 229–230, 266; truth and, 264
other, 3, 24, 35–36, 67, 92, 112, 179, 182, 221–222, 238–239, 250–251, 265–266, 272 n.3, 283; agent and, 182, 187; castration and, 70–71; desire and, 100 n.11, 101 n.29, 163–164; excess and, 26, 150; knowledge and, 163, 306–307; lack and, 71, 74–75, 286–287; mastery and, 275; production of, 174; shame of, 13–14, 102 n.38; signifier and, 97–98; subject and, 73–74, 91, 148. See also *Objet a*
Other Side of Psychoanalysis, The (Lacan), 2, 11–13, 21, 22, 25–27, 29, 51, 59, 96, 97–98, 130, 155, 220–224, 292
Our Posthuman Future (Fukyama), 244

Packard, Vance, 301–302
Panopticon, 278
Papert, Koenig, Lois, 302
Pascal, Blaise, 16–17

Paul, Saint, 111
perversion, 5, 46, 50–51, 70–71, 88, 90–91, 97–98, 103 n.42, 115, 264–265, 286–287, 289, 307
Petronius, 230–231
phallic signification, 46, 60, 75, 84–85, 153 n.10, 248
phallus, 36, 50–51, 61, 70–71, 73–78, 79, 81, 83, 297–298; mother and, 50 (*see also* Desire)
Phenomenology of Spirit, The (Hegel), 22, 132, 144, 146–148, 152, 154 n.14, 185, 190, 235
Phenomenon of Life: Towards a Philosophical Biology, The (Jonas), 243
philosophy, 1, 89, 181–182, 191–192, 217, 265–266, 272 n.4; bureaucrat and, 274; desire and, 154 n.13, 185; excess and, 151; Freud and, 88; Hegel and, 130–131, 137, 144, 150, 152; hysteric and, 145; master and, 139, 142, 182–184, 189; university and, 135–137; as withdrawal, 122
Plato, 140, 142, 145, 153 n.10, 161–162
Plus-de-jouir, 3, 33–34, 38, 44–45, 84, 132, 196, 214 n.2
Prager, Dennis, 175
Prigogine, Ilya, 191–192
primal horde, 41, 58–59, 61–62, 64–66, 223
Prince, Condé de, 16
product(s), 3, 162, 169, 171, 179, 249, 251, 261, 275, 284, 293, 304, 307; of discourse, 287; inversion and, 186; knowledge and, 145, 147; master's discourse and, 161–162; neurosis and, 72; as *objet a*, 296; performance and, 282–283; satisfaction and, 34; of slave, 200–201; surplus enjoyment and, 163; unconscious and, 56–57
prohibition, 42–43, 48 n.9, 259–260, 296, 310; desire and, 224–225; of enjoyment, 29, 38, 41; father and, 38, 64–65, 223–224; jouissance and, 34, 43, 59–60, 295, 313 n.33; on prohibiting, 4, 12–13, 46; subject and, 217–218, 308; as translated, 42–43, 46

Project for a Scientific Psychology (Freud), 266
"Proposal on Psychical Causality" (Lacan), 236
"Proposition of 9 October 1577 on the Psychoanalyst of the School" (Lacan), 258, 260
Proust, Marcel, 16
Prussia. *See* Hegel, G. W. F.
Psicoanalisi, La, 260
Psychoses, The (Lacan), 50
psychosis, 4, 46, 50–51, 60, 70–72, 77, 79, 84–85, 97–98, 246–247

Quackelbeen, Julien, 297–298
Question of Lay-Analysis, The (Freud), 88

Radiophonie (Lacan), 56, 184–185, 220–221, 249–250
Rameau's Nephew, 25, 214 n.10, 234, 237
Rancière, Jacques, 1
Rat man, 39
Reagan, Ronald, 205, 211, 213
real, 6, 48 n.10, 70, 73–74, 94–95, 108, 127 n.3, 197–198, 213, 220–221, 251, 254, 256–257, 285; father and, 29, 43, 216; Freud and, 230–231; hysteric and, 69; ideal ego as, 73, 76–78; as impossibility, 55–56, 58, 152, 168, 224; jouissance and, 31, 213, 264; law and, 114; as object, 309–310; power and, 278–279, 285–286; psychosis and, 245–246; shame and, 25; symbolic and, 220, 223; truth of, 75, 165–166, 167, 263
Reality in Advertising (Reeves), 300
Reeves, Rosser, 300–302
Reformation, 208, 242–243
Reik, Theodor, 89–90
Repetition(s), 32–34, 37–38, 141, 158, 162, 170–171, 199, 203–204, 224–225, 275–276, 301–302
Reveries of a Solitary Walker (Rousseau), 263, 265–266, 270
Rhetoric (Aristotle), 293
Rimbaud, Arthur, 264–265
Rocking the Ages (Yankelovich), 303
Roosevelt, Franklin, 245

Roosevelt, Teddy, 211
Rousseau, Jean-Jacques, 263–264, 266, 271

S_1, 21, 36, 90–91, 96, 98–99, 146, 153 n.9, 177, 179, 305; betrayal of, 97–98; discourse and, 93–95, 163; as emblem, 23; father and, 30, 35, 43; as master, 93, 110, 164–165, 187, 197–198, 258–259; philosophy and, 142; repetition and, 142, 198, 200; as singularity, 23; subject and, 36, 44–45, 91, 101 n.27; symbolic and, 92, 307; unary trait and, 157; as university discourse and, 151–152, 311, 312; value of, 18, 27, 259–260; Yahweh and, 183. *See also* Master signifier; Matheme
S_2, 30, 91, 97–98, 146, 153 n.9, 177, 179, 258–259; hysteric and, 67, 81, 145, 163, 207; philosophy and, 142; as prior to subject, 35–36, 43; as slave, 93, 133–134, 142; symbolic and, 92; university discourse and, 107, 151, 152, 202, 287, 311. *See also* Knowledge; Matheme
Sade, Marquis de, 101 n.24, 102 n.31
Santner, Eric, 110
Sartre, Jean-Paul, 13–14, 137; and existentialism, 22
Satiricon (Petronius), 230–231
Satyricon (Fellini), 230–231
Schiller, J. C. F. von, 234–235
Schmitt, Carl, 229
Schreber, Daniel Paul, 264
Schudson, Michael, 301
science, 22, 56–57, 139, 217, 220–221, 225, 232, 243, 251, 257, 260; discourse of, 255–257; emergence of, 183–184; of ethics, 162; knowledge and, 2, 258–259; myth and, 55–56; psychoanalysis, 89–90; of real, 85–86; subject and, 6, 249–250; as university discourse, 189
Scientific Advertising (Hopkins), 300
Searle, John, 280–282, 284–285
Sellin, Ernst, 215 n.18
Senatus Populusque Romanus, 26
separation, 38, 84, 97–98, 111, 114
Sévingé, Mme de, 16

sexuation, 4, 50–51, 59–60, 69, 72, 85–86, 87 n.32, 259–260; formulas of, 58, 70

shame, 6, 19, 21, 23–24, 26, 97–98, 230, 264; capitalism and, 12–13; die of, 11, 17–20, 96, 234, 265–266; father and, 43, 47; gaze and, 13–16, 17, 102 n.38; guilt and, 12, 231, 242, 245; honor and, 17, 25, 26–27; as shameful, 15, 25. *See also* Ashamed

Signifier(s), 20, 72, 83, 92–94, 100 n.15, 153 n.9, 163–164, 169, 179, 184–185, 196, 208, 212–213, 234, 249, 251, 258, 269, 306–307, 312; castration and, 204–205, 224; chain of, 43–45, 47 n.6, 93–94, 152, 156, 158, 287; consciousness and, 133, 189, 267–268; desire and, 295; function of, 44–45, 214 n.3; hysteric and, 69, 81–82, 84, 165–166; jouissance and, 30–34, 37–38, 42–44, 141, 158, 196–202, 209–210, 250–251, 261; knowledge and, 140, 160–162, 177 n.5; lack and, 268–269; mother and, 71; Name-of-the-Father and, 51, 61, 223; negativity and, 162, 166; shame and, 11, 97–98; signified and, 96–99, 278–279, 282–283, 297. *See also* S_1

Sloterdijk, Peter, 243

Smith, Adam, 203, 212

Smythe, Dallas, 311

Socrates, 182–185, 189

Sophocles, 41, 52–53, 58, 61

Soviet Union, 108–109, 293, 301

speech, 32, 55–56, 81, 84, 91, 93–94, 107, 143, 155, 193 n.4, 220, 222–223, 225, 240, 256–257, 279–281; agency of, 84

speech acts, 7, 93–94, 101 n.22, 180, 182, 274, 276, 278, 280, 288–290; conditions for, 283–284; as declarative formula for, 282

Spinoza, Baruch, 179, 188

Stalin, Joseph, 7, 108–109, 128 n.6

Starobinski, Jean, 264

State and Revolution (Lenin), 123

State of Exception, The (Agamben), 111

Stavrakakis, Yannis, 294, 299, 307, 310

Stengers, Isabelle, 191–192

Stock, Gregory, 246

Structural Study of Myth, The (Lévi-Strauss), 52

Studies on Hysteria (Freud), 39

subject, 4, 5, 19–22, 61, 66, 73, 76, 91, 93, 100 n.17, 101 n.27, 111, 129, 131, 153 n.5, 154 n.13, 170, 218–219, 234, 237, 244, 249, 250–251, 260; castration and, 60–61, 71, 238–239; desire and, 80, 93–94, 100 n.11, 101 n.29, 117, 249, 257; discourse of, 171, 251; as divided, 3, 33, 35, 37, 69, 84–85, 179, 190, 206, 230, 275, 282–285, 309 (*see also* $); Freud and, 48 n.10; hysteric and, 72, 75, 81–82, 147–148, 163–164, 207; jouissance and, 12, 31, 45, 141, 158, 196, 225, 297–298, 313 n.33; as Kantain, 243; knowledge and, 18, 110, 144, 146, 150, 152, 222–223, 269, 309–310; love and, 91; master and, 21, 24, 26, 116–117, 163, 165–166, 173, 195; Other and, 13, 16, 38, 229, 242, 266, 286–287; position of, 76–78, 135, 180, 259–260; S_1 and, 43; shame and, 14; speaking and, 90–91, 256–259, 285–286; suicide of, 240; superego and, 217–218, 289; symbolic and, 161–162, 192, 220, 294–295; theory of, 99 n.6. *See also* Signifier(s)

subjective, 6, 21–22, 50–51, 91, 108, 196, 204–205, 254, 258, 267–268, 275, 282–284, 288

"Subversion of the Subject and the Dialectic of Desire, The" (Lacan), 294–295

Superego, 37, 39, 110, 114, 209–210, 217–219, 238–239, 241, 256, 264, 289, 307–308, 311, 313 n.33

Surplus enjoyment. *See* Enjoyment

Surplus jouissance, 4, 6, 17, 141, 166, 170–171, 175, 177 n.4, 200, 201–202, 204–205, 207, 212, 261. *See also* Enjoyment; *Plus-de-jouir*

symbolic, 24, 48 n.10, 78–79, 94–95, 114, 119, 164–165, 196–197, 289–290, 307; castration and, 41, 43–44, 46, 50–51, 58–59, 63, 84, 163, 165–166, 204–205, 210; economy, 196; efficiency

symbolic (*continued*)
of, 112–113, 136, 288–289; energy, 198, 208–209; fantasy and, 97; father and, 83–84; identification and, 92, 100 n.15, 156; imaginary and, 55–56, 116–117, 173; matrix of, 53, 110, 216, 255; Name-of-the-Father and, 41–42; Oedipus complex and, 50–51, 260; order of, 46, 72, 84–85, 93–94, 100 nn.14, 17, 190–191, 192, 295; passion and, 21; real and, 29, 127 n.3, 167, 197–198, 213, 220, 223; subject and, 161–162
symptom, 11, 73–74, 83, 89, 108–109, 113, 131, 152, 171, 218–221, 229, 234, 250–251, 256–257, 259–260; hysteria and, 75, 83, 145, 148–149, 156–157, 163, 167
System of Objects, The (Baudrillard), 307

Tawney, R. H., 12
Taylor, Charles, 243–244
Television (Lacan), 22, 61, 239, 266
Théorie du sujet (Badiou), 189
Theory of Turin (Miller), 230
thermodynamics, 2, 140–141, 157, 160–161, 194 n.12, 198
Theweleit, Klaus, 41–42
Third critique (Kant), 208
Third Way. *See* New Labour
Thomas Aquinas, Saint, 123
Thomson, J. Walter, 300
Thoughts on War and Death (Freud), 213
Thousand Plateaus, A (Deleuze and Guattari), 189
Three Studies on Hegel (Adorno), 149–150
Tommy Hilfiger, 312
Totem and Taboo (Freud), 40, 52, 57–62, 64–66, 209, 222–223; as neurotic product, 64
transference, 74, 77–78, 94–95, 101 n.27, 103 n.42, 139, 150, 156–157, 201–202, 206, 218–219, 259–260; as counter/negative, 27, 150, 218–219
Treatise on the Passions (Descartes), 3
truth, 3, 76, 88, 99 n.2, 148–149, 163, 179, 194 n.13, 216, 225, 246–247, 261, 272 n.5, 284, 313 n.33; castration and, 43, 70, 223–224; consciousness and, 22–23; democracy and, 120–121; desire and, 73, 84, 115; fiction of, 74–75; as half-said, 266, 271; Hegel and, 129, 145–146, 232; hysteric and, 64, 69, 75, 81, 83–85, 163–167, 207; intimacy and, 6, 263, 265, 269; jouissance and, 6, 156, 196, 217, 222–223, 264; knowledge and, 67, 110, 115–116, 142, 147, 152, 200, 220–221, 233; love and, 95, 230–231; master and, 131, 136, 171, 277; myth and, 55–56; Oedipus and, 41; revolutionary and, 238; science and, 255, 256–257; speech acts as, 280, 282–283; subject and, 234, 267, 307
Twilight of the Gods (Wagner), 123–124

UCLA, 245–246
unary trait *(einziger Zug)*, 33, 45, 79, 100 n.17, 156–157
unconscious, 73, 143, 189, 217–218, 220–221, 233, 249–250, 256–257, 279–280, 313 n.33; analysand and, 251, 267–268; desire as, 56–57, 75, 220; enjoying and, 250–251; formation of, 51, 57, 74, 112–113; identification and, 78–79; intentionality and, 285; law and, 61; master signifier and, 110, 115–116; shame and, 15, 230–231
United States. *See* American(s)
university discourse, 5, 7, 52, 90–91, 93–94, 108, 109–110, 137, 173, 176, 183–187, 190, 194 n.16, 195, 208–209, 212, 221–222, 258, 278–279, 284, 289, 292, 304, 309, 311, 312; advertising and, 293–294, 309–310, 312; as bureaucratic, 107, 276–277, 285–286; capitalism and, 136, 169, 171, 183–184, 200–201, 203, 208; exploited and, 222–223; Hegel and, 135, 138; as hegemonic, 108–109, 277, 289–290; matheme of, 3, 168, 206, 293, 308; modernity and, 275, 285–286; New Labour and, 288; as producer of subjects, 187–188; and S_2, 202, 207, 287

Varela, Francisco J., 191–192
Vatel, François, 16, 18

Vertigo (Hitchcock), 126
Vietnam War, 195, 209, 212
Vincennes, University of, 1, 11, 15, 17, 21, 25, 230, 233, 292
voice, 46, 116–117, 242–243, 251, 253 n.33
Volkswagen, 294–295, 299, 305
Voltaire, 236

Wagner, Richard, 123–124
Wakeman, Frederic, 298
Weber, Max, 12, 203, 212–213
Wells, Rich, Greene, 298

West(ern), 7, 112, 206, 232, 242–243, 257. *See also* Capitalism
Widlocher, Daniel, 27, 28 n.20
Wittgenstein, Ludwig, 136
Wolf man, 39, 180–181

Yahweh. *See* God
Yankelovich Partners, 303

Zapatistas, 118, 123
Žižek, Slavoj, 149, 153 n.6, 190–191, 286–287, 293, 309–311

Library of Congress Cataloging-in-Publication Data
Jacques Lacan and the other side of psychoanalysis : reflections
on Seminar XVII / edited by Justin Clemens and Russell Grigg.
p. cm.— (SIC ; 6)
Includes bibliographical references and index.
ISBN 0-8223-3707-X (cloth : alk. paper)
ISBN 0-8223-3719-3 (pbk. : alk. paper)
1. Psychoanalysis. 2. Lacan, Jacques, 1901– Envers de la
psychanalyse.
[DNLM: 1. Lacan, Jacques, 1901– Envers de la psychanalyse.
2. Psychoanalysis WM 460 J19 2006] I. Clemens, Justin.
II. Grigg, Russell. III. SIC (Durham, N.C.) ; 6.
BF173.J28 2006   150.19'5—dc22   2005031589